Mike Meyers' Co

Introduction to Networking

Richard Alan McMahon, Sr.

McGraw-Hill/Osborne

New York Chicago San Francisco
Lisbon London Madrid Mexico City Milan
New Delhi San Juan Seoul Singapore Sydney Toronto

The McGraw·Hill Companies

McGraw-Hill/Osborne
2600 Tenth Street
Berkeley, California 94710
U.S.A.

To arrange bulk purchase discounts for sales promotions, premiums, or fund-raisers, please contact **McGraw-Hill/**Osborne at the above address. For information on translations or book distributors outside the U.S.A., please see the International Contact Information page immediately following the index of this book.

Introduction to Networking

34567890 QPD QPD 01987654

ISBN 0-07-222678-1

This book was composed with Corel VENTURA™ Publisher.

Publisher
BRANDON A. NORDIN

Vice President & Associate Publisher
SCOTT ROGERS

Acquisitions Editor
CHRISTOPHER C. JOHNSON

Senior Project Editors
BETSY MANINI, LEEANN PICKRELL

Acquisitions Coordinator
ATHENA HONORE

Technical Editors
FRED BISEL, BRIAN J. CARROLL,
JANE HOLCOMBE, NICK LAMANNA,
PAUL H. WILSON, TIMOTHY E. JENKINS

NWCET Skill Standards Consultant
LAURIE STEPHAN

Copy Editor
ANDY CARROLL

Proofreaders
STEFANY OTIS, LISA THEOBALD

Indexer
DAVID HEIRET

Computer Designers
KATHLEEN FAY EDWARDS,
ELIZABETH JANG

Illustrators
MELINDA MOORE LYTLE,
MICHAEL MUELLER,
LYSSA WALD

Series Designers
JOHN WALKER, PETER F. HANCIK

Cover Series Designer
GREG SCOTT

About the Author

Richard Alan McMahon, Sr., Major (USAF Ret) is a full-time lecturer in the Finance, Accounting, and Computer Information Systems (FACIS) Department at University of Houston, Downtown and specializes in teaching Introductory and Advanced Data Communications and Networking, Information Security Management, Systems Analysis, Project Management, Management Information Systems, and Introductory and Advanced Computer Applications, all with a heavy emphasis in hands-on instruction. Additionally, Rich and his partners opened a certification training center in the Galleria area of downtown Houston where Mike Meyers used to conduct his Train-the-Trainer sessions covering his A+ and N+ coursework. Rich authored 4 series and 11 textbooks on Windows XP for Prentice Hall and an additional textbook on Windows 2000 Security Design with EMC Paradigm.

Rich holds an M.B.A. from Hardin-Simmons University and recently enrolled in Argosy University's doctoral program, where he is working toward his D.B.A.

About the Series Editor

Michael Meyers is the industry's leading authority on A+ and Network+ certification. He is the president and cofounder of Total Seminars, LLC, a provider of PC and network repair seminars, books, videos, and courseware for thousands of organizations throughout the world. Mike has been involved in the computer and network repair industry since 1977 as a technician, instructor, author, consultant, and speaker. Author of several popular PC books and of A+ and Network+ courseware, Mike is also the series editor for the highly successful Mike Meyers' Certification Passport series as well as the new Mike Meyers' Computer Skills series, both published by McGraw-Hill/Osborne. Mike holds multiple industry certifications and considers the moniker "computer nerd" a compliment.

About the Contributor

Many thanks go to Eric Maiwald, who wrote Chapter 9, "Securing a Network." His expertise and invaluable contribution are very much appreciated.

Eric Maiwald is the chief technology officer for Fortrex Technologies. Mr. Maiwald oversees all security consulting and product implementations for Fortrex clients. He also manages the Fortrex Network Security Operations Center where all managed services are performed. He has personally been involved in performing assessments, developing policies, and implementing security solutions for large financial institutions, service firms, and manufacturers.

The International Information Systems Security Certification Consortium has certified Mr. Maiwald as an information systems security professional. He is a prominent speaker at several security conferences, is the author of *Network Security: A Beginner's Guide* (McGraw-Hill/Osborne, 2001), coauthor of *Security Planning & Disaster Recovery* (McGraw-Hill/Osborne, 2002), and was a contributing author of *Hacker's Challenge* (McGraw-Hill/Osborne, 2001).

■ About the Technical Editors and Peer Reviewers

This book was greatly influenced by the dedicated group of teachers and subject-matter experts who reviewed this book and whose suggestions made it so much better. To them we give our heartfelt thanks.

Fred Bisel (CCDP, CCAI, MCSE, MCT) is an instructor and system administrator at Craven Community College in New Bern, North Carolina. Mr. Bisel holds a B.S. in mathematics from East Kentucky University and an M.A. in education from East Carolina University. He is an accomplished banjo performer and recently placed second at the Teluride (Colorado) and MerlFest (North Carolina) banjo contests.

Brian J. Carroll (MCSE, MCT, and CCNA) is the national education director for the International Education Corporation, Irvine, California. Brian was a senior network engineer for a dot com. He has 18 years' teaching experience, 10 of which were as a tenured professor of information systems engineering and dean for California Baptist University, Riverside. Brian earned a B.S. from Southern Illinois University, Carbondale, and a J.D. from San Francisco Law School. He has published over 20 professional articles.

Jane Holcombe (A+, Network+, MCSE, MCT, CTT+, and CNA) is a pioneer in the field of PC support training. In 1983, she installed a LAN for her employer, a financial planning company. Since 1984, she has been an independent trainer, consultant, and course content author, creating and presenting courses on PC operating systems. Through the late 1980s and early 1990s, these courses were taught nationwide. She also coauthored a set of networking courses for the consulting staff of a large network vendor. In the early 1990s, she worked with both Novell and Microsoft server operating systems, finally focusing on the Microsoft operating system and achieving her MCSE certification for Windows NT 3.*x*, Windows NT 4.0, and Windows 2000.

Timothy E. Jenkins (B.S., A+, MCP, CCNA) has been teaching networking, hardware, and computer programming at ITT Technical Institute in San Bernardino, California, for five years. In addition to his teaching duties, Mr. Jenkins is the program chair over the Associate and Bachelor IT programs for the San Bernardino ITT campus. In addition, Mr. Jenkins is the campus network coordinator, campus newsletter editor, and is on the corporate curriculum development team. Tim graduated as the highest honor graduate in his class at ITT Tech and holds a degree in health science from Cal State San Bernardino. Most recently, he has been working on his M.A. in Instructional Technologies from Cal State San Bernardino.

Nicola (Nick) LaManna (M.Ed.) is currently the associate department chair for information technology and assistant professor at New England Institute for Technology, based in Warwick, R.I. He has worked in various positions in the computer networking field for approximately 12 years. He completed training in Novell Netware Engineering and was employed as a network administrator at Johnson and Wales University in Providence, R.I.

Paul H. Wilson is professor and department chair in the Telecommunications Management Department of DeVry University, Fremont, California campus. Mr. Wilson teaches computer networking, data communication, and personal computer management, and conducts his own consulting practice in these specialties as well. His professional background includes computer programming of systems involving railroad cost accounting, nuclear power plant maintenance, chemical manufacturing financial controls, and management of phosphate fertilizer manufacturing financial operations. Mr. Wilson holds a bachelor's degree from Lewis and Clark College and an M.B.A. from Pepperdine University. He has certified with Novell and Microsoft networking products.

■ Acknowledgments

Believe it or not, this book first needs to recognize Domino's pizza. After all, the academic bantering that eventually led to the creation of this book took place at a university pizza party put on by the McGraw-Hill representative, Herb Licon. Before I arrived (fashionably late) at the luncheon, our department's administrative secretary, Marie Cepeda, had already explained my interest in writing to Herb, and he was only too glad to champion the idea of me working with McGraw-Hill—somewhere. When Herb heard about the Mike Meyers series expanding its books into the academic arena, it was only natural to get us together, here in Houston where Herb, Mike, and I all reside.

As you probably already know, this *Introduction to Networking* is part of the newest of Mike Meyers' successful series of books. I was lucky enough to meet Mike on several occasions prior to making the book contract official. Each time, I walked away grateful for the chance to work with Mike on this series. If you ever get an opportunity to sit and talk (or even just to listen) to Mike, take it. You, too, will be glad, as I am, just to know Mike. It is even better to be part of this successful series with him and the Holcombes.

Chris Johnson ran herd over all of us once we were let loose. This book was only part of the total project—the entire series—that he got under way and pampered from start to finish. With the first three books in progress at the same time using the pedagogy and book design that Chris had developed, Chris did so much more than a normal acquisitions editor would ever take on. His master plan kept leading us in the right direction. He is to be commended for even finding the finish line, let alone dragging all of us there with this winner of a series. Thanks Chris.

This field is full of great ideas being penned on San Francisco hotel envelopes (Ethernet) or sketched on pie company napkins (Compaq's portable computer). Imagine if it were your job to take the envelopes and napkins from creative people (authors) and piece them together so they formed the book you now hold in your hands. The first line of editors performed just such a monumental task on each of these books, with the added task of mixing in the comments from every reviewer, as well. Athena Honore deserves a lot of credit for holding this whole end together. She had to have ten arms and three sets of eyes to deal with the many files that came her way. They got where they were supposed to be, so she did a great job getting us over all those hurdles. Robin Romer, Daniel Johnson, Rachel Brooke, Mary-Terese Cozzola, and even Chris Johnson each spent time massaging the manuscript with their developmental edit of the text you now see. Without them making sure it was technically accurate, and that it included the excellent comments from our reviewers, the next step would be wasted.

Then came Betsy Manini and her copyediting and proofreading team. I realize now that the job was not finished until the Editorial Services team was through crossing those *T*s and dotting those *I*s. I never knew how much such an effort would improve the flavor of the work being written. They tenaciously tweaked words and phrases with grammatical precision and consistency. By the time our creation (with Microsoft Word's Track Changes option turned on) got to Betsy, she, Andy Carroll, Stefany Otis, Lisa Theobald, and LeeAnn Pickrell had quite a job putting the finishing touches on an apparently moving target.

Of course, none of the above would matter if it weren't for the expertise of the production group. After all, they are the ones who make sure the page layout, art, and graphics are in the appealing package that you now find them. Quite frankly, they took hamburger and made it into steak (or coleslaw into a Caesar's salad for the vegetarians amongst us)! The book looks great and their efforts mustn't go without notice. Kathleen Edwards and Elizabeth Jang pieced the elements together into beautiful spreads, and Lyssa Wald, Melinda Moore Lytle, and Michael Mueller accepted only the best of the photos and screen shots and crafted my sketches into small works of art. It takes dedication to fit the pieces into a difficult jigsaw puzzle, so imagine the difficulty of piecing this project together with every piece having to be custom-made. Their efforts, like all the others mentioned above, should be heartily commended.

To all of you, I would like to express my deepest appreciation for a job well done. Thank you!

To my parents, Thomas F. McMahon, Sr. and Ruth Carraher McMahon, and to my wife's parents, David F. Kingston and Linda Spraggins Kingston who taught me perseverance;

To my family: Sheronna, Lauren Annalise, Ricky, Karen, Dan, Kim, Corey, Christine, Lance, and Cameron for their support and patience;

And to my champion at McGraw-Hill, Herb Licon;

I humbly dedicate this work to you all.

Rich

Information Technology Skill Standards and Your Curriculum

Standards-aligned curriculum is becoming a *de facto* requirement for schools everywhere in the United States today. Programs are required to be standards-aligned in order to show clearly that students are being taught and assessed consistently and to an agreed-upon set of skill and content standards. For those programs preparing students to enter the workforce, skill standards provide an excellent skeleton upon which to build courses.

Research has shown rich learning contexts improve learning and retention of knowledge. Students who learn in a real-world context are also better equipped to transfer their skills to the real world. The National Workforce Center for Emerging Technologies (NWCET) information technology (IT) skill standards provide the kind of real-world data that educators can use. Educators can draw from the skill standards to develop contextually rich assignments that help students situate their learning in specific work contexts with complex and real-world problems to solve.

IT skill standards provide a common language for industry and education so that building bridges between these two groups can be more efficient. The more industry recognizes what educational programs are doing, the easier it is for education to gain industry support. Schools that use a standards-aligned program are better prepared to gain support from industry for technical advisory boards, student internships, job shadows, faculty internships, and a host of other support resources.

IT skill standards provide increased portability of skills because of the common language. Other institutions can clearly identify the content and skills that graduates of a standards-aligned curriculum have acquired. Programs that are skill-standards–based will effectively oil the communication wheels between programs that traditionally have had difficulty agreeing on what has been taught and assessed.

The NWCET IT skill standards are the *de facto* national standards in information technology. Our skill standards are used by community and technical colleges and high schools across the nation. Major national professional organizations, such as COMP/TIA, recognize the IT skill standards and partner with the NWCET in a variety of skill standards–based projects.

NWCET and McGraw-Hill in Partnership

McGraw-Hill and the National Workforce Center for Emerging Technologies (NWCET) recognize the demands on educators in today's educational arena:

- To be responsive to increasing demands for accountability in terms of what students learn and how well they learn it
- To deal with more complex systems of articulation and transfer
- To partner with industry in order to give students better resources and more real-world contacts in their learning

McGraw-Hill and the NWCET have partnered with the goal of helping IT educators meet these demands by making the IT skill standards more easily available and ready to use. McGraw-Hill and the NWCET have developed three different products that will help you address the IT skill standards in your networking programs and courses:

- A crosswalk that highlights the IT skill standards addressed by the McGraw-Hill *Introduction to Networking* textbook

- A training document that helps instructors understand and use the features of a skill standards–aligned curriculum

- 10 skill standards–based activities with associated assessment tools

NWCET Background and Mission

In 1995, the National Science Foundation (NSF) designated and funded the National Workforce Center for Emerging Technologies as a National Center of Excellence in Advanced Technological Education. The Center was created to advance IT education and improve the supply, quality, and diversity of the IT workforce.

The NWCET has since become a leader in new designs for IT education, developing products, services, and best practices that provide timely, relevant, and lasting solutions to meet the needs of IT educators and the IT workforce. The NWCET translates the rapidly changing demands of the technology workplace into programs, curricula, courseware, and assessments that prepare students for current and future IT careers.

The NWCET is perhaps best known for its IT skill standards. Skill standards provide an agreement of what is expected in order for a student to be successful in a given career area. They provide a validated, industry-derived framework upon which educators can build curricula. Using industry skill standards as the foundation for curricula will result in a closer alignment between educational programs and workplace expectations, and will result in a better skilled workforce.

To support new and innovative IT programs and degrees, the NWCET (http://www.nwcet.org) provides other professional development opportunities for high school teachers and community college and university faculty. The Educator-to-Educator Institute (E2E) (http://e2e.nwcet.org), the training branch of the NWCET, is dedicated to helping IT educators achieve excellence in IT instruction. CyberCareers (http://www.cybercareers.org) is a web site oriented toward middle and high school students and teachers and provides a wide variety of career education materials, such as job descriptions and an IT Interest Inventory.

About This Book

■ Important Technology Skills

Information technology (IT) offers many career paths, leading to occupations in such fields as PC repair, network administration, telecommunications, Web development, graphic design, and desktop support. To become competent in any IT field, however, you need certain basic computer skills. The Mike Meyers' Computer Skills series builds a foundation for success in the IT field by introducing you to fundamental technology concepts and giving you essential computer skills.

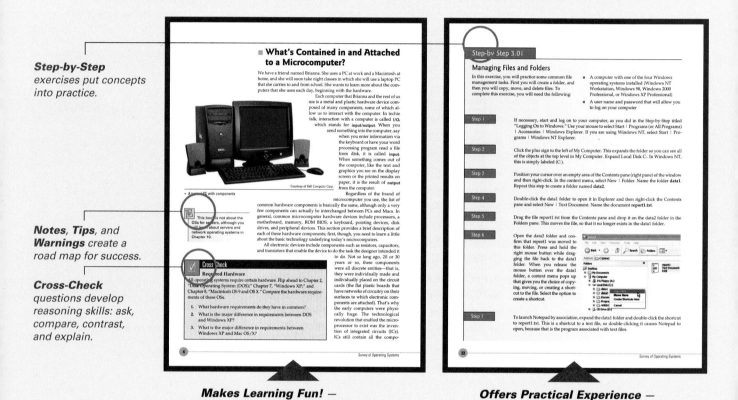

Step-by-Step exercises put concepts into practice.

Notes, Tips, and **Warnings** create a road map for success.

Cross-Check questions develop reasoning skills: ask, compare, contrast, and explain.

Makes Learning Fun! — Rich, colorful text and enhanced illustrations bring technical subjects to life.

Offers Practical Experience — Step-by-Step tutorials and lab assignments develop essential hands-on skills and put concepts in real-world contexts.

Proven Learning Method Keeps You on Track

The Mike Meyers' Computer Skills series is structured to give you a practical working knowledge of baseline IT skills and technologies. The series' active learning methodology guides you beyond mere recall and, through thought-provoking activities, labs, and sidebars, helps you develop critical thinking, diagnostic, and communication skills.

Effective Learning Tools

This colorful, pedagogically rich book is designed to make learning easy and enjoyable and to help you develop the skills and critical thinking abilities that will enable you to adapt to different job situations and troubleshoot problems.

Rich McMahon's proven ability to explain concepts in a clear, direct, even humorous way makes these books interesting, motivational, and fun.

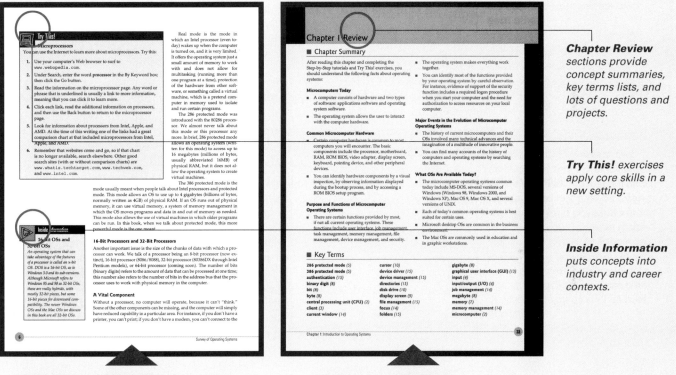

Chapter Review sections provide concept summaries, key terms lists, and lots of questions and projects.

Try This! exercises apply core skills in a new setting.

Inside Information puts concepts into industry and career contexts.

Engaging and Motivational —
Using a conversational style and proven instructional approach, the authors explain technical concepts in a clear, interesting way using real-world examples.

Robust Learning Tools —
Summaries, key term lists, quizzes, essay questions, and lab projects help you practice skills and measure progress.

Each chapter includes:

- **Learning Objectives** that set measurable goals for chapter-by-chapter progress
- **Four-Color Illustrations** that give you a clear picture of the technologies
- **Step-by-Step Tutorials** that teach you to perform essential tasks and procedures hands-on
- **Try This!**, **Cross-Check**, and **Inside Information** sidebars that encourage you to practice and apply concepts in real-world settings

- **Notes**, **Tips**, and **Warnings** that guide you through difficult areas
- **Chapter Summaries** and **Key Terms Lists** that provide you with an easy way to review important concepts and vocabulary
- **Challenging End-of-Chapter Tests** that include vocabulary-building exercises, multiple-choice questions, essay questions, and on-the-job lab projects

CONTENTS

FOREWORD FROM MIKE MEYERS

This book, like the other books in this series, is designed for exactly one function: to give you a broad introduction and overview of various aspects of the information technology (IT) world. If you're new to computers, then welcome! This book is for you. If you're trying to decide where you want to go within the big world of IT, then again welcome—this book will help you sort out the many options and figure out where your interests may or may not lie. Do you want to become a Microsoft Windows expert? Do you want to get into troubleshooting and repairing PCs? What about becoming a network administrator? These books will help you understand the many aspects of IT and the many jobs within the IT world that are available.

So how will this book help you understand what IT is all about? Well, let's start by exploring the text in front of you right now. Like all of the books in this series, it is written in a very relaxed, conversational style that's a pleasure to read. We've tossed the staid, boring technical writing style out the window and instead written as though we're speaking directly to you—because as far as we're concerned, we are. In this and the other books in this series, we aren't afraid of the occasional contraction, nor do we worry about staying in third person. We've pretty much dumped all those other dry, pedantic rules that most technical writing has reduced itself to. I've suffered reading those books, and I swore when it came time to put together this series that we were going to break that mold—and we have! With over a million copies now in print using this series' conversational style, we think a lot of folks agree with what we're doing.

Keep your finger on this page and leaf through the book for a moment. Isn't it beautiful? Sure, there are plenty of exercises and questions for you to use to practice your skills, but let the left side of your brain take a nap and let the right side appreciate just how attractive this book is. The four-color printing and all of the colorful elements give the book what I describe very scientifically as a "happy feeling"—akin to walking the aisle at a grocery store.

Last—and this is very important—you'll never find yourself lost in any of these books. You'll never get blindsided by a term that hasn't been defined earlier. You won't find yourself reading one topic and suddenly grinding gears as new, totally unrelated topics smack you in the face. Every topic leads from simple to complex, from broad to detailed, and from old to new, building concept upon concept while you read, making the book hard to put down. This is what I call *Flow*, and it's the most important aspect of these books.

So enjoy your reading. If you have any questions, feel free to contact me at michaelm@totalsem.com.

Mike Meyers

INTRODUCTION

■ What Will You Learn?

In this book, you'll learn what networks are and why they are helpful—why they are so very important that they are worth studying early in your career. You'll learn how networks function, and perhaps most important for your future peace of mind, you'll learn how to make them work and get them to do just what you want them to do. You'll learn how different companies' network operating systems (NOSs), and even different versions of an individual company's NOS, tackle the same problems. You'll learn where they are similar and where they are different. Best of all, you'll learn to be comfortable with almost any networking situation you'll encounter on the job.

This book is organized into ten chapters:

■ Chapter 1, *Introducing Basic Network Concepts*, will give you an overview of microcomputer hardware and will introduce you to the basic functions common to all operating systems. This stuff is important because one of the major functions of an operating system is to manage computer hardware.

■ Chapter 2, *Installing Network Hardware*, covers all of the physical components that are essential to connecting computers to a network, including the Internet. You'll learn about different network components, such as workstations, network servers, routers, cables, wireless systems, among many other things. You'll also get your hands dirty by learning how to install network interface cards and create a network cable connection.

■ Chapter 3, *Communicating Over Networks*, provides you with a fundamental introduction to how networks communicate and send data from one computer to another. You'll start with the bits and bytes of digital signals, work your way through computer addressing, delve into the essentials of communication protocols, and finally learn how to design a network.

■ Chapter 4, *Installing Network Operating Systems*, teaches you how to install three major network operating systems: Novell Netware 6.0 server, Windows 2000 Server, and Red Hat Linux Server. For each server, you'll work through similar steps to prepare your hardware for installation, verify its compatibility, check the configurations, and test its operation.

■ Chapter 5, *Accessing Networks*, is where you'll learn how to install and configure client software on network workstations. In this chapter, you'll learn how to install and configure three client-side operating systems: Windows XP Professional, Novell Client, and Red Hat Linux.

- Chapter 6, *Building a Directory Service*, covers the Windows operating system that combines the friendly, consumer-oriented versions of Windows with the robust nature of the Windows NT products. This chapter will give you the skills you'll need to install, configure, manage, and troubleshoot Windows 2000.

- Chapter 7, *Creating Network File Systems*, will teach you about storing data and applications for users to share on your classroom network. You will first learn about Novell's method for storing and retrieving these items. Next you will learn about the comparable filing system Microsoft uses in Active Directory (AD). Finally, you will use both of these filing systems to store items on your network.

- Chapter 8, *Printing Over a Network*, will teach you about network printing. You will create local printers and access those printers over a network. You will share printers and learn about Microsoft's printer-sharing techniques as well as become familiar with Novell NetWare print features.

- Chapter 9, *Securing a Network*, is a lesson you can't afford to miss. It's all about being aware of the risks and knowing how to plan for a secure network. This chapter will teach you how to do both and set you on the right road to network security.

- Chapter 10, *Managing a Network*, will teach you how users can help manage their own computers—by running utilities that check their disks or defragment their storage, by backing up their own files, and by viewing their active tasks using Task Manager. On your server, you will learn about using the Simple Network Management Protocol (SNMP), Performance console, and Network Monitor. You will also learn about the compression and quota-management tools available on NTFS volumes and how to use Novell's text-based commands and NetWare Loadable Modules (NLMs) at the NetWare server console. Finally, you will examine some of the features of specific NetWare utilities, such as MONITOR, DSREPAIR, and NWCONFIG.

■ You Will Learn to...

Working in the networking field often requires you to have an extensive and constantly updated encyclopedia of information. Starting out that way would require you to learn networking information at an enormous rate, similar to drinking water by putting your face in front of an opened fire hydrant! Rather, you will find that this book presents just the key points about networking, and will help guide you as you continue to explore the specifics of the field. This book is also designed to teach you basic skills that you'll need in order to be successful as you begin working with networks.

Walk and Talk Like a Pro

Each chapter starts with a list of learning objectives. These are followed by lucid explanations of each topic supported by a real-world, on-the-job scenario and enhanced by liberal use of graphics and tables. To give you hands-on experience and help you "walk the walk," each chapter contains detailed Step-by-Step tutorials and short Try This! exercises that enable you to practice the concepts. To help you "talk the talk," each chapter contains definitions of networking terms, summarized in a Key Terms list and compiled into a Glossary at the end of the book. Be ready for a Key Term Quiz at the end of each chapter!

Troubleshoot Like a Pro

While there is quite a bit of useful information in this book, a single book simply can't give you everything you need to know about networking. In addition to providing you with a solid introduction to the networking field, we'll also give you some of the tools that will help you help yourself, which is a valuable skill whether you're on the job or working at home. For example, we'll show you how to use the help files and perform updates to your new operating systems, and we'll teach you how to use the Internet to find even more information that will help you with potential troubleshooting problems.

Think Like a Pro

We've also included Inside Information sidebars, which provide insight into some of the subtleties of working with networks, and Cross Checks that help you understand how networking comes together. Notes and Tips are sprinkled throughout the chapters, and Warnings help prevent mishaps (or an emotional meltdown). At the end of each chapter, a Key Term Quiz, Multiple-Choice Quiz, and Essay Quiz help you measure what you've learned and hone your ability to present information on paper. The Lab Projects challenge you to independently complete tasks related to what you've just learned.

■ Resources for Teachers

Teachers are our heroes, to whom we give our thanks and for whom we have created a powerful collection of time-saving teaching tools. These tools are available on CD-ROM:

- An Instructor's Manual that maps to the organization of the textbook
- ExamView® Pro testbank software, which generates a wide array of paper or network-based tests, and features automatic grading
- Hundreds of questions, written by experienced IT instructors
- A wide variety of question types and difficulty levels, allowing teachers to customize each test to maximize student progress
- Engaging PowerPoint® slides on the lecture topics
- A crosswalk that highlights the IT skill standards addressed by the McGraw-Hill *Introduction to Networking* textbook
- A training document that helps instructors understand and use the features of a skill standards–aligned curriculum
- 10 skill standards–based activities with associated assessment tools

Introducing Basic Network Concepts

"In the beginning, there were no networks. Life was bad."

—MIKE MEYERS

In this chapter, you will learn how to:

■ **Identify human and computer networks**

■ **Describe the benefits of networks**

■ **Distinguish between the different types of networks**

Networks are everywhere—or so it seems. You can hardly do anything with data that does not involve a network. Like the human networks that we are all part of, computer networks let us share information and resources. In business, the reliance on networks is even more pervasive than in homes or schools. Networks help individuals and businesses alike save money, but they also help create income. Without a doubt, networking within the home will catch on over the next few years as it has in business. Soon, nearly all individuals in even moderately developed nations will have networked components throughout their homes. Those that don't will be *netologically* disadvantaged because they will not be able to learn or to function at the same level as those who are networked.

In this chapter, you'll begin by relating networks to situations and concepts you already know. Once you have a basic understanding of what networks are and what they can do, it helps if you can actually begin working with them. In fact, it is so helpful to learn the ropes of networking through hands-on guided practice that that's what is planned for you here. You will play the role of an employee in a fictional company, and you'll have to learn on the job. The more you *become* the person, the more you will learn about the need for and operation of computer networks.

■ Understanding Networks

Although you are probably taking this class to learn about computer networks, and some of you probably already know how important networks are to businesses that want to survive, we will begin this discussion as though you are an employee in a netologically disadvantaged (my term for those who have minimal network awareness) company. You might actually be an employee working for such a company and trying to help it out of that predicament, or you may know of people or companies that are in this sort of struggle.

Lauren has recently been hired as the computer manager for SinkRSwim Pools. Lauren is a certified networking administrator, but her new company unfortunately has only outdated computers. The owner recognized that the company's lack of growth was directly tied to the employees' lack of computer skills, so in her first meeting after being hired, Lauren was given the authority to purchase the additional computers and create the network she had proposed to the owner in her initial job interview. The owner gave her a six-month timeline in which to implement networking at SinkRSwim Pools in such a way that the workers will understand its use and welcome the new knowledge it requires. She was also informed that the thought of learning new computer skills frightened some long-term SinkRSwim Pools employees. The owner expects Lauren to help them become more at ease with the computers so they will be more likely to learn the necessary skills.

Lauren's first goal is to ease the workers' fears by teaching them about computers and showing them how a need for networks develops naturally. Lauren knows that if her fellow employees understand the concept of networking, the computer network will more likely be successful in the company. Lauren has decided to review basic network concepts with her coworkers as she works with them on their new computers.

Human Networks

In its broadest sense, a **network** consists of two or more entities, or objects, sharing resources and information. Although this book is about computer networks, there are networks that don't involve computers, and those networks are everywhere. You have grown accustomed to working with them, possibly without even knowing it.

It may not matter to you that, in a basic sense, sharing (giving or getting) is a fundamental aspect of networking. You just know that you do it.

Family Network

Most people belong to a family network in which related people share their resources and information. This sharing is bi-directional because even the youngest family members share information of some sort. As the family grows, so does the network.

Peer Network

Outside the family, there is a community that offers a wider array of resources than the typical family can provide. Naturally, it makes sense to

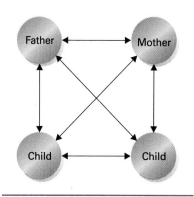

- A network connects members of a family together.

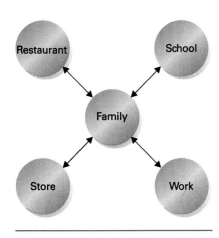

- The family network connects with the greater community.

In sidebars and the end-of-chapter exercises throughout this coursebook, you will be working with a real-world company called Technology Education and Acquisition Center of Houston (TEACH) that is currently undergoing a sudden expansion. In fact, it has just posted an announcement in the local newspaper, listing several available management positions within the company. It seems there is an opportunity to acquire another highly successful facility in another part of the state, and all the current employees are moving. Later in the chapter, you will find yourself role-playing as one of the replacement candidates vying for one of the company's high-paying positions.

connect the family to this community to take advantage of the wealth of resources available around town. This type of information/resource sharing can be as simple as loaning a hammer to a neighbor, car-pooling with work associates, or helping a friend with his or her homework. All of these activities involve sharing, or trading, resources. This kind of network is represented by a two-way relationship, a give and take among equals or peers.

Restaurant Network: The Client and the Server

So, in any type of human network, there's a lot of giving and taking. You're already more accustomed to the client/server perspective in networking than you realize. For instance, when you go to dinner at a restaurant, you become a customer, or **client**, enjoying the food and drink prepared and served to you by the restaurant. On the other hand, the waiter works as a **server**, controlling and providing his customers with access to resources in the form of placing orders for and delivering food items. The server knows that requests will be made of him (access is sought when an order is placed) and that he will service those making the requests (access is granted when the order is delivered).

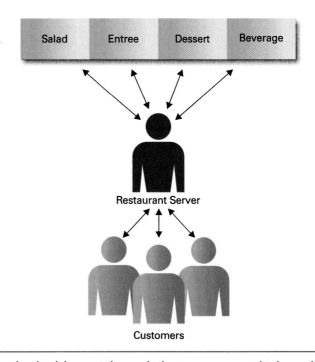

- In a dining situation, it is easy to know whether you are supposed to be serving or being served.

Contact Network

Anyone who has looked for a job knows that one of the best ways to find a job is to network. That is, create a list of friends and associates who will help you find the perfect job. The more people you meet and get to know, the better your chances of obtaining work. As you develop and nurture your career, this contact network will serve you best because your role in it will change as you gain more experience. Soon, you may be able to help the people who helped you. And as your personal and professional networks grow, so do your opportunities.

These examples of human networks should help you understand that networking is common between people and is not just an activity restricted to computers. However, this book will focus on computer networks—connecting computers and having them communicate with each other.

Computer Networks

A **computer network** consists of two or more computing devices that are connected in order to share the components of your network (its resources) and the information you store there, as shown in Figure 1.1. The most basic computer network (which consists of just two connected computers) can expand and become more usable when additional computers join and add their resources to those being shared.

The first computer, yours, is commonly referred to as your **local computer**. It is more likely to be used as a location where you do work, a **workstation**, than as a storage or controlling location, a server. As more and more computers are connected to a network and share their resources, the network becomes a more powerful tool, because employees using a network with more information and more capability are able to accomplish more through those added computers or additional resources.

The real power of networking computers becomes apparent if you envision your own network growing and then connecting it with other distinct networks, enabling communication and resource sharing across both networks. That is, one network can be connected to another network and become a more powerful tool because of the greater resources. For example,

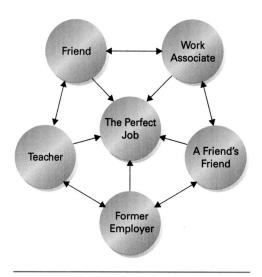

• The more people in your network, the better your chances of finding that perfect job.

For the remainder of this text, the term *network* will be used to mean *computer network*.

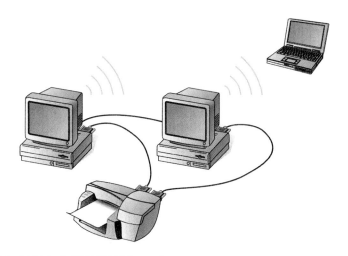

• **Figure 1.1**   A computer network can be as simple as two or more computers communicating.

you could connect the network you and your classmates develop for this course to similarly constructed networks from other introductory networking classes if you wanted them to share your information and networked resources. Those classes could be within your own school, or they could be anywhere in the world. Wherever that newly joined network is, the communication and resource sharing activities in that new network could then be shared with anyone connected to your network. All you have to do is join that new network's community or allow its members to join yours.

In addition, a company's cost of doing business can be reduced as a result of sharing **data** (defined as a piece or pieces of information) and resources. Instead of having individual copies of the data at several locations around the company, and needing to keep all of them similarly updated, a company using a network can have just one shared copy of that data and share it, needing to keep only that one set of data updated. Furthermore, sharing networked resources (like printers) means that more people can use a particular resource and a wider variety of resources (like different printers) can be used by each network user. Any time a company can do more with less, or buy fewer items to do the same job, its total costs are reduced, and it is able to make more money per dollar spent.

Network Plan

Networking computers first and tracking the connections later can quickly become confusing and unmanageable as you try to find which computer communicates with and shares resources with which other computers. In your human network, do you share everything with your friends? In your family network, would you want your parents or guardians to know your every thought? You have your information-sharing plan in your head, and it is important to keep track of it so you don't make a mistake and share something where it was not intended.

Similar concerns must be considered while designing a computer network. Before you even connect your first computers together, you should have a plan. A **network plan**, therefore, is a formally created product that shows all the network's components and the planned connections between them. Such a plan is also used to manage the various types of information. Your plan should show what types of information are stored where, and who is allowed to use each type.

Information Management

Your network plan should help you manage the information gathered, stored, and shared between your users. If you were given an empty three-drawer filing cabinet and told to use it to organize your company's information, you would have an excellent (although manual) example of a filing system that needs a plan. Having an overall guide that tells you who will be allowed access to the three drawers will help determine what you store in each one. Once you have that part of the plan, you could put the least-used information in the bottom drawer, the more-used in the middle drawer, and the most-used in the top drawer so that it is easier for your users to access their information. Knowing who needs to know what, and its corollary—who does not need to know what—lets you determine whether to lock a particular drawer, too.

Even when we discuss implementing a three-drawer manual filing system, the importance of having a network plan ahead of time becomes evident. If you put the limited-access material in a drawer open to all employees, how do you keep it secure? Additional security measures (like adding a lock to a drawer, or moving the secure information somewhere else) may be required later.

A networking plan could tell you that as specific types of sensitive data (like medical, personal, or payroll information) are gathered or grouped, they should be stored higher in the hierarchical structure (ranked from most sensitive to least sensitive), and this can save you time in the end. That plan should specify that the access requirements are stricter for sensitive data and reduce the number of people able to use specific types of information.

The distribution side of the networking plan, as opposed to the accumulation side of the plan discussed above, should spell out that the more an individual has access to the data in storage, the less they should be able to share groups of information entrusted to them. For example, you may not mind sharing your first name, but you would probably object to an instructor openly distributing all information in your school records to anyone requesting it.

> The **format**—or the strict requirements placed on the order and structure of how you enter data—is very important. The number 123456789, for instance, could be either a zip code or a Social Security number. If it is formatted as 123-45-6789, you know that it is a Social Security number. What would you do if you were told that your life depended on your making a payment to the bank on the date 010203? When would that payment be made? Would the payment date change if that date were in the year-month-day format? Of course it would, and the payment would be long overdue. Format, then, is important!

Information's Importance

If you think about the manual filing system we discussed using a filing cabinet, an important computing concept is easy to recognize. Some information is more important or more sensitive than the rest. It is usually obvious in real filing cabinet systems, because the top drawer is usually where the most sensitive information is stored, and it is locked. Few people in an organization have access to that information. For example, credit card or Social Security numbers are information that should be given the highest level of security—access to that information is given only to a limited number of people in a company. On the other hand, some information, such as Web pages, newsletters, and product information, is created for everyone to see, even outside a company. Figure 1.2 shows how this kind of information is organized into a **hierarchy of information**, where the most detailed information is found at the top and the more general, less secure information is located at the bottom. How much information would you be willing to provide about yourself to a perfect stranger? Country of birth? Sure. State of residence? Why not? But you might have second thoughts about advertising your street address or phone number to a stranger.

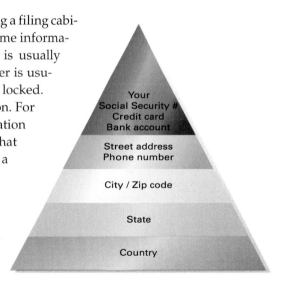

• **Figure 1.2** The hierarchy of information—The more specific the information becomes, the more restricted it should be. What kind of data would you be willing to give to a stranger?

Cross Check

Thinking About a Network Plan

You have just learned about the need to describe information management and data hierarchies in your network plan. It can be equally important when you receive data to know that such a plan is in place. Use what you have learned about creating a network plan as you answer the following questions:

1. If you knew that your school's (or your employer's) plan stipulated that sharing sensitive information was to be strictly controlled, and you agreed with those controls, how would that knowledge affect the degree of data sensitivity that you would be willing to share over that network's resources?

2. Although you might choose to share some (or all) of your personal information with selected classmates, would you feel comfortable if you thought your instructor planned on sharing your whole file freely with everyone in your class without your permission?

3. Even if it were not yet true, would the thought of your instructor sharing your information freely affect the amount of information you shared when someone else in authority on the network requested sensitive data?

The collection and proper manipulation of many seemingly unimportant pieces of information, and the effective tracking of them, makes information management on networks so important, just as when you are maintaining a manual filing system. A single piece of information in a data field, such as your first name, can seem unimportant. However, by combining your first name with other pieces of related information, like your last name, address, age, gender, and phone number (stored in other data fields), the pieces can be put together to create a data record, which can accurately describe something (or someone) that is important—like you. Finally, combining similar records (such as records describing all your classmates) creates a file that, because it contains sensitive information from more than one source, is more sensitive than a single record.

Information sharing, therefore, has serious security issues to be considered, and network access to data must be evaluated carefully so that only those who need it can access it. Security will be discussed in more depth in Chapter 9.

■ Identifying the Benefits of Networks

Ricky finds himself pondering the question, "What are networks used for?" He is the second person brought aboard SinkRSwim Pools to enhance its

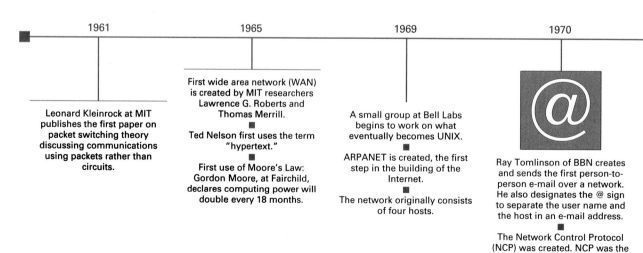

1961
Leonard Kleinrock at MIT publishes the first paper on packet switching theory discussing communications using packets rather than circuits.

1965
First wide area network (WAN) is created by MIT researchers Lawrence G. Roberts and Thomas Merrill.
■
Ted Nelson first uses the term "hypertext."
■
First use of Moore's Law: Gordon Moore, at Fairchild, declares computing power will double every 18 months.

1969
A small group at Bell Labs begins to work on what eventually becomes UNIX.
■
ARPANET is created, the first step in the building of the Internet.
■
The network originally consists of four hosts.

1970
Ray Tomlinson of BBN creates and sends the first person-to-person e-mail over a network. He also designates the @ sign to separate the user name and the host in an e-mail address.
■
The Network Control Protocol (NCP) was created. NCP was the first standardized network protocol used by ARPANET.

network use. Remember, that's where Lauren is creating a network to replace the company's outdated computers. Ricky volunteered to help Lauren explain the benefits of networking to the company's workers as part of his computer class project at school. The workers already have the new computers Lauren ordered and are happily doing more with them, but Ricky is helping Lauren network them and is encouraging the workers to use the network.

Ricky remembers Mike's words at the opening of this chapter: "In the beginning there were no networks. Life was bad." This may have meant one thing to Mike when he said it, but the beginning for these workers is right now. They haven't had networks, and they don't see why they should need them. Ricky decides to discuss the historical development of computers and show how they helped other businesses.

In the early days of the personal computer (PC), during the late '70s and early '80s, often a PC was used as a **stand-alone computer** and operated independently from other computers, as shown in Figure 1.3. When, over the span of just those few years, their use proliferated and more PCs were found relatively close to each other, users began sharing information. The information was either printed out or copied from one computer to another using backup or storage devices, such as tapes, disks, or other digital storage media.

The printout or the storage device was then physically carried to another computer where the information was reentered or copied from the portable media into the next computer. This process was referred to as a **sneakernet** because users actually had to walk from computer to computer. It was

● **Figure 1.3**   Stand-alone computers are operated independently.

1973	1974	1975	1976

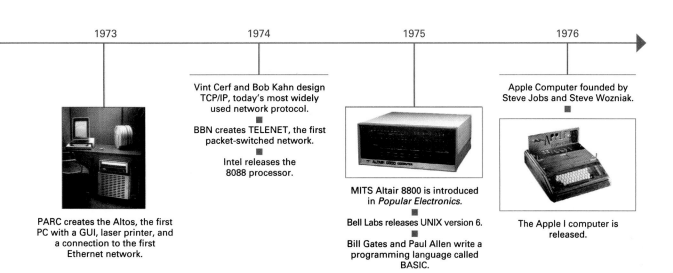

Vint Cerf and Bob Kahn design TCP/IP, today's most widely used network protocol.
■
BBN creates TELENET, the first packet-switched network.
■
Intel releases the 8088 processor.

Apple Computer founded by Steve Jobs and Steve Wozniak.
■

MITS Altair 8800 is introduced in *Popular Electronics*.

PARC creates the Altos, the first PC with a GUI, laser printer, and a connection to the first Ethernet network.

Bell Labs releases UNIX version 6.
■
Bill Gates and Paul Allen write a programming language called BASIC.

The Apple I computer is released.

- One sneakernet alternative was the floppy disk, which was used to transfer data between computers that were not networked.

probably the cheapest type of network—unless the computers were large distances apart or the information needed to be shared among many computers. Other drawbacks to sneakernets were that printouts were often bulky, and the storage devices could hold a relatively small amount of data compared to the large amount of output users produced.

Once computers were connected by networks, information sharing increased dramatically. People found that more data helped them make better decisions, and companies started saving money. Many original networks were designed to facilitate communication, but they were quickly expanded as businesses noticed increased productivity and reduced costs.

Sharing Information

Computers increase your ability to communicate. Once you begin working with a computer, you are likely to become more productive. However, what do you do with that increased productivity if you are not connected to anyone? Communication requires not only someone with information to share but also someone on the other end with whom to share it. Companies don't benefit by creating sheer volumes of output—they benefit when the increased output helps them make better decisions or increases the likelihood of increased income. Having your computers networked allows you to do both with your newfound increases.

The initial reason for developing most computer networks was to assist users with sharing their increased output, especially between computers in the same general vicinity, as shown in Figure 1.4. However, users wanted not only to share information with others, they wanted to communicate about that information after someone else had it, too. In addition to transmitting the user's original information, computer networks enabled those users to discuss what was being transmitted, and this resulted in even more communication. Additional network communications techniques thus came into being, such as e-mail and video conferencing. Furthermore, with the increases in the sizes of networks, sharing no longer had to be concerned with proximity. The use of networks has effectively erased distance and

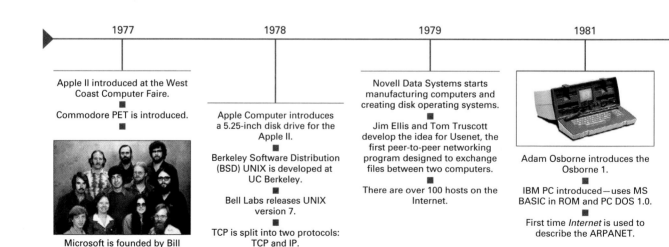

1977	1978	1979	1981
Apple II introduced at the West Coast Computer Faire. ∎ Commodore PET is introduced. ∎	Apple Computer introduces a 5.25-inch disk drive for the Apple II. ∎ Berkeley Software Distribution (BSD) UNIX is developed at UC Berkeley. ∎ Bell Labs releases UNIX version 7. ∎ TCP is split into two protocols: TCP and IP.	Novell Data Systems starts manufacturing computers and creating disk operating systems. ∎ Jim Ellis and Tom Truscott develop the idea for Usenet, the first peer-to-peer networking program designed to exchange files between two computers. ∎ There are over 100 hosts on the Internet.	Adam Osborne introduces the Osborne 1. ∎ IBM PC introduced—uses MS BASIC in ROM and PC DOS 1.0. ∎ First time *Internet* is used to describe the ARPANET.

Microsoft is founded by Bill Gates (bottom left) and Paul Allen (bottom right).

• **Figure 1.4**   Computer communication—Two computers in the same general vicinity should be able to communicate.

time constraints. You can communicate almost instantly to anywhere in the world that is connected to your network.

Networks are an effective way to communicate. Using networks, companies can send the same information to large numbers of employees or customers quickly and efficiently. Examples include company newsletters and announcements for employees, as well as advertisements and purchase information for customers. Also, individual employees are more likely to communicate with larger numbers of individuals both inside and outside the company using **e-mail**, an electronic means of communicating that is similar to mail but done on computers, usually over the Internet, over networks. E-mail is the most commonly used feature of the Internet, and its use is growing dramatically. In fact, e-mail is fast becoming the primary choice for much of our daily communication.

Sharing Resources

In the sneakernet era, users spent huge amounts of time attempting to share their resources. They had to physically distribute files that others needed. Expenditures for printers and other attached computer components rose

> The ability of networks to be joined together to form larger networks has resulted in what is called the *Internet*—a worldwide collection of connected computers able to communicate with each other.

> You should be aware that there is next to no privacy when sending e-mail. Your electronic message can not only be intercepted and read anywhere along its route to your ultimate recipient, but it can later be forwarded, without your permission, to any number of additional recipients. You should, therefore, use care in what you say as well as how you say it.

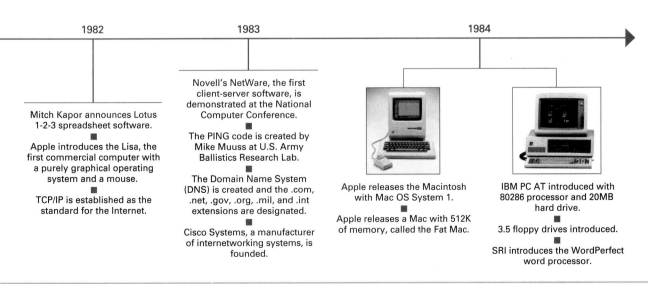

rapidly while the individual components themselves were not being used to their full capacity. On top of that, the hard disk storage on each local computer began filling up, partly because everyone had a copy of every document. One copy of that data, and even the applications that produced it, could more efficiently be stored in a single location and shared over a network.

The ability to share resources was another reason networks were created, and it is still one of the main purposes for using networks. The inevitable technology creep (the continuing need for additional investment in technology that is required to stay current) extends the computer user's involvement in technology because companies expect employees to learn new systems as they are installed. Companies also look for ways to make the best use of their investments by sharing the purchased resources among multiple departments. Let's look at some of the resources that are commonly shared over computer networks.

Peripherals

Many companies start with multiple stand-alone computers. Not too long after the initial computer purchase, however, additional components that attach to a computer, called **peripherals**, like printers, scanners, and speakers, are purchased and are connected to that computer to expand its use (see Figure 1.5). When there are multiple users and computers, it soon becomes apparent that the peripheral devices are seldom fully utilized. Money can be saved if some of these peripherals are shared, instead of having to purchase a separate set for each computer. Networking enables the sharing of peripherals.

The ability to share printers was very often enough of a cost savings for companies to invest in implementing and supporting a simple network. The company could then also realize additional cost savings as it shared additional

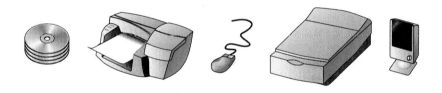

• **Figure 1.5**   Common network peripherals

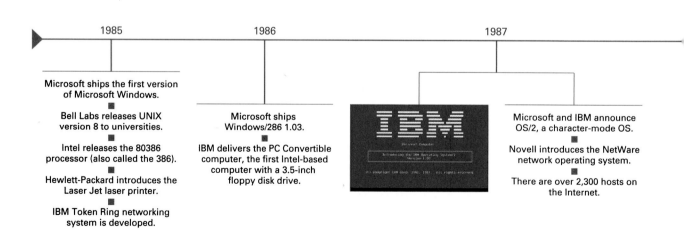

1985
- Microsoft ships the first version of Microsoft Windows.
- Bell Labs releases UNIX version 8 to universities.
- Intel releases the 80386 processor (also called the 386).
- Hewlett-Packard introduces the Laser Jet laser printer.
- IBM Token Ring networking system is developed.

1986
- Microsoft ships Windows/286 1.03.
- IBM delivers the PC Convertible computer, the first Intel-based computer with a 3.5-inch floppy disk drive.

1987
- Microsoft and IBM announce OS/2, a character-mode OS.
- Novell introduces the NetWare network operating system.
- There are over 2,300 hosts on the Internet.

peripheral devices, such as faxes, modems, scanners, plotters, and virtually any other device that connects to computers. Sharing peripherals often ends up producing significant cost savings and more than justifies the expense of adding a network.

Storage

Data was being loaded on the computers of every fledgling network user as they expanded their network use. Users quickly ran out of space on their own local computers, so the people in charge of the networks began devising ways to store data centrally so that it was accessible to any user who needed it. Large amounts of storage capacity, usually in fast, very powerful computers, were set up to act as storage locations for this data where access to it could be controlled by the person storing the data.

Applications

Cost and space savings are achieved when computer users can centrally store their software **applications**—the computer **programs** (organized sets of computer instructions) that make a user's computer do what needs to be done. Applications, such as those used for preparing taxes, creating text documents, or playing computer games, have grown in complexity and size and often take up considerable local storage. Installing an application once on a network and then sharing it cuts down on the storage space required when multiple users need the same application.

Unfortunately, there are still several problems with this type of arrangement. Some applications work fine with different setups for each user (different choices for screen settings and other custom features), but normally all such settings must be the same for all users. Sometimes, applications still function better when installed on a user's local computer.

Assisting Collaboration

Once you have digital information and the ability to share it instantly with others over networks, you can have multiple people working on the same process collectively. Much of the initial communication about computer-produced products that occurred during and immediately after the sneakernet era dealt

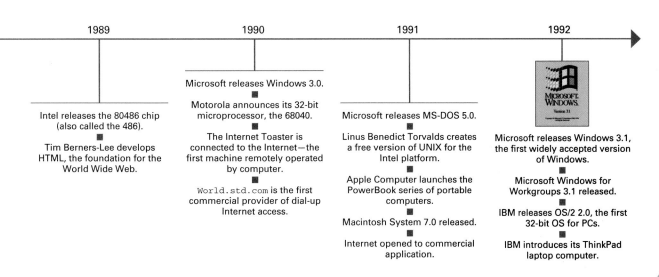

1989

1990

1991

1992

Intel releases the 80486 chip (also called the 486).

Tim Berners-Lee develops HTML, the foundation for the World Wide Web.

Microsoft releases Windows 3.0.

Motorola announces its 32-bit microprocessor, the 68040.

The Internet Toaster is connected to the Internet—the first machine remotely operated by computer.

World.std.com is the first commercial provider of dial-up Internet access.

Microsoft releases MS-DOS 5.0.

Linus Benedict Torvalds creates a free version of UNIX for the Intel platform.

Apple Computer launches the PowerBook series of portable computers.

Macintosh System 7.0 released.

Internet opened to commercial application.

Microsoft releases Windows 3.1, the first widely accepted version of Windows.

Microsoft Windows for Workgroups 3.1 released.

IBM releases OS/2 2.0, the first 32-bit OS for PCs.

IBM introduces its ThinkPad laptop computer.

with coworker **collaboration**, with coworkers discussing each other's work or possibly even exchanging opinions about what other users had created. Those early computer users found that once they created something and sent it out for review, the comments returned often led to important adjustments that would improve the original product. Such collaboration assisted the widespread use of computers because it provided a tangible benefit that businesses could associate with the increased costs of installing computers in the first place.

Many software makers took this early form of collaboration into consideration and added that feature to the capabilities of their software. The newest versions of the applications included in Microsoft's Office suite (such as Word, Access, Excel, and PowerPoint) allow multiple users to access and make changes to the same document at the same time. That way, all users can work together on the original document, and changes made by any collaborating member are immediately posted within the document. A more powerful implementation of this concept can be found in an application designed to facilitate collaboration, such as Microsoft's Terminal Server (see `http://www.microsoft.com/windows2000/technologies/terminal/default.asp` for more information).

Facilitating Centralized Management

Just connecting computers to a network meant that some sort of similarity existed among them (or else the computers would not be able to communicate), and a maintenance capability may have been available in the early networks. However, it wasn't until much later (in the mid '90s) that maintenance personnel started using networks to assist with the management tasks associated with the network's operation and maintenance.

It came about as a direct result of standardization and interoperability, which meant computers worked the same way and could work with each other. This was a drastic change to the original networks, where all the different networked components had different computer programs, or **software** (a set of instructions that control the operation of a computer) running them. Having more similarities meant lower support costs. These savings were usually due to **economies of scale** brought about by buying more similar computers and obtaining a lower per-unit cost. Companies soon began

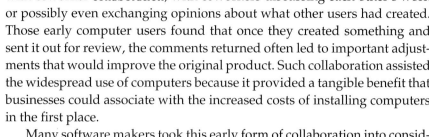

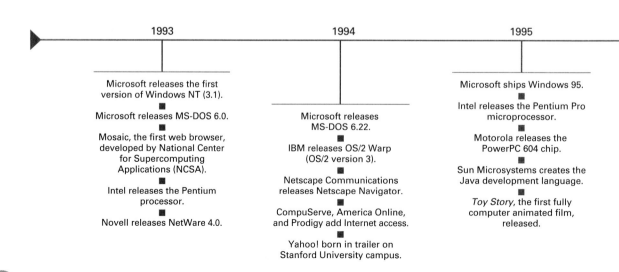

1993	1994	1995
Microsoft releases the first version of Windows NT (3.1).		Microsoft ships Windows 95.
Microsoft releases MS-DOS 6.0.	Microsoft releases MS-DOS 6.22.	Intel releases the Pentium Pro microprocessor.
Mosaic, the first web browser, developed by National Center for Supercomputing Applications (NCSA).	IBM releases OS/2 Warp (OS/2 version 3).	Motorola releases the PowerPC 604 chip.
Intel releases the Pentium processor.	Netscape Communications releases Netscape Navigator.	Sun Microsystems creates the Java development language.
Novell releases NetWare 4.0.	CompuServe, America Online, and Prodigy add Internet access.	*Toy Story*, the first fully computer animated film, released.
	Yahoo! born in trailer on Stanford University campus.	

directing technicians to purchase similar equipment to obtain the benefit of those savings. Once that happened, the network could be used to help maintain those similar components, and this further increased efficiency and reduced the total amount companies would spend on a particular component over that equipment's usable lifetime, called **total cost of ownership (TCO)**.

Managing Software

Using the network helped reduce software costs. Savings occurred when all users on a network used the same software and when software was bought in bulk quantities for a discount. Centralizing the installation of that software also reduced operation costs because the installations could be accomplished remotely—over the network. The computer programs that were needed to perform the installations were stored on servers and made accessible over the network. The maintenance personnel would then simply log on to the network from a client computer and install the needed applications using the installation software stored on the server.

Within the past few years, even more savings have been achieved by having the centralized server initiate the software installations or updates on the client computers without the need for maintenance personnel to actually visit any of the clients.

Maintaining the Network

Purchasing similar equipment for use on the network meant that network maintenance costs were reduced because there were fewer dissimilar components. Maintenance workers no longer had to attend numerous training sessions on many different components, which meant they could spend more time maintaining the actual components.

Backing Up Data

Along those same lines, a network minimizes the time spent backing up (saving extra copies, called **backups**, of) necessary files. In the event of a hardware or software failure that causes information or applications to be lost, vital information and necessary applications can be restored if sufficient backups exist. The backup process is normally a regular activity in a company,

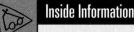
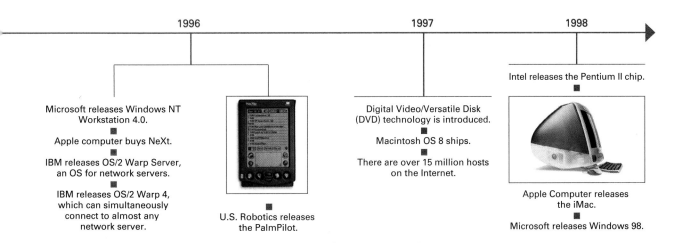

1996

Microsoft releases Windows NT Workstation 4.0.

Apple computer buys NeXt.

IBM releases OS/2 Warp Server, an OS for network servers.

IBM releases OS/2 Warp 4, which can simultaneously connect to almost any network server.

U.S. Robotics releases the PalmPilot.

1997

Digital Video/Versatile Disk (DVD) technology is introduced.

Macintosh OS 8 ships.

There are over 15 million hosts on the Internet.

1998

Intel releases the Pentium II chip.

Apple Computer releases the iMac.

Microsoft releases Windows 98.

and all transactions between scheduled backups are recorded so that the files can be restored as completely as possible. Technicians can access the backup files and recorded transactions from a central location without having to physically visit the source computers.

■ Distinguishing Between Network Classifications

Lauren may have been hired into her networking administration position at SinkRSwim Pools by a forward-thinking company owner, but she has to remember that it was that forward-thinking manager who kept his workers away from the increases in technology and did not furnish them with computers until now. She knows that even though she was given a budget, she will still have to get her network approved by her new boss. Therefore, Lauren will only get the network she has designed by increasing her new boss's knowledge about the different types of networks and convincing him that the network is necessary as designed. She decides to explain the different ways networks can be classified so she can elicit his input and support to come up with the choice she has already decided upon for the company's network.

Classifying Networks by Their Geography

Networks are frequently classified according to the geographical boundaries the network spans. Two basic geographical designations for networks—local area network (LAN) and wide area network (WAN)—are the most common. A third designation, metropolitan area network (MAN), is also used, although its use has become clouded (because it might not be a clear-cut classification anymore) as networks continue connecting to the Internet.

There is much current debate about the usefulness of any of the three geographical classifications (LAN, MAN, or WAN) now that the Internet can effectively join all computers.

These three classifications, unlike the other methods used to describe networks, are based upon the specific levels of technology they use when going from one level to the other. The three geographical classifications are discussed next because the geographical concepts and the increased emphasis they place on technology as you go from one level to the next still apply.

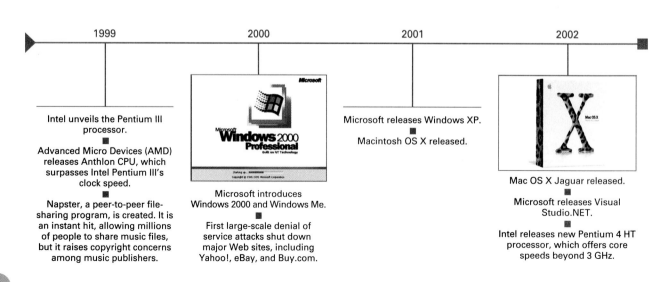

1999
Intel unveils the Pentium III processor.
■
Advanced Micro Devices (AMD) releases Anthlon CPU, which surpasses Intel Pentium III's clock speed.
■
Napster, a peer-to-peer file-sharing program, is created. It is an instant hit, allowing millions of people to share music files, but it raises copyright concerns among music publishers.

2000
Microsoft introduces Windows 2000 and Windows Me.
■
First large-scale denial of service attacks shut down major Web sites, including Yahoo!, eBay, and Buy.com.

2001
Microsoft releases Windows XP.
■
Macintosh OS X released.

2002
Mac OS X Jaguar released.
■
Microsoft releases Visual Studio.NET.
■
Intel releases new Pentium 4 HT processor, which offers core speeds beyond 3 GHz.

Local Area Network (LAN)

If the network is contained within a relatively small area, such as a classroom, school, or single building, as shown in Figure 1.6, it is commonly referred to as a **local area network (LAN)**. This type of network has the lowest cost and least overall capability of the three geographic classifications. Because the pieces of equipment in a LAN are in relatively close proximity, LANs are inexpensive to install. Despite their decreased capability, however, their closeness and resultant low costs typically result in the use of the fastest technology on a LAN. Thus, this network classification usually has the highest speed components and fastest communications equipment before the other network classifications see such equipment using the same speeds. This is because it takes less overall investment to get the smaller network running the faster equipment. LANs, therefore, are commonly considered the building blocks for creating larger networks.

Metropolitan Area Network (MAN)

As the computers get further apart, a LAN becomes more difficult to install, and additional measures such as additional communications equipment may need to be employed. When the network spans the distance of a typical metropolitan city, as shown in Figure 1.7, it can be referred to as a **metropolitan area network (MAN)**. Although this term is beginning to lose its popular use, the concept of the network outgrowing its local confines and requiring additional resources still applies. Much of the same technology, such as the fast networking components and communications equipment used in LANs, can be used in MANs, but more are required, so this classification is not quite as technologically advanced as are LANs. Although the speeds achieved in a MAN are typically as high as in a LAN, it requires high-speed connections, such as fiber optics. Increasing the distance and the technology levels increases the relative installation and operation costs of MANs.

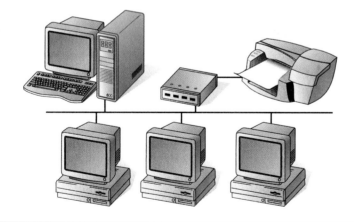

● **Figure 1.6**   A LAN covers a relatively small distance.

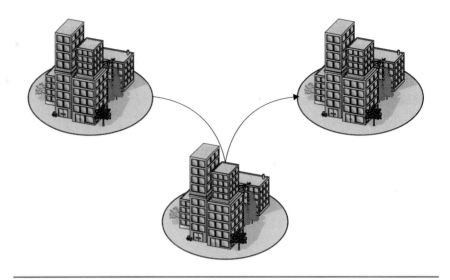

• Figure 1.7 The MAN covers a somewhat wider area than a LAN.

Wide Area Network (WAN)

The MAN outgrows its usefulness when the network must expand beyond the confines of the typical metropolitan area. When the network spans a larger area, as shown in Figure 1.8, it is classified as a **wide area network (WAN)**. Because of the extensive distances over which WANs communicate, they use long-distance telecommunications networks for their connections, which increases the costs of the network. The Internet is just a giant WAN.

Classifying Networks by Component Roles

Another method used to classify networks focuses on the roles the networked computers play in the network's operation, and more specifically on which computer controls that operation. There are two basic types of role classifications for networks—peer-to-peer networks and server-based networks. The difference between the two revolves around which computer is in charge of the network. A third classification, client-based networks, has come into existence because of the increased capabilities of the typical client computer.

• Figure 1.8   The WAN covers an extremely wide area and involves numerous transmission technologies.

Peer-to-Peer Networks

A peer is considered an equal. All computers on a **peer-to-peer network** can be considered equals, as shown in Figure 1.9. That is to say, no one computer is in charge of the network's operation. Each computer controls its own information and is capable of functioning as either a client or a server depending on which is needed at the time.

Peer-to-peer networks are popular as home networks and for use in small companies because they are inexpensive and easy to install. Most **operating systems** (the software that runs the basic computer functionality) come with peer-to-peer networking capability built in. The only other cost involved with setting up a peer-to-peer network comes into play if a computer does not have a network interface card, or NIC (the device that physically connects your computer to your network's cabling), already installed.

Typical initial peer-to-peer networking involves no security measures. Rather, each peer simply shares its resources and allows others open access to them. In fact, a peer-to-peer network becomes difficult to manage when more and more security is added to the resources. This is because users control their own security by adding password protection to each share they create. **Shares** are any resources users control on their computers, such as document folders, printers, and other peripherals. Each shared resource can actually have its own password. Someone wanting access to numerous shared resources has to remember many passwords. Security on a peer-to-peer network can quickly become complex and confusing.

Try This!
Determine Organizational Needs

It's time to determine the computer and networking needs of your company. Try this:

1. Refer to the TEACH organizational chart (see Lab Project 1.3, at the end of this chapter) and analyze it to determine how many computers the organization should have for its executive, supervisory, and support personnel.

2. Use the organizational chart itself, or a copy of the chart, to mark the location of each management workstation with the letter *W* enclosed in a green circle. For now, disregard the possible use of portable computers in your assessment.

3. Using the geographical classification possibilities, determine the TEACH network's classification and mark the location of where you would put servers. Mark the server locations with the letter *S* enclosed in a red triangle.

4. At the bottom of the TEACH organizational chart, write the total number of servers and workstations you determined were necessary based upon your analysis.

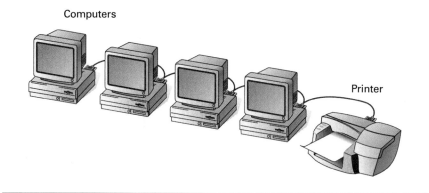

• **Figure 1.9**   A peer-to-peer network. Peer-to-peer networks have no centralized control.

While peer-to-peer networks are inexpensive to set up, they are extremely limited in scope. The accepted maximum number of peers that can operate on a peer-to-peer network is ten. They are, therefore, not appropriate for larger, more secure networks.

Server-Based Networks

Unlike peer-to-peer networks that operate without central control and are difficult to secure, a **server-based network** offers centralized control and is designed for secured operations, as shown in Figure 1.10. While there are still both clients and servers on a server-based network, a dedicated server controls the network. A **dedicated server** is one that, for all practical purposes, operates solely as a server.

A dedicated server on a server-based network services its network clients by storing data, applications, and other resources, and then providing access to those resources when called for by a client. When a client requests a resource such as a document, the server sends the whole resource (the document) over the network to the client, where it is processed and later returned to the server for continued storage.

Dedicated servers can also control the entire network's security from one central location or share that control with other specially configured servers. This central network control also contributes to the economies of scale discussed under the "Facilitating Centralized Management" section earlier in this chapter (using similar equipment results in cheaper equipment prices and fewer training costs) and makes the server-based network the dominant networking model used in networks today.

Most servers can actually operate as clients but rarely ever do, because such use may interfere with their server capability, and they are usually not in an accessible location. Typically, once a server is set up, it is secured in a location where users cannot access it. Only the network administrator should have access to a server. Therefore, users do not operate it as a workstation, and the client functionality of servers is rarely employed.

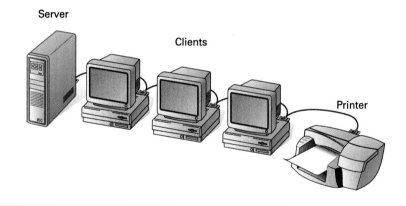

Server

Clients

Printer

● **Figure 1.10**   A server-based network. Server-based networks involve centralized control.

Client-Based Networks

Client-based networks are a further refinement to the concept of a server-based network that relieves the heavy burden on the network's capacity resulting from frequent server-performed transactions. A client-based network takes better advantage of the server's powerful processors and of the increasingly powerful computers used in typical workstations. A client-based network utilizes a client workstation's power in processing some functions locally while requesting additional processing from a server whenever it is needed for increased speed.

Client-based network servers process requests from clients and return just the results, rather than sending the original resource to the client to be processed and returned after computations are complete. Client-based networks, therefore, take advantage of the powerful processing capabilities of both the client and the server, as shown in Figure 1.11. This type of arrangement may include application servers (where entire computer programs are shared from the server) and communications servers (where e-mail and other communications media are operated).

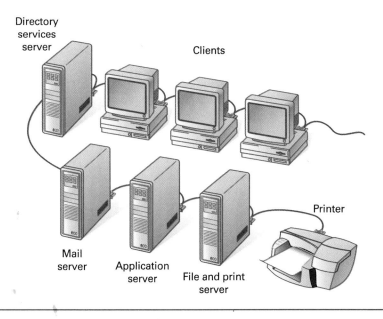

• **Figure 1.11**   A client-based network. A client-based network takes advantage of the power of both the server and the client alike.

Chapter 1 Review

■ Chapter Summary

After reading this chapter and completing the Try This! exercises, you should understand the following facts about networking:

Identify Human and Computer Networks

- A network consists of two or more entities sharing resources and information.

- Examples of basic networks include your human network, school lunchrooms, restaurant dining, and business contact development.

- The capability to share is enhanced when information is stored on computers.

- Computer networks consist of two or more computers that are connected and able to communicate.

- Networked computers share resources and information.

- Powerful networks result when additional computers are added to the communication possibilities.

- As more and more data becomes available over a network, some kind of a control system must be established.

- The hierarchy of data should be used in network planning.

- Access to data stored higher up in this chain is more strictly controlled, which means fewer people can view that data.

- *Data* is defined as a piece or pieces of information.

- The collection, proper manipulation, and effective tracking of data makes information management on networks so important.

Describe the Benefits of Networks

- Computers operated independently from others are known as stand-alone computers.

- *Sneakernet* was the term used for running data from one computer to another on disk.

- Most computer networks develop to facilitate communication, initially to share output and later to communicate through e-mail.

- The ability to share resources is another main purpose for initiating networks.

- Peripherals are additional components that attach to computers to expand their use.

- Sharing peripherals, such as printers, often offered enough of a cost savings for companies to invest in networks.

- Large computers can be set up as storage locations where data is offloaded and access to it is controlled by the person storing the data.

- Installing an application on a network and then sharing its use cuts down on the storage space required when multiple users need the same application.

- Coworkers discussing each other's work, or collaboration, assisted the widespread use of computers.

- Networks help centralize the management of software and maintenance of computers, such as installing upgrades and backing up data.

Distinguish Between the Different Types of Networks

- Networks are frequently classified according to the geographical boundaries spanned.

- A network contained within a relatively small area, such as a classroom, school, or single building, is commonly referred to as a local area network.

- A network that spans the distance of a typical metropolitan area is sometimes referred to as a metropolitan area network.

- A network covering a larger area than a single city is classified as a wide area network.

- Another method used to classify networks focuses on which computer controls the network's operation.

- All computers on a peer-to-peer network can be considered equal.

- Peer-to-peer networks are popular as home networks and for use in small companies because they are inexpensive and easy to install.

- Server-based networks offer central control and are designed for secured operations.

- A dedicated server operates solely as a server by storing data, applications, and other resources, and providing access to those resources when called for by a client.
- Client-based network servers process requests from clients and return just the results.
- Client-based networks take advantage of their own powerful processors as well as the increasingly powerful computers used as typical workstations.

■ Key Terms List

applications *(11)*	format *(5)*	programs *(11)*
backups *(13)*	hierarchy of information *(5)*	server *(2)*
client *(2)*	local area network (LAN) *(15)*	server-based network *(18)*
client-based networks *(19)*	local computer *(3)*	shares *(17)*
collaboration *(12)*	metropolitan area network (MAN) *(15)*	sneakernet *(7)*
computer network *(3)*		software *(12)*
data *(4)*	network *(1)*	stand-alone computer *(7)*
dedicated server *(18)*	network plan *(4)*	total cost of ownership (TCO) *(13)*
economies of scale *(12)*	operating systems *(17)*	wide area network (WAN) *(16)*
e-mail *(9)*	peer-to-peer network *(17)*	workstation *(3)*
	peripherals *(10)*	

■ Key Term Quiz

Use terms from the Key Terms List to complete the following sentences. Not all the terms will be used.

1. A(n) _network_ consists of two or more entities, or objects, sharing resources and information.

2. A(n) _server_ controls and provides access to resources.

3. The _network plan_ is the plan used when controlling data access in the higher levels of accumulated data storage.

4. When strict requirements are placed on the order and structure of how data is entered, that information's _heirarchy_ is said to be important.

5. A computer operating independently from other computers is called a(n) _stand-alone computer_

6. The process of physically carrying data from one computer and entering it into another computer came to be known as a(n) _sneakernet_ .

7. Additional components attached to a computer to expand its use are called _peripherals_ .

8. A user's own computer is commonly referred to as a(n) _workstation_ .

9. The lowest geographical network classification, also considered the building block when creating larger networks, is the _LAN_ .

10. The role-based network classification where all computers can be considered equal and no one computer is in charge of the network's operation is a(n) _peer to peer network_

■ Multiple Choice Quiz

1. A network consists of what minimum number of entities sharing resources and information?
   a. One
   b. Two
   c. Three
   d. Ten

2. In network terms, your ability to decide whether to share your food in the school's lunchroom

puts you mostly in which of the following positions?

a. Client

b. Client/server

c. Peer-to-peer

d. None of the above

3. A waiter in a restaurant fulfills which of the following roles?

a. Client

b. Server

c. Peer

d. All of the above

4. Which of the following is required before a computer network is present?

a. Two or more computing devices

b. Connections between devices

c. Electronic resources and information to share

d. All of the above

5. What should be done before connecting the first computers when initiating cross communication between computers?

a. Plan

b. Request permission

c. Grant permission

d. Expand

6. Which of the following is true regarding the hierarchy of data?

a. Data stored higher should be shared freely

b. Access requirements are stricter at lower levels

c. More people should have access to the highest level

d. The higher your access, the less you should share

7. Whether a nine-digit number is easily recognized as a zip code or a Social Security number is determined by which of the following?

a. Its magnitude

b. The sum of the digits

c. Its format

d. Its use

8. Which of the following is the most often used feature of the largest known WAN?

a. Exchange music

b. E-mail

c. Games

d. Centralized maintenance

9. Which of the following *cannot* be considered a peripheral device?

a. Computers

b. Printers

c. Modems

d. Scanners

10. Which of the following is *not* a purpose for a network?

a. Assist collaboration

b. Share resources

c. Inhibit communication

d. Centralize management

11. The cost savings usually brought about due to buying increased numbers of an item involves:

a. Economies of scale

b. Network collaboration

c. Communicated price comparisons

d. Client/server relations

12. Which of the following is *not* a reason for reduced maintenance costs when using networks?

a. Fewer dissimilar components

b. Training

c. Backups

d. Less frequent software upgrades

13. Which of the following is a geographical network classification?

a. Client

b. WAN

c. Server

d. Peer-to-peer

14. Which of the following describes a network where all computers are considered equal with no one computer in charge?

a. Client

b. WAN

    c. Server

    d. Peer-to-peer

15. The Internet can be classified as a giant:

    a. LAN

    b. WAN

    c. Server

    d. Client

■ Essay Quiz

1. Let's say that you were the one hired by SinkRSwim Pools in this chapter instead of Lauren. If a coworker asked you to explain yourself after you used the phrase *network of computers*, what would you say to her? Elaborate so that a novice would understand completely.

2. Chaos is happening within your network. Security was discussed when you started working at your current job, but not much emphasis was placed on it at first. Now, confidential company information is appearing in competitors' planning sessions. You remember the warning you were given by your supervisor about devising a plan. Fully discuss the concept that a hierarchy of data must be established.

3. Assume that you are a member of the TEACH organization's training department. Make out a purchase order requesting that a new training lab in the TEACH training center be joined to the network. Fully explain on your purchase order why it is necessary to join this new lab to the network and what existing components the lab will rely upon once it is connected.

4. Explain the concept of a *network client* and, after analyzing the TEACH organizational chart once again, determine the maximum number of network clients you would expect to have on that company's entire network.

5. Ricky is still out there helping Lauren enlist the cooperation of the SinkRSwim Pools workers by having them become network users. Help him come up with convincing arguments that will make those workers want to join their new workstations to the network as soon as they take delivery. Remember, they are computer novices and do not yet have access to their computers, and don't forget to be convincing.

Lab Projects

• Lab Project 1.1

In this project, you are going to use your personal information and apply for the TEACH employment opportunity discussed later in Lab Project 1.3. You will be developing a resume and a job application form. The steps that follow identify the information you need in your resume, along with an example of an application format that has been used at TEACH in the past. Plan how you will complete both your resume and the application form, and then create both items manually. Remember that although you are applying for a job that interests you, someone else may be selected. You should ensure that your qualifications make you eligible for at least two alternative positions.

You will need the following:

- Bright blue and black ink pens.
- Blank 8½ × 11 paper.
- A ruler for creating straight edges.
- Your own personal information gathered in this chapter.
- The research information you gathered about the networking profession.
- Your job and school history (made up, if you wish).
- Three references (made up, if you wish).

Then do the following:

1. Design your own application form using the best sample you can find on the Web as a guide if you'd like. Create the form yourself, by hand, with bright blue lines and black-ink printed lettering, and make it look as professional as you can.

2. After you have chosen the TEACH position you would most like to fill, complete your form as an actual TEACH application, using at least the following information on your newly created form.

Be sure to include:

Name (last, first, middle initial)

Street address

City, state, zip code

Phone number

Education—List in reverse chronological order all classes taken in the past year, giving teachers' names, grade for the class, and the school.

References—List at least three character references (excluding anyone related to you or under 25 years of age).

State whether or not you are physically capable of performing the work required to fill the position you have chosen.

• Lab Project 1.2

Now you will create a resume and submit it, along with the application you created in Lab Project 1.1, to your instructor. Using those resumes and application forms, your instructor will choose the company president. All other positions in TEACH will be filled by that new president, acting as the hiring official, by choosing from the remaining applications according to your instructor's criteria discussed in class.

You will need the following materials:

- Your application form from Lab Project 1.1.

- A lab computer running a suitable word processing application and connected to a suitable printer.

- A data or distribution CD to use in your test of the Startup disk you create.

Then create a resume using the following TEACH resume information and action verbs list.

TEACH Resume Information   Your TEACH resume is a one-page "word snapshot" of yourself that you share with potential employers when trying to convince them to invite you in for an interview. It should be neat, clear, and concise, and should accurately portray all your qualifications for the position you are seeking. You should use action words as much as possible in your resume to show what you did and the results of your actions.

TEACH's format includes a requirement that you clearly state your objective concerning which job

you would like to obtain. Your finished resume will also have a one-inch margin formed by a black inked box that you must draw by hand.

1. Include the following major categories in your resume:

Objective	Education History
Employment History	Job Qualifications
Hobbies	Personal Information
Computer Expertise	

2. Strive to use action verbs in your resume; here are some samples you might use:

accomplished	achieved
analyzed	coordinated
created	designed
directed	eliminated
established	evaluated
improved	initiated
launched	motivated
organized	performed
planned	proposed
reduced	reorganized
revised	simplified
solved	supported
translated	

3. Use your own discretion when creating your resume layout. Do some research to become aware of the current resume philosophy regarding the length and data you want to show. Remember, though, that your resume is

a snapshot of you and what you are bringing to the company. Occasionally, you will run into an interviewer who is intimidated by what you have on the table, and you must be aware of that, too.

④ Submit your completed application and your resume to your instructor when requested.

⑤ Plan to be present when your application is reviewed by the hiring official—your instructor or designated lead student—and prepare

yourself for that review by asking yourself hypothetical sets of questions about the position you have chosen.

Note: If you want to apply for a particular position but know that you do not meet the job prerequisites, you may have to role-play just enough so that you qualify for that position, but don't get carried away and spoil the application process by claiming unrealistic years of experience or technical expertise that would actually make you over-qualified.

• Lab Project 1.3

You now know what networks are, and what their purposes can be in typical companies. You have also been partially introduced to the fact that you will become a working member of a fictional company—TEACH in this case. It is time to better introduce you to TEACH's personnel and relate the company's present network status to what you have learned.

A company's organizational chart can often be used to reveal network requirements. Refer to TEACH's organizational chart, shown in the following illustration. When reading the following sections, locate each person's position within the company

as it is discussed. Remember, this scenario is fictitious. You may also have to refer back to this TEACH organizational chart after you have your position so you can confirm your job relationships based on your location within the organization. You should also note that the names used indicate the user login name conventions you should set up with your network.

Headquarters   The president and chief executive officer (CEO), RichardM, spent years working in the training industry before starting the new TEACH corporation. Just over ten years ago, RichardM and the vice president, his wife SheronnaM, started the company and formed the executive management of TEACH when the previous occupants of the training center requested a bailout. Many things have changed since that time, but the corporation remains a family operation with their son, RickyM, the head of corporate administration, and daughter, AnnaliseM, the manager of the sales department. AnnaliseM recently worked as a teacher in the public school system for many years and came back to TEACH to help increase sales. The last employee at the corporate office is the receptionist,

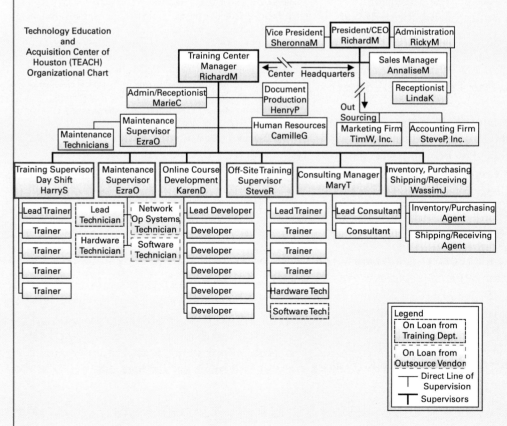

LindaK, who performs much of the company's data entry while acting as the focal point for all customer on-site interaction.

Training Center   All other corporate activities are accomplished in the separately maintained training center section. These include training-center management (two shifts), document production, off-site training development, maintenance, web development, content development, processing, inventory control, center administration, and operation of an independent consulting department. RichardM, temporarily also acting as the training manager, brought with him to the center significant previous management training and experience, and a high level of involvement in computer technology. RichardM's night-shift manager until just recently was HarryS, who was promoted two months ago from the manuscript-processing department. HarryS and his trainers just came back to the day shift until after the present sales slump and business needs again require a night shift's coverage.

EzraO is the center's maintenance department supervisor, where he also supervises the document production section run by HenryP. Both EzraO and HenryP have been with the company from its formation in 1992. KarenD, the online course development manager, has a master's degree in computer science and has worked directly with RichardM on many projects in the past. CamilleG is the human resources manager, assists with inventory control, and has significant experience with training center operations at all levels. MaryT is the training center's consulting manager.

SteveR was just recently put in charge of off-site training. Inventory control, purchasing, and shipping/receiving are handled by WassimJ, who recently transferred to the center from one of the vendors that previously supplied TEACH off-site trainers. Training-center administration functions are handled by MarieC, who also acts as the purchasing representative, controlling all input and output documents. In addition, there are 20 hourly employees working at the center in their respective departments.

Now that you have some background information about TEACH, you should be aware of the company's employment needs and begin thinking about being "hired" into one of those impending va-

cancies. In this activity, you will view the announced vacancy in TEACH and begin investigating and making some decisions about which position will best fit your desired network involvement.

You will need the following materials:

- The TEACH Help Wanted advertisement (shown below)

- Access to the Internet (in the classroom, at home, or somewhere on campus)

- A copy of your own personal information gathered earlier in this chapter

Then read the TEACH employment announcement below and decide which of the listed jobs you might be able to apply for based upon what you want to do in this course. Remember, you will be assuming that role for the rest of the course. However, you can later apply for another position that is more advanced. List two alternative choices.

Help Wanted

Small technology training center in need of entire training team to replace a recently transferred group of highly qualified, dedicated trainers. Positions available immediately include: (1) Training Center Maintenance Supervisor to supervise four technicians and oversee operation of four server bays, (2) Online Development Supervisor to oversee six employees and manage operation of two web servers, (3) Swing-shift Training Manager, (4) Production Manager to control in-process printing activities involved with training material development, (5) Inventory Control agent, (6) Receptionist, (7) Sales Manager, (8) Consulting Manager, (9) Administration Manager, (10) Purchasing Manager, (11) Human Resources Manager, (12) Vice President, (13) and a substitute President/CEO. Additionally, a new marketing consulting firm, accounting firm, and legal firm are needed for outsource responsibilities. A manager capable of operating an off-site education department and another to initiate and maintain a new Research and Development Department are also needed.

Interested Individuals should apply in person at TEACH.

A hand-designed application and a TEACH-oriented resume must be submitted.

1 Open your Internet browser and initiate a search using the words "Occupational Outlook Handbook" as shown in the following illustration. This will search the Internet and return information that may assist you with deciding which job will best suit you. Your computer's desktop and your Internet browser will likely look different from those used in this and all other exercises throughout this text. That should not affect your results.

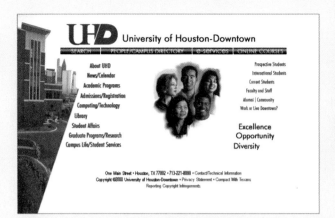

② Scroll through the returned results and locate the one for *Occupational Outlook Handbook*. It will likely be the first one in your list. Click the Occupational Outlook Handbook's link to go to that site. If, for some reason, it is not returned in your search, enter `http://www.bls.gov/oco/` in your browser's address field and press the ENTER key.

③ Click the Occupational Outlook Handbook's link to go to that site. Once there, enter the term "networking" in the Search by Occupation window field in the upper-right hand corner of the web site, as shown next.

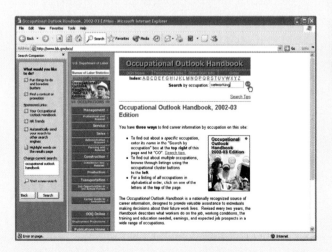

④ Scroll to and click the return link entitled Systems Analysts, Computer Scientists, and Database Operators/Administrators.

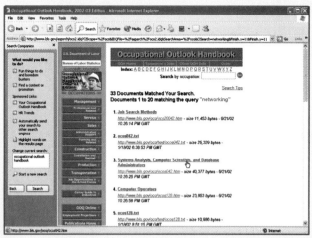

⑤ Read the article on this group of computer careers. Pay particular attention to the section on networking, shown in the following illustration, and the other sections on Working Conditions, Employment, Training, Job Outlook, and Earnings. Apply what you read to the decision you are trying to make regarding your TEACH employment possibilities.

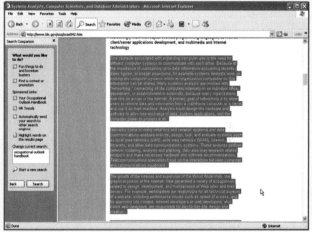

⑥ Prepare a summary of this site's information, and submit a copy of your work to your instructor, along with four other summaries of similar sites you locate by following the links at the bottom of this initial site. Keep your information handy in case you need it again during this course. Additional links you might use to obtain information are `http://computerjobs.com` and `http://www.dice.com`.

chapter 2 Installing Network Hardware

*"One computer does not a
network make."*

TWENTIETH-CENTURY VERSION OF
INSCRUTABLE ANCIENT WISDOM

In this chapter, you will learn how to:

- **Describe typical network components**
- **Distinguish between different types of network cabling**
- **Install and configure a network interface card**

I t is helpful for you to understand the definition of networks by relating them to something you already understood like you did in Chapter I, but you should also know what goes into creating one as well. How do you recognize computer networks? What do you need if you want to put one together? What can you do with one once you have it? These are some of the questions you should be able to answer when you understand computer networks. Once you understand them, you should be able to connect the pieces and form your own network.

In this chapter, you will learn the basic structure of computer networks. You'll begin with an introduction to the basic components that exist in all computer networks and examine how they function together. Next, you will learn about the fundamental network components—servers, clients, and workstations. From there, you will explore the fundamental hardware used when networking computers, and you'll learn to recognize different types of network cabling. Then, you will create the network cabling that you will need to connect your workstation to the network. Finally, you will examine some of the components that can be connected to your network to help extend its functionality.

■ Describing Typical Network Components

Remember Lauren from SinkRSwim Pools in the first chapter? Well, she was very successful in her task of getting the basic concepts of networking across to her new coworkers. Now they want to know more. Don't they always? They want to learn what goes into creating networks. Lauren began by telling them that all computer networks have the same basic pieces, or components.

The Basic Components

There are four basic components of a computer network. They are your computer, the electronic data you want to share, at least one other computer to share your data with, and the physical connection between the computers.

Your Computer

You have the first basic component of a network when you have a stand-alone computer. It might be your school lab's workstation or your home computer. No matter where the computer is, though, the goal in using a computer is typically to enter some kind of information into the computer one time and then be able to use that information as many times as you want later in such a way as to take advantage of a computer's speed. Otherwise, you might as well re-create the data fresh each time you need it. The information you enter might be actual data entries made into a database or it might be something more in the form of a program or application you might write for others to use. You might even create documents, load applications someone else wrote, or play games they created, but the central theme here is that all of them allow you to take advantage of the computer's speed. Networked computers, then, let you use even more information because you have access to data stored in multiple locations.

Although computers are fast and you can do tremendous things with a single computer, you reap major benefits by connecting computers in a network. When working at a computer, you will almost always want to share your work with someone at another computer. Simply using that first network component, a computer, leads to the need for the other three basic components of a computer network so that you can allow other users to access your data and use it at other networked locations.

Computer Components Most personal computers are made up of four main pieces that may or may not be physically separate: the monitor, the keyboard, the mouse (or laptop's touch pad), and the system unit. The keyboard and mouse are input devices, and the monitor is an output device.

The **monitor** is just a video display that gives the computer a means of communicating with the user. The monitor connects to your computer and displays the actions you are performing on your computer. In Windows operating systems, the monitor is an integral part of the system and displays choices and available actions for the user. In some types of computers, such as bank teller machines, a computer's monitor can also be used to **input**, or enter, data into a computer.

• A flat panel computer monitor

The **keyboard** is simply a means of communicating with the computer. By pressing the keys, you issue commands to the computer. Usually, the keyboard is operated like a typewriter. However, on keyboards there are additional multiple-keystroke combinations (such as CTRL-ALT-DEL) that can be used to invoke special features. You can also use keys that are not on a typewriter (like the CTRL key or the ALT key) to create special characters that replace the normal letters shown on each keyboard's key.

• A keyboard

The **mouse** provides a method of communicating with the computer that is sometimes more convenient than the keyboard. It is simply a means of pointing to something on screen and communicating with the computer so that the computer acts on the specified object. The mouse converts up-and-down and left-and-right motions to vectors on the computer's screen, and it usually directs an arrow (or another graphic depiction) shown on screen. This arrow or graphic is called a *cursor*.

The system unit can really be considered the heart of the computer. The **system unit** houses the essential electronic circuitry of the computer, such as the **central processing unit (CPU)**, read-only memory (ROM), and random access memory (RAM). Additionally, all added components, such as video cards, compact disc (CD) players, floppy disk drives, hard disk drives, and soundcards are also located in the system unit.

• A mouse, like the keyboard, is a type of input device.

One of the most important things to remember about RAM is that it starts fresh (empty!) whenever power is turned on. Think of it as a very fast scratch pad where the computer does its work, but it goes away when power is turned off. That is why you lose your work in a power failure if you have not saved it to a more permanent storage medium, such as your hard drive or a floppy disk.

• The system unit, to which the monitor, keyboard, and mouse are connected, contains the brains of the computer.

Electronic Data

The second basic component of a computer network is the electronic data that is created and stored for later retrieval to take advantage of the computer's speed.

In the classroom setting and in most computer installations, storing data on a computer is more convenient than storing handwritten documents like those initially found in your instructor's record of information discussed in Chapter 1. You already started storing your own information, and additional material when applying for an employment position. That electronically stored data will be used throughout this course.

Cross Check

Sharing Information

Use the data you have stored in your computer about yourself and assume that your classroom computers are not yet connected together to form a network when responding to the following points:

1. Describe three methods that could be used to share the information stored in your computer such that your classmates' computers will contain copies of your data.

2. Describe how you could share your information on another network that is not physically connected to yours.

Additional Computers

An additional computer is the third network component, and it lets you share your stored information. **Network data** is information you wish to share over networked computers.

Connection Medium

The fourth basic component of a computer network is the connection between each of the computers involved in the network. The computers have to be connected somehow so they can share the data you have stored. Although this component is the last discussed in this chapter, it could be argued that the connection, also called the **networking medium**, is the most important. It is over this link that you send your data to another computer. You'll see, in the discussion that follows, that the connection is actually made up of the networking medium and a network interface.

Network Component Functionality

You now have a basic network. You have the data that you want to share, and you have at least two linked computers: one that stores your data and one or more others that will access the data. The fundamental components are in place; now you need to understand how these components function as a network.

Consider the human networks you've experienced in your own environment (such as the restaurant's client and server model mentioned in Chapter 1) and then think about what you have in your lab. You'll see that these fundamental components are available in your classroom, and they fulfill the basic functions of networked computers.

You want the computer that has your data to "serve it up" to other computers. You effectively become a restaurant and your computer the server. The computers requesting your information

Cross Check

A Networking Comparison

When thinking about networks, keep in mind the comparison to a restaurant that you learned about in Chapter 1.

1. In networking terms, what do you become when entering the restaurant?

2. From a networking perspective, what is the staff member who waits on you during your meal?

• This IBM p Series server is designed to run large scale networks and Internet services.

• When connected to a network, a printer becomes a network client.

become your clients as they seek access to your data. In this simple example, that second computer may just start out as a workstation, but it becomes a client when it requests services from your computer. Your computer is then a server.

Server

A **network server** (generally just called a *server*) is a computer that offers services and resources to clients, workstations, and other servers over a computer network. Typically, the computers used as servers are some of the strongest and fastest computers on the network. They may even be designed specifically as servers, such as the IBM p Series server shown here, and they commonly have multiple processors and larger hard drives, in addition to having large amounts of RAM.

A server provides centralized management of resources, security, and expanded access to networked resources for other computers on the network, as shown in Figure 2.1.

Client

A **network client** (often just called a *client*) is a device on a computer network that requests services or resources from a server. Clients can be printers, workstations, servers, or any other device connected to the computers on a network. The most common network clients are workstations.

Workstation

A workstation is a computer that is able to operate independently of the network and manage its own files and processing. In a typical network, most computers are stand-alone workstations able to function without the network. They are connected to the network so they have access to networked

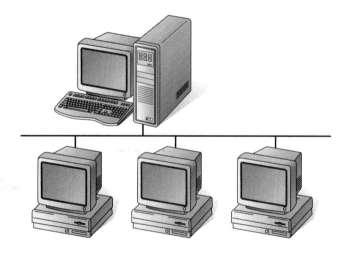

• **Figure 2.1**   A server

resources should those resources be needed. The availability of using the additional security measures and the possibility of incorporating the centralized management that are part of using networked resources are two of the main reasons workstations join a network.

Courtesy HP and Apple Computer

• A Compaq notebook computer and an Apple iMac both can serve as workstations.

Network Connectivity

Once you acquire a server with something to share, at least one client who needs something that is sharable, such as a workstation or a printer, and the data that you want to share with that client (or any other clients), you have the majority of the basic network's essential components. You have the "who needs to get information or services from whom" and the "what needs to communicate where," but something very important is still missing.

The pathway between the computers (or resources) and some kind of interface connecting the computers to the network have not yet been taken into account. Since each of your networked computers need to be connected, this pathway component along with its interface are essential portions of a network.

Communication Medium

Deciding how to connect your networked computers involves selecting the **communication medium**. This is the physical path between your networked resources and normally takes the form of coaxial cable (cable similar to wiring used for cable TV) or **twisted-pair wiring** (cabling similar to that used for telephone wiring). More recently, **fiber-optic cabling** (insulated glass or hard plastic fibers through which light passes and transfers data) has gained widespread acceptance as a network communication medium. A **wireless medium** (using infrared or radio waves between network components) is also growing in popularity.

The principal hardware components that make up your network are shown connected with an unspecified type of wiring (as opposed to wireless) in Figure 2.2. A server (top left) is connected to a print server (top center) sharing its printer (top right). It is also connected to various network

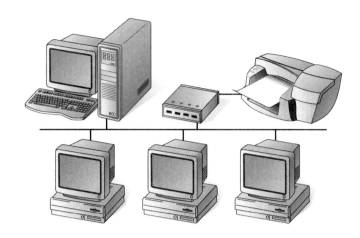

● **Figure 2.2**   A typical network

clients (bottom row). In this simplistic view of a network, notice that no detail is provided as to how the wiring connects to the components. You need to know more about these connections.

Network Interface Cards

The components of the network may be shown wired to each other in Figure 2.2, but the network connection has not been specified. You must decide how you are going to connect your computers to the network medium.

● A network interface card

To connect the networked components to the physical cabling, your clients will require a **network interface card (NIC)**, also called a *network board*. The NIC plugs directly into a computer's system unit and provides a networking connection point. The NIC both provides the physical connection where you plug in your wiring (or other networking medium) to the networked device, and it is the device that ultimately creates and sends the signal from one networked device to the next.

Concentrators

You create your network by connecting your computer to the network cabling through its network interface card. However, where do you go next? Your cable only has two ends, so unless you have enough NICs in your computer to connect to every device on the network, you will need some way to connect to the various other resources you want to share.

Putting it in simple terms, just as a single garden hose cannot supply water to multiple locations, a single networking cable cannot physically connect your computer to more than one other resource. However, if you connect that garden hose to a box with several outlets where you can connect other garden hoses, you can get your water to more than one other location. On your network, there is a similar connection device, called a network **concentrator**, which allows you to connect multiple cables together so you can make numerous connections to your networked resources.

Hub A **hub** is a type of concentrator. It acts as a central meeting point where your cables join so that information can travel to all the other resources throughout your network. Hubs are usually simple box-like devices with several wiring ports that can be used to receive data and pass it on to any device connected to another one of those connection ports. If your computer had enough **ports**, or connection points, to plug in sufficient NICs for all of the resources on your network, there would be no need to use a hub as a concentrator.

Copyright © 1995–2003, 3Com Corporation

- Hub/wiring concentrator

As you can imagine, it is more economical to use hubs for additional network connections than to add additional ports to computers. Computer manufacturers have no way of knowing how many connections you need, and it is much simpler for data to be sent by one computer and received by all other computers connected to a concentrator, or hub.

Hubs were once the only mechanism capable of acting as a concentrator. They were widely used in early networking and could be found in most computer networks. In fact, because of their simple design, hubs rarely wear out and you will encounter them in many networks as they still serve their initial purpose. However, while hubs provided the necessary additional connections, they sent all information to every device, and this ended up using much of the network capacity. Something was needed that worked a bit differently.

Switches Hubs, as concentrators, helped networks grow. It became easy to connect two or more computers. However, additional features had to be added to network concentrators so that they could reduce network communication (or **message traffic**). The hub's replacement needed to be able to communicate with individual clients rather than send every message to every client on the network.

The next form of concentrator was the **switch**. While it looked like the hub and provided a centralized connection like the hub, adding switches reduced network traffic because they added the capability of network monitoring and selective configuration. Shared data could be sent directly to an individual resource rather than to every networked resource at the same time. These additional features originally added to the cost of using concentrators, but as prices dropped and technology advanced, switches became more economical to use than the simpler hub.

Bridges Networks continued to expand, and they needed to be connected to other networks, often requiring connections between different networking cabling types. Switches were no longer the answer. What was needed was a mechanism that connected dissimilar networks together.

Such a device, called a **bridge**, was created so that networks could consist of different segments and information could be passed from one segment to another, regardless of whether dissimilar network cable types were involved in the process, shown in Figure 2.3. The bridge's main purpose was to join two or more separate networks that use the same networking language, called a **protocol**. (Now the use of bridges is fast disappearing in favor of better switches and newer concentrators called routers.)

Routers A **router** is the most sophisticated of the concentrators discussed here because it is able to read specific portions of messages and send them directly to their intended destinations. These destinations can even be in separate networks that may be contained within a larger network as seen in Figure 2.4. Thus, information can go directly from network 1 to network 8 without anyone else receiving the traffic involved with the information's transmittal. Furthermore, a router can select the best path based on specified restrictions (lowest cost or fastest time) and networks being served by a router are not all required to use the same protocol. Because they are able to separate segments of large networks, routers are frequently used to add security to sensitive networked resources, effectively isolating them from the view of unauthorized network users.

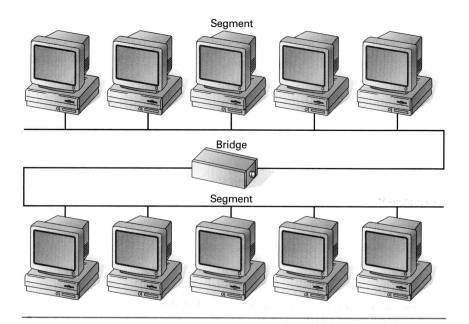

• **Figure 2.3**   A bridge segments a network.

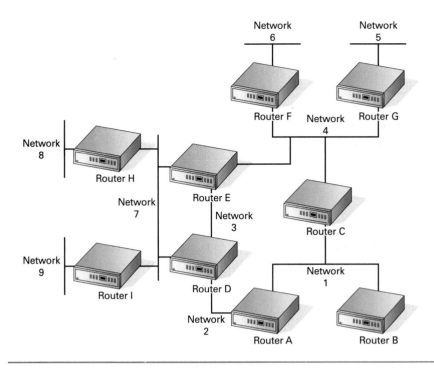

• **Figure 2.4** Networks are separated by routers.

Distinguishing Between Different Types of Cabling

Network cabling is the physical connection that runs between your networked resources. You should become familiar with the four basic types of networking medium mentioned earlier—coaxial cable, twisted-pair wire, fiber-optic cable, and wireless—and recognize each type when you see it. The different cable types will be compared to each other by considering their capabilities for transmitting Ethernet signals.

Coaxial Cable

Coaxial cable gets its name from its physical construction. Unlike most electronic signal wiring, which uses two distinct and separable wires to transmit electrical signals (one wire with a solid core for one direction, and a second wire with a braided mesh for the opposite direction), coaxial cable may use two conductors for signal flow, but it is constructed in such a way that the two conductors share the same axis. (*Co* indicates the two conductors, and *axial* indicates the same axis, hence, the name coaxial.) What this means is that one conductor is physically inside the other. Furthermore, unlike most other wiring, the two coaxial conductors cannot be easily separated.

Coaxial cable (or *coax*) is similar to the cable television wiring that connects to your television, except that it has a slightly different rating because it carries a different type of electrical signal—network communication instead of television signals. Thick coax cable, or **thicknet** as it is commonly called, was the first widely used network-cabling medium. Thicknet cable is approximately half an inch in diameter and carries an Ethernet signal reliably for up to 500 meters (1,650 feet).

Looking at a cross-section of coax cable, as shown in Figure 2.5, you can see two layers of electrical conductor—a solid copper core and a braided or foil (or both) copper shielding, separated by a third layer of non-conducting, fairly rigid insulator material. All of that is coated with a protective cable-jacket casing that is also non-conductive. There are two types of coaxial cable used on networked computers, thicknet and thinnet. Although both are created using the same concept, thicknet uses a primitive vampire tap connection, which is no longer widely used and will not be discussed further in this section. Let's take a look now at thicknet's replacement—thinnet.

Thin coax cable came into use shortly after thicknet. Since it did essentially the same job (although limited to a shorter distance) while weighing and costing significantly less, the use of thin coax or **thinnet**, quickly outpaced its predecessor. Thinnet cable is approximately a quarter inch in diameter and carries an Ethernet signal reliably for up to 185 meters (610 feet).

Coaxial cable is used to connect computers in a line from one to another, called **daisy chaining**. At each end of a thinnet coax cable, there is a twisting barrel-like connection called a **BNC connector**, and at each network interface card, there is a separate T-connector inserted into the BNC connector and twisted into place, as shown in the T-connector illustration. The thinnet cable is used to connect one computer to the next. At both ends of the daisy chain, another type of connector is twisted into the T-connector to terminate the signal. This **terminator** is just a device that absorbs any residual signal at the end of the network and ensures that the signal does not bounce back over the cable medium where it would cause signaling errors on the network.

- Thinnet coaxial cable; both ends of a length of thinnet cable

- A BNC T-connector showing a terminator and typical wiring connector

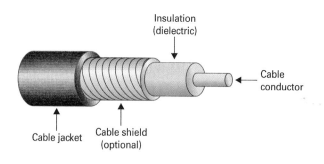

Insulation (dielectric)

Cable conductor

Cable jacket

Cable shield (optional)

- **Figure 2.5**   A cross-section of a coaxial cable shows its layers.

Twisted Pair

Twisted-pair (TP) wire is similar to the telephone wire in your home, except that it normally has eight individually insulated wires bundled together instead of the four in telephone wire. TP is constructed such that those eight wires are grouped as four pairs inside a protective casing. Additionally, each of the two wires in each pair is wrapped around each other, or *twisted*. Furthermore, there are two types of TP—shielded and unshielded (STP and UTP). Both are inexpensive to install and easy to maintain. STP has added insulation as a result of the layer of foil surrounding the pairs inside the outer casing, as shown in the illustration. UTP is now the most commonly used network-cabling medium.

- A layer of foil surrounds the pairs inside a shielded twisted-pair cable.

Try This!

Network Cable Creation

Ask your instructor for a 3-inch piece of Cat-5 twisted-pair cable and a pair of scissors, so you can find out how difficult it is to create a network cabling connection. Try this:

1. Using the scissors, cut back the twisted-pair cable's covering. Without untwisting the wires, separate the cable into its four pairs of wires. Count the number of twists in each of the four pairs of wires.

2. Untwist and straighten out just the first inch of each pair of wires. Lay the four pairs of wires on the table from left to right in front of you, mentally number them from 1 to 4, and note that each pair has wires A and B. Decide which you want to use as A and which will be B (which wire is used as A or B does not matter at this point but you will need to stick with your decision from this point forward).

3. Take pair number 1 in your right hand and, using only the untwisted section, align wires A and B beside and touching each other, and pinch them between your left index finger and your left thumb.

4. Take pair number 2 in your right hand and, using only the untwisted section, align wire A beside and touching the rightmost of the two wires from pair 1 already being pinched in your left hand.

5. Take pair number 3 in your right hand and, using only the untwisted section, align wire B beside and touching the rightmost of the three wires from pairs 1 and 2 already being pinched in your left hand.

6. Align wire B from pair 2 beside and touching the rightmost of the current four wires being pinched in your left hand.

7. Align wire A from pair 3 beside and touching the rightmost of the current five wires being pinched in your left hand.

8. Take pair 4 in your right hand and, using only the untwisted section, align wires A and B beside and touching the rightmost of the current six wires being pinched in your left hand.

If you have the ends of the eight wires aligned perfectly such that the 1-inch untwisted end of each wire is straight and butted up against the wire next to it as the four pairs are pinched between your fingers, you understand the difficulty cabling workers face when creating a network connection.

Fiber Optics

One of the newer mediums for transmitting network data is fiber-optic material. Fiber-optic cable consists of a central fiber-optic core surrounded, much like the core of a coax cable, with a cladding material, and coated with a protective plastic covering. The central fiber-optic core is highly refined plastic or glass that has a high degree of light transmission capability. The core is surrounded by a cladding material that reflects bouncing light back inward to the central glass core so that it increases the distance signals can travel.

Unlike the wiring discussed up to this point, fiber-optic cable does not send or receive electrical signals for data transmissions. Instead, data is converted into light signals and transmitted down the fiber-optic cable. Either lasers or other light-producing mechanisms, such as light-emitting diodes (LEDs) are used as the source of light. Using lasers is more dependable but more costly, so most fiber-optic networks use LEDs as their light source. After the data is converted to a light signal and sent down the fiber-optic cable, it must be converted back to data at the other end of the cable. A second strand of fiber is used as the return conductor.

• A piece of fiber-optic cable

Wireless

Another of the newer network transmission mediums incorporates wireless connections. Two of the most common reasons for using wireless networking are mobility and convenience. Most of the wireless networks use either infrared or radio waves, but there are also other options, such as microwave and satellite networks. When people travel extensively, they often need network access from wherever they may be located. With a laptop computer and a network access point, shown in Figure 2.6, a traveler has the same dual-conductor capability (the ability to transmit and receive) found in the other network cabling mediums and therefore has the potential for network access whenever a wireless network is within range. Physical connections, such as wiring, are not practical in all locations where mobile network users may be found.

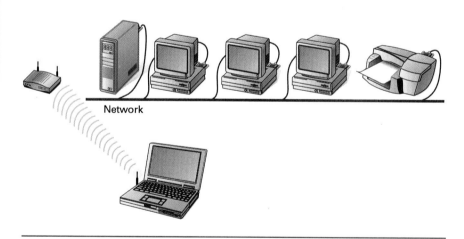

Network

• **Figure 2.6**   A wireless portable computer connecting to a cabled network access point

Creating a Straight-Through Cable

Now that you have an idea about what networks are and how they are cabled together, it's time to connect some computers and begin networking over your own cables. In this activity, you will create your own **straight-through network cable** using two **RJ-45 connectors** (the most common connector used in networking today) to connect your computer to the network concentrator—probably a hub in this case.

To complete this exercise, you will need the following items:

- One network interface card (NIC) per computer or networked device

- RJ-45 connectors (one for each planned cable end, plus lots of spares for practice)

- Cat-5 unshielded twisted-pair (UTP) wire (sufficient wire should be available for short pieces of "practice" cable in addition to the wiring you will make to link your computer to the server connection)

- RJ-45 wire **crimping tool** (used to fasten the connector to the cable)

- Wire cutters

- 10Base-T wire **continuity tester** (used to check the capability for signal flow over the cable)

- Hub or switch (with sufficient capacity to connect each classroom computer to the server)

Step 1

Obtain a length of Cat-5 twisted-pair cable from your instructor. Depending on where the instructor wants to use your cable, you should end up with one that is typically anywhere from 6 to 100 feet long. Note that the maximum Cat-5 UTP cable segment distance is 100 meters (about 325 feet).

Step 2

Being careful not to nick the insulation off the internal twisted pairs of wire inside the Cat-5 cable piece, make a cut in the outer covering 3/8 inch from one of the ends. This should expose the internal four pairs of twisted wiring inside the external cover.

Note: When cutting and stripping the ends of cables to install networking connections, you may want to trim more than the 3/8 inch that is allowable for the final connection. You should remember, however, that you must trim the wires to the 3/8-inch length before finishing.

Step 3

Pull off the entire external cover surrounding the twisted pairs, but don't untwist the pairs. Make sure you keep each pair of wires together and, if you cut the casing back too far, as shown here, trim the individual pairs to the desired 3/8-inch length. In this illustration of a UTP cable, each pair has a different number of twists.

Step 4

Note whether the internal wires have solid or striped colors on the plastic coating. The colors (or striping) will play an important role when connecting the wires to the RJ-45 connectors.

Untwist the exposed 3/8-inch section of each pair of wires. Notice that the pairs of wires were twisted together but that the spacing of the twists on one pair was different from the spacing of the twists on another pair. These twists help filter out interference from one pair to another.

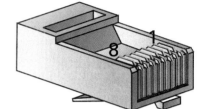

Prepare the RJ-45 connector, shown in the illustration, by turning it around so that the flat side is toward you and the plastic tang is away from you and pointing down. Pin 1 will be to your left.

Arrange the single wires for insertion into the RJ-45 connector in the following straight-through cable order (commonly called its pinout) from left to right, and pinch all eight wires close together and side by side between your index finger and your thumb. Note that the colors of the wires will depend on whether striped or solid-colored wiring is used.

Pinouts for Straight-Through Cable

Pin	If Striped-Colored Wiring:	If Solid-Colored Wiring:
1	White/Orange	Green
2	Orange	Yellow
3	White/Green	Blue
4	Blue	Red
5	White/Blue	Black
6	Green	Orange
7	White/Brown	Brown
8	Brown	Gray

Note: *In addition to the availability of striped or solid-colored wiring, the different specifications of wiring you see may have various other color coded wires. However, the relative position of the wiring remains the same. Match your actual colors with those given in the exercise, use them consistently and the process will still work properly.*

Slide all eight wires completely into the open end of your RJ-45 connector. They are properly seated in the RJ-45 when you can look through it and see the ends of the wires behind the small metallic knives that cut into the wiring to form the connection, as shown here.

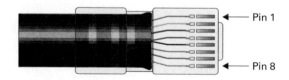

Make sure that the wires are all completely pushed up against the top end inside the RJ-45 and that the external covering of the wire is inside the connector. The wire's covering will give the cable support and help keep the smaller wires from being pulled out if the cable is tugged.

| Step 10 | When your wire is inserted properly, have it checked by your instructor. When told to proceed, use the crimping tool to crimp your RJ-45. It can now be used as one end of a network connection. Get instructor confirmation before continuing with the other end of your RJ-45 connector. |
| Step 11 | If your instructor tells you to continue making a straight-through cable, repeat the process beginning with Step 2. When you get back to this point after crimping the second end, test your cable using the cable tester. If it passes the continuity check, you have a working cable. |

If your instructor tells you to hold on to your cable after adding the first RJ-45 connector so you can later create a **crossover network cable**, used to connect two computers or two hubs directly, store the cable for now, but be able to retrieve it when you get to Lab Project 2.2.

Congratulations

Congratulate yourself. You have just completed a wiring task that would have cost the school approximately $2.50 per foot if a network-wiring specialist had made the cables. As you can see, becoming a network-wiring specialist could prepare you for a lucrative career should you choose that path, and provided you could find sufficient numbers of wiring projects requiring your talents. Completing your first network cable and understanding its use may be just what it takes to start you down the network-wiring career path. However, understanding cabling is just one important part of a networking position's requirements. The next thing to do is look at how you connect your computer to the network using the cable you just created.

■ Installing and Configuring a Network Interface Card

There should be plenty of network cables for everyone in your class now that you have all become familiar with adding RJ-45 ends to network cable. Now you need network interface cards in your computers so that you can connect them together as you form your network. If your instructor did not strip the NICs out of the computers before you installed Windows, your system may already recognize your network interface card. If that is the case, and there are two computers on the network talking to each other, you can skip this section and wait while the other individuals install NICs into their classroom computers.

Otherwise, it is time to install a NIC so you can continue with your networking project. In case you forgot, the network interface card is a small circuit board that plugs into an expansion port on the motherboard in your computer's system unit. That circuit board allows your computer to "speak" over the network and lets it be "heard" by other computers on the network.

Install a Network Interface Card

In the following steps, you will be working on the inside of your computer. Make sure you follow all safety precautions.

To complete this exercise, you will need the following:

- One network interface card (NIC) per computer or networked device

- Computer running Windows 98 or higher
- Screwdriver
- Crossover network cable

Step 1

Remove the computer's cover and choose an empty expansion slot appropriate for the type of NIC card you are installing. Observe safety precautions when removing the cover from your computer.

Warning: The computer operates with voltages that can be lethal. Before you remove the computer cover, observe the following steps to protect yourself and those around you, and to prevent damage to the system's components:

- *Turn off the computer, and unplug the unit from its power source.*
- *Disconnect all cables connected to the system unit.*
- *Remove any jewelry from your hands and wrists, or anything that may dangle into your working environment.*
- *Use only insulated or nonconductive tools.*

Step 2

Remove the expansion slot's back plate (if one has been installed) and insert the NIC into the expansion slot. Secure it with the screw that you removed from the expansion slot's back plate. The NIC is shown installed here.

Note: Make sure that the NIC is securely seated in the expansion slot. It may take firm downward pressure to ensure proper installation. When correctly seated, the gold fingers on the bottom edge of the NIC will not be visible.

Step 3

Replace the computer's cover and reconnect all cables to the computer. Then connect a crossover networking cable from your computer to another computer in your classroom.

Step 4

Turn the computer on. Windows 98, NT, 2000, or XP Workstation installed on a Pentium computer will detect the new NIC's presence and will initiate driver installation.

Warning: Immediately shut down the computer if there is any evidence of smoke upon initial startup. The metal fingers inside the plastic slots could be bent when items such as a NIC are installed. If the bent fingers touch each other, overheating may occur and a sudden release of smoke may result.

Step 5

If your NIC is not recognized by your computer upon startup, your instructor will have to initiate troubleshooting procedures. Other steps, such as installing a driver or contacting the manufacturer of either your computer or the NIC or both, may be necessary.

Step 6

If the NIC is installed properly and Windows properly recognizes the card, your Windows desktop will include a **Network Neighborhood icon**. Right-click the Network Neighborhood icon and select Properties.

Network Neighborhood

Open
Explore
Find Computer...

Map Network Drive...
Disconnect Network Drive...

Create Shortcut
Rename

Properties

Step 7

In the Network window (also called a **dialog box** because you use them to tell Windows what settings to change), select Client for Microsoft Networks and click the File and Print Sharing button.

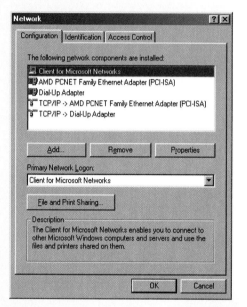

Check both boxes in the File and Print Sharing dialog box. This allows you to give others access to your files and to print using your printers.

Step 8

Right-click the Network Neighborhood icon and select Properties again. Click the Add button. In the Select Network Component Type dialog box, select Protocol and click the Add button. In the Select Network Protocol dialog box, select Microsoft in the left pane and highlight NetBEUI in the right pane, as shown in the following illustration. Click OK to install the **NetBEUI** protocol. (NetBEUI is a networking language spoken by your computer, and it is selected for its easy configuration and its speed). Your computer will have to be restarted after installation.

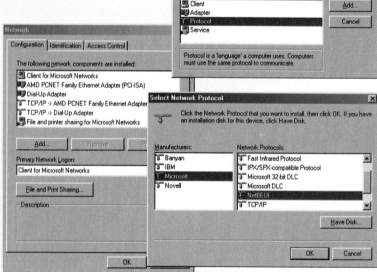

Step 9

After restarting and double-clicking the Network Neighborhood icon, you should see the other computer you are networked to if the computer has already shared at least one file.

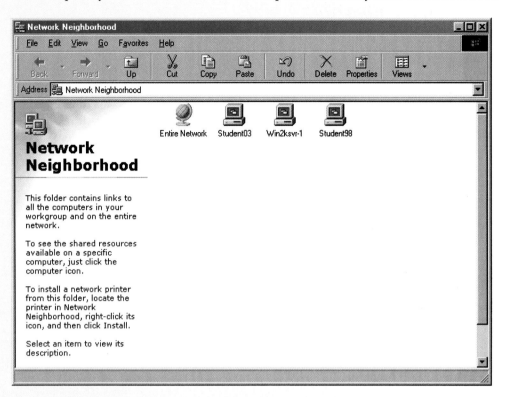

Step 10

If nothing has been shared on either computer, click on the C: drive, select File | Sharing from the menus, and click the Shared As option button to activate sharing.

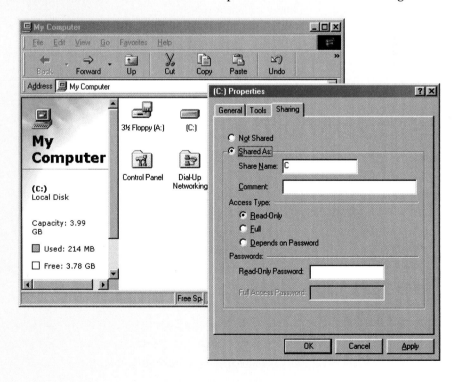

Chapter 2 Review

■ Chapter Summary

After reading this chapter and completing the Step-by-Step tutorials and Try This! exercise, you should understand the following facts about your network's development:

Describe Typical Network Components

■ Once you have data that you want to share, two computers to share it, and wiring or other medium connecting them, you have the basic components of a computer network.

■ The computer able to "serve up" information is commonly referred to as the server.

■ The other computers on the network are clients, because they are requesting services or resources from the server, and these clients are commonly stand-alone workstations.

Distinguish Between Different Types of Network Cabling

■ The networked computers are interconnected with cabling.

■ Those connections are comprised of twisted-pair wiring, coaxial cabling, or fiber-optic cabling.

A wireless medium using infrared or radio waves is also growing in popularity.

■ The cabling connects the computers through network interface cards or network boards, which act as both translators and physical connectors for the network.

■ A hub serves as a concentrator so many clients can connect to a server.

■ Switches, bridges, and routers also act as centralized connections in a network and furnish additional services for passing information around the network.

■ This chapter also had classroom participants make network cables from Cat-5 cable.

■ RJ-45 connectors and crimping tools were used to connect properly sequenced wiring into either a straight-through cable or a crossover cable.

Install and Configure a Network Interface Card

■ The network interface card was installed and configured, and a network protocol was set up, allowing a basic network connection to be made, demonstrating networking capability.

■ Key Terms

attenuation *(37)*
BNC connector *(38)*
bridge *(36)*
Cat-5 *(37)*
central processing unit (CPU) *(30)*
coaxial cable *(37)*
communication medium *(33)*
concentrator *(34)*
continuity tester *(41)*
crimping tool *(41)*
crossover network cable *(43)*
daisy chaining *(38)*
dialog box *(46)*
electromagnetic interference (EMI) *(37)*

Ethernet *(37)*
fiber-optic cabling *(33)*
hub *(35)*
input *(29)*
keyboard *(30)*
message traffic *(35)*
monitor *(29)*
mouse *(30)*
NetBEUI *(46)*
network client *(32)*
network data *(31)*
networking medium *(31)*
network interface card (NIC) *(34)*
Network Neighborhood icon *(45)*
network server *(32)*

ports *(35)*
protocol *(36)*
random access memory (RAM) *(33)*
RJ-45 connectors *(41)*
router *(36)*
straight-through network cable *(41)*
switch *(35)*
system unit *(30)*
terminator *(38)*
thicknet *(38)*
thinnet *(38)*
twisted-pair wiring *(33)*
wireless *(33)*

Key Term Quiz

Use the preceding vocabulary terms to complete the following sentences. Not all the terms will be used.

1. Used extensively in typical networks as one of the four main parts of computers, the box-like component that houses the majority of the electrical pieces of a desktop computer is called _____.

2. On a network using thinnet cabling, the device that absorbs any residual signal at the end of the network and ensures that the signal does not bounce back over the cable is called a(n) _____.

3. The general term for the connection between computers on a network is the _____.

4. The computer networking component that offers its services and/or its resources to clients over a computer network is called the _____.

5. When your computer has electricity applied, the _____ is activated and acts as a "thinking location" for the computer's "thought" processes.

6. A workstation connected to a network is the most common example of a(n) _____.

7. The connection between your networking medium and your computer is called the _____.

8. The first type of network concentrator, which was called a(n) _____, simply acted as a central meeting point where cables joined to share information so it could travel to all other resources throughout the network.

9. When computers "speak" to each other, they are using what is known as a(n) _____.

10. The individual pairs of wires inside Category 5 cabling are twisted to reduce the effects of _____.

Multiple-Choice Quiz

1. Which of the following is not one of the four main parts of a typical desktop computer?

   a. Mouse

   b. Keyboard

   c. Monitor

   d. Consolidated processing unit

2. Which of the following basic components of a computer network is created and stored for later retrieval to take advantage of the computer's speed?

   a. Your computer

   b. Electronic data

   c. Other computers

   d. Connection medium

3. Which of the following is defined as information you wish to share over connected computers?

   a. Classified data

   b. Hierarchy of data

   c. Network data

   d. Personnel data

4. Which of the following is/are basic components of a computer network?

   a. Your computer

   b. Electronic data

   c. Connection medium

   d. All of the above

5. Increasing which of the following components inside your computer's system unit will allow more concurrent processing to be accomplished at the same time?

   a. Random access memory

   b. Electronic data

   c. Network interface cards

   d. Connection ports

6. All of the following network resources can be considered network clients *except*:

   a. Printers

   b. Workstations

   c. Servers

   d. Processors

7. Which of the following is *not* a reason for a workstation to join a network?
   a. Security
   b. Independent operation
   c. Centralized management
   d. Sharing networked resources

8. The communication medium used on the first computer networks was:
   a. Shielded twisted pair
   b. Fiber-optic cable
   c. Coaxial cable
   d. Unshielded twisted pair

9. Connecting which of the following components between your computer and its networking medium completes the physical path between you and the other networked computers?
   a. Network interface card
   b. Processor
   c. Connection port
   d. Random access memory

10. Which of the following components creates and sends the signal from one networked device to the next?
    a. Random access memory
    b. Electronic data
    c. Network interface card
    d. Connection ports

11. Of the following network concentrator devices, which is most like the garden hose sharing water through a box with several other outlets connected to other garden hoses?

    a. Bridge
    b. Switch
    c. Router
    d. Hub

12. Of the following network concentrator devices, which connects networks using different network cabling types but the same network protocol?
    a. Bridge
    b. Switch
    c. Router
    d. Hub

13. Attenuation involves:
    a. Weakening the effects of EMI
    b. Weakening signals over a distance
    c. Strengthening the effects of EMI
    d. Strengthening signals over short distances

14. Which of the following cabling mediums has/have more than one conductor?
    a. Coax
    b. Fiber optics
    c. UTP
    d. Wireless

15. What is the distance you should trim back the insulation from the end of a Cat-5 UTP wire when adding an RJ-45 connector?
    a. 1 inch
    b. 3 inches
    c. 1½ inch
    d. 3/8 inch

■ Essay Quiz

1. You have just been promoted to your TEACH training lab's Network Neighborhood Watch program and put in charge of a computer upgrade that involves everyone in your class working inside their system units. What should you remind each of your classmates of before they open the cover of any computer?

2. You are in a hurry on a high-profile rollout of a new network at a client's worksite. Lanesha, your normal training assistant for classes you offer at the TEACH facility, asks you to explain the difference between a straight-through cable and a crossover cable. What quick answer can you give Lanesha that satisfies her curiosity until you can better answer her question in the TEACH training labs?

3. Keithon sent you on a service call to help Jolecelle, one of your TEACH coworkers, replace an inoperative network interface card. After you replace the card, how can you tell if her computer recognizes the new network interface card after Windows starts?

4. You have been asked to work with Steve in the Accounting firm that handles all TEACH's payroll and customer account payments. Steve has requested that you and seven other coworkers reenter numerous pieces of financial data and send them over the network from student stations in the training section. How would the wire twists in the twisted-pair cable running between the training section and the headquarters section affect your actions?

5. What must you do on Huong's computer (in the TEACH headquarters office) before Shandra (working on a computer in the TEACH training facility) can see and access Huong's resources?

Lab Projects

• Lab Project 2.1

This project involves inventorying all the networked resources in your computer lab that you will be using in this course. You should continue the role-playing process and design your own inventory form to use on the equipment you would work with in your position within the TEACH organization. The following steps will provide you with a basic procedure to use when conducting your inventory. Plan how you will ensure that all equipment is listed on the inventory only once and that it shows up in the proper location within the TEACH structure.

You will need the following:

■ Bright blue and black ink pens

■ Blank 8½ × 11 paper

■ Ruler for creating straight edges

■ Company information for the position you were "hired" into in Chapter 1

■ Access to the computer lab's networked resources

■ A flashlight to help with reading serial or model numbers

Then, do the following:

1. Write a procedure for conducting an inventory of the typical computer lab. Include steps to ensure all networked resources are contained within the inventory.

2. Using your inventory procedures, conduct the inventory and record any additional steps needed to accomplish the task. Update the procedures as appropriate with any necessary steps discovered during the inventory process.

3. Ensure that sufficient information is recorded about the items (model and serial number) to determine how many of each are available in the lab. In the event an update becomes necessary for a particular item, you need to know how many you have to purchase and install. Depending on the number of students in your class, you may need to perform this inventory on multiple computers to ensure that all networked equipment is included in the inventory. You should also include important information about your computer that may affect your use of the network, such as processor, RAM, NIC, and peripherals.

4. Your procedures should also include a method to visibly confirm whether a particular item has been included in your inventory.

5. As a class, decide how often your inventory will be verified against actual equipment locations. This may be an important step if you are allowed to move equipment from one location to another.

• Lab Project 2.2

This project involves creating an additional type of networking cable that you may need when configuring your network. The straight-through cable you created in Step-by-Step 2.01 connects a computer or networked resource to a hub. Occasionally, however, you may want to connect one computer's NIC directly to another computer's NIC, or you may want to connect one hub to another hub. In these instances, you may need what is called a *crossover cable*. The following steps contain the information you need to create such a cable. By following them, you will create your own crossover network cable and be able to connect two computers or two concentrators directly to one another.

You will need the following:

- One network interface card (NIC) per computer or networked device

- RJ-45 connectors (one for each planned cable end, plus lots of spares for practice)

- Cat-5 unshielded twisted-pair (UTP) wire (sufficient wire should be available for short pieces of "practice" cable in addition to the wiring you will make to link your computer to the other computer)

- RJ-45 wire crimping tool

- Wire cutters

- 10Base-T wire continuity tester

Warning: Whenever working with computer wiring or electrical components, be sure to use antistatic procedures. Your lab instructions may include use of antistatic wrist straps that release static buildup to a ground wire attached to the metal frame of your computer. If not, you should make sure to discharge any built-up static in your body by touching the computer's metal frame.

Then do the following:

① Obtain a length of Cat-5 twisted-pair cable with a straight-through connector already installed on one end from your instructor (or create one as explained in Step-by-Step 2.01 earlier in the chapter).

② Being careful not to nick the insulation off the internal twisted pairs of wire inside the Cat-5 cable, make a cut in the outer covering 3/8 inch from the end without a connector. This should expose the internal four pairs of twisted wiring inside the external cover.

③ Pull off the external cover from the twisted pairs but don't untwist the pairs. Make sure you keep each pair of wires together and, if you cut the casing back too far, trim the individual pairs to the desired 3/8-inch length.

④ Note whether the internal wires have solid or striped colors on the plastic coating. The colors (or striping) will play an important role when connecting the wires to the connectors.

⑤ Untwist the exposed 3/8-inch section of each pair of wires. Notice that the spacing of the twists on one pair of wires was different from the spacing of the twists on another pair. These twists help filter out interference from one pair to another.

⑥ Prepare the RJ-45 connector by turning it so that the flat side is toward you and the plastic tang is away from you and pointing down. Pin 1 is to your left.

⑦ Arrange the single wires for insertion into the RJ-45 connector in the crossover cable order listed in the following table from left to right. Pinch all eight wires close together and side by side between your index finger and your thumb.

Pinouts for Crossover Cable (One End Only!)		
Pin	If Striped-Colored Wiring:	If Solid-Colored Wiring:
1	White/Green	Blue
2	Green	Orange
3	White/Orange	Green
4	Blue	Red
5	White/Blue	Black
6	Orange	Yellow
7	White/Brown	Brown
8	Brown	Gray

⑧ Slide all eight wires completely into the open end of your RJ-45 connector. It is properly seated in the RJ-45 when you can look through it and see the ends of the wires behind the small metallic spurs that cut into the wiring to form the connection (see the crossover connector wiring shown in the following illustration).

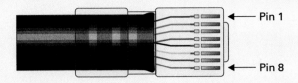

Pin 1

Pin 8

9 Make sure that the wires are all completely pushed up against the top end inside the RJ-45 and that the external covering of the wire is inside the connector. The wire's covering will give the cable support and help keep the smaller wires from being pulled out if the cable is tugged.

10 When your wire is inserted properly, have it checked by your instructor and, when told to proceed, use the crimping tool to crimp your RJ-45.

11 After crimping this second end, test your cable using the cable tester and note the expected test results for crossover cables. If it passes the continuity check, you have a working crossover cable.

12 Mark this wire with some sort of tag to differentiate it from your straight-through cables.

Communicating Over Networks

In this chapter, you will learn how to:

- **Understand network communication**
- **Decipher computer addressing**
- **Describe network communication protocols**
- **Design networks**

You have seen what networks are and what makes up the typical component listing for networks. You know that networks are intended for sending digitized messages (such as documents, photos, and the very common means of communication: e-mail) and sharing a computer's peripheral equipment. You also know that those messages and networked equipment are meant to be shared or controlled using network software and hardware. All of this involves computers communicating with each other, so you'll need to take a closer look at that digitized form of communication to better understand its effect on your network. In this chapter, you will start by looking at what constitutes effective communication and then investigate how the necessary network components can be located and employed for conducting this communication within your own network.

You will begin by learning about the digital "language" computers use to communicate. That language uses a binary communication system, which is often represented in a shorthand that might be a new counting system for you—hexadecimal. You will then create your own code and attempt to send digital messages. Different character codes will be discussed using an updated character code of your own as an example. Since the point of sending a message is that someone receive it, addressing schemes will then be studied with an emphasis on determining how a single computer is located on the network. Each computer has a network address, and the components of that address will be discussed along with a few common network layout possibilities.

Understanding Network Communication

As Ricky learned when he took a speech class in school, members of any kind of network cannot effectively communicate unless there is a sender, a receiver, a message, and a method of transmission (a *medium*). This became especially evident to him when he stood up in front of his first audience long before joining the SinkRSwim Pools organization. He tried to use every medium available to him, including speaking more loudly as we all tend to do when we are sure that the audience does not understand what we are saying. He hoped his instructor would think he got his message across to those few who were actually listening.

Years later, it became painfully obvious to Ricky that the message he sent should have been in a form that his classmates could have understood more easily. His audience didn't understand the words he was using, and speaking more loudly didn't help the situation. Ricky realized that in order to communicate well, he and his classmates needed to speak the same language. Without that common language, the result was the blank stare of a missed message. Add another layer between the sender and receiver, such as a translator, and communication can be even less effective.

Ricky found that his realization held true when his dog barked at intruders in his back yard. Ricky knew there was a message. Moreover, his dog knew what the message was. Still, Ricky kept asking "What is it, boy?" as if the dog could clarify the message if he was given another opportunity.

The principles of network communication are basically the same as those Ricky learned in his speech class. There has to be a sender, a receiver, a message, and a medium. In this book's first chapter, you saw that a network has senders and receivers—the servers and clients found on networks—and that they can change roles based upon whose needs are being met at the time. Then, in Chapter 2, you started to look at transmission mediums. Since the message is also a requirement for communication, you need to know something about what it says over the network.

Computer Signals

When two computers communicate or "speak" on a network, they exchange **digital** signals, as shown in Figure 3.1. Each signal instance, or digit, is represented by a distinct (or discrete) state, such as representing those states using either 0 volts or plus 1 volt sent as a signal. A single digital signal would then contain only one of those two states (or any distinguishable either/or condition, such as on or off), and the transition from one to the other would be instantaneous. A digital signal cannot be interpreted as anything other than one of the two agreed-upon states.

Digital signals have a **finite** (countable) number of states, which makes them different from **analog** signals, which have an **infinite** (not countable) number of states, as shown in Figure 3.2. In an analog signal, there is a gradual transition from one state to another with an infinite number of transition instances along the signal.

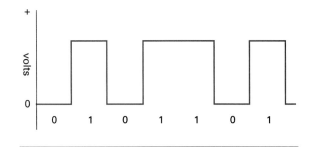

● **Figure 3.1**   A digital signal with seven digits

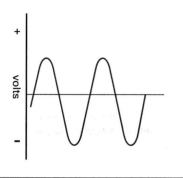

• **Figure 3.2** An analog signal

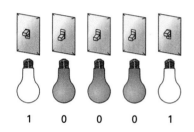

1   0   0   0   1

• Light signals

Digital **states** can be likened to a pitch-dark room where a 150 watt light is suddenly illuminated or extinguished. The two states are definitely distinct, and each is immediately discernible. The computer equates the presence of an electrical signal with "on" and represents it with a 1, whereas it equates the absence of an electrical signal with "off" and represents it with a 0.

A system that uses only the numbers 0 and 1 is called a **binary** system. Computers can rapidly differentiate between these two distinct (binary) digital states and communicate using this language.

Try a little practical experiment using the International Morse Code, shown in Figure 3.3, and your classroom light switch (or a flashlight) to send a message.

1. Leaving plenty of space between your letters, print out a short message on a sheet of paper.

2. Horizontally, and beneath each letter, add its International Morse Code equivalent in dots and dashes.

3. Assign all other class members the responsibility of decoding your message.

4. Go to your classroom light switch (or use a flashlight).

5. Flip the light switch on or off to send one full letter at a time— without referring back to your paper (remember: it may be dark).

6. Complete the transmission of your message and have your classmates decode it without any discussion.

7. Compare their results with your message to see if they understood your text.

When a receiving computer "listens" to the network medium, and the medium's initial state changes from not carrying a signal (interpreted as 0) to carrying a signal, the listening computer can interpret this changed state as representing a transmitted digital 1. Remove that signal and the receiving computer will interpret that changed state as a digital 0. These changed states must occur over an agreed period of time or the computer will either not understand them or interpret them incorrectly.

If the 150 watt bulb in that pitch-dark room were to be hooked up to a **rheostat** (a device used to gradually adjust electrical current) instead of an on/off switch, the difference between analog and digital would be immediately apparent. When you turn or slide the rheostat, the light is actually "on," but there is an infinite number of such "on" positions ranging from all the way off to all the way on. Each of those positions corresponds to the infinite number of points along the gradual slope of an analog signal.

A	· —	S	· · ·
B	— · · ·	T	—
C	— · — ·	U	· · —
D	— · ·	V	· · · —
E	·	W	· — —
F	· · — ·	X	— · · —
G	— — ·	Y	— · — —
H	· · · ·	Z	— — · ·
I	· ·	1	· — — — —
J	· — — —	2	· · — — —
K	— · —	3	· · · — —
L	· — · ·	4	· · · · —
M	— —	5	· · · · ·
N	— ·	6	— · · · ·
O	— — —	7	— — · · ·
P	· — — ·	8	— — — · ·
Q	— — · —	9	— — — — ·
R	· — ·	0	— — — — —

• **Figure 3.3** International Morse Code

Introduction to Networking

Digital to Analog Conversion

Digital information is used in all computer communication, so it may seem strange to hear that computers can communicate over telephone lines even though most telephone lines are capable of carrying only analog signals. Another piece of equipment is necessary to convert the sending computer's digital signal to an analog signal (a process called **modulate**) and then to convert the analog signal back to a digital signal that the receiving computer can recognize (**demodulate**), as shown in Figure 3.4. This piece of equipment is called a **modem**, a name that comes from combining the words modulate and demodulate.

Modem

• Figure 3.4   A modem converts digital signals to analog for the sender and from analog to digital for the receiver.

Bits

 A bit is a single instance of a digital signal (the word being a combination of *binary* and *digit*). That is, a bit is the individual "on" or "off" that is represented by the corresponding 1 or 0. You can think of a bit as an electrical signal sent down a cable (the most common type of network transmission medium). This image is effective because it is easy to envision someone either sending or receiving a bulging, swiftly traveling electrical pulse through those wires.

Bits can also be sent using other means. They can be represented by other medium states, such as the relative signal strength of light pulses or radio waves. The computer can interpret the positive states—such as the presence of a light pulse or radio wave—as a binary 1. The absence of light or sound waves can be interpreted as a binary 0.

Bits by themselves don't do a lot for us. It's true that, because they are binary, they can be transmitted to and interpreted by the receiving computer very quickly. A bunch of bits, though, is nothing but a bunch of bits. Without some semblance of order, there is no message. A bit becomes important to computers only when it is combined with other bits to create different characters, much as we combine different strokes of a pen or pencil to form letters and numbers.

Bytes

When you first learned how to write, you had to be taught that a grander scheme, your alphabet (or other character set), had to be used before your writing meant anything. The same is true for digital communication. There has to be a way of organizing the bits or they would be nothing more than randomly dispersed, unrecognizable

 Cross Check

Sending and Receiving

Answer the following questions using what you have learned about senders and receivers:

1. What role does a modem play in enabling communication between computer senders and receivers?

2. What is the impact of using a modem on the overall effectiveness of the network's communication?

Cross Check

Transmitting Mediums

Use what you learned about transmission mediums in Chapters 1 and 2 of this text to answer the following questions:

1. What is the transmission medium used when transmitting light pulses as information signals over a network?

2. What is the term for the type of network medium that transmits network information using radio waves?

1 0 1 1 1 0 1 1

● **Figure 3.5** A byte's eight digital signals

A playful way to remember the difference between bits and bytes is to think of bits as "itty BITty." Then, remember that a byte is really just "a mouthful" of bits.

Inside Information

Character Standard Codes

Computers use a character code to translate from the binary information to characters people can read. Although the data is recorded within the computer in machine code consisting of all 1's and 0's, displaying it that way to humans would be useless. Standard output character sets were introduced to solve this problem.

The most accepted character set is ASCII (American Standard Code for Information Interchange, pronounced "ask-ee"), which was finalized in 1968 and is still in use today. Another set, developed by IBM for its mainframe computers, is EBCDIC (Extended Binary Coded Decimal Interchange Code, pronounced "eb-see-dik"). EBCDIC uses a slightly different conversion system to choose the characters it displays to the user. Prior to either of these standards, each equipment manufacturer used its own character conversion. Development of a standard helped make the equipment interchangeable.

gibberish. Much like when your scratching on paper (or sometimes walls) turned from simple lines and shapes into crudely formed letters, a computer can communicate when it combines groups of bits into the "letters" of its own alphabet (or other character set).

The letters and characters used to write the different languages around the world are difficult to form, oddly shaped, and often easily mistaken for something else. A computer cannot function properly using such an alphabet. Instead, uniformity and precision are the rule. Every character in the digital alphabet needs the same number of "strokes" or digits, and early designs for computer characters settled on seven bits. Currently, the octet (a group of eight) is used to provide the most desirable binary character capability. Each character the computer uses to communicate contains eight distinct bits as shown in Figure 3.5. That eight-bit character is called a byte.

Since the original computers were designed by and planned for English-speaking users, the original 7-bit code's 128 available characters were sufficient to represent the Roman alphabet, the numbers (0–9), and the other characters needed for English. The international appeal of the computer forced the addition of another bit, and as a result, each byte can now be used to represent up to 256 characters, digits, or symbols on a computer. Unicode was also created and allows us to represent all languages on a computer simply by using two bytes per character. Now, every language can easily be represented on computers.

Cross Check

Changed Code

As you can see by looking at the International Morse Code chart in Figure 3.3, shown earlier, no consideration was given to keeping characters the same length. Keep in mind the fact that computer character codes must have all eight bits filled before they can be recognized, and answer the following questions:

1. How many bits would have to be set aside in order to represent the International Morse Code's character coding, as shown in Figure 3.3, without making any changes?

2. If the International Morse Code's character coding were to be changed such that all available spaces in a character (places where dots or dashes *could* be used) had to be filled, and no two characters could be represented by the same code, how many digits would then have to be used in order to represent the *New and Improved* character code?

3. Develop your own *New and Improved* character code to meet the preceding requirements using either a 1 for a dot and a 0 for a dash, or the other way around. Hint: You may need to develop a character to represent a blank space in a coded message.

Messages

When a computer communicates with itself or with another computer, it assembles its characters (groups of bytes) into words, complete statements, and other digitized data meaningful to other computers. Combining bits and bytes, then, is the process that forms the foundation of all computer communication. ~~A computer's ability to quickly string bits together as bytes that are then sent over the network for other computers to receive and interpret is really what networking is all about.~~

Step-by-Step 3.01

Create and Send a Computer Message

Now that you understand the concept of digital communication and the use of bits and bytes, see if you can create and effectively send a message. In this activity, you will form a team and will develop your own character code and message translation mechanism in an attempt to get someone at the opposite end of your classroom to accomplish a simple task. To complete this exercise, you will need the following items:

- One floppy disk (or Zip disk)
- One computer for each "step" along the message path, with Windows and Microsoft Word installed
- Sufficient 8½ × 11-inch paper and pencils to formulate encoded messages

- A set of simple tasks (provided to your instructor with this course's setup materials)
- At least 8 "process" students, one (or more) assigned to each step in the procedure
- Someone (preferably the instructor) to act as the role setter
- Five copies of each of the two possible outcomes (one using dashes as 1's and dots as 0's, and the other using dashes as 0's and dots as 1's) from the previous Changed Code Cross Check exercise
- At least two "communicator" students (people designated as Communicators for the Communication-Out and Communication-In)

Step 1

Your team should have the coding assistant create message-coding sheets by turning the page horizontally and drawing five boxes across the top of the page (approximately ½ inch tall by 1 inch long), leaving a ½-inch space between and above the boxes. Number the boxes 1 to 5 from left to right. One inch below the boxes, draw ten horizontal lines across the paper and leave ½ inch of space between the lines as shown in the illustration.

Step 2

Decide which of the two *New and Improved* coding schemes to use—one where dots are changed to 0's (and dashes to 1's) or where dots are changed to 1's (and dashes to 0's). Then, enter the code for a 0 in box number 1 along the top edge of the message-coding sheet using the respective five-digit code that has been chosen.

Step 3	The Communication-Out person, using the appropriate coding scheme indicated by the coded 0 in box number 1, should write out a short action message (using the instructor-provided activities) intended for Communicator-In on the other side of the room. It should be written on a separate piece of paper and use at least five but not more than ten words. When the message is successfully interpreted, the receiver will perform the requested action.

Step 3

The Communication-Out person, using the appropriate coding scheme indicated by the coded 0 in box number 1, should write out a short action message (using the instructor-provided activities) intended for Communicator-In on the other side of the room. It should be written on a separate piece of paper and use at least five but not more than ten words. When the message is successfully interpreted, the receiver will perform the requested action.

Step 4

The encoding team should encode the message on a third sheet of paper using the coding scheme identified in box number 1. Use a separate line for each word. Code each character using the appropriate five-bit code but decide whether to write the characters from right to left or left to right. In box number 2, encode the word *read* using the appropriate direction and the coding scheme from box 1.

Step 5

The scrambling team should then enter the coded message on the message-formatting sheet with one word per line after properly encoding either the word *up* or *down* in box 3 to indicate whether the message starts on line 10 or 1. The number 1, 2, or 3 should also be encoded in box 4 to indicate which is the first word and which successive words to read (1 means start with the first word and read one word at a time, 2 means start with the second word and read every other word, and 3 means start with the third word and read every third word).

Step 6

The role setter (instructor) shall properly encode either an *A* (to act) or a *P* (to pass) the action message in box number 5. If the role setter encodes *P* to pass, the Communicator-In has the option of passing the action and returning it to the sender who shall immediately perform the requested action. An *A* indicates that the action must be immediately acted upon by the receiver.

Step 7

The role setter then transfers the completely encoded message to the disseminator who should check the message format and ensure that all required entries are made. If not, the message should be discarded and the originating team must send the same message again. If the message is valid, the disseminator displays the message-coding sheet for the descramblers, who each use boxes 1, 3, and 4 to interpret and copy the encoded words in the proper sequence onto a separate sheet of paper.

Step 8

The de-scramblers then transfer their copy of the message to separate decoders who, using the information from the encoded box 2 direction, decode the individual words in the message and provide it to their Communicator-In who reviews it for applicability. If it is not addressed to their Communicator-In, they take no action. Otherwise, they decide, based on the coded entry in box 5, whether to Act or Pass the message, and the appropriate person or group (depending on what the task was) takes the directed action.

■ Deciphering Computer Addressing

The TEACH organization has numerous computers that are networked together. You and your coworkers have grown accustomed to using your computers to tap into all of the networked resources within the company's equipment pool and to sharing your files, folders, and other computer documents with anyone you choose.

Suppose when you applied for a job at TEACH, you were hired to replace MarieC, the chief of the administration department and head receptionist for the entire training center. In that position, you would want control over the company-related materials that could be viewed on the network. Additionally, you'd like to know that something you send to a specific individual is received only by that individual and not by anyone else on the network. You have learned why computers need to be connected into networks, and how computers communicate over a network. Now you need to know how one computer can actually get in touch with another computer.

If you mail a letter to someone, they have an address that must be used to correctly get the letter to their location. Networked computers also have addresses, and these networking addresses can be broken down into smaller components.

Unique Addresses

Accurately storing and retrieving data over a network depends heavily on each device having a unique address, with an exact name (using the correct format) and storage path (that points to the address) so that the unique address correctly finds the device. Following a particular path when trying to locate a device should result in there only being one such device at the final location. If there are two devices with the same address, a system that relies on unique addressing for storage and retrieval cannot work.

You can apply the unique addressing concept to your life at school. The office personnel should be able to check their records at any given point in time and be able to identify exactly where you are supposed to be located. Even in the rare instances when two students have exactly the same name (including middle names) there are ways for instructors and administrators to uniquely identify the individual students, such as using the school's student numbers or the students' social security numbers.

Think back to classes you have taken in the past. You may remember a situation where two people shared the same name. During the first few days, the instructor probably experienced "unique addressing" difficulties when one student's name was called and two people responded. Usually there was some obvious difference between the two, and everyone grew accustomed to the problem and compensated for it in some way. Maybe one of them went by a nickname, or by their middle name, or had a "1" or "2" placed after their name. In some way, those students were differentiated and a method was devised to address them properly.

The TV sitcom Newhart once poked fun at just such a situation, and that comedic moment became one of the most memorable of the series. The scene involved one person introducing his family members and not recognizing that his circumstances were just a bit odd. He entered and made introductions by declaring, "Hi, I'm Larry. This is my brother Daryl, and this is my other brother Daryl."

You'd have no difficulty delivering mail (or data) to Larry in this situation. However, would you know which Daryl to hand a package to if it were sent simply to Daryl? You would have an addressing problem. That's why addresses on a network must be unique.

Courtesy of 3Com

● **Figure 3.6**   The MAC address is a 12-digit number that can sometimes be found on the network interface card (NIC).

Physical Address

The physical address is the first element of a computer's network address and typically comes from a special serial number assigned to a component (the network interface card) installed inside the computer itself. The numbers are controlled by the networking industry's regulating organization, the Institute of Electrical and Electronics Engineers (**IEEE**, commonly referred to as the "I-triple-E"). The equipment manufacturer requests a block of unique 48-bit binary numbers and then assigns a separate number to each network interface card (NIC) it creates. Thus, no number can ever be reused, and each computer gets to have a unique **physical address**.

On the networks where you will likely be working, that physical address is the means by which your computer will gain access to the networking medium. It is also called the Media Access Control address, or **MAC address.** The first 24 bits of the MAC address assigned to a NIC are set by the IEEE to identify the manufacturer. The second 24 bits are used for a unique serial number that is assigned to the individual network interface cards by the manufacturer. As a matter of convenience, these numbers are referred to in their shorthand hexadecimal notation, usually on the serial number side of your network interface card, as shown in Figure 3.6. The physical (or MAC) address is also sometimes referred to as the **hardware address**.

Hexadecimal Notation

Hexadecimal notation (hex), shown in Table 3.1, is a numbering system that uses **base 16** instead of the customary base 10. That is, there are 16 **alphanumeric** characters (the letters A through F are added) instead of the usual 10 numeric digits. Hex is a shorthand way of writing binary numbers—there is a single hex digit equivalent for each four digits of a binary number. It takes four binary digits to represent the numbers 0 through 16, but the same range can be represented with a single hex digit.

Take the 48-bit binary number used in the MAC address. Working with the actual binary MAC address would involve 48 1's and 0's strung together. Not too appealing. The hex equivalent of a 48-digit binary number is a 12-digit hex number, a system which is a bit easier to use. (This comes from 48 being divided by the 4 binary digits that a hex digit can represent.) Imagine yourself turning individual lights in a bank of four light bulbs on and off to create the sixteen binary digit combinations in a 4-bit number, as shown in Table 3.1.

Table 3.1	Hexadecimal Number Conversion Table	
Hex	**On/Off Light Equivalent**	**Binary**
0	All lights off	0000
1	Only fourth light on	0001
2	Only third light on	0010
3	Third and fourth lights on	0011
4	Only second light on	0100
5	Second and fourth lights on	0101
6	Second and third lights on	0110
7	Second, third, and fourth lights on	0111
8	Only first light on	1000
9	First and fourth lights on	1001
A	First and third lights on	1010
B	First, third, and fourth lights on	1011
C	First and second lights on	1100
D	First, second, and fourth lights on	1101
E	First, second, and third lights on	1110
F	All lights on	1111

MAC Addressing

You should know how a NIC's MAC address is actually implemented within your computer and be able to convert that coded number to the actual binary address it represents. In this exercise, you will need the following:

■ A computer running Windows 9*x*, 2000, or XP,

or

■ An instructor-provided demonstration network interface card with a visible MAC address

Step 1

Do one of the following:

■ At your Windows 9*x* computer, click the Start button and select RUN. Type **CMD** and press ENTER, and then type **WINIPCFG** and press ENTER again. Copy down the 12-character hexadecimal Adapter Address provided in the display, and close your open windows.

■ At your Windows NT/2000/XP computer, click the Start button and select RUN. Type **CMD** and press ENTER, and then type **IPCONFIG/ALL** and press ENTER again. Copy down the 12-character hexadecimal Physical Address provided in the display, as shown in the illustration, and close your open windows.

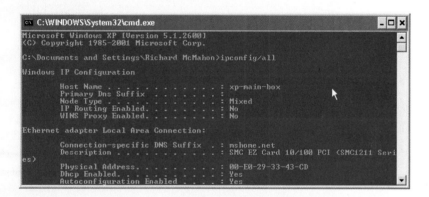

Step 2

Open your computer's calculator by selecting Start | Programs | Accessories | Calculator. When the calculator appears, select View | Scientific and then click the Hex option button as shown here.

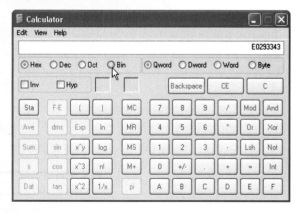

Enter the hexadecimal MAC address you obtained in Step 1. Note that **leading zeros** (those to the left of your number) will not be displayed if you try typing them into your calculator or when the results of a calculation are displayed.

Step 3	Click the calculator's Bin option to display your MAC address in its binary digit form.

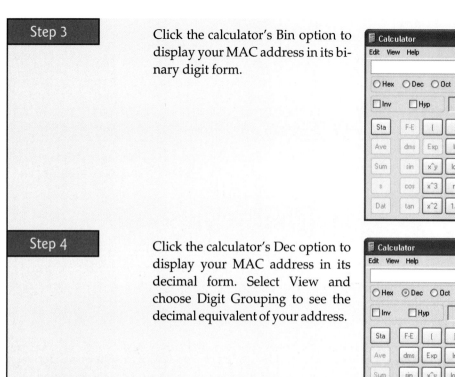

Step 4	Click the calculator's Dec option to display your MAC address in its decimal form. Select View and choose Digit Grouping to see the decimal equivalent of your address.

Node Address

Along with the hardware address, some networks also require a unique **node address** for every computer on that particular network. Although machines already have individual MAC addresses, adding a node address to the MAC helps locate those randomly generated numbers just as a street name helps group the houses in a neighborhood. If you work with Novell NetWare's earlier versions, you will need to create node addresses.

This node address scheme will work well for all communication between computers on the same Novell local area network, but these node addresses are only unique within the network. Another step is necessary for communicating beyond the boundaries of that Novell network. Since each node address is only useful within the specific network to which it is attached, another number is arbitrarily assigned to each network by the network servers when they communicate with other networks.

Network Address

The combination of node address (if one is used) and MAC address then becomes the computer's **network address,** and it must uniquely identify a specific computer to all others on the network. This unique address is how network messages are directed to specific computers and how those computers determine whether specific messages apply to them.

• Figure 3.7 If the address of the message does not match the address of the workstation, it keeps going until it finds the right computer.

When a message is sent, it is addressed to a particular computer or workstation. As each message travels through the network, the network interface card will read the address of the message. If the message is not addressed to that workstation, the message will be ignored. However, if the address of the message matches the workstation address, the message will be received and read by the workstation (see Figure 3.7).

Although they may use different types of addressing, such as static (like the MAC address mentioned above), dynamic (where addresses are configured by servers controlling the network), or configurable (where addresses are set by installers and remain changeable depending on the circumstances), all computer networks must ensure that addresses are guaranteed to be unique.

Network Address Implementation

The uniqueness of network addresses ensures that effective communication takes place, but how is that address used on the network? When one computer wants to communicate with another computer within its own network, a **source address** is created, which specifies where the transmitted information originates. Likewise, a **destination address** is created, which specifies the information's destination. Both the source and destination addresses are then added to the data being transmitted to make sure that the message is routed properly. If the receiving computer determines that the message is directed to someone else, it is simply discarded or passed along, depending on the type of network. Otherwise, it is examined by the receiver. In either case, if it is not completely understood, the receiver asks the sender to retransmit the message. When it is completely understood and intended for the receiving computer, that receiving computer then acknowledges receipt, and the sending computer no longer needs to consider repeating the transmission.

Download IEEE Standards

From your reading, you should already gather that the IEEE is an influential organization in the networking field. Their **standards**, or rules, are far-reaching and always changing. Normally the IEEE standards are only available to you on the Internet through the IEEE, itself, if you have paid a subscription for the service. In an effort to "Close the digital divide," the IEEE has partnered with industry leaders to make the standards available free. However, the free version is not always the latest. If you want the most recent, you still have to pay for a subscription. Otherwise, six months after they are released, the rules are posted to the free site.

In this activity, you will connect to the IEEE web site and download several IEEE standards. To complete this exercise, you will need the following items:

- An operational computer that is connected to the Internet
- External storage media such as floppy or Zip disks
- Adobe Acrobat Reader loaded on your computer

If Adobe Acrobat Reader is not currently loaded, you can obtain and load it onto your computer from the following site: `http://www.adobe.com/products/acrobat/readstep2.html`.

Step 1

Log on to a computer, open your browser, type **http://standards.ieee.org/getieee802/** into the Address window, and press ENTER. Once you agree to their terms and conditions for each standard, you can view (and save) the online copies. Although they are not the latest versions, these copies of the standards offer you an excellent opportunity to use actual documentation in subsequent exercises.

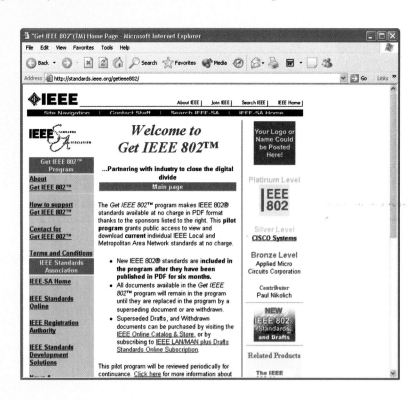

Step 2

Use the scroll bar on the right if necessary and view the IEEE Working Groups section (in the lower-left corner of the web site). Click on the first document (802), as shown here.

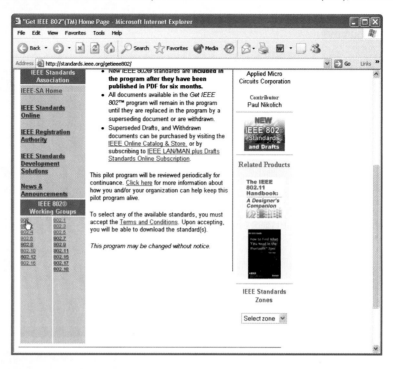

Step 3

Whenever a document is returned, as shown in the following illustration, glance through it and save it to your storage device (floppy or Zip disk) before clicking the Back arrow (in the top left of your browser) to return to the document listing so you can go through the saving process for each of the other available documents. If a committee web site is returned, use the back arrow to return to the Document Listing page and select another document to save.

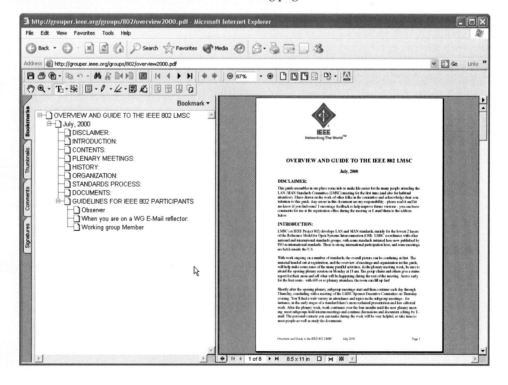

Note: Because of IEEE rules about using this online documentation, copies of all documents may not be available. If a document was released within the last six months, it will not be available through this free online service.

Step 4

Although some of the listed documents may not be available because of the IEEE rules, make sure you download the 2000 version of 802.3, shown in the following illustration. (You obtain it at the following address: `http://standards.ieee.org/getieee802/portfolio.html?agree=ACCEPT`; then click on the download section's 802.3 listing and choose the latest IEEE 802.3 link, agree to the terms and conditions, and wait the few minutes it may take to transfer the almost 1600 pages to your computer.)

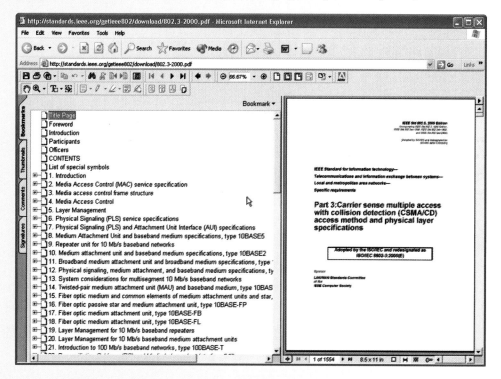

Cross Check

Using the IEEE 802.3 Specifications

Use the IEEE 802.3 document you downloaded in Step-by-Step 3.03 and have stored in either your computer or your external storage (floppy or Zip disk) when answering the following questions.

1. Locate section 3.2.3, "Address fields," in the document, and find out how many address fields are contained in each MAC frame, or message, and how many bits are actually used to transmit each of those addresses.

2. Locate section 3.4, "Invalid MAC frame," in the document and list the conditions that must be met for a MAC message to be declared invalid.

Describe Network Communication Protocols

Do you remember Ricky raising his voice when he realized that his audience wasn't understanding his message? Ricky broke a human communication rule—don't yell at people if you want them to voluntarily listen to you. Network communication has similar rules, and many of them are decisions made by the communicator when attempting to communicate. Aren't you taught to look at people when you speak with them, to talk in a pleasant tone, to speak slowly, and to communicate in such a way that your listener will understand? Those are just a few of the rules we follow when conversing.

Along with the rules for effective communication that Ricky carelessly overlooked, there were other decisions that he was unaware of when preparing his classroom speech. Many of those decisions had to do with deciding on a purpose for delivering his speech and then deciding how to deliver his message effectively. Ricky had to design his speech, and you must, similarly, design your network.

Recall that network communication relies on ~~networked resources transmitting digital messages over a networking medium to other networked resources~~. Just as in human communication, there are rules involved when communicating over networks. Break those rules and others may hear you but they might not understand or listen to your message.

Network Communication Decisions

You have already seen that messages are made up of characters, that characters are simply bytes, that bytes are formed by combining bits, and that bits are really just organized binary signals. You also learned that messages will flow from one resource to another over a networking medium as long as you know the recipient's unique address. However, does effective network communication automatically happen if you have characters, a networking medium connecting resources, and unique addresses? Hardly.

Think back to the confusion that ensued when you tried sending simple messages across the room using your own Morse Code adaptation. You had everything you needed to communicate effectively, but it still was not easy. What were you missing? What other decisions had to be made? The following sections look at just a few of the additional decisions that you must make before effective communication can take place.

Language to Use

When you formulate a mental image of Ricky delivering his speech, in what language do you "hear" his message? Did you give much thought to that? With global mobility being so easy nowadays, many of your classmates could probably get up in front of the room and deliver a speech in a language that you, and many around you, would not understand? Languages, however, are simply compilations of rules, with each language having its own rules. Try to apply rules from one language when speaking another and confusion usually results.

To effectively communicate over a network, you must select a set of language rules from the thousands of sets that have all been developed for network communication. Those sets of rules are called protocols. Two of the earlier networking languages, or protocols, were **NetBIOS** (Network Basic Input/Output System) and NetBEUI (NetBIOS Extended User Interface). These protocols were developed by IBM for use on early networks.

Much like human language, protocols are continually updated as they are used. NetBIOS, initially a networking solution developed by IBM to reside in a computer's memory during operation, has transformed and now provides significantly more than simple networking. IBM extended the development of NetBIOS with its release of NetBEUI, and Microsoft popularized this new release by including NetBEUI in its first attempts at networking.

NetBEUI is still recommended for use on very small networks, and it is still probably the fastest popular small network protocol because of Microsoft's extensive distribution system. However, its early reliance on broadcasting message traffic to all networked resources (or nodes) became a drawback as the numbers of those resources on a single network increased dramatically. Most of the network's transmission capability was used up carrying pointless message traffic. Network communication slowed to a crawl, and potentially important messages could not go any faster than the traffic surrounding them. Something had to be done to cut down on those broadcasts and speed up the flow of traffic.

Step-by-Step 3.04

Locating the NetBEUI Protocol

On a Windows 9*x*, NT, or 2000 computer that is already network-capable, use the Network Neighborhood icon to locate the NetBEUI protocol. For this exercise, you will need *one* of the following:

- A Networked Win9*x* workstation
- Or a WinNT workstation
- Or Win2k workstation

Step 1

Right-click the Network Neighborhood icon on your desktop, and select Properties from the drop-down menu. If this icon is not available, ask your instructor for assistance.

Write down the items in the Network dialog box, and click the Add button. Depending on your computer's configuration, you may have to use the scroll bar (if one is available) to view all the items currently installed on your computer.

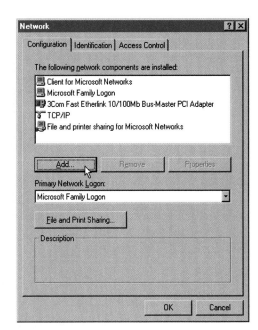

In the Select Network Component Type dialog box, select Protocol, and click the Add button.

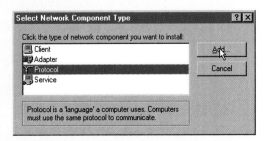

In the Select Network Protocol dialog box, select Microsoft in the Manufacturers selection box on the left, scroll to and select NetBEUI in the Network Protocols selection box on the right.

If you have permission from your instructor, click OK to add the protocol, and continue with these steps. If you don't have permission, click Cancel to return to the desktop without adding the protocol, and skip the remainder of these steps.

Warning: Up through this point in the procedure no changes have been made to your computer. Clicking Cancel disregards your pending changes while clicking OK implements them. Make sure you have permission to change your computer before clicking the OK button.

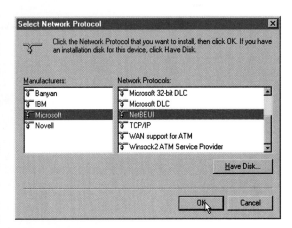

Step 5	If you have permission and have added the NetBEUI protocol to your computer, verify that the NetBEUI protocol icon is present in your Network dialog box's list of installed network components, and then click OK.	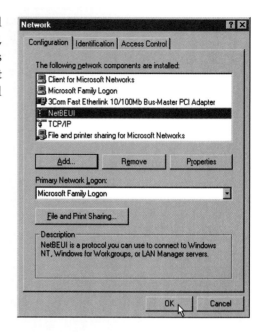

Step 6	In the System Settings Change dialog box, click Yes to restart your computer.	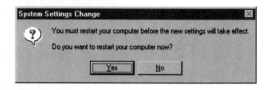

Broadcasting Versus Routing

Early networking involved digital messages that were simply broadcast over the networking medium to anything listening. Because networks were small when IBM first developed NetBIOS and NetBEUI, it was good for all computers to listen for any communication and extremely good if they actually all heard something. Sending messages directly to the resource for which it was intended—routing the messages—did not really enter into the first networking initiatives. However, very soon routing had to be taken into account.

When you worked through your in-class message creation exercise in Step-by-Step 3.01, you used a form of routing when you coded pieces of information in the various boxes at the top of the message. When that message was decoded, different groups of people on the receiving end focused their attention only on their assigned sections of the message. They decoded their segment of the message, invoked the applicable procedures based on what they thought the message told them,

 Cross Check

Transmitting a Message

Think back to the process you used when transmitting your message from one side of the classroom to the other, and answer the following questions:

1. Describe three components built into your message-formatting sheet from Step-by-Step 3.01 that helped the students on the receiving end decipher your message and get it to its ultimate user.

2. Describe how you could alter the form such that only your intended team would decode the message if multiple sets of decoding teams were given the same encoded message.

and passed their interpretation, along with the original message, on to the next step in the process. That decoding process relied on your message's formatting—the specific character order or location used when transferring information.

Message Format

Just as in English, simply being able to create the individual characters of the alphabet does not guarantee skillful communicative ability. The rules for combining those characters into words, words into sentences, and sentences into paragraphs must be mastered. Those rules specify how you format your message, and they are really the mechanism that transforms simple computer signals sent as individual characters into a complex language. In fact, by using those very same characters, you can communicate in several different languages simply by altering the set of rules you use to combine them. Much the same way, a network designer's choice of the various protocols available can be based upon the needs of the networked community and how the networked resources are to be shared. Fortunately, once you make the decision to use a particular protocol, many of the formatting decisions are already made for you.

The concept of formatting is simple—it is the combining of mutually acceptable characters such that messages can be exchanged. That simple concept is at the basis of all network communications, even though the way it is implemented within the various network protocols can be complex. Think back to the format you used when you sent a message using Morse Code earlier in the chapter. Your receiver would not have been able to decipher your message without knowing ahead of time how you put it together. They needed to know what information was in those five boxes at the top before they could interpret the rest of the message.

Layered Communications

When network communication was in its infancy, almost everything was proprietary. If you bought an operating system that was network-capable, every component of your network would have to use that same operating system. Nobody else's would work with the one you had. It amounted to mass confusion if you tried adding dissimilar components to the system or connecting to a different type of system at the opposite end. That's because there were no rules for how one system would work with another.

The solution came in the form of a recommendation from an international agency. That agency, the International Standards Organization (**ISO**), suggested the use of a standard layered model to explain network communication. They further recommended that their reference model's standards be open and made available to everyone so that interconnectivity between different systems would be more likely to occur. The ISO named their reference model the Open Systems Interconnection (**OSI**) model. The idea was both simple and radical, but their goal was to enhance the likelihood of effective network communication and they succeeded.

OSI Reference Model Concept

The OSI model simplifies complex networking activities by grouping the steps in the process into seven separate task layers (the Physical, Data Link,

Learn more about the OSI model and how it works by going to http://www.learntcpip.com/ and selecting "How the OSI Model Works." This is a 36-minute presentation.

Although there are many ways to remember the seven layers of the OSI reference model, one of the most common uses the first letter from the names of each of the layers: Please Do Not Throw Sausage Pizza Away.

Table 3.2	Layers in the OSI Model	
Number	**Name**	**Function**
Layer 1	Physical layer	Consists of the networking media (wiring and interconnections) and the components necessary to transmit a signal from one end to the other
Layer 2	Data Link layer	Packages the data so that it can be transmitted over the Physical layer
Layer 3	Network layer	Separates the data into frames and determines the route the data will take to its destination
Layer 4	Transport layer	Makes sure data packets are sequenced properly and do not contain any errors
Layer 5	Session layer	Maintains a connected link, called a session, between the two communicating ends
Layer 6	Presentation layer	Determines the format used for communication and compresses, encrypts, or converts the data as necessary for the protocol in use
Layer 7	Application layer	Completes or initiates the actions being communicated

Network, Transport, Session, Presentation, and Application layers), as outlined in Table 3.2. By dividing the process into smaller tasks, it is easier for vendors to perfect smaller pieces of the problem.

Internet Communications

Networking advances came about and a move toward international standards was possible because of work the U.S. military had done developing what came to be called the Internet. Many of the enhancements to networking capabilities today are available to us because of the development of the Internet. The military's need was to ensure the survival of military command and control using interconnected (and often unused) computer capacity around the country.

Because the most widely used networking configuration is that used for Internet communications, that setup is the one you will examine most in this book. The Internet primarily operates using TCP/IP, so you will be exposed to some of its basic concepts. Other Internet protocols include FTP, SMTP, and HTTP, and these will be examined along with two other vendor configurations: Novell's IPX/SPX and Apple Computer's AppleTalk.

Although the seven layers of the OSI model describe typical actions undertaken during network communication, the demarcation between the layers and the total number of layers is unimportant as long as all the actions are accomplished. In addition to the OSI model, there are several other models available, such as those from the Department of Defense, Apple, and Novell. In fact, a revised model might be more in line with actual practice on

Inside Information

OSI Model— A Radical Departure

What made the OSI model radical was the recommendation that it be open to anybody. The intent was to give everyone the same information so nobody would have an economic advantage, and it was also more likely that the standards would be used if they were given away. Once the standards were used, specialization within the OSI layers could occur, because vendors knew what the connectivity expectations were for each of the other layers. If a new product, for instance, could speed up or simplify a layer in the middle of the OSI reference model (sometimes called the OSI stack), the vendor could concentrate on working with that layer exclusively and would only have to worry about data formats used by the adjacent layers. That is, as long as the data could be received from the lower layer and be handed off properly to the next layer, vendors could work their magic any way they saw fit within the layer (or layers) they were trying to enhance.

today's Internet. A new model with only five layers would be a bit easier to understand than the OSI model. You could simply group the top three layers of the OSI model together and consider them all part of a larger Application layer, while keeping the other four OSI layers intact. In actual practice, the top three OSI layers are typically housed inside the communicating computers anyway, so grouping them together and handling them in one step would be a practical solution.

Transmission Control Protocol/Internet Protocol (TCP/IP)

As this section's name implies, **TCP/IP** (Transmission Control Protocol/Internet Protocol) is actually more than just a single protocol. In fact, it is what is known as a protocol suite—more than one protocol working together to accomplish a particular task. TCP/IP has become the language of the Internet, and its use is a prerequisite to Internet access. It has been in use since the days when the Internet was strictly military and was referred to as **ARPANET** (Advanced Research Projects Agency Network). The combined TCP/IP protocol is the most widely used protocol in the world because it acts as the Transport and Network layer protocols used by everyone on the Internet.

Transmission Control Protocol (TCP)

The Transmission Control Protocol (TCP) links the Application layer to the Network layer (which means that TCP works at the Transport layer) and makes sure the data is correctly sized, that it is properly put in packets, and that it is sequenced in the right order upon receipt. Establishing the connection between the sending and receiving ends of the Application layer and ensuring that the data is received and properly resequenced makes TCP a reliable, or **connection-oriented**, protocol.

Internet Protocol (IP)

The Internet Protocol (IP) is a set of rules that are more concerned with sending a message to the correct address than with whether the data actually makes it to that receiver. It is, therefore, a **connectionless protocol**, which means that it is an unreliable protocol. IP will send its information regardless of whether the receiver is there or not. Of primary importance to IP's set of rules is the creation and maintenance of an addressing scheme, known as IP addressing. IP operates at the OSI's third layer—the Network layer—so it is responsible for selecting the best route for each message to travel on its way to the receiver.

Although it did not start out that way, all computers now connecting to the Internet must do so using an IP address. These addresses are managed by the Internet Corporation for Assigned Names and Numbers (ICANN), which accepts applications for and issues unique numbers or blocks of numbers as required. Each IP address is a unique 4-byte (or 32-bit) number formatted such that each byte (or 8-bit segment) is separated by a period. An example would be the address 100.100.100.100 (which would be read as "100 dot 100 dot 100 dot 100"). IP addresses can be assigned statically to individual computers or they can be assigned dynamically.

- **Static addressing** One way a network administrator can implement IP addresses is to assign individual addresses to specific computers. Each of these addresses would then be referred to as a

Although reference models such as the OSI and DOD are handy conceptualizations of how specific segments of networking should work together, protocols are actual sets of rules used when effecting that communication. Some protocols predate those reference models.

static address. As long as there is a record of where each IP address is assigned and none are installed twice, troubleshooting address problems is a matter of looking up where the number comes from and going to that computer. However, when computer locations change, or if there are frequent IP address changes, the likelihood of two computers accidentally having the same number is increased. When that happens, the first machine on the network is granted the number's use whether it is the rightful owner of that address or not. Locating an incorrectly implemented number can be difficult, and if you make frequent changes, keeping an accurate record may take an extensive investment in manpower.

- **Dynamic addressing** Another way an administrator can implement IP addressing on a network is to use **dynamic addressing**. This is done using the Dynamic Host Configuration Protocol (**DHCP**), which is a set of rules that allow a group of computers to effectively lease IP numbers to network members on an as-needed basis. A pool of IP numbers is made available to the network through a DHCP server, and when computers start, their configuration has them request an IP number from that server, which leases a number, provided one is available, to the computer starting up. When a computer's lease expires, another computer can use that IP number if it is needed. DHCP is somewhat easier for networking newcomers to implement on a network than static addressing but additional software (the DHCP server) must be running on the network already.

> One thing to remember is that a DHCP server cannot itself be issued an IP address from another DHCP server. Its IP address must be static.

User Datagram Protocol (UDP)

An alternative to TCP for communicating at the Transport layer is User Datagram Protocol (**UDP**). UDP is a connectionless protocol (like IP) that operates at the Transport layer. It can actually be faster than TCP in some instances because, as a connectionless protocol, it does not have to open a connection with the receiver, and it does not have to do any error correction. Both of these functions are performed by TCP—a connection-oriented, or reliable, protocol—and they take additional overhead in the form of added steps, and they may slow down transmissions as a result. However, in cases of large messages and faulty connections, errors may occur and retransmissions may ultimately make TCP faster than UDP in the long run. UDP does no checks to ensure receipt so it never does automatic retransmission. Missed messages may, therefore, result in slower communication over UDP.

> The difference between TCP and UDP (reliable versus connectionless communication) is similar to the difference between sending a letter with a stamped, self-addressed envelope for return correspondence and sending an unsigned postcard. They both get the message across, but the letter sender wants to make sure that the message got there while the postcard sender just assumes that it arrived.

Domain Name Service (DNS)

An alternative to using the IP address method for locating resources on the Internet is by using the Domain Name Service (**DNS**) combined with a site's Uniform Resource Locator (**URL**). URLs are specially formatted names, like www.microsoft.com, and they are regulated by ICANN.

While IP addressing is accomplished at the Network layer of the OSI model, DNS operates at the Application layer. It is like a giant phone book where you can find an IP address by knowing the URL. Or you can provide an IP address, and the DNS server will link it to the URL.

Thousands of DNS servers exist to furnish users with IP addresses. When a user types a URL into a web browser, a request is sent to any listening DNS server to furnish the corresponding IP address. As long as the URL is listed in a listening DNS server, the correct IP address will be returned and the communication will occur.

Domain names are sort of like people's given names. The family name is to the right and the given name is to the left. In the domain naming system, there are upper-level naming groups, (such as com, net, org, edu, gov, and mil) that are shown on the right side of the URL. To the left of those naming groups the domain names become more and more specific. For example, with the domain name microsoft.com, the major grouping of "com" is made more specific by adding the name of the business you are seeking within com. In this case, that business is Microsoft.

File Transfer Protocol (FTP)

If you work with the Internet much at all, you have probably found that transferring files is a common occurrence. Browsers are actually applications that are typically capable of transferring files using the Hypertext Transfer Protocol (HTTP) with a web server at one end and your browser at the other, but it's not a very efficient way to get the job done. Browsers are specifically designed for sending requests and receiving linked web pages and not for sending or receiving files.

As you have seen, however, there are many protocols for special purposes. Transferring files is the specialty of the **File Transfer Protocol (FTP)**, which also operates using a client at the Application layer and a server (in this case, an FTP server) at the opposite end. The FTP server usually has files available for distribution to anyone logging into the server (and many of the files are compressed so they take up less room and transfer faster). Many FTP servers allow anonymous logins, while others require passwords and proper authentication. It is also possible to send files to an FTP site, making the process of exchanging large pieces of information fast and simple.

Simple Mail Transfer Protocol (SMTP)

The Simple Mail Transfer Protocol (**SMTP**) is a set of rules that regulate the sending of e-mail across the Internet, where it is then stored on a user's mail server. Suppose you send an e-mail to a friend. In order to read the e-mail, your friend must use an e-mail program (at the Application layer) and invoke another set of rules in the form of either the Post Office Protocol (**POP**) or the Internet Message Access Protocol (**IMAP**). Those protocols bring text messages to the computer so your friend can read them. In addition, e-mail often includes attachments, such as graphics or documents. These attachments must be handled by an SMTP extension called Multipurpose Internet Mail Extensions (MIME), which converts each attachment into a coded form similar to text so it can be transferred over SMTP, and then converts it back prior to reading.

Intranet/Extranet Communications

Because the networking concepts of the OSI model are the same no matter how your network is actually connected, you can use the Internet configuration

Inside Information

URLs

You almost never see it, but at the end of every URL you type, there is supposed to be another dot (.). If you were being completely accurate, Microsoft's address is really "www dot microsoft dot com dot". That final dot signifies the root of the tree, or its beginning. Since all computers on the Internet, by definition, are connected together, it makes sense that all URLs share the same root. However, the system is smart enough to interpret the dot on everything you type, even if you forget to add it. Try adding it sometime. Your system will thank you. It will be one less thing that it has to correct for you.

(using TCP/IP) to set up your network even if you don't have a direct connection to the Internet (such as that available through an Internet Service Provider). When you don't have an Internet connection but use the Internet communications techniques anyway, you are said to be conducting intranet communications. You are communicating over your own network without going over the Internet. All the same features are available, such as using TCP/IP, being able to FTP someone, and even being able to use both Network News and e-mail. All of these items will have to be maintained by someone on your network, but they will operate just the same as they would on the Internet. You just can't connect to anyone outside of your own network.

When two or more such intranets are networked without any of them being connected to the Internet, it is called an extranet.

Designing Networks

When deciding to implement a networking solution, many things need to be taken into consideration, and important decisions must be made early in the planning process. Some networks, especially small ones, just happen when two or more computers are joined together, possibly to fill a temporary need. However, those types of networks typically grow and usually result in unnecessary conflicts or expansion constraints that could have been avoided if thorough planning had initially occurred. On the other hand, if you have sufficient time, the needs of all networked resources should be adequately considered when planning and making decisions prior to physically laying out your network. Each of these steps will be examined next.

Network Needs

Sometimes when people start working on networked computers, the real reason for the network's existence is forgotten. Often, when people are promoted to elevated IT positions in a company and actually become responsible for administering the company's network, they start thinking that the network exists simply for them to maintain. Their primary goal becomes maintenance, but it's the type of maintenance that makes it easy for them to maintain the network rather than the type that keeps the systems operating at peak efficiency for the users.

There is a subtle difference there, but an important one. On one hand, the goal could be to keep the systems up and running at any cost, while making them as easy for the user to operate as possible. On the other hand, the goal could be less user-friendly and be simply to keep the systems operational with the least amount of downtime caused by the user actually using the computers. Unfortunately, some administrators give the impression that they would really like their jobs if it were not for all the users bothering them. Administrators who think like that are missing the point. They have forgotten why their networks came about in the first place.

However, it may also be too simplistic to say that the only reason networks exist is for the users. Companies usually install networks so their employees can use them as tools to help make more money for the company. That profit then covers the cost of adding or maintaining the network. The almighty administrator mentioned in the last paragraph does have a point. It would cost less to maintain the system if there were no users, but there would be no return on the investment, and that administrator would soon be out of a job. There needs to be a balance.

Network Choices

Remembering that there needs to be a balance between network availability to the user and the cost of providing the service, there are quite a few choices that go into setting up a network. The sooner in the process you make those choices, the less likely it is that there will be unnecessary (and costly) changes as the network expands. Some of the items that must be considered are budget, users, application, security, and growth.

Network Budget

The budget will probably be the most important consideration (from the company's perspective) when planning a network. While it may be true that the biggest and best equipment will be requested by both user and administrator alike, the fact that the total cost of the network must be less than the projected earnings from its use will impose an economic limit for installing and maintaining a network.

Network Users

The next most important consideration is the user. There are several questions that must be considered:

- Are the users trained and capable, or will they likely cause system problems because of inexperience with the networked resources?

- How many users are going to be able to use the system, and how many of those will be on the system at any one given time?

- When will their peak access occur, and how important is it that they obtain service right away upon initially logging on to the system?

- What is the maximum capacity that the network should be designed to handle before the user experiences significant delays in its use?

Network Application

Associated closely with knowing the network user (and tied directly to the income capacity of the network) is knowing how the network will be used and for what reasons it will be accessed. These facts determine both the means for producing the network's output (printers, faxes, monitors, speakers, etc.) as well as the tools that go into producing it (computer programs, user training, connectivity with others, etc.).

Network Security

Security is the subject of an entire chapter later in this text, but it stands to reason that it requires tremendous consideration early in the planning process. A system that is easily available to everyone from any location could impose severe economic hardships on the company if it were hacked or maliciously attacked. A general rule is to add as much security as is necessary, but only as much security as is necessary.

Network Growth

Networks rarely shrink, and users never have as much capability as they would like. Those are facts in the IT field. Another fact is that any new equipment will quickly become outdated and will most likely need to be replaced within two years. As a result, any system installed should allow for future growth, and allowances should be made for technological advances as well as for incorporating more resources (which includes both users and peripheral equipment) into the network.

Network Layout

The physical layout or geometric pattern formed by the arrangement of interconnected computers within a network is referred to as its **topology**. It deals strictly with how computers connect together.

Looking at the TEACH network's physical connections lets you determine where the components are located and how they are connected to each other—only the layout of the physical equipment should be considered. This will not give you any indication of the logical flow through those components—the TEACH network's logical flow may not actually follow the physical configuration. That is determined by the connecting equipment's design (whether it uses hubs, switches, or routers), by the design of the cabling used to make the connections, and by the software (or hardware) used for each of the network's member computers. There are three very common types of physical topologies: the bus, ring, and star topologies.

> If asked to create a network design, you would most likely be deciding on your network's physical connections, or its topology.

Bus Topology

In a **bus topology**, all computers are attached to and listen for communication over what amounts to a single strand of wire with direct connections to each computer along the bus, as shown in Figure 3.8. This is called daisy-chaining computers together. Computers in the resulting chain are not responsible for signal regeneration.

The main connection in a bus topology is also called the **bus** or **backbone**, and every end on the bus must be either connected to a computer or **terminated** with a special attachment that absorbs the signal at the ends of the cable.

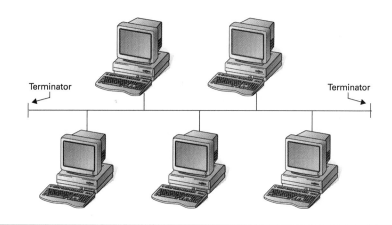

• **Figure 3.8**   Bus topology

Ring Topology

In a **ring topology**, the computers are attached to each other in a large circle, as shown in Figure 3.9. The signal flows around the circle to the next station but stops if that circle is broken or the station is not operating properly. Each station has both a receiver and a transmitter, and each therefore acts as a signal repeater when passing the signal to the next station. Since each station serves as a signal regenerator, the ring topology supports greater distances between the stations before signals deteriorate and become unreliable.

In a ring, the signal is passed in one direction only, and if one station is not operating properly, it is simply bypassed. However, a break anywhere in the circle completely stops the ring topology from communicating at all until the ring is reestablished. Because the ring becomes totally unusable with even a single break, physical rings are rarely used today.

Star Topology

The **star topology** is the most common topology used now, mainly because it is the easiest to maintain. At the center is the hub, and each computer has a direct connection to the hub, as shown in Figure 3.10. The hub, since it is connected to all other network segments, receives the network signals from every segment and transmits them to the rest of the connected network segments. When this topology was first used, the hub components simply passed the signals to connected network segments. However, as you have seen in earlier chapters, newer hubs are able to direct communication to specific recipients who are connected to the same hub. Furthermore, hubs can be connected to other hubs to increase the size and capacity of a network.

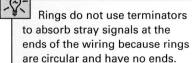

Rings do not use terminators to absorb stray signals at the ends of the wiring because rings are circular and have no ends.

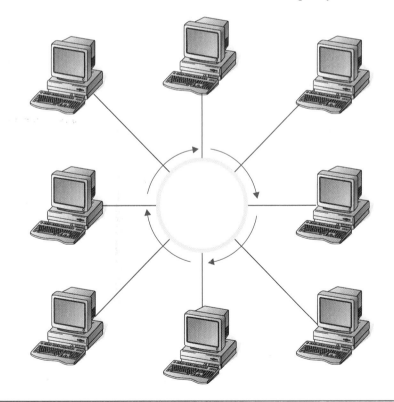

• **Figure 3.9** Ring topology

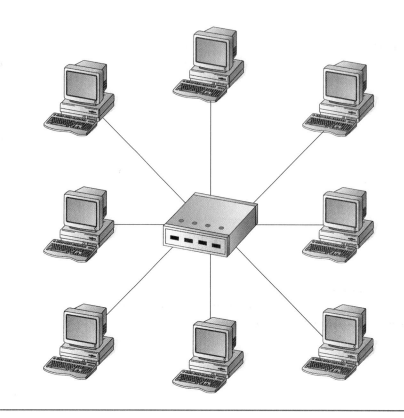

• Figure 3.10   Star topology

Hubs play an important role in the star topology because all network communications passes through the hub on its way to each of the spoke-like connections of the star. This creates a slight increase in cabling costs, but it makes the system relatively easy to troubleshoot. If no workstations can communicate, it is likely that the hub has stopped working. However, if only one machine can't communicate, it is highly probable that the problem is a failure in that single machine's connection to the hub.

Step-by-Step 3.05

Implementing a TCP/IP Network

Although your classroom's network may already work properly, it is important that you understand how to implement a network where one does not exist. (*Note: Skip this activity if you do not have instructor permission to implement changes to your classroom's networked computers.*)

In this activity, you will delete your current networking configuration and restart your computer. This will simulate installing a NIC on a non-networked computer and joining that computer to an existing network.

To complete this exercise you will need the following items:

- Classroom lab environment with sufficient networked workstations (Windows 98, ME, or 2000) for each student

- At least one computer left untouched and operating as a DHCP server

- Use of the MSHOME workgroup

Step 1

Right-click the Network Neighborhood icon on your desktop, select Properties, and then select each of the networking components currently installed in the Network dialog box and click the Remove button to delete them.

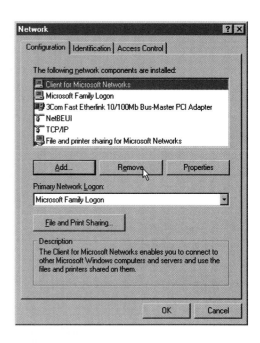

Step 2

Click OK to close the Network dialog box, and click Yes to restart your computer. If more than one hardware profile exists on your workstation and you are presented with a confirmation dialog box, click OK to confirm the removal of your NIC from all current profiles. Depending on which operating system you have installed on your computer, this may require you to restart your workstation more than once.

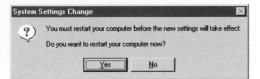

Verify that your computer has located what appears to it to be a newly installed networking capacity by ensuring that the Network Neighborhood icon reappears on your desktop (your computer will recognize that a NIC is installed and that there are no settings for it, so the networking capacity will seem to be new to the computer).

Step 3

Once again, right-click on the Network Neighborhood icon and select Properties. Verify that basic network components have been reinstalled by the operating system by looking in the installed components window on the Configuration tab of the Network dialog box.

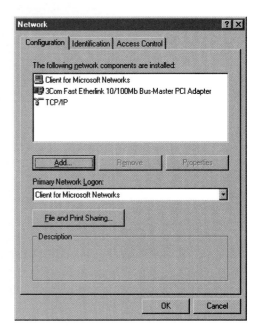

Step 4

Highlight the Client for Microsoft Networks component, and click the Properties button. Verify that there are no entries in the Logon Validation section of the Client for Microsoft Networks Properties dialog box, and then click Cancel.

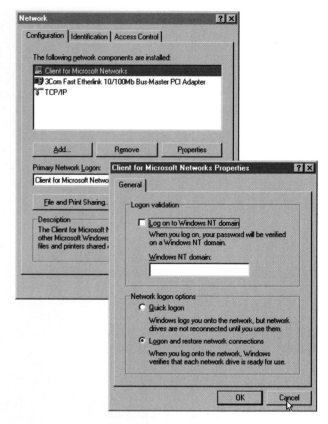

Step 5

Highlight the TCP/IP entry in the installed components window of the Network dialog box, and click the Properties button. Verify that the Obtain an IP Address Automatically option is selected in the TCP/IP Properties dialog box, and click OK.

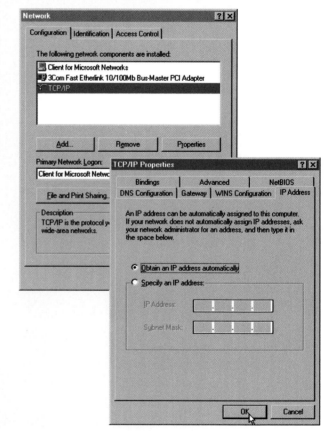

Step 6	Click the Identification tab of the Network dialog box. Verify (or enter) the appropriate workstation and workgroup information for your computer.

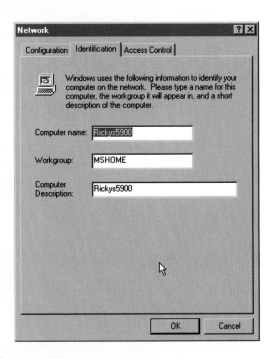

Step 7	Click the Access Control tab of the Network dialog box and ensure that the Share-Level Access Control option is selected.

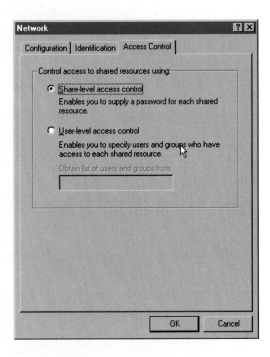

Step 8

Click the Configuration tab of the Network dialog box, and click the File and Print Sharing button. Check both options in the File and Print Sharing dialog box, and then click OK to install file and printer sharing on your computer.

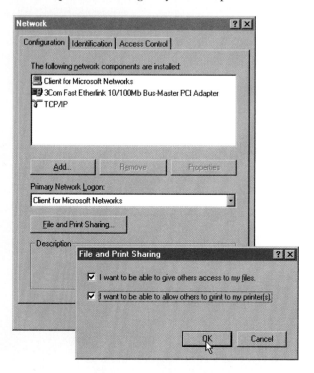

Step 9

Verify that the File and Printer Sharing for Microsoft Networks component has been installed by looking in the installed components window on the Configuration tab of the Network dialog box. Click OK to implement all pending changes on your computer.

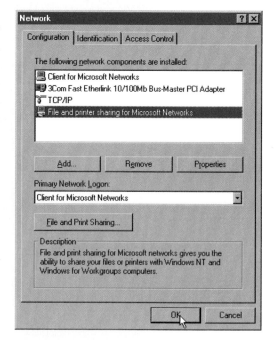

Step 10

Click OK to confirm restarting your computer. Depending on the configuration of your workstation, you may have to click the Start button and log off your computer and then log back on to implement your networking capability. This is especially true if your computer uses Windows 98.

Chapter 3 Review

Chapter Summary

After reading this chapter and completing the Step-by-Step tutorials and Cross Checks, you should understand the following facts about networking:

Understand Network Communication

- Communication involves a sender, a receiver, a message, and a medium.

- Digital information "spoken" on a network is made up of bits and bytes that are combined and interpreted at the other end as a computer's "words."

- A bit is a single digit and a byte is made up of eight bits.

- A system of communication that uses eight bits per character can have up to 256 characters in its alphabet.

- A computer's language system that uses only the numbers zero and one is called a binary communication system.

- A modem converts digital information to analog and analog information back to digital.

Decipher Computer Addressing

- The system of addressing on computer networks depends on having unique addresses for each networked object.

- Network messages are sent over the network and picked up at the appropriate physical, hardware, or node address.

- MAC addresses are usually located on a computer's NIC, which have unique numbers added by their manufacturers.

- Computer communication over networks requires the source address of the sender and the destination address of the intended receiver.

- Hexadecimal notation is a base-16 counting system, where there are 16 alphanumeric characters instead of just the 10 numeric characters in the standard base-10 system.

Describe Network Communication Protocols

- There are thousands of network protocols available, and each is a set of rules, making up a language, which can be used to communicate on a network.

- NetBIOS and NetBEUI are two early broadcasting protocols developed by IBM for use on the small networks in existence at the time.

- Routing involves directing communication directly to a resource.

- Using a protocol's rules you apply formatting that alters simple computer signals sent as individual characters into a complex but understandable language.

- The International Standards Organization (ISO) recommended the use of its Open Systems Interconnection (OSI) model as a solution to dissimilar networking components.

- The OSI reference model uses seven layers—Physical, Data Link, Network, Transport, Session, Presentation, and Application.

- Additional reference models have been created by the Department of Defense, Apple, and Novell, just to name a few.

- Transmission Control Protocol/Internet Protocol (TCP/IP), the language of the Internet, is actually a protocol suite made up of two separate protocols—TCP and IP.

- TCP is a connection-oriented, or reliable, protocol.

- IP is a connectionless, or unreliable, protocol.

- The Internet Corporation for Assigned Names and Numbers (ICANN) assigns IP addresses and tracks Uniform Resource Locator (URL) names to the Domain Name Service (DNS) server that connects a resource's name to its IP address.

- IP addresses can be implemented as static numbers or can be dynamically assigned using a Dynamic Host Configuration Protocol (DHCP) server.

- User Datagram Protocol (UDP) is a connectionless Transport-layer protocol.

- A URL consists of an upper-level naming type (com, net, or org) at the right end of its name and specific identifiers at the left.

- File Transfer Protocol (FTP) is a fast protocol used for transferring files over a network.

- Simple Mail Transfer Protocol (SMTP) is the e-mail protocol used on the Internet.

- When considering a network, the budget, users, application, security, and potential for growth are among the primary considerations you should base your decisions on.

Design Networks

- Topology refers to the physical layout or arrangement of computers in a network.

- The three most common topologies are the bus, ring, and star topologies.

Key Terms

alphanumeric *(62)*	extranet *(78)*	physical address *(62)*
analog *(55)*	fault intolerant *(81)*	POP *(77)*
ARPANET *(75)*	fault tolerant *(81)*	protocol suite *(75)*
ASCII *(58)*	File Transfer Protocol (FTP) *(77)*	rheostat *(56)*
backbone *(80)*	finite *(55)*	ring topology *(81)*
base 16 *(62)*	hardware address *(62)*	routing *(72)*
binary *(56)*	hexadecimal notation *(62)*	SMTP *(77)*
bit *(57)*	IEEE *(62)*	source address *(65)*
bus *(80)*	IMAP *(77)*	standards *(66)*
bus topology *(80)*	infinite *(55)*	star topology *(81)*
byte *(58)*	intranet *(78)*	states *(56)*
connectionless *(75)*	ISO *(73)*	static address *(76)*
connection-oriented *(75)*	leading zeros *(63)*	TCP/IP *(75)*
demodulate *(57)*	MAC address *(62)*	terminated *(80)*
destination address *(65)*	modem *(57)*	topology *(80)*
DHCP *(76)*	modulate *(57)*	UDP *(76)*
digital *(55)*	NetBIOS *(70)*	unique address *(61)*
DNS *(76)*	network address *(64)*	URL *(76)*
dynamic addressing *(76)*	node address *(64)*	
EBCDIC *(58)*	OSI *(73)*	

Key Term Quiz

Use the preceding vocabulary terms to complete the following sentences. Not all the terms will be used.

1. When computers communicate, they exchange _____ signals, which means that each signal instance is represented by a distinct state.

2. It is impossible to count an analog signal's _____ number of states.

3. A system that uses only the numbers zero and one is called a(n) _____ system.

4. The words modulate and demodulate have been combined to form the term _____, which is a piece of equipment that converts digital signals to analog and analog signals back to digital.

5. A device used to gradually adjust electrical current is called a(n) _____.

6. The most accepted of the standard output character sets is _____.

7. Accurately storing and retrieving data over a network depends heavily on each device having a(n) _____, with an exact name and storage path.

8. The _____ is a 48-bit number, commonly called the MAC address, and is assigned to a NIC by its manufacturer.

9. The physical layout or arrangement of computers is referred to as a network's _____.

10. If a system can withstand one or more failures and still operate at some lesser degree of total capacity, it is said to be somewhat _____.

■ Multiple-Choice Quiz

1. Which of the following essential elements of effective communication is missing when a networked computer being addressed is turned off?

   a. Speaker

   b. Listener

   c. Medium

   d. Message

2. In digital communication, how many signal instances are represented by a single distinct state?

   a. One

   b. Two

   c. Sixteen

   d. Infinity

3. A decimal number 10 is equivalent to which of the following in hex?

   a. F

   b. 9

   c. C

   d. A

4. In an analog signal, which of the following terms can be used to describe its transition from one state to another?

   a. Finite

   b. Gradual

   c. Binary

   d. Decimal

5. Using a 4-bit binary character scheme expressed using the on (1) or off (0) positions, which of the following would be interpreted as the hexadecimal alphanumeric character E?

   a. 1011

   b. 1001

   c. 1110

   d. 0111

6. The single on or off that is transmitted as an electrical signal down a cable to another computer can be which of the following? (More than one answer may apply.)

   a. 1

   b. 0

   c. Bit

   d. Byte

7. Which of the following are *not* reasonable signals used when transmitting digital information as medium states?

   a. Electrical current

   b. Magnetic inductance

   c. Light pulses

   d. Radio waves

8. Using an 8-bit binary character system, how many characters, digits, and symbols are available for computer communication?

   a. 256

   b. 128

   c. 16

   d. 26

9. Who determined the character set used in computers prior to ASCII or EBCDIC?

   a. The U.S. government

   b. The network administrator

   c. The user

   d. The manufacturer

10. Which of the following violate(s) the unique address concept?

   a. Misdirected mail

   b. Twins with the same name in the same class at school

   c. Two people that look alike in the same class at school

   d. A computer's NIC with the same MAC address as another computer's physical address

11. How many hexadecimal characters does it take to represent a 48-bit MAC address?

   a. 12

   b. 16

   c. 8

   d. 6

12. The manufacturer's identity code for the MAC address represented by the decimal number 188,900,977,659,375 is

   a. F23CB9

   b. 12E0F2

   c. FEDCBA

   d. ABCDEF

13. On a Windows 98 machine, using which of the following will *not* result in the system returning information that includes your MAC address?

   a. IPCONFIG/ALL

   b. IPCONFIG

   c. WINIPCONFIG

   d. WINIPCONFIG/ALL

14. How many leading zeros will be displayed in a 48-bit binary MAC address with a value of a digital 1 if it is used within a network on a star topology?

   a. 47

   b. 23

   c. 11

   d. None

15. Which of the following networking topologies is fault intolerant?

   a. Star

   b. Ring

   c. Bus

   d. None

■ Essay Quiz

1. How do computers speak to each other on a network?

2. Explain the networking address scheme.

3. Define the term "topology," and list the different topology types.

4. What can stop computers set up with a ring topology from communicating?

5. What is the most commonly used topology in the classroom?

Lab Projects

Time to roll up your sleeves and apply what you've learned. The following lab projects will enable you to practice the concepts discussed in this chapter.

• Lab Project 3.1

You have been asked to assist your networking administrator in the TEACH organization in deciding which topology (or topologies) to use in the different locations around the company. You have been asked to draw your solution to this problem and explain the reasons for your selections.

You will need the following:

- A computer lab with sufficient computers for each class member
- Blank 8½ × 11 paper
- Ruler for creating straight edges
- The TEACH organizational chart

Do the following:

1. Determine the layout of the computers that will be used within your training center.
2. Determine the layout of the computers that will be used within your HQ.
3. Choose the best connectivity method for use between the training center and your HQ.
4. Explain your design to your class.

• Lab Project 3.2

You were hired by EzraO as a network hardware technician in the TEACH organization. You have been told that your network has a backbone, a ring, and a star used in different locations around the company. You have been told to help reply to several maintenance calls that have recently surfaced. Numerous callers have reported that their network connections have been lost and they are no longer able to perform their work. Ezra told you just before he left for the evening that he had verified that the servers on each side of the network's backbone are both communicating properly.

You will need the following materials:

- A computer lab with computers for each class member
- Blank 8½ × 11 paper
- Ruler for creating straight edges
- The TEACH organizational chart

Do the following:

1. Examine the layout you created in Lab Project 3.1 for the computers you used within your training center.
2. Examine the layout you created in Lab Project 3.1 for the computers you used within your HQ.
3. Examine the connectivity method you used between the training center and your HQ.
4. Determine the most likely solution to the current problem with your users' computers.
5. Explain your reasoning to your class, and specify a troubleshooting methodology that you would use to fix the problem from this point.

Installing Network Operating Systems

"You can't have everything. Where would you put it?"
—STEVEN WRIGHT

In this chapter, you will learn how to:

- **Install and configure Novell NetWare 6.0 server**
- **Install and configure Windows 2000 Server**
- **Install and configure Red Hat Linux 7.3 server**

Now that you have a good idea about what networks are and how they can benefit you, it's time to put together your own network and get started working on it. You have information to store, multiple users, and more than one computer to share information with, so you have a need for a network.

Normally, your servers will be the strongest, fastest, and most powerful computers that your company can afford. They are the central point of all the company's users, and everyone on the network must use them for authentication, storage, retrieval, printing, and running network applications. Your servers should be fast and capable of handling high-capacity load levels. When it comes to server selection, the more powerful, the better. For your classroom servers, however, you will probably have computers similar to those at your workstations as long as they meet the minimum requirements for the particular software you are installing.

In this chapter, you will install three different operating systems. Novell's NetWare 6, a server-only network operating system; Microsoft's Windows 2000 Server, a server that can also be used in the workstation mode; and Red Hat's Linux 7 server, a less expensive alternative to using Microsoft products. For each different server, you will work through similar steps to prepare your hardware for the installation: verifying its compatibility, checking its configuration, and testing its operation. There are subtle differences between these three sets of preparation sections, and you should complete the particular network operating system's steps before you actually begin installing any of these servers.

■ Installing and Configuring Novell NetWare 6

Once you have decided to use Novell networking products, you should acquire the applicable version of the Novell NetWare network operating system. NetWare 6 is the version used here because it is currently the most recent release. While the installation procedures given here will not make you an expert on using Novell's product, their use will enable you to build an operational NetWare server.

Preparing for the Installation

Careful preparation for a server installation will make the task much easier. While servers are not the easiest things to install, making sure they meet the requirements, operate properly, and include all the necessary drivers can help ensure consistent trouble-free operation.

In nearly all Novell classes, the instructor recounts the legend of the "lost server." According to the legend, during an equipment audit done years after an office reconstruction project, a server viewable on the network was finally found inside a small walled-off room that had been thought to be empty and no longer necessary. The server was abandoned in that room but it never failed. That installation was probably accomplished using procedures like those that follow.

Remember, if you intend to take the Certified Novell Administrator exam, it is more important to know the official minimum hardware requirements according to Novell's documentation than it is to know what "really" works. Novell's official minimum requirements are based on extensive product testing, and you must know those minimum requirements when you take their test, even though you may have successfully installed it on systems with less than the minimum requirements.

Checking Hardware Compatibility

First, you need a computer to act as the server. In your classroom setting, the server will probably be more powerful than the workstations, but not as powerful as would be needed in a typical company. In fact, Novell lists two sets of hardware requirements—minimum and recommended—and almost all companies use more than the recommended hardware requirements. While the minimum hardware requirements specify the absolute minimums that you must have if you want the software to operate properly, meeting the higher requirements will further reduce the possibility of your having difficulty with the operating system. Since no business's livelihood will depend on the installation you'll do in this chapter, your server will not need as much power as the recommended requirements specify. Simply getting the software running so that you can gain familiarity with its use is often sufficient in a lab situation, so you can use the lesser of the two minimums.

Novell NetWare 6's minimum requirements include a server-class computer with a Pentium II or compatible AMD K7 processor and 256 megabytes (MB) of RAM. Novell's servers also use a DOS **boot partition** (a separate section on the hard disk where the DOS startup files are located), and NetWare 6 requires its boot partition to be at least 200MB with an

---

☑ **Cross Check**

Server Capabilities

Use the information about networks from Chapters 1, 2, and 3 when answering the following questions:

1. Describe three benefits that users would receive from the addition of more servers to a network.

2. Describe three benefits that could be achieved by a software manufacturer if its networking operating system only operated as a server and did not have to operate as a workstation.

additional 200MB of available space. In addition, there must be at least 2GB (gigabytes) of available hard disk space for the **SYS volume** (where the system files are located).

Meeting these minimum requirements with a classroom server will be sufficient for the exercises in this text. However, most companies use Novell's recommended hardware requirements as their real minimums. Novell's recommended hardware requirements include a Pentium III or compatible 700 MHz processor, 512MB of RAM, a boot partition of at least 1GB, and at least 4GB of available hard disk space for the SYS volume.

Checking Hardware Configuration

For any installation of NetWare 6, Novell requires a CD-ROM drive, an SVGA display adapter and monitor, and a network interface card. For NetWare 6, Novell also recommends a USB, PS/2, or serial mouse. In addition, for the workstations (typically Windows XP or 2000 Professional) supported by the network server, Novell recommends using the most recent version of its client software.

Testing Server Hardware

In order to test that your server's hardware functions properly, it is a good practice to rebuild your selected computer's hard disk drive and start with a fresh installation (a new, or clean, install) so that nothing remains on your hard drive from a previous system. The newer Novell products allow you to wipe your hard drive clean by booting from the CD and building all new **partitions** (separate storage areas on hard disk drives) during the installation, but it is good to know how to run these procedures for older equipment and to understand what the newer Novell products are performing automatically for you. Either way, you will end up with the **primary DOS partition** (the area on the hard disk that, once set to be active, is used by the operating system during computer startup) being the only partition on your hard drive when you start the server installation.

Using FDISK to Remove Partitions   You should use FDISK (the DOS command for partitioning fixed disks) to delete all the existing partitions on your hard disk, including the primary DOS partitions, and recreate only a single primary DOS partition. When you are prompted for the size of the partition, change the setting from 100 percent to 500MB. That partition size will work when you install NetWare 6 as your server's network operating system. During the NetWare 6 install, the amount used will be the default 200MB.

Step-by-Step 4.01

Using FDISK

Your processor retrieves the data you store on the hard drive based on its file system. In this exercise, you will erase everything on your workstation's disk and reformat it as specified in the following steps.

Warning: Do not proceed with this section until your instructor tells you to do so. This procedure can result in irreparable damage to someone else's files.

To complete this exercise, you will need the following items:

- DOS install disks (6.22 or 6.21)
- Computer with a hard disk drive that can be totally erased

Step 1

Insert the DOS diskette number 1 into the 3½-inch floppy disk drive and restart the computer by turning it off and then back on. This ensures that the computer goes through a **cold start** and that all settings are reinitialized. (This is sometimes also called a cold boot.)

Step 2

The computer will start up from the floppy disk, and in the Welcome to Setup screen it will warn you about backing up your files before proceeding.

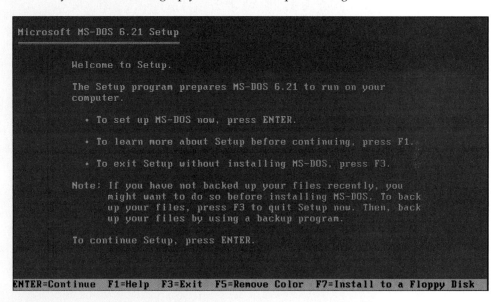

Step 3

Exit from the DOS setup by pressing F3, and exit from the Exiting Setup dialog box by pressing F3 again, and you should end up at a DOS A: prompt.

At the A: prompt, enter the DOS command **FDISK** by typing **fdisk** and pressing ENTER. The resulting FDISK Options screen gives you options to create partitions on your **fixed disks** (your hard disk drives).

```
                          MS-DOS Version 6
                       Fixed Disk Setup Program
                  (C)Copyright Microsoft Corp. 1983 - 1993

                            FDISK Options
                                  0
        Current fixed disk drive: 1

        Choose one of the following:

        1. Create DOS partition or Logical DOS Drive
        2. Set active partition
        3. Delete partition or Logical DOS Drive
        4. Display partition information




        Enter choice: [1]





        Press Esc to exit FDISK
```

Choose option 4 to open the Display Partition Information screen, which shows information about your currently installed partitions. This step-by-step procedure accomplishes only a single partition's removal, but you should delete all partitions. Note the partitions that are on your disk so that you can delete each one. Press ESC to return to the previous screen when finished.

```
                        Display Partition Information

        Current fixed disk drive: 1

        Partition  Status   Type    Volume Label  Mbytes   System   Usage
          C: 1       A    PRI DOS                   502    UNKNOWN   25%




        Total disk space is 2047 Mbytes (1 Mbyte = 1048576 bytes)







        Press Esc to continue_
```

Step 6

Choose option 1 in the FDISK Options screen, and press ENTER to get to the Delete Primary DOS Partition screen, shown here. The screen includes a warning that the data in the primary DOS partition will be lost. You have to designate the partition, enter the partition's name, and confirm this command before the computer will allow you to delete the partition.

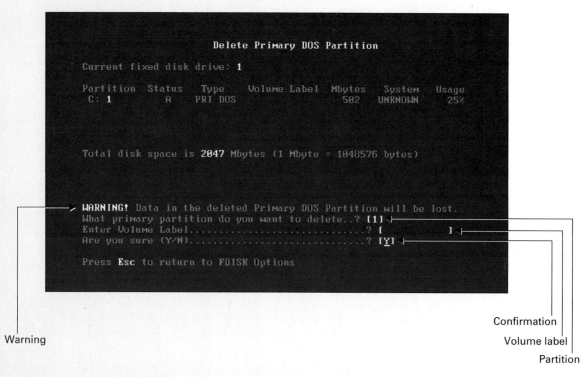

```
                    Delete Primary DOS Partition

Current fixed disk drive: 1

Partition  Status  Type    Volume Label   Mbytes   System    Usage
  C: 1       A     PRI DOS                  502     UNKNOWN     25%




Total disk space is 2047 Mbytes (1 Mbyte = 1048576 bytes)




WARNING! Data in the deleted Primary DOS Partition will be lost.
What primary partition do you want to delete..? [1]
Enter Volume Label............................? [          ]
Are you sure (Y/N)............................? [Y]

Press Esc to return to FDISK Options
```

Confirmation
Volume label
Partition

Warning

Press ESC to return to the FDISK Options screen, shown in Step 4 of this exercise.

Step 7

Choose option 1 in the FDISK Options screen, which will take you to the Create Primary DOS Partition screen. Type **N** to choose a setting other than 100 percent of the drive, and press ENTER.

Step 8

In the next Create Primary DOS Partition screen, you can specify the name for and size of the partition. Type **500** for the amount of available hard disk space the computer should use for the DOS partition and press ENTER.

Step 9

Press ESC to return to the FDISK Options screen, select 2 to set an **active partition**, (the partition used for startup) and press ENTER. Note the warning that the primary DOS partition must be turned on, or active, before it can be used for startup.

Step 10

In the Set Active Partition screen, type **1** to set your new DOS partition as active, press ENTER. Then press ESC to return through the FDISK screens to the initial FDISK Options screen, and press ESC again to exit FDISK.

Removing Windows NT Boot Loader on FAT Partition

If your system is on a FAT partition, you must remove the **Windows NT boot loader** (the initial segment of the NT operating system that loads into a computer and boots the system in Windows NT) and files. To remove a boot loader on a FAT partition, follow these steps:

1. Boot the drive with a Windows 9*x* or DOS system diskette that has a **SYS.COM** file (the DOS file containing the operating system commands) on it.

2. Transfer the system file from the diskette to the hard drive partition by typing **SYS C:** (a command that directs the computer to transfer the operating system to the C: drive) from the A: prompt.

3. Remove the diskette and restart the computer.

4. Delete the following files from the C: drive:
   - C:\PAGEFILE.SYS
   - C:\BOOT.INI
   - All files whose names begin with "NT" (i.e., NT*.*)
   - C:\BOOTSECT.DOS
   - The \WINNT_ROOT folder
   - The \WINDOWS NT folder in the \PROGRAM FILES folder

Removing NT Partitions Should you decide that you want to reuse a Windows NT or 2000 server or workstation as a NetWare server, you may find it difficult to remove NT prior to reformatting the drive. You should check your NT drive with FDISK as explained in Step-by-Step 4.01 to verify whether your system is on a **FAT** (file allocation table) partition or an **NTFS** (NTFS file system) partition. A FAT partition should have its Windows NT boot loader removed so it can be repartitioned and an NTFS partition should simply be removed using the install floppy disks.

Installing Your Drivers You should install DOS onto your rebuilt server's hard disk drive using the DOS 6.21 or 6.22 setup disks and any drivers you have for your equipment. During the actual NetWare 6 installation, the special version of DOS that Novell includes with its installation software package (**NDOS**) will overwrite the test configurations you have installed on the drive and will automatically select updated drivers. If you were to install either NetWare 5 or NetWare 4.11, you would be required to use your driver disks.

Since the NetWare operating systems we are discussing all install from CD-ROMs, you should run the installation software for your CD-ROM drive to install your CD-ROM's drivers in DOS. Your installations of DOS and NetWare will both go more smoothly if you connect both your hard drive and your CD-ROM drive directly to your motherboard as IDE drives, rather than using disk controller cards. There will be fewer configuration errors when the installer needs to know which driver to use. Since this connection is done inside your system unit, you should ask your instructor about how your computer is configured.

You should also load your mouse drivers because they are needed with NetWare 5 and NetWare 6 file servers. In NetWare 4.11 and earlier versions, the user interface was simply text-based, and you entered information through typing text commands into a console. With the advent of Windows, however, users have become accustomed to working with graphical interfaces, using a mouse to point at icons and click on objects instead of typing text commands. Novell's NetWare 5 and 6 are more graphically-oriented interfaces and they include graphical user interfaces (GUIs) that involve the use of a mouse. Server console operation has thus become more user friendly.

You should also have your network interface card's installation disks available when you start the server installation because you may need your network card settings if NetWare does not automatically locate your network card. You should check whether your NIC manufacturer has an updated NetWare driver. Most manufacturers have new drivers available on

Installing the mouse software and including the drivers in your DOS setup statements ensures that the mouse will work when NetWare 6's graphical user interface launches. That, coupled with remembering whether your mouse is a PS/2 version or connected via one of your communications ports (usually COM1 or COM2) so you make the right selection when asked, will prevent your having to reinstall NetWare 6. Otherwise, you will be in a "Mouseless Mode" during and after server installation. While it is possible to navigate with the keyboard, you will probably have to install a serial mouse later.

the Internet, and your instructor has probably already checked the Web for your driver's availability.

Testing Other Hardware The final hardware items you will need for your network installation are a hub and the network wiring so that you can connect the server to your other workstations. Unless you still have sufficient unused ports on hubs currently connecting your network, you will need to add any newly created classroom computers to ports on an additional hub or switch.

Try This!

Removing Windows NT from an NTFS Partition

If your system is on an NTFS partition, you need to remove Windows NT from the partition. To easily remove NT from the partition, try this:

1. Boot the drive with the Windows NT (or Windows 2000) setup diskettes.
2. Continue the NT installation until asked to verify the partitions used for your NT system. Select the **NTFS** partition and press D to delete it.
3. Press F3 to exit setup.
4. Exit the setup, repartition the drive, and load DOS.

For each of these new connections, you will need the network wiring to join the new computers to the network. If you are working through these exercises at home and still have one of the crossover cables you made in Chapter 2, you can use it to connect your single computer directly to your server and bypass the need for a hub or switch.

Finally, you will need any other storage media planned for your network, and any printers or other peripherals that will be used.

Step-by-Step 4.02

Installing NetWare 6

If you have carefully prepared for the installation, your computer should be ready for Novell's NetWare 6 network operating system. Novell's NetWare 6 has one installation method with several options for different types of installations. Your server needs for the classroom situation are relatively small, so one of the simplest installations will suffice. Later, you might rebuild your server and use a more customized installation.

In this exercise, you will install NetWare from CD-ROM, and this will erase everything on your workstation's disk drive and reformat it with a 200MB DOS partition. It will also configure your server to use the Internet Protocol (IP) and will create a new Novell Directory Services (NDS) tree.

Warning: Do not proceed with this section until your instructor tells you to do so. This procedure can result in irreparable damage to someone else's files.

To complete this exercise, you will need the following items:

- Computer with a hard disk drive that can be totally erased
- NetWare 6 network operating system software and sufficient licenses (evaluation copies are available at http://www.novell.com/products/netware/nw6_eval.html)
- DOS install disks (version 6.22 or 6.21), if the computer does not boot from CD, or a bootable floppy if DOS is not available (created using MKFLOPPY.BAT found in the INSTALL directory of the NetWare 6 operating system CD)
- CD-ROM drive with drivers if the computer does not boot from CD
- Mouse with drivers
- Network interface card with drivers
- Hub or switch
- Networking cables
- Network IP addresses and naming convention

Step 1

Insert the Novell NetWare 6 operating system CD into your computer's CD drive and restart the computer by turning it off and then back on. This reboots the computer, ensures that it goes through a cold start with all settings reinitialized, and displays the first installation dialog box, where you will choose the installation language.

Note: In this first text portion of the installation process, you move around the screen using the TAB key or your arrow keys.

Step 2

Press ENTER to install in English, and press ENTER again to read the license agreement. Read the agreement and press ESC to return to the previous screen. Then scroll to the Accept License Agreement option and press ENTER.

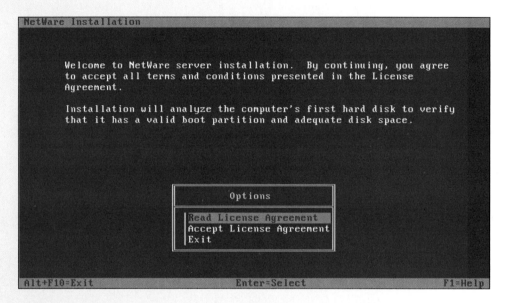

Step 3

Confirm the option to create a new boot partition by pressing ENTER.

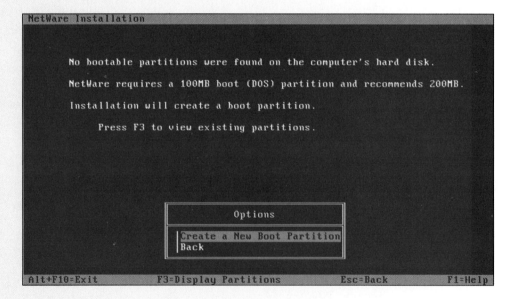

Step 4

Accept the default boot partition settings by pressing ENTER to continue. In the next window, read the warning about removing all data, volumes, and partitions on that first hard disk, and then scroll to the Continue option and press ENTER again.

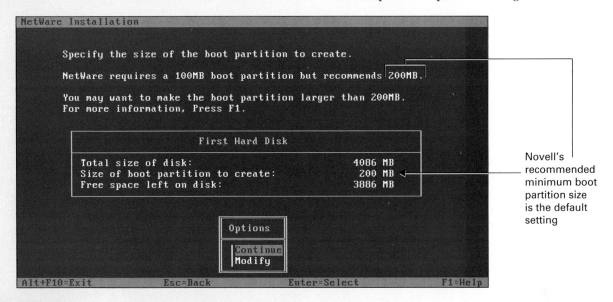

Novell's recommended minimum boot partition size is the default setting

Step 5

After the default boot partition settings are implemented and a new boot partition is created, agree to the requirement to reboot by pressing any key to continue. After the computer restarts, the new boot partition will be formatted, and you are required to read the next license agreement and accept it by pressing F10.

Step 6

There are two install options—Express and Custom. To switch from one to the other, highlight the option and press ENTER. The Express install is the fastest and requires the least amount of information to be entered. However, selecting the Custom option and not changing any of the available options implements the Express setup while allowing you to verify your settings. Select Custom and press ENTER.

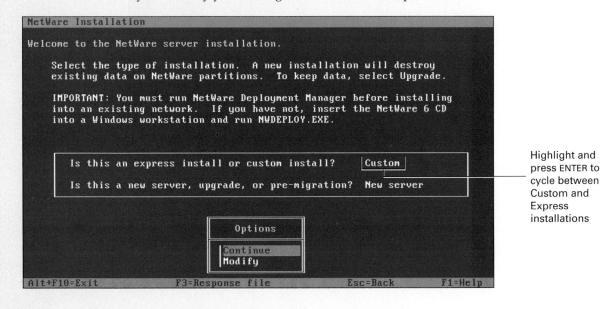

Highlight and press ENTER to cycle between Custom and Express installations

Step 7

Verify your server settings, regional information, mouse type, and video mode by selecting the Continue option and pressing ENTER in the next several windows. Monitor the small File Copy Status window on your screen as the setup copies into place the files it needs for the installation.

Step 8

Verify your device drivers and network boards by selecting the Continue option and pressing ENTER in the next several windows. Then the setup will load the drivers, save the system information, and look for the disk devices it will use for the installation.

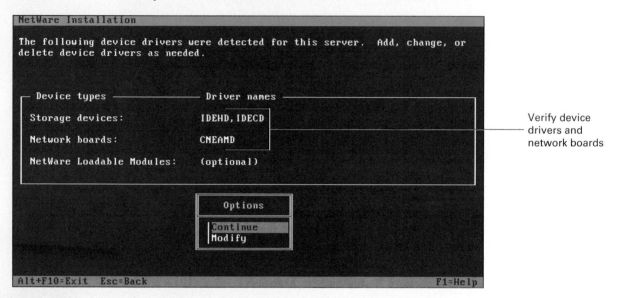

Verify device drivers and network boards

Step 9

Verify the volume SYS and partition size that will be used during the installation by selecting the Continue option and pressing ENTER. The system will spend several minutes performing system transfers as the installation proceeds.

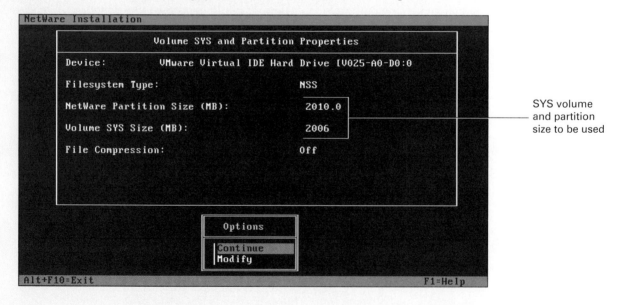

SYS volume and partition size to be used

Introduction to Networking

Step 10

At the end of this portion of the file copying process, the server reboots, leaves the text-based mode, and enters the graphical mode to finish copying files. You will notice a distinct change in the appearance of your installation screen, and your mouse will become active.

Step 11

In the Server Properties window, enter **NW6_Svr1** as the name of your server, but increase the number at the end of the server name for each additional student creating a server so that each server has a unique name in your lab. Then click the Next button. Use the browse button in the Encryption window to locate your operating system's license, and click Next.

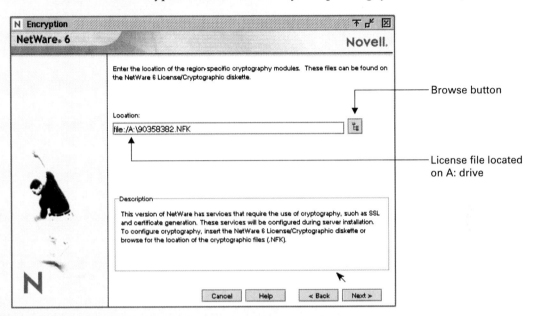

Step 12

In the Protocols window check the IP check box, set the IP address, subnet mask, and router IP address provided by your instructor, and click Next.

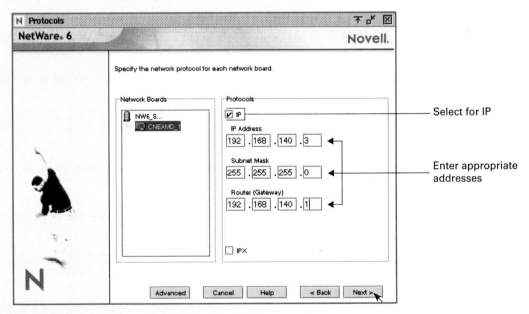

Step 13

After setup checks for duplicate servers, you can enter your host name, domain name, and the IP address of your name server in the Domain Name Service window. Then click Next.

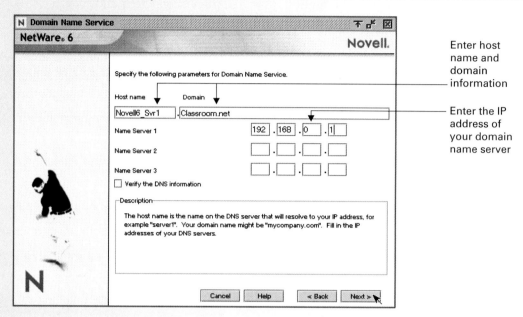

Enter host name and domain information

Enter the IP address of your domain name server

Step 14

In the Time Zone window, select your time zone and turn on the daylight saving time option if applicable by checking the check box. Then click Next. In the NDS Install window that follows, check the New NDS Tree check box and click Next.

Step 15

In the next NDS Install window, enter the information provided by your instructor for your particular server and click Next.

Caution: Be sure to remember your password. You may have to completely rebuild the computer's operating system to get past the password security if you forget the password.

Tree name

Context where the server will be located

Administrator's user name

Context where the Admin user will be located

Hidden password and password verification

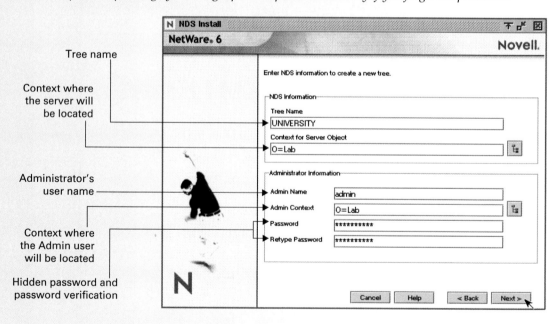

Introduction to Networking

Step 16

In the final NDS Install window, confirm the information that will be used when creating your server and click Next. In the Licenses window that follows, use the browse button, if necessary, to locate the license file that will be used when creating your server. Then click Next.

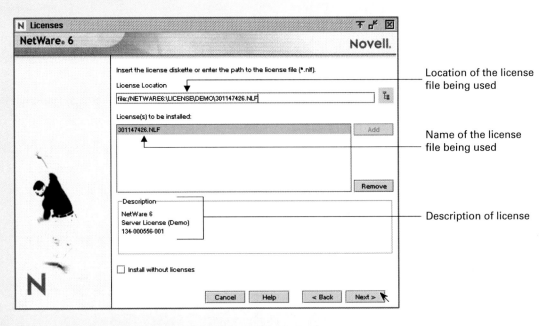

Location of the license file being used

Name of the license file being used

Description of license

Step 17

In the Summary window, confirm the products that will be installed when creating your server and click Next. The setup program will then begin creating your server and will display a progress bar to indicate its progress.

In the Installation Complete window, click Yes to restart your server. Upon restarting, your server will be operational when it displays the Novell NetWare 6 server graphical interface.

Installation Complete

Congratulations. You have completed your server's installation and now have an operational Novell NetWare 6 server at your disposal. The usefulness of your new server will depend on the speed of its processor and on how much space it has remaining on its hard drive.

The server you built will be important for you during the remainder of this course, but its speed and capacity will not. Server speed and capacity, however, are very important when you create Novell NetWare servers for your future (or current) employer's environment in an actual production setting. Usually this type of server does not need rebuilding, and a newcomer may wait a long time before installing another. It is good to get the practice now.

You can get a listing of many of Novell 6's console commands by entering the command **HELP** at the System Console window and pressing ENTER. Half of the list will appear, and you can view the other half by pressing any key. Press the ESC key to exit the Help screen and return to the System Console.

Running Directory Services Repair

It is always a good idea, after building or making extensive changes to a Novell server, to run directory services repair (**DSREPAIR**). This NetWare Loadable Module (**NLM**) checks and repairs your **server directory** (the index inside the operating system that keeps track of your server objects).

To run DSREPAIR, try this:

1. Start your new Novell server.

2. From the GUI desktop, press CTRL+ESC to go to the Current Screens window, and enter the selection number for the system console.

3. In the System Console screen, type in **DSREPAIR** and press ENTER to initiate the NLM.

4. In the Available Options window, select the Unattended Full Repair option, and press ENTER to start the repair process.

5. Watch your screen for the functionality checks that are done. The full repair should take just a few seconds to complete.

6. Press ENTER to continue, and select Yes in the Exit DSREPAIR window and press ENTER again. This will return you to the Current Screens window where you can stop or type the command **STARTX** to restart the console GUI.

■ Installing and Configuring Windows 2000 Server

If you decide to use Microsoft networking products, you should acquire the applicable version of Microsoft's networking operating system. In this chapter, Windows 2000 Server is the version that has been chosen because it is one of Microsoft's most current network operating system releases, and it is the entry-level version of Microsoft's Windows 2000 Server lineup. While the installation procedures given here will not make you an expert on using Microsoft's network operating systems, they will build you an operational Windows 2000 Server.

Cross Check

Naming Conventions

When you install components on your network, some thought should be given to the naming conventions used for each of the different types of objects—especially servers. You have already added a Novell NetWare 6 server, and you are now going to add a Microsoft Windows 2000 Server. Use the information you already know about network design from Chapter 1 when answering the following questions.

1. Should the naming convention used for your different types of servers be based on geographical location or some other means of differentiating them? Explain.

2. Since your classroom setup actually has all the servers in the same location as the workstations, which different topologies could be used? Explain.

Preparing for the Installation

Although you must carefully prepare for a Windows 2000 (often called Win2k) Server installation, it is not nearly as important as when you are preparing to install a NetWare server. However, making sure the server machine meets the requirements, operates properly, and includes all the necessary drivers can help ensure consistent trouble-free operation.

Checking Hardware Compatibility

The first things you need are computers to act as your servers. Because these servers will be used in a classroom, they will probably be similar to your workstations and won't be as powerful as most companies would need. Like Novell, Microsoft also lists two sets of requirements for each of its operating systems—minimum and recommended. The standard practice when actually using these products is to consider the recommended requirements (which are always greater than the minimums) as the real minimums, and then add a comfort level above that for added safety.

In your lab, you will be lucky if you meet the Microsoft minimums. This should not hamper your efforts, though, because simply seeing the server run will give you important experience.

The Microsoft minimums for Windows 2000 Server require a 32-bit computer with a Pentium 133 MHz processor, 128MB of RAM, and at least one hard disk where the system root (usually C:\WINNT) can be located on a partition with at least 671MB of available hard disk space.

Checking Hardware Configuration

Microsoft recommends using a 12x CD-ROM drive for installations, but they can be done over a network instead, assuming a network interface card is installed. You also need an SVGA display adapter, a network interface card, and an MS-DOS–based operating system if you are installing over a network using the installation files stored on a Windows server. You'll also need the most recent version of the network operating system software that you plan to install. Microsoft also recommends a mouse or other pointing device. If your CD-ROM drive is not bootable, you'll need a high-density 3½-inch floppy drive to use for the installation.

Try This!

Finding Microsoft Help

If you need information about Windows 2000 Server, you can always go to Microsoft's online Help service. To locate online assistance for Windows 2000 Server, try this:

1. Log on to your computer and open your browser. Go to the following link: `http://www.microsoft.com/windows2000/en/server/help/`.

2. Search through the available topics to locate the necessary information.

3. Exit your browser and close all windows when completed.

Microsoft also offers another product that will help you decide whether your equipment will be supported by its operating system. On the install CD there is a file (hcl.txt in the Support folder) that contains its Hardware Compatibility List (or **HCL**). That list contains the names of all the hardware that has passed Microsoft's hardware compatibility tests prior to the software's release. An updated version of that list can be reviewed before installing a server. It can be found on the Microsoft web site at `http://www.microsoft.com/hwdq/hcl/`, where you can search for the products or the categories of products you want to verify.

Remember, if you intend to take the Microsoft certification exams, it is more important to know the official Microsoft minimums rather than what you may come to consider the "real" minimums. Microsoft's official minimums are based on extensive product testing and intended reliability. You must know the stated minimum and recommended requirements when you take their test even though you may have successfully installed the software in settings with less than the stated minimums.

Testing Server Hardware

In order to test that your server's hardware functions properly, it is a good idea to rebuild your selected computer's hard disk drive and start with a fresh installation (a new install done so that nothing remains on your hard drive from a previous system). Although the newer Windows products allow you to wipe your hard drive clean by booting from the CD (or by using the set of four installation diskettes) and building all new partitions during the installation, it is good to know these procedures for older equipment, and to understand what is and is not performed automatically for you. That way, you will end up with the primary DOS partition being the only partition on your hard drive when you start the server installation.

Step-by-Step 4.03

Creating Windows 2000 Server Boot Disks

Although the installation package for Windows 2000 Server includes a set of four installation 3½-inch floppy diskettes, you can make a new set at any time if you have the installation CD-ROM. In this exercise, you will create a new set of installation floppies on a Windows 9*x* computer.

To complete this exercise, you will need the following items:

- Computer already running a Windows 9*x* operating system

- Windows 2000 Server installation CD-ROM
- Four blank 3½-inch floppy diskettes
- CD-ROM drive

Step 1

Insert the Windows 2000 Server installation CD-ROM into an operational computer running one of the Windows 9*x* operating systems. The CD should run automatically (commonly called AUTORUN or AutoPlay on Windows XP). Otherwise, open the CD and click on the Setup **executable** (a program with a .exe filename extension that you can run, or execute, to perform a task).

Step 2

In the Microsoft Windows 2000 CD dialog box, click No and then click the Browse This CD option in the Microsoft Windows 2000 CD window.

Step 3

Double-click the Bootdisk folder on your installation CD, and double-click the Makeboot.exe executable. This will start creating your floppies in a DOS environment.

(You should use the Makeboot.exe file to create boot disks on Windows 9x computers, but use the Makebt32.exe file when creating these disks on a Windows NT 4, 2000, or XP computer.)

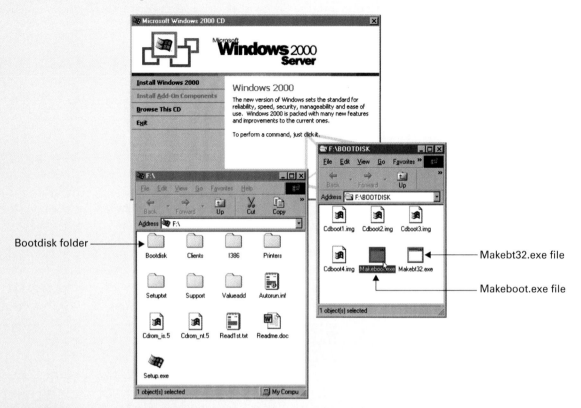

Bootdisk folder

Makebt32.exe file

Makeboot.exe file

Step 4

Enter the letter of the drive you will be copying to (usually A:), get the four floppy disks ready, and label the first floppy disk "Windows 2000 Boot Disk." Insert the first disk into the floppy disk drive, and press any key to begin, as shown here.

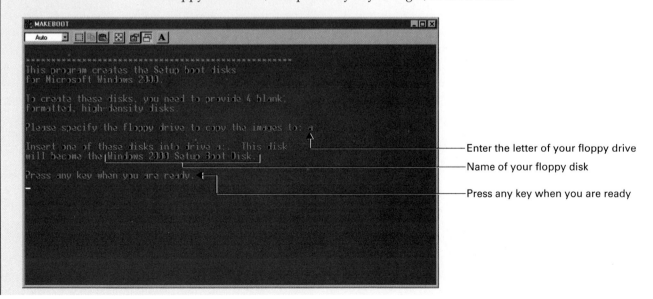

Enter the letter of your floppy drive

Name of your floppy disk

Press any key when you are ready

Step 5

As each disk finishes, ensure that the screen does not show that any errors were found, remove the completed disk, and use the information provided on screen to label the next three disks (Windows 2000 Setup Disk #2, then #3, and finally #4). Then insert each labeled floppy diskette into the floppy disk drive after the previous one is finished, and press any key to begin, starting with Windows 2000 Setup Disk #2.

Step 6

When the fourth disk has finished, and you have the on-screen report that the setup boot disks have been created successfully, close all open windows, remove the fourth disk, and remove your installation CD.

Using FDISK to Remove Partitions   You should use FDISK to delete all the existing partitions on your hard disk, including the primary DOS partition, and re-create a primary DOS partition. When you are prompted for the size of the partition, change the setting from 100 percent to 500MB. That partition size will work no matter whether you are installing Novell or Microsoft software on the computer. FDISK procedures can be found in Step-by-Step 4.01, earlier in this chapter.

Removing NT Partitions   Should you decide that you want to reuse a Windows NT or 2000 server or workstation as a Windows 2000 Server, you do not have to remove the NT partitions prior to installing your new operating system. You should check your NT drive with FDISK as explained in Step-by-Step 4.01 to verify whether your system is on a FAT partition or an NTFS partition. A FAT partition can be converted to an NTFS partition after installation, but an NTFS partition can simply be reused during installation. In either case, you can completely remove all partitions during the installation procedure. Procedures for removing the partitions can be found in the "Using FDISK to Remove Partitions" section in the Novell server installation portion of this chapter.

Installing Your Drivers   You should continue to install DOS onto your rebuilt server's hard disk drive by following the simple installation steps contained in the DOS 6.21 or 6.22 setup disks, and you should try out any drivers you have for your equipment. During the actual Windows 2000 Server installation, the system uses its extensive driver base and may overwrite the drive configurations you installed, as it automatically selects updated drivers.

Since Windows 2000 Server installs using CD-ROMs, you should run the installation software for your CD-ROM drive to install your CD-ROM's drivers in DOS. Your installation will go more smoothly if you connect both your hard drive and your CD-ROM drive directly to your motherboard as IDE drives, rather than using disk controller cards. There will be fewer configuration errors when the installer needs to know which driver to use. Furthermore, your computer should be configured so that one of its options allows you to boot from the CD-ROM drive. Since this connection is done inside your system unit, you should ask your instructor about how your computer is configured.

 Try This!

Boot Diskettes

If your computer is running Windows NT, Windows 2000, or Windows XP you will need to create your four installation floppy diskettes using the Makebt32.exe file. To create your installation floppy diskettes, try this:

1. Insert your Windows 2000 Server installation CD-ROM into your computer's CD drive.

2. Use the same procedures as in Step-by-Step 4.03, except use the Makebt32.exe file.

You should also load your mouse drivers to ensure that the mouse works for your graphical user interface (GUI). In the past, the user interface was simply text-based, and you entered information by typing text commands into a console. Now with the more graphically oriented interfaces, such as Windows 2000 Server, users have become accustomed to working with graphical interfaces—pointing at icons and clicking on objects instead of typing text commands. Operating server consoles have thus become more user friendly.

Your network interface card's installation disks should also be available when you start installing the server software because you may need your network card settings. You should confirm that your NIC manufacturer has an updated Windows 2000 Server driver. Most manufacturers have new drivers available on the Internet, and your instructor has probably already checked the Web for your driver's availability.

Testing Other Hardware   The final hardware items you will need for your network installation are a hub and any network wiring necessary to connect the server to the other workstations. Unless you still have sufficient unused ports on the hubs currently connecting your network, you will need to add any newly created classroom computers to ports on an additional hub or switch.

For each of those new connections, you will also need network wiring to join the new computers to the network. If you are working through these exercises at home and still have one of the crossover cables you made in Chapter 2, you can use it to connect a single computer directly to your server and bypass the need for a hub or switch.

Finally, you will need any other storage media planned for your network, and any printers or other peripherals that will be used.

Step-by-Step 4.04

Installing Windows 2000 Server

If you have carefully prepared, your computer should be ready for Microsoft's Windows 2000 Server network operating system. Windows 2000 Server is usually installed using the CD-ROM drive, but it can be installed over a network using a shared network drive.

Your server needs in the classroom are relatively small, so one of the simplest installations will suffice—you might choose to rebuild your server and use a more customized installation later. In this exercise, you will install Windows 2000 Server from a CD-ROM, and this will erase everything on your workstation's disk drive, reformat it with an NTFS partition, configure your server to use the IP protocol, and create a new Windows 2000 Server.

Warning: Do not proceed with this section until your instructor tells you to do so. This procedure can result in irreparable damage to someone else's files.

To complete this exercise, you will need the following items:

- Computer with a hard disk drive that can be totally erased

- Windows 2000 Server network operating system CD and sufficient licenses

- DOS install disks (6.22 or 6.21) if the computer does not boot from CD, or bootable floppies if DOS not available (created using the Bootdisk folder on the operating system install CD)

- CD-ROM drive with drivers if the computer does not boot from CD
- Mouse with drivers
- Network interface card and drivers

- Hub or switch
- Networking cables
- Network IP addresses and naming convention

Step 1

Insert the Windows 2000 Server operating system CD into your computer's CD drive and restart the computer by turning it off and then back on. This reboots the computer and ensures that it goes through a cold start with all settings reinitialized. The setup process checks your hardware configuration, opens the Windows setup screen, and displays the Welcome to Setup screen, where you decide whether to continue setting up your computer.

Step 2

Press ENTER to continue with the setup, and press C in the next screen to confirm that you want to write over any existing material on the hard disk. Read the license agreement, press PAGE DOWN to read the terms, and then press F8 to agree to the license agreement. Then, as shown in the following illustration, press ENTER to confirm that you want to set up Windows 2000 on the selected item.

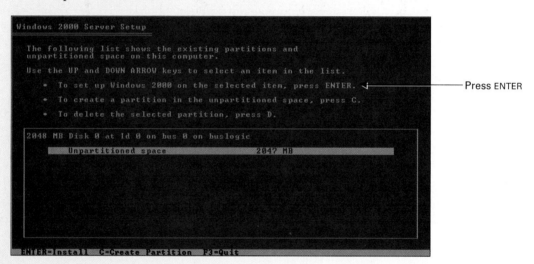

Press ENTER

Step 3

Select the default Format The Partition Using The NTFS File System by pressing ENTER to continue. Setup continues through several processes and you can see a progress bar on the screen that you can monitor while it is formatting the partition, examining your disks, copying files to your Windows 2000 installation folders, and then initializing your configuration prior to rebooting the system.

Step 4

After setup initializes your configuration, it signals to you that it will reboot your computer in 15 seconds. You can press ENTER to restart the computer immediately or wait for setup's automatic reboot.

Step 5

After the computer restarts, your system will pass through several different startup screens, which will bring you to the Welcome to the Windows 2000 Setup Wizard dialog box. Use your mouse and click Next to continue the setup process.

Step 6

The setup wizard will install your devices and stop at the Regional Settings dialog box, where you can review and customize your settings and then click Next when you are ready to proceed. In the following dialog box, enter your name and organization, as shown here, and click Next to continue.

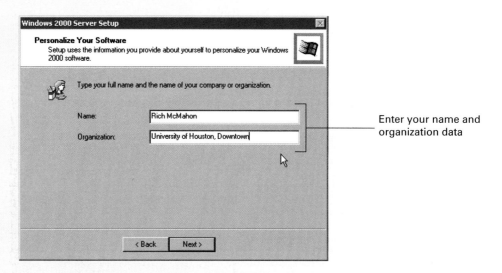

Enter your name and organization data

Step 7

Enter your 25-character product key from the yellow sticker on the back of your CD case, and then click Next. Be very careful typing in the exact characters given in the product key—some of the characters are easily misread. If your product key is rejected as invalid, recheck your entry, reenter the sections as required, and click Next again.

Step 8

In the Licensing Modes dialog box, select the licensing mode your network will be using from the two options (Per Server or Per Seat), and click Next. If you select the Per Server mode, you should enter the number of concurrent connections your licensing arrangements allow.

Select the applicable option for your licensing mode

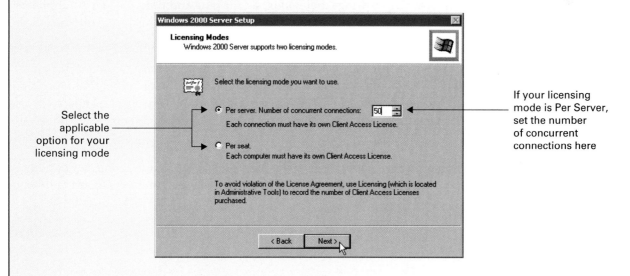

If your licensing mode is Per Server, set the number of concurrent connections here

Step 9

Enter your computer name and your administrator password (twice, to confirm it) and then click Next. The administrator account is the most powerful account on the system and this **administrator password** allows a user to log in as that powerful position. It should be protected.

Caution: Be sure to remember your password. You may have to completely rebuild the computer's operating system to get past the password security if you forget the password.

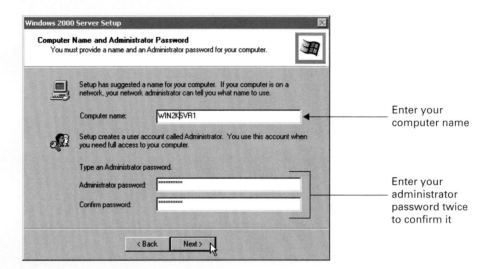

Step 10

Accept or configure your Windows 2000 components. Use the scroll bar on the right side of the window to view additional components, and click the details button to see the items chosen within those components. Click Next when you are satisfied with the configuration.

Step 11

In the Date and Time Settings dialog box, set the date and time, choose the applicable time zone, and select the daylight saving option if required. Click Next to accept the settings.

Step 12

Setup then installs your networking components, and in the Networking Settings dialog box provides you with the choice of using Typical Settings or Custom Settings. Choose Typical Settings unless your instructor tells you otherwise. Click Next to continue.

Step 13

In the Workgroup or Computer Domain dialog box, enter your workgroup or domain name if you have one. If you have not been provided with your workgroup or domain name, you should ask your instructor before proceeding. Click Next to continue.

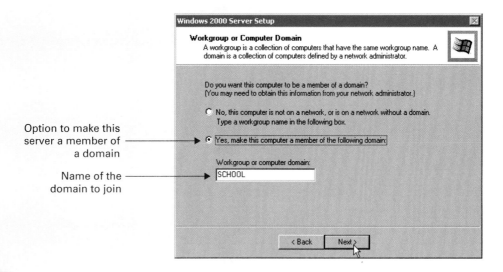

Option to make this
server a member of
a domain

Name of the
domain to join

Enter the user name and password for the user who is authorized to join the machine to the domain (if you entered a workgroup or domain name) and click OK.

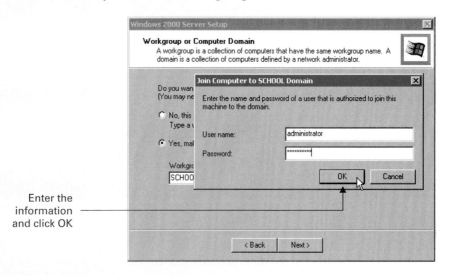

Enter the
information
and click OK

Setup then displays several wait screens as it installs components and Start menu items, registers components, saves settings, and removes any temporary files it used. Then it displays the Completing the Windows 2000 Setup Wizard dialog box, at which point you should remove your CD from the drive and click the Finish button to restart your computer.

When the Welcome to Windows dialog box is displayed, press CTRL+ALT+DE-LETE to initiate the logon to your new server. When the Log On to Windows dialog box appears, enter your administrator password, and click OK to log on to your new server as the administrator.

Try This!

Installing the Latest Windows 2000 Service Pack

It is always a good idea, after building or making extensive changes to a Windows 2000 Server, to install the latest **service pack** (an update to the operating system made available by Microsoft). To install the latest service pack, try this:

1. Start your new Windows 2000 Server as Administrator.

2. Start your browser and go to `http://www.microsoft.com/windows2000/`.

3. Click on the link for the latest service pack and follow the links to download the service pack.

Installation Complete

Congratulations. You have completed your second server installation and now, assuming you did both installations on different computers, you have an operational Windows 2000 Server at your disposal in addition to the NetWare server you created earlier. The usefulness of this newest server depends on the speed of its processor and on how much remaining space it has on its hard drive.

The server's speed and capacity are not very important for the remainder of this course, but they are very important when you create Windows servers in an employer's actual production setting. The knowledge you gain from installing these Windows 2000 Servers in the classroom will give you an understanding of how they are created. Usually these servers do not need frequent rebuilding, so a newcomer may wait a long time before installing another.

■ Installing and Configuring Red Hat Linux

A relative newcomer to the server field gives you yet another choice when selecting your networking products. Red Hat Linux worked its way into the industry by providing free software, and it has developed that product line into a very viable alternative. Once you decide to use Red Hat Linux products on your network, you should acquire the latest version of the server software. Red Hat Linux 7.3 was used to demonstrate this vendor's network operating system. While the installation procedures given here will not make you an expert on using Red Hat Linux products, they will build you an operational Red Hat Linux server.

Preparing for the Installation

You must carefully prepare for a Red Hat Linux server installation as you would for a NetWare or Windows server installation to avoid as many problems as possible. The Red Hat Linux installation process has most of the input screens earlier in the setup process than in either Microsoft or Novell setups, but the software setup itself is not as thorough in deciding what components make up your system so it can determine what new things it needs to install. Therefore, when getting ready to set up your server, make sure the computer meets the requirements, operates properly, and includes all the necessary drivers. This will help ensure a complete setup and consistent trouble-free operation after installation.

Checking Hardware Compatibility

As with the other two operating systems, you need a computer to act as the server. Again, because this server will be used in a classroom, it will probably be similar to your workstations and won't be as powerful as most companies would need a server to be. Like Novell and Microsoft, Red Hat Linux also gives different sets of requirements for its operating systems. Since they can also operate in just a text-only mode (that doesn't need a graphical user interface), some of the Red Hat Linux requirements have minimum requirements, recommended requirements, and also text-mode requirements. Unlike the other operating systems, however, most of Red Hat's documentation is available on the company's web site. Keep this URL handy during the installation and when operating your server: `http://www.redhat.com/docs/manuals`.

In your lab, you will be lucky if you meet the Red Hat Linux minimum requirements, but this should not hamper your efforts. With this operating system, as with any other products you learn about in the classroom, simply seeing it run will give you important experience. The minimum requirements for a Red Hat Linux server are a Pentium class computer with a Pentium 200 MHz processor, 32MB of RAM for a text-mode installation and 64MB for graphical mode (but 96MB are recommended). The installation also requires at least 650MB of hard disk space or 4.5GB of available hard disk space for a full install (plus additional space for any files you will be storing on the server).

Red Hat Linux, like Microsoft Windows 2000, includes another product that will help you decide whether your equipment will be supported by its operating system. On its web site is a Hardware Compatibility List (HCL) at `http://www.redhat.com/hcl/`. That list identifies all the hardware that has passed Red Hat's **Ready Tests** (Red Hat's equivalent of Microsoft's extensive component compatibility testing) before the latest software's release. This list should be reviewed before installing a server. It lists alternative search techniques that you can use when searching through the listed products that are compatible with the latest release of the operating system.

In addition, the installation guide on the Red Hat web site includes a form that gives you a systems requirement table (Table 2.1 in the guide), listing the items you should have information about prior to beginning the installation. This form can be found in the guide at `http://www.redhat.com/docs/manuals/linux/rhl-7-3-manual/install-guide/`.

Checking Hardware Configuration

Linux recommends using a boot-enabled CD-ROM drive for installations but provides alternative boot methods as well. You will need a high-density 3½-inch floppy drive for the installation if your CD is not bootable. You also need information about your monitor and display adapter and the network operating system

Cross Check

Purposes of Networks

Use the information you already know from Chapters 1 and 2 about the purposes of networks to answer the following questions:

1. Which of the main purposes for networks will this Linux server likely satisfy?
2. All your computers are required to communicate with each other, so based on the installations of the other two servers, which protocol will you be choosing for your Linux server? Why?

software that you plan to install. For the graphical installation, you should also have a mouse.

Testing Server Hardware

In order to test that your server's hardware functions properly, it is a good idea to rebuild your selected computer's hard disk drive and start with a fresh installation (a new install done so that nothing remains on your hard drive from a previous system). Although Red Hat Linux products wipe your hard drive clean by booting from the CD and building all new partitions during the installation (and deleting any unnecessary partitions to get the required free space), it is good to know how to perform these procedures for older equipment, and to understand what is and is not performed automatically for you. When you do this, you will end up with the primary DOS partition being the only partition on your hard drive when you start the server installation.

Using FDISK to Remove Partitions   You should use FDISK (the DOS command for partitioning fixed disks) to delete all the existing partitions, including the primary DOS partition, and recreate only a primary DOS partition. When you are prompted for the size of the partition, change the setting from 100 percent to 500MB. That partition size will work no matter whether you install Linux, Novell, or Microsoft server software. However, during the server installation, all partitions in the needed space will be removed. The FDISK procedures can be found in Step-by-Step 4.01, earlier in this chapter.

Removing NT Partitions   Should you decide that you want to reuse a Windows NT or 2000 server or workstation as a Linux server, you do not have to remove the NT partitions prior to installing your new operating system. You should still check your drive with FDISK as explained in Step-by-Step 4.01 to verify proper operation but you will completely remove all partitions during the Linux operating system's installation procedure. Procedures for removing the partitions can be found in the section entitled "Using FDISK to Remove Partitions" in the Novell server installation section of this chapter.

Installing Your Drivers   You should continue to install DOS onto your rebuilt server's hard disk drive by following the simple installation steps found in the DOS 6.21 or 6.22 setup disks, and you should try out any drivers you have for your equipment. During the actual Red Hat Linux server installation, the installer uses its extensive driver base and may overwrite the drive configurations you installed as it automatically selects updated drivers.

Since Red Hat Linux server installations use CD-ROMs, you should run the installation software for your CD-ROM drive to install your CD-ROM drivers in DOS. Your installation will go more smoothly if you connect both your hard drive and your CD-ROM drive directly to your motherboard as IDE drives, rather than using the disk controller cards found in older equipment. There will be fewer configuration errors when the installer needs to know which driver to use. Your computer should also be configured so that one of its options includes booting from the CD-ROM drive. Since this connection is done inside your system unit, you should ask your instructor about how your computer is configured.

You should also load your mouse drivers to ensure that the mouse works for your graphical user interface (GUI). In the past, the user interface was simply text-based, and you entered information by typing text commands into a console. Now with the more graphically oriented interfaces, such as **GNOME** and **KDE**, that are available for Red Hat Linux servers, users are becoming more accustomed to working with graphical interfaces—pointing at icons and clicking on objects instead of typing text commands. Operating server consoles has thus become more user friendly. You'll see these newer graphical interfaces during the installation when you are asked to select the packages (which are actually sets of available applications). The Linux installer will piece together the customized environment you choose.

Your network interface card's installation disks should also be available when you start installing the server software because you may need the network card settings. You should confirm that your NIC manufacturer has an updated driver. Most manufacturers have new drivers available on the Internet, and your instructor has probably already checked the Web for your driver's availability.

Testing Other Hardware   The final hardware items you will need for your network installation are a hub and any network wiring necessary to connect the server to other workstations. Unless you still have sufficient room on hubs currently on your network, you will need to connect your new lab computers to an additional hub or switch.

For each new connection, you will need network wiring to join the new computers to the network. If you are working through these exercises at home and still have one of the crossover cables you made in Chapter 2, you can use it to connect your single computer directly to the server and bypass the need for a hub or switch.

Finally, you will need any other storage media planned for your network, and any printers or other peripherals that will be used. You should also find out whether a firewall will be used anywhere on the network and, if so, what kind and where.

Some Linux Specifics

One of the main attractions of using Linux that its supporters point to is its open source code. That means you can not only view the operating system's actual programming code, but you can change it as well. Unlike Microsoft and Novell, which protect their program code, you are encouraged to look at how things work in Linux and to make changes to nearly anything you want. You are then encouraged to share your changes with all other Linux users. Since you are forbidden to sell the software, such changes are seen simply as a way of creating better software for everyone.

One result of this open source code is very evident during the installation of your server software, as you can choose the packages of applications you want to install on your server to create your desired environment. Some of the most evident choices involve the different user interfaces (text-based, GNOME, or GNU, for example), different file systems (Novell's file system or the Windows file system, for example), and different server functions (such as a news server). Each of these can be configured during setup, and your instructor will likely give you any required settings that differ from the default recommendations.

Inside Information

To Firewall or Not to Firewall

The term firewall *comes from building construction and refers to an extra-strong, fire-retardant wall that is designed to protect people from places where fires are more likely to occur, such as in electrical rooms. Such a wall is intended to slow the spread of a fire should one develop, so that any occupants can safely escape.*

In the computer world, firewalls are generally added between the public Internet and private computers or networks. Adding a firewall thus protects network users from outsiders accessing the network and possibly harming its resources. Although it is not normally done, you could add a firewall to each computer protecting it from anything on the outside. Installing and configuring this firewall hardware is normally an administrator function.

Another Linux feature is that it allows you to choose your type of boot loader. Boot loaders start your operating system on your hard drive, and Linux offers numerous choices, including the option to not use a boot loader at all. If one is not used, your computer should boot up using a floppy disk (which you can also choose to create during your installation).

After you decide to use a boot loader, you get to choose between the LILO (Linux Loader) and GRUB (Grand Unified Bootloader) boot loaders. Choose the older LILO to provide legacy support for older equipment, or choose the newer GRUB, which is the default loader, for newer systems. You also have the choice of where you want your boot loader to be loaded from. By default, the system looks to the Master Boot Record (MBR) during startup, but you can also locate the boot loader on your computer's root partition and direct the computer to look there instead.

Linux also provides partitioning choices during installation. This used to be quite cumbersome, as you had to assign a starting point on your hard drive where your operating system and its associated storage would be located, in addition to allocating sufficient disk space to incorporate any required functionality provided for during your installation. While you can still perform this type of manual configuration using either the Disk DRUID tool (Red Hat's interactive manual disk partitioning tool) or the Red Hat FDISK option (a partitioning tool similar to the MS-DOS FDISK command), the installer now includes an automatic setup option. You should use automatic partitioning unless you are well versed in the partitioning process or you receive extensive directions from the person in charge of maintaining your computers.

Step-by-Step 4.05

Installing Linux 7.3 Server

If you have carefully prepared, your computer should be ready for Red Hat Linux's network operating system. Red Hat Linux's server setup has one installation method that includes several options for different types of installations.

Your server needs in the classroom are relatively small, so one of the simplest installations will suffice, and you will be able to simply accept most of the default settings as you create your basic server. Later, you might rebuild your server and use a more customized installation. In this exercise, you will install Red Hat Linux 7.3 from a CD-ROM, and this will erase everything on your workstation's disk drive and reformat it, configure your server to use IP, and create a new Red Hat Linux server.

Warning: Do not proceed with this section until your instructor tells you to do so. This procedure can result in irreparable damage to someone else's files.

To complete this exercise, you will need the following items:

- Computer with a hard disk drive that can be totally erased

- Red Hat Linux's network operating system software

- DOS install disks (6.22 or 6.21) if the computer does not boot from CD, or bootable floppy if DOS is not available (created using the boot.img file found in the IMAGES directory on the Red Hat Linux operating system CD)

- CD-ROM drive with drivers if the computer does not boot from CD
- Mouse with drivers
- Network interface card and drivers

- Graphics card information
- Hub or switch
- Networking cables
- Network IP addresses and naming convention

Step 1

Insert the Red Hat Linux 7.3 operating system CD into the your computer's CD drive and restart the computer by turning it off and then back on. This reboots the computer, ensures that it goes through a cold start with all settings reinitialized, and displays the first installation dialog box, where you can choose the installation mode, as shown here. If you just press ENTER, the setup will automatically start with the default settings.

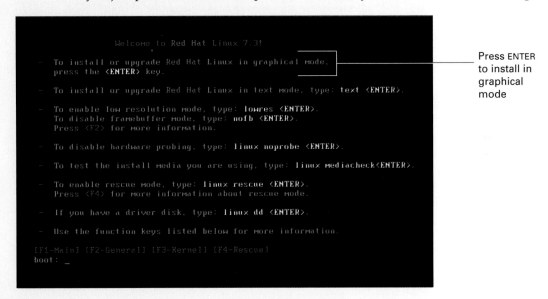

Press ENTER to install in graphical mode

Step 2

The Red Hat Linux setup will take you through several screens, starting with text-based line entries, then basic blue-screen dialog boxes, and finally the higher resolution graphical implementation with the Red Hat logo.

Step 3

Decide whether you want to use the Help screen during the installation, and click on the Next button in the Welcome to Red Hat Linux dialog box to initiate the installation. The screen shots used in this exercise show the Help feature displayed. You can also display this information at any time during the installation by pressing the Help button. Use the scroll bar on the side of the screen to view additional information, and click the Hide Help button if you no longer want the Help information displayed.

When the Language Selection window appears, choose the appropriate languages and click Next.

Step 4

In the Keyboard Configuration window, select the appropriate configuration and click Next. In the Mouse Configuration window, select your mouse configuration and click Next.

Step 5

In the Installation Type window, select the Server option and click Next. In the Disk Partitioning Setup window (see next illustration), click the Help button and read the information provided. Select automatic partitioning (unless your instructor tells you to manually partition your drives and provides you with detailed instructions for either Disk DRUID or FDISK), and click Next.

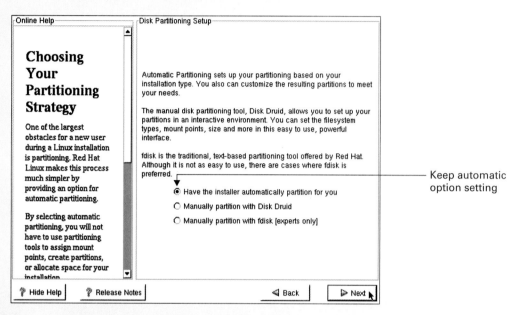

Step 6

Confirm the drive initialization by clicking Yes in the dialog box that is displayed, and then read the three partitioning options in the Automatic Partitioning window (if you chose that option earlier). These methods involve removing just the Linux partitions, removing all partitions, or leaving all partitions intact so that your new installation is built in a new partition using any free space that exists on your hard drive. Unless your instructor tells you otherwise, you should select the Remove All Partitions on This System option. Once you have made your selection, click Next.

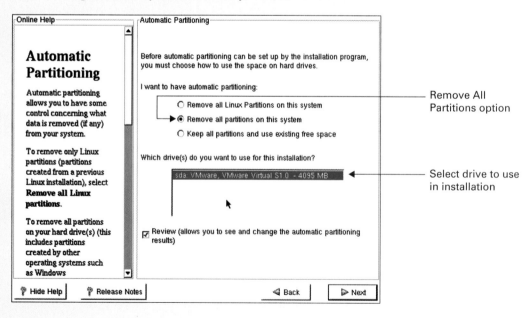

Introduction to Networking

Step 7

If the option you selected involves removing partitions, click the Yes button to confirm that you want to go ahead. In the Disk Setup window, verify the location where you want Red Hat Linux installed, and click Next.

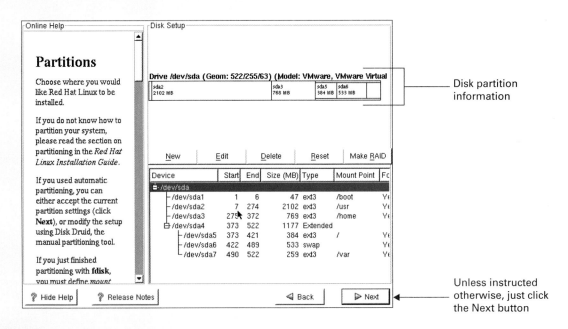

Disk partition information

Unless instructed otherwise, just click the Next button

Step 8

Unless your instructor tells you otherwise, keep the default settings in the Boot Loader Configuration window, and click Next. This keeps GRUB as your boot loader and locates it in the Master Boot Record using the filename displayed in the following illustration.

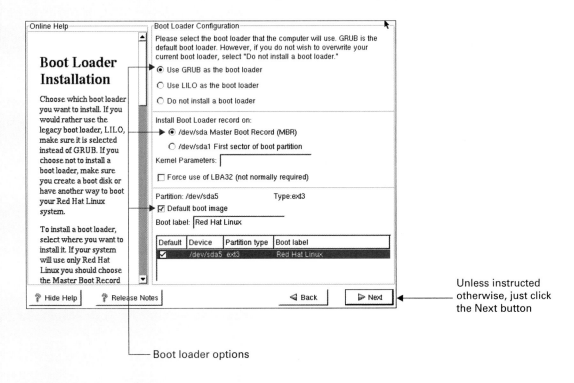

Unless instructed otherwise, just click the Next button

Boot loader options

Step 9

In the Boot Loader Password Configuration window, type and verify a boot loader password if you intend to use one, and click Next. Assigning a password to the boot loader feature ensures that users are not able to reboot your computer without authorization.

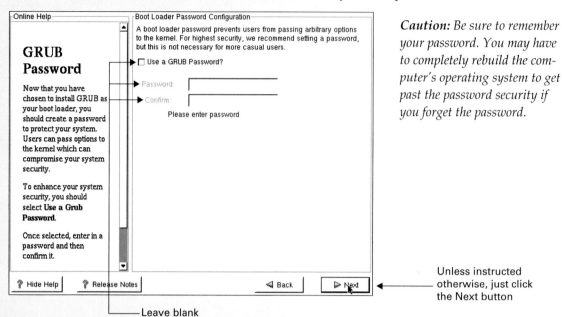

Caution: Be sure to remember your password. You may have to completely rebuild the computer's operating system to get past the password security if you forget the password.

Step 10

In the Network Configuration window, select the Activate on Boot option to start your network interface card when you turn on your computer. Select the Configure Using DHCP (Dynamic Host Configuration Protocol) option to allow a properly configured server to automatically assign an IP address to each networked computer. Finally, confirm or configure any remaining settings provided by your instructor, and click Next to continue. Notice in the following illustration that the configuration shows each of your network connections (eth0 in this example) in its own window and lets you set up each one separately. If your network will use static IP addresses, uncheck the DHCP option and insert any information provided by your instructor in the applicable remaining fields.

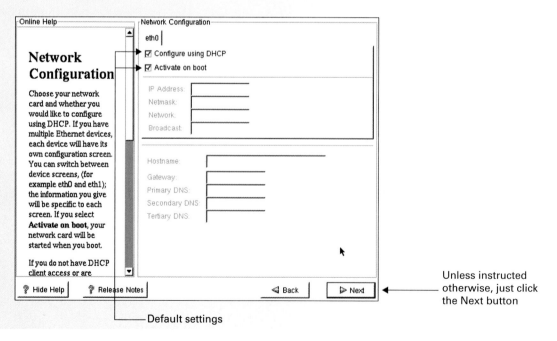

Step 11

In the Firewall Configuration window, confirm or configure your settings. Clicking the Help button displays the Firewall Help information shown in the following illustration, which includes the definition of and uses for a firewall. As shown, your server will use a medium security firewall with a set of customized rules that allows incoming DHCP requests to be accepted by your server. Remember that a firewall keeps unwanted connections out of your network and only allows those connections you specify—DHCP requests in this case. Notice too that you can turn the firewall completely off, or you can increase the security level and even use a default set of rules. Your firewall decisions should be verified with your instructor before making any changes. Click Next to continue.

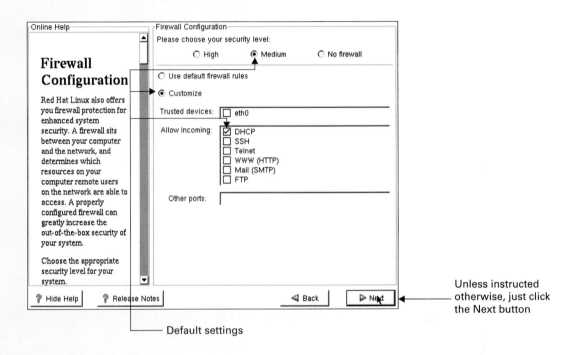

Unless instructed otherwise, just click the Next button

Default settings

Step 12

In the Additional Language Support window, verify or select your configuration and click Next. In the Time Zone Selection window, select your time zone and click Next.

Step 13

In the Account Configuration window, enter and verify your root administrator password. Then click Add to create a new login account for yourself, enter the appropriate information, and click OK and then Next. As you can see from the Help information for this window, setting up this account (and its password) is one of the most important aspects of your installation. The root user account has complete control of the system, and with it you can install the packages (applications) that control and run on your system. Because this account is so powerful, you should use the root user account only when administration activities are necessary. Unauthorized use of that account will then be less likely because of its less frequent use.

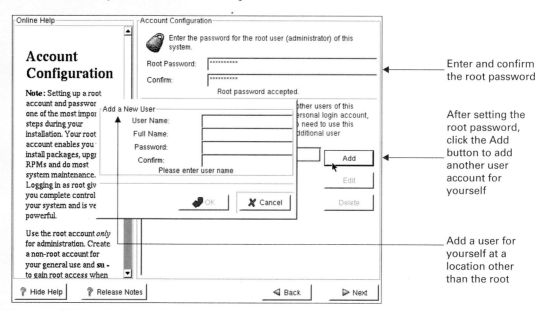

Enter and confirm the root password

After setting the root password, click the Add button to add another user account for yourself

Add a user for yourself at a location other than the root

Step 14

In the Package Group Selection window, select the package groups (or applications) that will be installed when creating your server. Linux calls its graphical interface the X Window System (either the classic or the newer system) and that interface must be used with either the GNOME or the KDE graphical user interfaces, as they simulate the Windows desktop environment. Notice that you also get to choose between the different types of server application packages that you wish to use on your computer (such as the news server or various file servers). Click Next to continue.

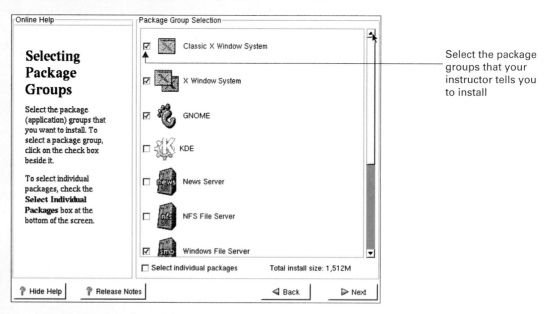

Select the package groups that your instructor tells you to install

Step 15

In the Graphical Interface (X) Configuration window, use the vendor selection triangles and the scroll bar to locate and verify that the appropriate graphics adapter has been selected for your server. If the correct information has not automatically been configured, select the appropriate adapter and specify the amount of RAM contained on your video card. This is an important step—your video configuration must be correct or the graphical user interface will not function properly. Notice, the Skip X Configuration check box at the bottom of the window. This option is used if you want to use only a text-based user interface and do not wish to activate any GUI environments. Click Next to continue.

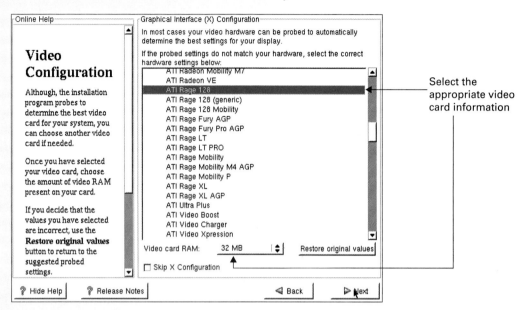

Step 16

In the About to Install window, click Next to start the actual server installation. Monitor the installation on the Installing Packages screen. When the first installation CD is completed, remove it, replace it with the second CD, and click OK.

Step 17

When the Boot Disk Creation window is displayed, insert a non-write-protected blank 3 ½-inch HD diskette into your floppy disk drive and click Next to have the system create a boot disk. Remember to remove the disk when it is completed. You should take this opportunity to create a boot disk in case there are startup difficulties later. Should your server fail to start, you can insert this boot disk and perform an emergency startup.

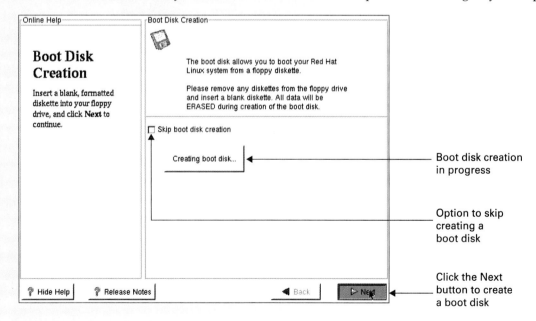

Step 18

In the Monitor Configuration window, select your monitor and click Next. When the Customize Graphics Configuration window appears, you can set or test your graphics configuration, choose your desktop environment (if there are multiple choices available), and choose your login type. This is another point at which you can decide whether to use GUI or text-based operations—during startup in this instance. This window also lets you sample different screen resolutions and color depths to see the display that best suits your needs and to test those configurations prior to completing the software installation. Once you are satisfied, click Next to continue.

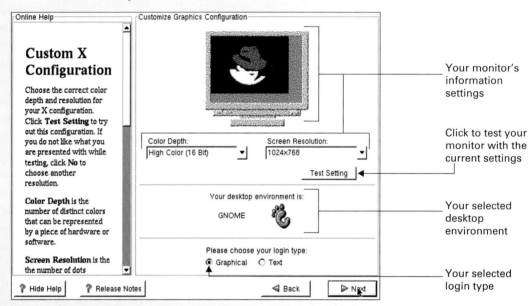

Your monitor's information settings

Click to test your monitor with the current settings

Your selected desktop environment

Your selected login type

Step 19

In the Congratulations window click the Exit button. Upon restarting your computer, your server will offer you a choice of available installation options that you can highlight and press ENTER to select. The default settings will automatically be selected if you do not make a selection. Your server will provide you with either the graphical logon screen or, as shown here, a text-based logon to your new server.

Type your user name and then your password to log in to the server

Installation Complete

Congratulations. You have completed your third server installation and have now added an operational Red Hat Linux server to your NetWare 6 and Windows 2000 servers (assuming you did all three installations on different computers).

The experience you gained here will transfer to any other server installation you may undertake. While the steps may not be exactly the same, they will be similar enough that you will be somewhat familiar with the process, and you will have an easier time than when you installed your first server in class. The knowledge you gained from installing these Linux servers will give you an understanding of how they are created. Usually this type of server does not need rebuilding, and a newcomer may wait a long time before installing another.

Chapter 4 Review

■ Chapter Summary

After reading this chapter and completing the Step-by-Step tutorials and Try This! exercises, you should understand the following points about networking.

Install and Configure Novell NetWare 6.0 Server

- Servers are usually the fastest and most powerful computers a company can afford.

- Novell NetWare is a server-only network operating system; Microsoft Windows 2000 Server is a server operating system that can also be used in workstation mode; and Red Hat Linux provides a low-cost alternative to using Microsoft's operating system products.

- When preparing to install a server, check the hardware compatibility, check its configuration (possibly removing any NT partitions, if applicable), and test your hardware.

- Novell NetWare 6 minimum hardware requirements include a Pentium II processor with 256MB of RAM and at least 2GB of available hard disk space.

- Vendors specify their hardware requirements specifying the required minimums that you must have and recommended minimums that they think you should have.

- When installing a server, it is a good idea to start with a fresh installation.

- Use the DOS command FDISK when partitioning fixed disks.

- Use a cold start when initiating a server installation to ensure all settings are reinitialized.

- You must accept an operating system's license agreement in order to continue with the setup process.

- The procedures you learned when installing these servers will be similar to those you will use in an employer's production environment.

Install and Configure Windows 2000 Server

- Microsoft servers are a bit easier to install than Novell servers.

- Microsoft requires a 32-bit computer with a Pentium 133 MHz processor, 128MB of RAM, and at least 671MB of available hard disk space.

- Check Microsoft's Hardware Compatibility List to ensure your equipment will be supported by the operating system.

- The newer operating systems allow you to wipe your hard drive clean by booting from the installation CD and building all new partitions during the installation.

- Windows 2000 Server is usually installed using the CD-ROM drive but can be installed over a network using a shared network drive.

Install and Configure Red Hat Linux 7.3 Server

- Most of Red Hat Linux's setup input screens occur early in the installation process.

- The Red Hat Linux setup includes a text-mode installation option with separate minimum requirements.

- Red Hat Linux offers most of the necessary documentation on its web site.

- Red Hat Linux requires a Pentium 200 MHz processor, either 32MB or 64MB of RAM, depending on whether you do a text-mode or graphical-mode installation, and at least 650MB of available hard disk space.

- Check the Red Hat Linux Hardware Compatibility List to ensure that your equipment will be supported by the operating system.

- The installation guide on Red Hat's web site includes a systems requirement table listing that you can print and fill in with your system installation for use during setup.

- Red Hat Linux can be installed using a boot-enabled CD-ROM drive or by creating a boot diskette using the tools provided on the CD.

- Red Hat Linux includes options to install two graphical interfaces—GNOME and KDE.

- Use the file boot.img found in the Images directory to create your bootable floppy for a Red Hat Linux installation.

■ Key Terms

active partition (97)
administrator password (114)
boot partition (93)
cold start (95)
DSREPAIR (106)
executable (108)
FAT (98)
FDISK (96)

fixed disks (96)
GNOME (119)
HCL (107)
KDE (119)
NDOS (98)
NLM (106)
NTFS (98)
partitions (94)

primary DOS partition (94)
Ready Tests (117)
server directory (106)
service pack (116)
SYS C: (98)
SYS.COM (98)
SYS volume (94)
Windows NT boot loader (98)

■ Key Term Quiz

Use the preceding vocabulary terms to complete the following sentences. Not all of the terms will be used.

1. When you perform a new installation of a server's operating system, it is a good practice to check the operating system vendor's web site to see if a new _____ has been released to update your new system.

2. The Windows operating system uses the only active _____ when starting up.

3. A(n) _____ consists of turning the computer off and then back on so that all settings are reinitialized.

4. The DOS command _____ is used to create partitions on your hard disk drives.

5. The partition used for starting up must be set such that it is a(n) _____, or turned on, before it can be used to start the computer.

6. When installing Novell NetWare 6 on your computer, the type of partition that may need to have a Windows NT boot loader removed before it can be repartitioned is the _____ partition.

7. The _____ file is the DOS file that contains the operating system's commands.

8. _____ is Novell's version of DOS and it is included with Novell's installation software package.

9. Use Microsoft's _____ to check your equipment to see if it has passed Microsoft's extensive testing program.

10. The Red Hat Linux graphical interfaces _____ and _____ allow users to point at icons with a mouse and click objects instead of typing in text commands.

■ Multiple-Choice Quiz

1. Which of the following is a server-only operating system?

   a. Windows 2000

   b. Novell 6.0

   c. Red Hat Linux 7.3

   d. DOS

2. Which of the following is (are) not a stated minimum requirement for a Novell 6.0 server?

   a. Pentium III processor

   b. 256MB of RAM

   c. Server-class computer

   d. At least 2GB of available hard disk space

3. Which of the following hardware items is (are) required when installing a Novell 6 server?

   a. CD-ROM drive

   b. SVGA display adapter

   c. Network interface card

   d. USB, PS/2, or serial mouse

4. Which of the following should be accomplished before initially setting up a new server?

   a. Start with a fresh installation

   b. Rebuild your hard disk drive

c. Use FDISK to delete all but the primary partition

d. Create two primary DOS partitions

5. When removing a primary DOS partition from a fixed disk, which of the following steps must be accomplished before it can be deleted?

   a. Designate the partition

   b. Enter the partition's name

   c. Press the ESC key

   d. Confirm the delete command

6. How many DOS partitions can be concurrently set to active?

   a. 4

   b. 3

   c. 2

   d. 1

7. Which of the following are the two install options available when installing Novell's NetWare 6?

   a. Express

   b. Full

   c. Partial

   d. Custom

8. The required boot partition needed for a Novell NetWare 6 installation is:

   a. 200MB

   b. 2GB

   c. 100MB

   d. 1GB

9. What must occur after the initial file copying process of a Novell NetWare 6 installation, before the installer can leave the text-based mode and enter the graphical mode to finish copying the files?

   a. Down the server

   b. The server must reboot

   c. You must select Text to Graphics

   d. GNOME must be installed

10. Which of the following protocols is (are) available during a Novell NetWare 6 installation?

    a. IPX/SPX

    b. IPX

    c. IP

    d. NETBEUI

11. Which of the following represent Microsoft minimum requirements necessary to install the Windows 2000 Server operating system?

    a. Pentium II processor

    b. 256MB of RAM

    c. 32-bit computer

    d. 12x CD-ROM drive

12. Where can Microsoft's Hardware Compatibility List be found?

    a. On the install CD in the root directory

    b. On the Microsoft web site

    c. At http://www.hcl.com/hwdq/hcl

    d. In the install CD's Support folder

13. On a fresh installation of Windows 2000 Server, what key do you press to continue the installation after you have received the warning about setup detecting that your computer is running an operating system incompatible with Windows 2000?

    a. ESC

    b. F10

    c. ENTER

    d. C

14. Which of the following is offered as the default partition in a Windows 2000 Server fresh installation?

    a. NTFS

    b. NDS

    c. FAT

    d. FAT32

15. Which of the following is (are) not a hardware requirement when installing a Red Hat Linux 7.3 server?

    a. Boot-enabled CD-ROM drive

    b. Pentium 200 MHz processor

    c. 128MB of RAM

    d. At least 650MB of hard disk space for a full installation

■ Essay Quiz

1. In your own words, explain how you would convince a novice networking specialist to reformat and rebuild the hard disk drive of a computer that will be used as a new server on your network.

2. Based upon your experiences with the three server installations, defend or refute the following statement: "A graphical user interface lets a user accomplish more."

3. Compare the Novell graphical server console with Microsoft's server desktop.

4. Explain why the computer used as a server is usually the fastest and most powerful computer in an organization.

5. Describe the processes used in all three operating systems when inputting your administrator password.

Lab Projects

Time to roll up your sleeves and apply what you've learned. The following lab projects will let you practice the concepts discussed in this chapter.

• Lab Project 4.1

In your position at SinkRSwim Pools, you have been asked to rebuild a server that just recently had its hard drive fail. The hardware supplier delivered the new hard drive's warranty replacement, and it has already been installed in the server. You have been asked to format the drive with a 500MB boot partition, and to build a Novell NetWare 6 server using the express setup. Your server was running Novell NetWare 5 at the time it failed, so your company has decided to replace it with NetWare 6 now.

You will need the following:

- A lab computer that meets the Novell NetWare 6 minimum hardware requirements

- Novell NetWare 6 installation CD
- A set of DOS 6.21 or 6.22 diskettes
- A boot-enabled CD-ROM drive

Then do the following:

1. Use FDISK to repartition your new drive.
2. Insert the setup CD into the CD-ROM drive and reboot your system.
3. Continue the setup using the express setup procedures.
4. Test your server when it arrives at the graphical server console screen.

• Lab Project 4.2

Your supervisor at SinkRSwim Pools just came to you when she found out you had performed several server installations in your networking classes at school. There have been complaints that users are unable to work with their files stored on a Windows NT 4.0 server from their Windows 98 workstations. The server was partitioned into two NTFS partitions

when it was created, and the decision has been made to rebuild that computer completely using the Windows 2000 Server operating system, and to partition it using FAT instead of NTFS. All necessary files and accounts have already been safely transferred to other company servers, so you can perform a fresh installation.

You will need the following materials:

- The user name and password for the administrator account on the former Windows NT 4 server

- The Windows 2000 Server installation CD-ROM

- The set of four Windows 2000 Server boot diskettes created in the "Boot Diskettes" Try This!

- A boot-enabled CD-ROM drive

Then do the following:

1. Use FDISK to repartition your new drive to 500MB.

2. Insert the setup CD into the CD-ROM drive and reboot your system.

3. Continue the setup using the default setup configurations.

4. Test your server when it reboots to the Welcome to Windows dialog box.

• Lab Project 4.3

You were recently given one of the company's spare computers and told to use it to learn the Red Hat Linux text-mode installation procedure so you can present it in a class you will be giving to the company's other employees. There has been a lot of employee interest in learning Linux and installing it on their older computers at home to use as additional servers. Your supervisor knows that she should take advantage of any employee interest in working with additional technology, so she has volunteered your services to foster that interest. You should perform a text-mode installation of Red Hat Linux 7.3 and practice it so you can perform the installation with no problems in your group training session. All the employees have already verified that their equipment meets the minimum requirements for the operating system.

You will need the following materials:

- An operational lab computer with the same configuration used in the original Linux installation in Step-by-Step 4.05.

- Red Hat Linux's network operating system installation CD set

Then do the following:

1. Insert the operating system's CD in your CD-ROM drive and restart your computer.

2. At the first Welcome to Red Hat Linux screen type **TEXT** before pressing the ENTER key. This will initiate the text-based installation where you navigate to your selections using the TAB key or the arrow keys.

3. Follow the same installation procedures used in Step-by-Step 4.05 except at Step 14 make sure the Classic X, GNOME, and KDE Group packages are deselected in the Package Group Selection window before pressing the Next button.

4. In the Video Configuration window, select the Skip X Configuration option at the bottom of the screen.

5. Accept all default settings for the remainder of the installation.

6. Restart your computer when your installation is complete.

Accessing Networks

*"Work, work, work, is the
main thing."*
—ABRAHAM LINCOLN

In this chapter, you will learn
how to:

- **Install and configure
  Windows XP Professional**
- **Install and configure
  Novell Client**
- **Install and configure
  Red Hat Linux**

In previous chapters you have learned how a network develops from the need
to share information between computers. You also learned how to build your
own servers—NetWare, Windows, and Red Hat Linux. In order to start using
your new servers and complete the network, however, you need one more element.
Right now, you have servers, connections, and information to share, but the
piece you are missing is the client.

In this chapter, you will install client software on your computers. You will
finish creating your own classroom network and put the servers you built in
the previous chapter to work. First, you will create a Windows XP Professional
workstation. Windows is the most commonly used workstation, and Windows XP
operating system is Microsoft's latest release. Once Windows is installed, you
will install the Novell Client software on that workstation, which will allow the
Windows workstation to access the Novell server. Finally, you will install Red
Hat Linux on a workstation to create an alternative Windows-like workstation.

■ Installing and Configuring Windows XP Professional

Servers, servers everywhere, but not a client in sight! That can be how it feels when you watch a network develop. At SinkRSwim Pools, Lauren and Ricky are installing new networking technologies. They have heard of the storage capabilities that will be available and are eager to put them to use. Lauren has installed the server operating systems on the SinkRSwim Pools computers, and those new servers are functioning properly in the locations where she and Ricky think they are most needed. She now believes it is time to add the clients and properly integrate them into her overall plan.

Lauren has already decided to install Windows XP Professional, rather than the more limited Windows XP Home, because of the additional networking capabilities afforded by using the more powerful version. Ricky has done his job well, and all the employees are eager to learn more and start using the new workstation capabilities in combination with the new servers.

Preparing for Installation

Computer users are generally more interested in how well their computer system operates than anything else. Whatever you can do to help keep their computers trouble-free will make their lives, and yours, much easier. Therefore, the time you spend preparing their workstations may benefit you more in the end than the time spent preparing for a server installation. Since you will be installing Microsoft's newest operating system, Windows XP Professional, the installation should be quite easy compared to any previous Windows version.

In addition to the computers you installed your server operating systems on, you will need separate computers on which you can install your workstation software. Workstation software allows those computers to act as your network clients. These workstations will then be used as your classroom student stations for the remainder of the semester.

The workstation computers you have to work with may be at or below many of the hardware requirements necessary to properly install your workstation operating system software. Servers are usually the most powerful computers on a company's network, but workstation computers running the same operating system don't usually need as much power. The computers you use for your workstations will undoubtedly be less capable than the computers you used for your servers.

 Its newest workstation software, Microsoft's Windows XP was initially released in two versions—**Windows XP Home** (for use in typical households, and including only limited networking capability) and **Windows XP Professional** (for use in company situations, including extended networking capability). This text expects the use of the Professional version. Currently there is no server version of the Windows XP operating system.

Try This!

Find Online Help for Windows XP

If you need information about either version of Windows XP, you can start your search on Microsoft's Windows XP web site. For an easy way to locate information about Windows XP Professional, try this:

1. Log on to your computer and open your browser.

2. Go to the following link: `http://www.microsoft.com/windowsxp/default.asp`.

3. Point to the Windows XP link at the upper left of the page to reveal links to all the current Windows XP editions and select Windows XP Professional. Links on this page may change frequently but should remain relatively easy for you to locate your version.

4. Click any of the links and search through the topics to locate the information you need.

Consider Hardware Requirements

Think back to the server installations in Chapter 4 and recall the different installation requirements given by the software manufacturers.

1. What are the names of the two sets of hardware requirements that Microsoft gives for each of its operating systems?

2. Explain what the actual standard practice is regarding these installation requirements when users try to achieve a comfort level.

Although Microsoft indicates that not meeting the minimum hardware requirements may limit its performance, a Windows XP Professional workstation can run on relatively low-powered equipment. As long as you install on a computer with the following requirements, the operating system should run properly:

- An Intel Pentium/Celeron family or AMD K6/Athalon/Duron family 233 MHz (single or dual) processor

- 64MB of RAM

- At least one hard disk where the **systemroot** (the main folder containing your Windows XP operating system files, which is usually C:\Windows) can be located on a partition with at least 1.5 gigabytes of available hard disk space

You may need more hard disk space if your installation procedures involve installing over the network, but this is not the recommended procedure for this course.

A better hardware configuration that follows Microsoft's recommended minimums will include a PC with a 300 MHz (single or dual) processor and 128MB of RAM.

Checking Hardware Compatibility

The Windows XP installation CD includes an option that will help you decide whether your computer equipment will be supported by the Windows XP Professional operating system. If you activate the install CD on a computer running an upgradeable Windows version (Windows 98, Windows NT 4.0 Workstation, Windows 2000 Professional, or Windows XP Home), one of the options listed is Check System Compatibility, as shown in Figure 5.1.

The options shown in Figure 5.1 are not available if you start your Windows XP Professional installation by booting from your installation CD-ROM. Additionally, upgrading from either Windows NT 4.0 Workstation or Windows 2000 Professional requires the service packs for those operating systems to be installed prior to initiating the upgrade to Windows XP Professional.

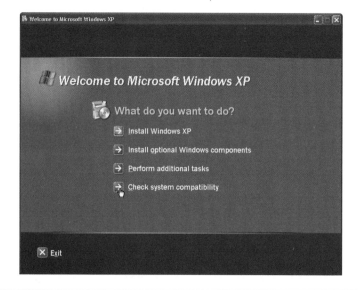

• **Figure 5.1**   The Windows XP installation CD includes a compatibility verification option.

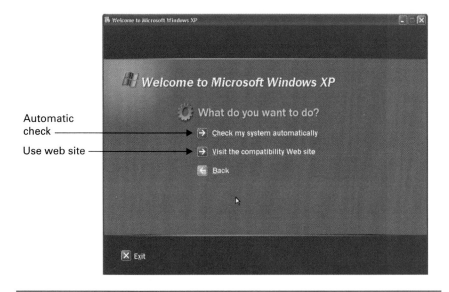

Automatic check

Use web site

• Figure 5.2 The Windows XP installation CD includes an automatic compatibility verification option.

Automatic Compatibility Check   Selecting the Check System Compatibility option gives you the choices, shown in Figure 5.2, of either checking your system automatically or visiting the Microsoft compatibility web site. Provided your Windows version can be upgraded, clicking the Check My System Automatically option will check your system and provide you with a list of incompatible components. It also provides you with remedies for correcting these incompatibility problems. If your system is not an **upgradeable system** (one that can be upgraded with the current version of the software), using this option simply reports that your system cannot be upgraded.

Web Site Compatibility Check   Selecting the second option, Visit the Compatibility Web Site, sends you to a Microsoft link that may catch you by surprise. It looks like a new catalog site instead of the text-based HCL site you might expect to encounter. However, that catalog site is actually the newest rendition of Microsoft's HCL, and it includes ad-like depictions of the approved equipment instead of just a textual listing of the hardware that had passed Microsoft's hardware compatibility tests prior to the software's release.

The text listing can be found on the Microsoft FTP site at `ftp://ftp.microsoft.com/services/whdq/hcl/`. (See a sample of the new Windows Catalog shown in Figure 5.3.) There, you can actually download any of the updated HCL text files Microsoft keeps available. Remember, you should check all hardware you intend to use in your system prior to installing Windows XP Professional on your system.

Checking Hardware Configuration

Microsoft recommends using a CD drive or **DVD** drive (a higher-capacity removable storage device) for installations. Also, if you have a network interface

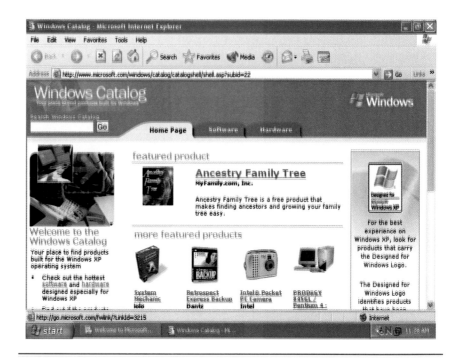

• **Figure 5.3**   Microsoft's new catalog-style HCL

card installed and enough extra hard disk space, your installations can be accomplished over a network. You will also need an SVGA display adapter that supports an 800×600 resolution and the workstation operating system

---

Try This!

Downloading a Windows XP Boot Disk

If you are unable to boot from your CD drive and need to start the Windows XP installation using the **setup boot disks**, you can locate them on Microsoft's Support web site (http://support.microsoft.com/). To locate the information about these disks, download the creation file, and then create a set of floppies, try this:

1. Log on to your computer, open your browser, and go to the following link: http://support.microsoft.com/.

2. In the Search the Knowledge Base text box in the upper-left corner of the web page, enter **Obtaining Windows XP Setup Boot Disks** and click the green arrow. (The **Knowledge Base** is Microsoft's searchable online information database.)

3. Click the link that best matches your search phrase. In this case, you should select the link for Obtaining Windows XP Setup Boot Disks.

4. Scroll down the web page to locate the link for Windows XP Professional in the appropriate language, click the link, and read the information provided.

5. Scroll down to and follow the instructions at the bottom of the page (or right-click the Download link and select Save As) and direct your computer to save the file to your desktop.

6. When the download is finished, double-click the file and follow the instructions to build your set of Windows XP setup boot disks using six high density, blank, formatted floppy disks.

Try This!

Cannot Boot from CD

If your computer does not allow you to boot from your CD, Microsoft suggests that you run the installation from an earlier version of Windows. From that installation you then access AUTORUN.INF on the CD to invoke Windows' **AutoRun** capability (where the operating system looks on the CD for an AUTORUN.INF and self-starts immediately when it is inserted in the CD drive) or you can manually start the CD's setup program. You can then start the Windows XP installation from within that operating system.

To begin a Windows XP installation when you cannot boot from a CD, try this:

1. Run your computer using a previous Windows operating system.

2. Insert your Windows XP Professional installation CD into your computer's CD drive.

3. If your CD's AUTORUN.INF file starts the installation process, follow the instructions in Step-by-Step 5.01. Note: you can also disable the AutoRun capability by holding down the SHIFT key while inserting your CD.

4. If the installation does not automatically start, click the Start button, select Run, and type **D:\setup** (use the identifier for your CD drive in place of the D). Then follow the instructions in Step-by-Step 5.01.

software that you plan to install. Microsoft also recommends a mouse or other pointing device. Additionally, you need a high-density 3½-inch floppy drive if your CD is not bootable and floppy disks are used for the installation.

Testing Workstation Hardware

In Chapter 4, you learned that you should test your server's hardware by re-building it and starting with a fresh installation (a new install done so that nothing remains on your hard drive from any previous systems), although doing so is not an absolute requirement. Starting with a fresh disk can be accomplished by using the DOS FDISK command and then totally rebuild-ing your hard disk drive prior to installation, just as you did with your servers.

This rebuilding of the hard drive can also be done during an installation of Windows XP from CD—the installer allows you to wipe your hard drive clean and build all new partitions during the installation. You will use that procedure in this chapter so that you will gain practice performing both types of setups. You will then be able to decide your preference for future installations.

Inside Information

What Happened to Windows XP Setup Boot Disks?

Something happened to the setup boot disks that were commonly used when installing the Win-dows NT-based operating systems on machines where the computer did not boot from a CD drive. They disappeared. Early informa-tion suggested the disk images, like those you created for Windows 2000 Server in Chapter 4, would be available on the Windows XP installation CD. However, even though the installation instructions still refer to using setup disks, the option to create them is not avail-able on the CD. Instead, you must download a single executable file from Microsoft's support web site that you can run to create a set of six installation floppy boot disks.

According to the information on that page, boot disks are a thing of the past and will no longer be available. All installations in the future will either be network-based or be done using CDs.

Installing Windows XP Professional

If you have carefully prepared, your computer should be ready for the installation of Microsoft's Windows XP Professional operating system. Microsoft recommends performing this installation using the CD drive. It can also be installed over a network using a shared network drive or even using a set of boot floppy disks. In this exercise, you will perform the setup using a CD-booted installation that will erase everything on your computer's disk drive and will reformat the drive with an NTFS partition. You will also set up your workstation so that it will use the IP protocol.

Warning: Do not proceed with this section until your instructor tells you to do so. This procedure can result in irreparable damage to someone else's files.

To complete this exercise, you will need the following items:

- Operational computer with an NIC installed and a hard disk drive that can be totally erased
- Windows XP Professional operating system software CD
- Bootable CD drive
- Workstation IP addresses and the naming convention used on your network

Step 1

Insert the Windows XP Professional operating system CD into your computer's CD drive and restart the computer by turning it off and then back on. This reboots the computer and ensures that it goes through a cold start with all settings reinitialized.

Step 2

When your system asks you to press any key to boot from the CD, Microsoft suggests pressing the SPACEBAR. The installation program (called Setup) starts by checking your hardware configuration, and then it displays the Welcome to Setup screen, where you decide whether to continue setting up your computer. Press ENTER to continue.

Note: You will notice that the installation procedure for Windows XP Professional is very similar to the procedures you used when installing Windows 2000 Server in Chapter 4. This is because both operating systems use the same technology, which has simply been updated from the Windows NT 4.0 operating system.

```
Windows XP Professional Setup

    Welcome to Setup.

    This portion of the Setup program prepares Microsoft(R)
    Windows(R) XP to run on your computer.

        •  To set up Windows XP now, press ENTER.

        •  To repair a Windows XP installation using
           Recovery Console, press R.

        •  To quit Setup without installing Windows XP, press F3.




    ENTER=Continue   R=Repair   F3=Quit
```

Step 3

Read the license agreement shown below, pressing PAGE DOWN to see the remainder of the agreement. Press F8 to agree to the license agreement.

Press F8
to agree

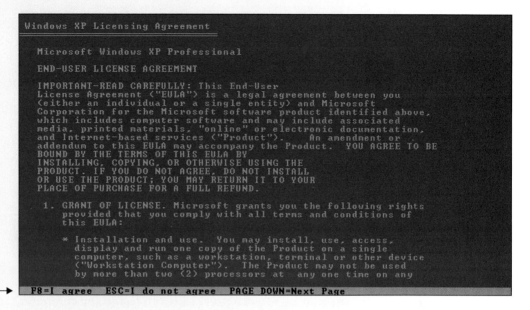

Step 4

If a partition already exists on your hard drive, highlight it, and press D to delete it. Confirm your intention to delete it (and all other existing partitions), and press C to create a new partition.

If you do not wish to delete the partition, press C to create a new partition for Windows XP on the selected partition.

Press D
to delete
partitions

Highlight
partition
to use

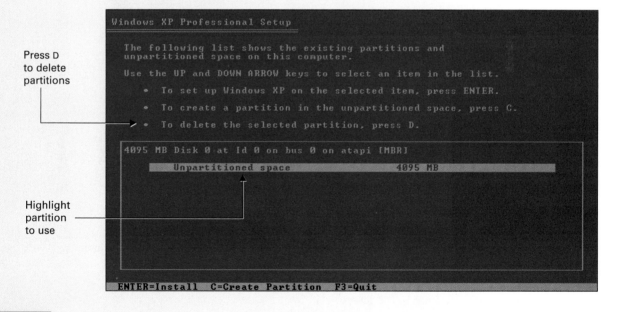

Step 5

Select the option to format the partition using the NTFS file system and press ENTER to continue. Setup will continue through several processes to format the partition, examine your disks, copy files to your Windows XP installation folders, and then initialize your configuration prior to rebooting the system.

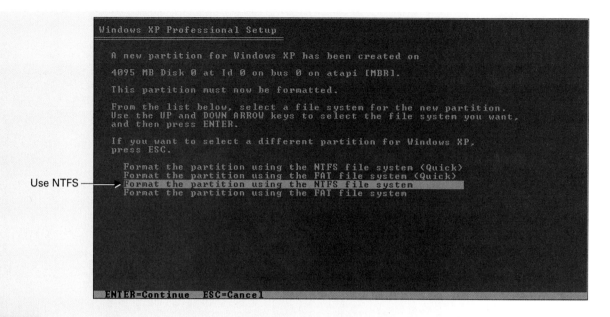

Step 6

After Setup initializes your configuration, it will signal you that it will reboot your computer in 15 seconds. You can press ENTER to restart the computer sooner or accept Setup's automatic reboot.

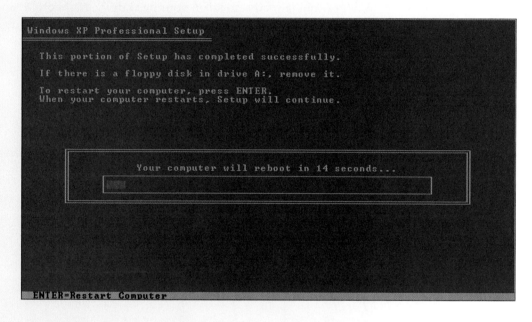

Step 7

After the computer restarts, your system will pass through several different startup screens and will bring you to the Windows XP Professional Setup status window, shown next. The remaining steps and your current status are displayed with a variety of different messages in the right panel, and eventually a time line is displayed in the bottom-left section of the screen.

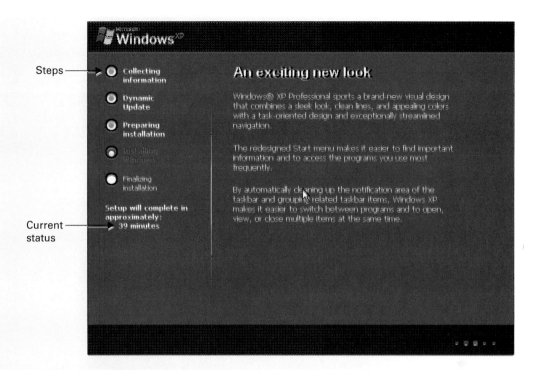

Steps

Current status

Step 8

The Setup wizard installs your devices and stops for your first input decision at the Regional and Language Options dialog box. At this point, you can review and customize your settings and then click Next to proceed with Setup.

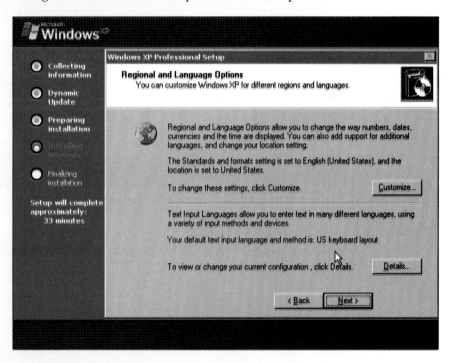

Step 9

In the Personalize Your Software dialog box, enter your name and organization and click Next to continue. In the following dialog box, enter your 25-character product key from the yellow sticker on the back of your CD case. Click Next to continue.

Tip: Be very careful typing in the exact characters given in the product key. Some of them are easily misread. If your product key is rejected as invalid, recheck your entry, reenter the sections as required, and click Next again.

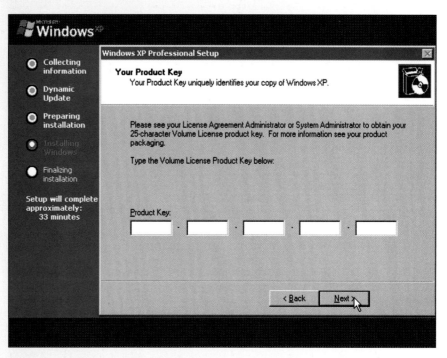

Step 10

In the Computer Name and Administrator Password dialog box, enter your computer name and the password for the workstation administrator account (twice for confirmation). Click Next to continue.

*Caution: The **workstation administrator account** is the first account added to your operating system and is the most powerful account on your workstation. This administrator password allows any user to log on to this local computer as the administrator and so should be protected.*

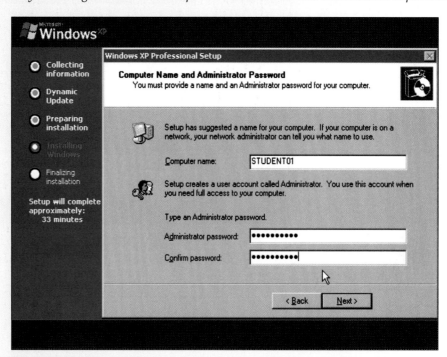

Step 11

In the Date and Time Settings dialog box, correct the date and time if necessary, choose the applicable time zone, and select the daylight saving option if required. Then click Next.

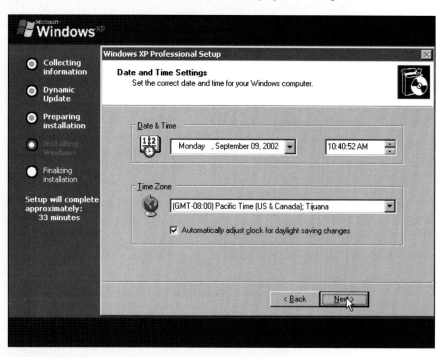

Step 12

Setup will then return you to the Windows XP Professional Setup status window until the Networking Settings dialog box gives you the choice between using Typical Settings or Custom Settings. Choose Typical Settings unless your instructor tells you otherwise, and then click Next.

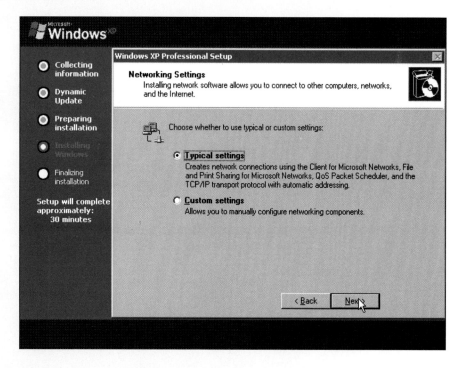

In the Workgroup or Computer Domain dialog box, enter your workgroup or domain name if you have one, as shown here, and click Next.

Tip: If you have not been provided with your workgroup or domain name, you should request instructor assistance before proceeding.

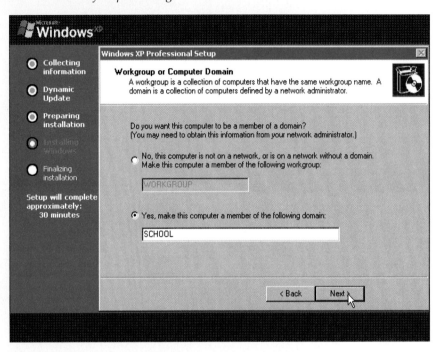

Enter the user name and password for the user who is authorized to join the machine to the domain (if you entered your workgroup or domain name), as shown here. Click OK to continue.

Tip: If you have difficulty joining a domain during the installation, Microsoft suggests using the default workgroup configuration and joining the correct domain after the installation is complete.

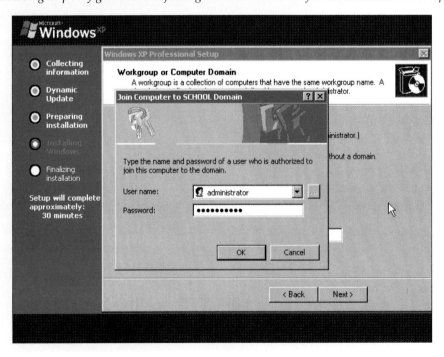

Step 15

Setup then redisplays the Windows XP Professional Setup status window as it installs components and Start menu items, registers components, saves settings, and removes any temporary files it used. Then it restarts the computer and provides you with the Log On to Windows dialog box.

Step 16

Enter your administrator password and click OK to log on to your new workstation as the local computer's administrator. Then click the Start button, as shown here, to view your new workstation's Start menu.

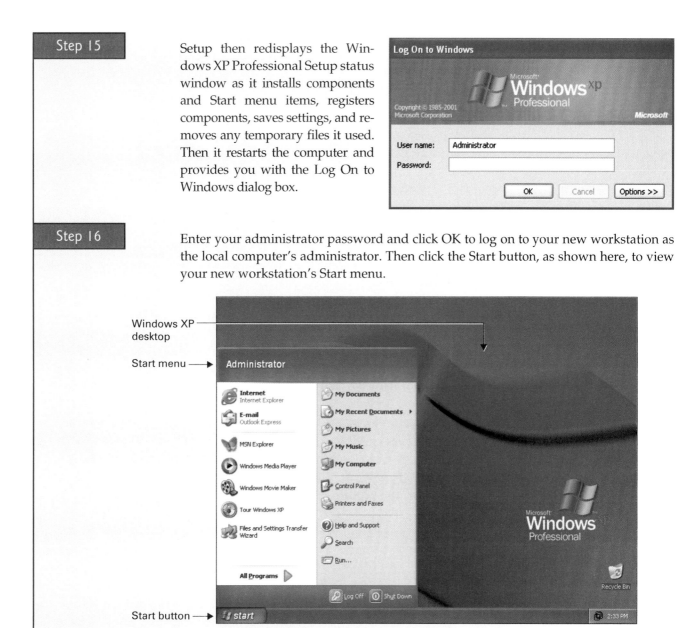

Installation Complete

Congratulations. You have completed your first client installation and you have an operational Windows XP Professional workstation that you can use in conjunction with the servers you created in Chapter 4. During this installation, you should have noticed that the setup procedure required less input from you than the server software installation required. Microsoft did this intentionally to cut the time required to install these systems. This new version of Windows is more capable of sensing your installed equipment and therefore requires less intervention on your part. This makes for a faster installation.

Because your lab computers may have the very minimum acceptable hardware, they may have a very limited capability or may work slowly. The speed of the workstations you build using these techniques will depend on the speed of the workstations' processors, how much RAM is installed on the computers, and how much space remains available on their hard drives. Regardless of how fast or useful your classroom workstations may prove to be, though, the procedures you employed here will help you when you install operating systems in the future.

■ Installing and Configuring Novell Client

If you have a NetWare server on your network, you won't know it is there unless you either work from the server's own console or have Novell Client installed on your workstation. **Novell Client** software runs on Windows workstations and allows them to operate as Novell clients and connect to NetWare servers.

Lauren knew this, and that is why she instructed Ricky to first create the workstations using Windows XP Professional. Now that the workstations are operational, Ricky plans to install the Novell Client software on each one, following the very simple installation instructions. The whole process is easy if you install the client on a recently installed workstation, because during the installation process you will have already verified the computer's hardware.

Try This!

Latest Service Pack

As you did with your new Windows 2000 server in Chapter 4, it is a good idea, after installing this computer's workstation operating system, to install the latest Microsoft service pack (the latest consolidated update to the operating system can be found at `http://www.microsoft.com/windowsxp/default.asp`).

To install the latest service pack, try this:

1. Start your new Windows XP Professional workstation as Administrator.

2. Start your browser and go to `http://www.microsoft.com/windowsxp/pro/downloads/default.asp`.

3. Click the link to the latest service pack, click that service pack's Express Installation link, and click the Windows XP SP's link to open the Windows Update web site.

4. Click the Scan for Updates green arrow to scan your computer and then review the updates found. This scan should return the recommendation to install the SP and any other updates currently available. If more than one item is available, check only the SP option at this time and click the Install Now button to start the installation.

5. Follow the instructions used in Chapter 4 to install the latest service pack to your newly installed Windows 2000 Server, and when the installation finishes, click the Finish button to restart your workstation.

Preparing for Installation

If you have just completed installing Windows XP Professional or you want to install the client on another Windows XP Professional computer, you can proceed immediately with your Novell Client installation because your hardware exceeds the requirements for the client software.

If you are about to install Novell Client on a computer running a different version of Windows, however, you should verify that your equipment meets or exceeds the minimum stated requirements before beginning any installation. This will be similar to the installation you will perform in Step-by-Step 5.02 (but using Novell Client 3.32 for Windows 95/98 software instead). That way, you will save yourself troubleshooting time when installations fail because those minimums were not met.

Checking Hardware Compatibility

The latest version of Novell Client (currently version 4.83) for Windows NT, 2000, and XP requires at least a Windows NT 4.0 operating system (with service pack 3 or later installed) and at least 24MB of RAM. Both Windows 2000 and Windows XP machines have more than these minimums, so they are also acceptable.

Checking Hardware Configuration

Once you have an operational Windows XP Professional workstation connected to your classroom network, no additional hardware configuration requirements must be met prior to installing Novell Client. Although it is not needed for the client software installation, you could ensure that your NetWare 6 server, set up in Chapter 4, is connected to your classroom network and is functioning properly.

Testing Client Hardware

The testing of the client hardware is adequately completed once you finish your Windows XP Professional installation. However, you should make sure you update your new Windows workstation with any available updates, including all service packs, prior to installing your Novell Client software. Your Windows XP Professional computer coupled with the networking capability of the NetWare 6 server will allow you to utilize the powerful networking features of Novell's software.

Try This!

Latest Novell Client

Although the Novell Client software used in this chapter was the latest at the time of writing, you should verify that you have the latest version available when you do your actual installations. You can locate the latest version on the Novell web site (www.novell.com/download). To download the latest client software, try this:

1. Log on to your computer and open your browser.

2. Go to the following link: http://www.novell.com/download.

3. In the Search for a Product Download drop-down lists in the upper portion of the web page, select Novell Client as the product and Windows XP as the platform, and click the Submit Search button. Alternatively, you can simply click the link to the software if it is listed in the top 10 downloads section that is located in the lower half of the web page.

4. If you submitted the search, continue locating the latest client version; otherwise, click the top 10 link to go directly to the software download.

5. Follow any additional links to the desired version, and save the software to your desktop.

6. Create a new folder named Novell Client, and move your newly downloaded file to that folder.

7. Open the new Novell Client folder, double-click the downloaded client file, and direct the unzipped files to be stored within your new Novell Client folder.

Step-by-Step 5.02

Installing Novell Client

Your workstation computer should now be ready for installing the Novell Client software.

Warning: Do not proceed with this section until your instructor tells you to do so. This procedure may install unnecessary networking client software and affect existing users' access to their computers.

To complete this exercise you will need the following items:

- Operational Windows XP Professional computer
- The downloaded Novell Client software

Locate and double-click the setupnw.exe file (created when you unzipped the down-loaded Novell Client file) in the Novell Client folder you created on your desktop in the "Latest Novell Client" Try This! exercise.

Warning: *You will not be able to install the Novell Client software if your Local Area Connection Properties dialog box is open. Ensure that this dialog box is closed before proceeding with your installation.*

If you install Novell's client software from CD, you must choose your installation language and the proper version (Windows 9*x* or NT) before proceeding, as indicated in the re-mainder of this procedure.

Leave the installation option set to the Typical Installation default, and click the In-stall button, as shown here.

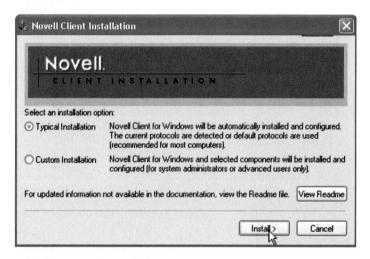

Very quickly, you will see a status window showing you that the installation is in progress. Click the Reboot button when the Installation Complete dialog box appears.

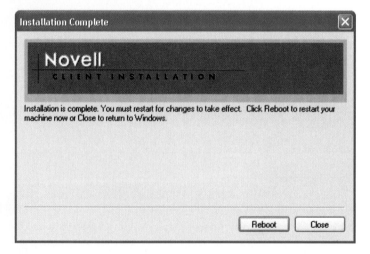

Step 4

When the computer restarts, you will be presented with the Novell Client's Begin Login screen in the middle of your blank Windows XP desktop. Press the CTRL+ALT+DELETE key combination as requested to initiate your login.

Step 5

At this point, you can simply log in to your workstation and skip the remainder of this exercise by entering your Windows XP user name and password and checking the Workstation Only option before clicking OK.

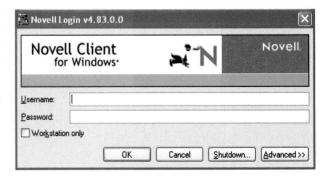

Step 6

Since you have already built a NetWare 6 server and attached it to your network, you can log in to your server by entering your NetWare user name and password. Ensure that the Workstation Only option is not selected, and click the Advanced button to reveal additional login information tabs and drop-down boxes.

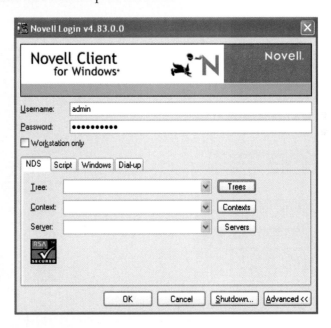

Step 7

Click the Trees button to reveal the Novell trees on your network. Highlight the tree you created when you built your NetWare 6 server, and click OK to add that tree to the Tree drop-down box in the Novell Login dialog box.

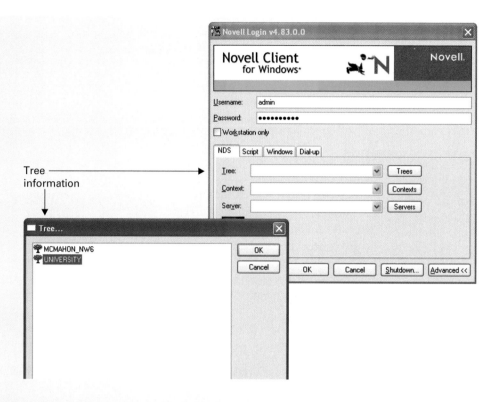

Tree
information

Step 8

Click the Contexts button to reveal the context you used on your tree when creating your NetWare server. Highlight that context and click OK to add that context to the Context drop-down box in the Novell Login dialog box.

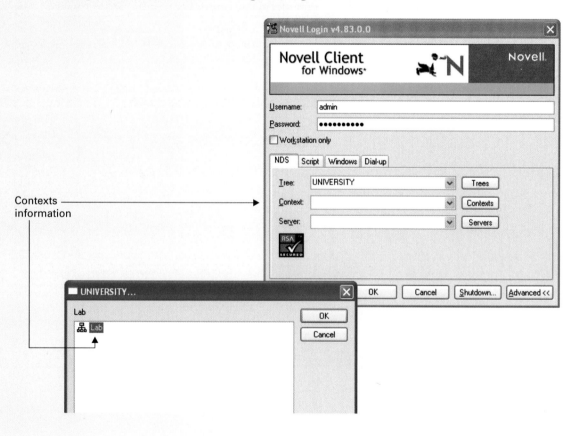

Contexts
information

Click the Servers button to reveal your NetWare server. Highlight that server, as shown here, and click OK to add that server to the Server drop-down box in the Novell Login dialog box.

Servers
information

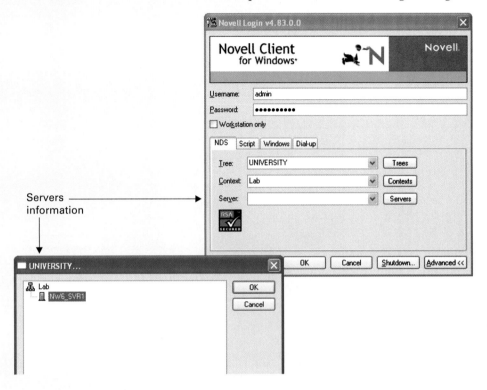

Click the Windows tab to reveal the Windows Login Information section of the Novell Login dialog box. Enter your Windows XP Professional local user name, and verify that the From box indicates the name of your local workstation. Click OK to log in to both your Novell server and your Windows XP workstation.

Tip: *If your Novell and Windows passwords are different, Novell Client will offer you the option of* **password synchronization***, which changes your Windows password to match your Novell password. This will give you a* **one-step login***, requiring only a single password entry for two or more logins.*

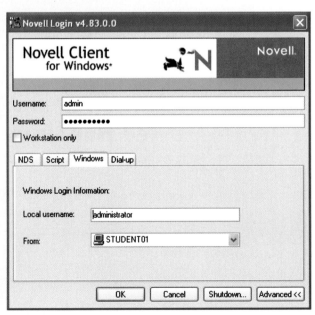

You can verify that you are properly logged in to both systems by ensuring that your workstation now includes a **Novell Services icon** (a red *N* in the taskbar's notification area). Once it is added by the installation program, you can right-click the icon to view the Novell Services shortcut menu and confirm that the client software is operating properly.

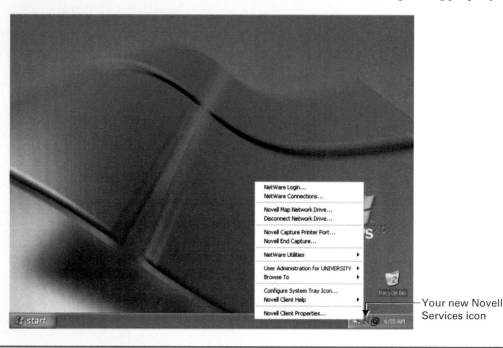

Your new Novell Services icon

Installation Complete

Congratulations. You have completed your second client installation and can now use your Windows XP Professional workstation to work with your Novell server. The usefulness of this client capability will depend on the speeds of both your server and your workstation processors, and on how much remaining space either has on its hard drive. However, regardless of how useful this capability turns out to be for you in this class, the procedure you just completed is similar to how you will create other workstations for Novell servers in the future. While the steps may not be exactly the same, you will be somewhat familiar with the process and will have an easier time with each new implementation.

■ Installing and Configuring Red Hat Linux

Ricky likes working with the Red Hat Linux server, and because both server and workstation software are on the same Red Hat Linux installation CD, he wants everyone at SinkRSwim Pools to be aware that an alternative workstation is available for networked users. Therefore, he intends to add several Red Hat Linux workstations in various locations around the company. Ricky realizes that a major drawback to using Linux as the workstation operating system is that he will not be able to install the same applications his workers currently use on their Windows workstations. Still, he believes it is important that the workers have additional options.

He already has the latest version of the software and, like you, he is experienced with Red Hat Linux's installation procedures. Although he does not consider himself an expert, he is comfortable that the knowledge gained building his server will be useful when he creates the workstations. You, too, will see that the procedures are extremely similar, and you should have no trouble at all installing a Red Hat Linux workstation.

Cross Check

Purpose of Networks

Use the information you learned in Chapters 1 and 2 about the purposes of networks when answering the following questions.

1. Which of the main purposes for networks will this Linux workstation likely satisfy?

2. All of your computers are required to communicate with each other, so based on the installations of the other computers on your network, which protocol will you be choosing for your Linux workstation? Why?

Preparing for the Installation

In order for the installation to go as smoothly as possible, you must carefully prepare for a Red Hat Linux workstation installation as you did for installing your server and your Windows XP Professional workstation operating systems. You should make sure that your hardware meets the program requirements, operates properly, and includes all the necessary drivers. This will help ensure a complete setup and consistent, trouble-free operation afterward.

Checking Hardware Compatibility

As with the other operating systems you have already installed, you need a computer on which to install this software, and because it is for classroom use, it won't need to be as powerful as the workstations used in most companies. As with Red Hat servers, Red Hat Linux workstation also has a text-only mode (that does not use a graphical interface), so minimum requirements, recommended requirements, and text-mode requirements are necessary for the hardware.

Unlike that of other operating systems, most of Red Hat's documentation is available on the company's web site. Use the following link to get the documentation: http://www.redhat.com/docs/manuals.

For a Red Hat Linux workstation used in a classroom setting, the vendor's minimums require the use of a computer with a Pentium 200 MHz processor and 32MB of RAM

Try This!

Red Hat Online Documentation

Red Hat provides you with online documentation for its products. You can locate information on its web site about the different types of installations (called *classes*) that you can install using the latest Red Hat software. To view information about the different classes, try this:

1. Log on to your Windows XP Professional client and open your browser.

2. Go to the following link: http://www.redhat.com/docs/manuals.

3. Click the Red Hat Linux link, scroll through the available manuals, and then locate and click the link to the x86 Installation Guide. Note that if you want to download a copy of the manual to your desktop, you could right-click the PDF link (located right below the file name) and save the entire Installation Guide's file to your desktop for later use.

4. In the Red Hat Linux Table of Contents, scroll down to "Which Installation Class Is Best For You?" in section one, and click that link.

5. Read the section and decide which installation class you will be using for your classroom computers.

for a text-mode installation or 64MB for graphical mode (96MB is recommended). The installation also requires at least 650MB of hard disk space or 4.5GB of available hard disk space for a full install, plus additional space for any files you will be storing on the server.

As you did before you installed the Red Hat Linux server, you should visit the section of Red Hat's web site that posts the Hardware Compatibility List (HCL): http://www.redhat.com/hcl/. That list identifies all the hardware that passed Red Hat's Ready Tests prior to the latest software's release. You should review that updated version of the list before you install the workstation operating system. In addition, remember that a systems requirement table lists the things you should know before beginning the installation. This table can be found in Chapter 2 of the Installation Guide.

Checking Hardware Configuration

As you'll remember from your Linux server installation, Red Hat recommends using a boot-enabled CD drive for all installations of its software, but it provides alternative boot methods as well. You will need a high-density 3½-inch floppy drive if your CD is not bootable or is not being used for the installation.

You will also need information about your monitor and display adapter. For the graphical installation, you should also have a mouse.

Testing Workstation Hardware

In order to test your workstation's hardware, it is a good practice to rebuild your selected computer's hard disk drive and start with a fresh installation rather than an update. However, as you know from your server installation, Red Hat Linux products wipe your hard drive clean by booting from the CD and building all new partitions during the installation. Unlike the server installation (which you could also use when installing a workstation), where you used FDISK manually, removed the NT partitions, and installed DOS, in this installation you will use an alternative method where you simply use the Red Hat Linux CD to initiate your installation.

Step-by-Step 5.03

Installing Linux 7.3

If you have carefully prepared, the computer you selected for this workstation should now be ready for Red Hat Linux's workstation operating system. You are already familiar with how Red Hat Linux's setup process has one installation method with several options, and once again, you will use the simplest installation. In this exercise, you will perform a CD-based installation that will erase everything on your workstation's disk drive and

reformat it, configure your workstation to use IP, and create a new Red Hat Linux workstation.

Warning: Do not proceed with this section until your instructor tells you to do so. This procedure can result in irreparable damage to someone else's files.

To complete this exercise, you will need the following items:

- Computer with a hard disk drive that can be totally erased

- Red Hat Linux's operating system software
- Bootable floppy disks if DOS is not available, created using boot.img found in the IMAGES directory on the Red Hat Linux operating system CD
- CD drive (with drivers if the computer does not boot from CD)

- Mouse for the graphical configuration
- Network interface card
- Graphics card information
- Network IP addresses and naming convention

Step 1

Insert the Red Hat Linux operating system CD into your computer's CD drive and re-start the computer by turning it off and then back on. This reboots the computer, ensures that it goes through a cold start with all settings reinitialized, and brings up the first installation dialog box where you can choose the installation mode. If you do not make a selection, the setup process will automatically start with the default settings.

Note: Since you have already completed a Red Hat Linux installation and most of the screens are the same, only those specifically applicable to a workstation's installation will be provided in these Step-by-Step procedures. Other images of the Red Hat Linux installer screens can be found in Chapter 4.

Step 2

The Red Hat Linux setup process displays several initial screens starting with text-based line entries, then basic blue-screen dialog boxes, and finally the higher resolution graphics implementation shown using the Red Hat logo.

Step 3

Decide whether you want to use the Help screen during the installation. You may not need it for this installation (since you have done the server installation), so you can click the Hide Help button in the Welcome dialog box. You can always click the Show Help button at any point during the installation should you feel you need that added assistance. Click Next to initiate the installation.

Step 4

In the Language Selection window, choose the appropriate languages and click Next. In the Keyboard Configuration window, highlight the appropriate configuration and click Next. In the Mouse Configuration window, highlight your mouse configuration and click Next.

Step 5

In the Installation Type window, select Workstation and click Next.

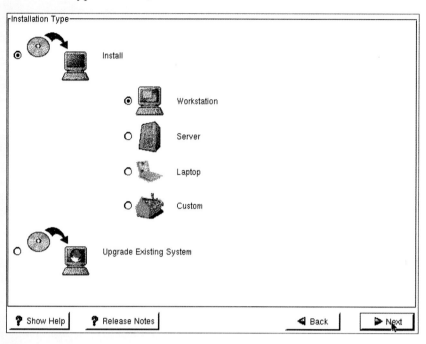

Step 6

In the Disk Partition Setup window, choose the way you want partitioning set up and click Next. Click Yes to confirm that you want to initialize the drive.

In the Automatic Partitioning window, choose the method you want used for automatic partitioning, and click Next. Click Yes to confirm that you want to remove the partition.

Step 7

In the Disk Setup window, verify the location where you want Red Hat Linux installed, and click Next. Verify the information in the Boot Loader Configuration window, and click Next. In the Boot Loader Password Configuration window, type and verify a boot loader password, and click Next.

Step 8

In the Network Configuration window, keep the default settings of Configure Using DHCP and Activate on Boot, as shown here, and click Next.

```
┌Network Configuration──────────────────────────────┐
│ eth0 |                                             │
│ ☑ Configure using DHCP                             │
│ ☑ Activate on boot                                 │
│                                                    │
│  IP Address:  [          ]                         │
│  Netmask:     [          ]                         │
│  Network:     [          ]                         │
│  Broadcast:   [          ]                         │
│                                                    │
│  Hostname:    [                ]                   │
│  Gateway:     [          ]            ▶            │
│  Primary DNS: [          ]                         │
│  Secondary DNS:[         ]                         │
│  Tertiary DNS:[          ]                         │
│                                                    │
│ ? Show Help   ? Release Notes    ◀ Back   ▶ Next  │
└────────────────────────────────────────────────────┘
```

In the Firewall Configuration window, confirm or configure your settings, and click Next. In the Additional Language Support window, verify or select your configuration, and click Next. In the Time Zone Selection window, confirm or select your time zone, and click Next.

In the Account Configuration window, enter and verify your root administrator password. Create an additional new user login account for yourself, and click OK. Click Next to continue.

In the Package Group Selection window, select the GNOME and KDE packages to be installed on your workstation, as shown here, and click Next.

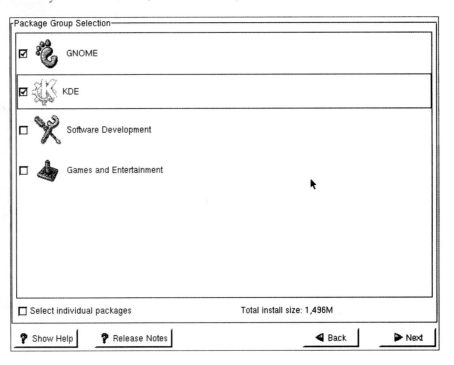

In the Graphical Interface (X) Configuration window, use the small triangle next to your vendor's selection and the scroll bar to locate the appropriate graphics adapter for your workstation. Specify the amount of RAM on your video card, and click Next to continue.

In the About to Install window, click Next to start the actual installation, and monitor the installation on the Installing Packages screen. When the first installation CD is completed, replace it with the second installation CD, and click OK.

When you come to the Boot Disk Creation window, if you need a floppy boot disk, insert a non-write-protected blank 3½-inch, high-density disk into your floppy disk drive, and click Next. If you don't need a floppy boot disk, click the Skip Boot Disk Creation option and click Next. If you create one, remember to remove the boot disk when it is completed.

In the Monitor Configuration window, locate and highlight your monitor, and click Next.

In the Customize Graphics Configuration window, set or test your graphics configuration, choose your login type, choose your desktop environment if multiple choices are available, and click Next. When the Congratulations window appears, click the Exit button.

Step 15

Upon restarting, your workstation will offer you a choice of available installation options that you can highlight and press ENTER to select. The default setting will be selected automatically if you simply press ENTER without making another selection.

Your system will provide you with either the graphical logon or a text-based logon to your new workstation.

Installation Complete

Congratulations. You have completed your third client installation and have now added an operational Red Hat Linux workstation to your network. The usefulness of this third client depends, as usual, on the speed of its processor and on how much remaining space it has on its hard drive. Once again, you should recognize that regardless of how useful this workstation may be to you now, the procedure you just completed will be the same as you will use to create other such workstations in the future. The experience you gained here will transfer to any other installations you undertake.

■ Chapter Summary

After reading this chapter and completing the Step-by-Step tutorials, the Cross Checks, and Try This! exercises, you should understand the following facts about networking:

Install and Configure Windows XP Professional

- Windows XP was initially released in two versions—Home and Professional.

- Keeping a user's computer trouble-free makes everyone's life easier.

- The Windows XP installation process is the easiest yet, compared with previous Windows versions.

- Information on Windows XP can be found on Microsoft's web site—www.microsoft.com/windowsxp/default.asp.

- Workstation computers do not need to be as capable or powerful as those used as servers.

- The minimum Microsoft requirements for installing Windows XP Professional include a computer with an Intel Pentium/Celeron family or AMD K6/Athalon/Duron family 233 MHz (single or dual) processor, 64MB of RAM, and at least one hard disk where the systemroot (usually C:\WINNT) can be located on a partition with at least 1.5GB of available hard disk space.

- When installing Windows XP Professional on a computer with another upgradeable operating system already installed, an automatic system verification option is available.

- Upgradeable Windows versions include Windows 98, Windows NT 4.0 Workstation, Windows 2000 Professional, and Windows XP Home.

- Service packs are required on upgrades from NT 4.0 Workstation and Windows 2000 Professional systems.

- Microsoft provides online access to both a graphical catalog-type HCL web site and text versions of the HCL on an FTP site. Check all your hardware using your choice of the available HCL versions.

- Microsoft recommends using a CD or DVD drive for installations.

- Boot setup disks are no longer available on Microsoft's Windows XP installation CD.

- You can wipe your hard drive and build all necessary partitions during your Windows XP Professional installation.

- If your system does not boot from a CD, Microsoft suggests running another upgradeable version of Windows and installing from within that system.

- You can also create and use a set of six boot setup disks to perform the installation startup.

- If you have trouble joining a domain during installation, simply join the default workgroup and join the domain later.

- The Windows XP installation process involves significantly fewer user interactions during the setup process, which results in a faster workstation installation.

- When you finish installing a new operating system, it is a good idea to check for updates, such as service packs.

Install and Configure Novell Client

- You cannot access your server on your network from non-NetWare computers unless they have Novell Client installed.

- Novell Client runs on Windows workstations so they can connect to Novell servers.

- Novell Client software provides a very simple installation process.

- Windows XP Professional more than meets the requirements for Novell Client software, so you can immediately start your client installation on a Windows XP Professional computer.

- You can download the latest version of the client software from the Novell web site.

- Novell Client requires at least the Window NT 4.0 operating system (with service pack 3 installed) but also installs on Windows 2000 and Windows XP computers.

- Make sure your Local Area Connection Properties dialog box is closed before starting your Novell Client installation.

- After completing the Novell Client installation, you are presented with a different initial login screen when you start your Windows XP Professional computer.

- Upon logging in to your Windows XP Professional computer, you can elect to log in to just your Windows environment or choose the more extensive login that connects you to the Novell server as well.

- When you log in to your computer through Novell Client using different passwords for Novell and Windows, you are given the option of changing your Windows password to match your Novell password for a single login entry.

Install and Configure Red Hat Linux

- The Red Hat Linux installation CDs include both the server software and the workstation software.

- Most of Red Hat Linux's setup input screens occur early in the installation process.

- The Red Hat Linux setup also includes a text-mode installation option with applicable minimum requirements.

- Red Hat offers most of the necessary documentation on its web site.

- Red Hat Linux requires a Pentium 200 MHz processor, either 32MB or 64MB of RAM depending on whether you do a text or graphic installation, and at least 650MB of available hard disk space.

- Check the Red Hat Linux Hardware Compatibility List to ensure your equipment will be supported by the operating system.

- The installation guide on Red Hat's web site includes a systems requirement table that you can print and fill in with your system installation for use during setup.

- Red Hat Linux can be installed using a boot-enabled CD drive or using the provisions on the installation CD to create a boot disk.

- Use the boot.img file found in the IMAGES directory to create your bootable floppy for a Red Hat Linux installation.

■ Key Terms

AutoRun (139)	**one-step login** (153)	**Windows XP Home** (135)
DVD (137)	**password synchronization** (153)	**Windows XP Professional** (135)
Knowledge Base (138)	**setup boot disks** (138)	**workstation administrator**
Novell Client (148)	**systemroot** (136)	**account** (144)
Novell Services icon (154)	**upgradeable system** (137)	

■ Key Term Quiz

Use the preceding vocabulary terms to complete the sentences that follow. Not all the terms will be used.

1. If you are unable to boot from your CD drive and need to start the Windows XP installation using a set of floppy disks, you can locate _____ on Microsoft's Support web site (http://support.microsoft.com/).

2. The version of Windows XP that has extensive networking capability and is intended for use in company environments is called _____.

3. The main folder containing your Windows XP operating system files is the _____.

4. A computer that is running a previous version of the Windows operating system that can have Windows XP Professional installed without removing the existing operating system is said to have a(n) _____ installed.

5. A(n) _____ is a higher capacity removable storage device than a CD.

6. The name for Microsoft's searchable online database where you can find information about

boot floppy disks for Windows XP Professional installations is called the _____.

7. If your CD driver has _____ capability, simply inserting a CD into the drive causes it to self-start immediately.

8. The first account added to your Windows XP Professional operating system is the _____.

9. The software added to a workstation so that the computer can operate using a networked Novell server is called _____.

10. When logging in to a Novell server using a workstation with the proper software installed, you will be offered the _____ option, where the software changes your Windows password to match your Novell password.

■ Multiple-Choice Quiz

1. Which of the following Windows versions is one of Microsoft's newest workstation operating systems?
   a. Windows XP Household
   b. Windows XP Professional
   c. Windows 2000 Professional
   d. Windows 2000 Workstation

2. Which of the following versions of Windows is upgradeable to one of Microsoft's newest workstation operating systems?
   a. Windows NT Server
   b. Windows 2000 Server
   c. Windows XP Household
   d. Windows 2000 Professional

3. Which of the following is a link to a Microsoft web site where information about the different versions of Windows XP can be found?
   a. `microsoft.com/windowsxp/default.asp`
   b. `downloads.microsoft.com/windowsxp/default.htm`
   c. `www.microsoft.com/windowXP/default.html`
   d. `ftp.microsoft.com/windows/xp/default.asp`

4. Which of the following is true regarding computers used for workstations?
   a. Novell Client requires a powerful Novell workstation computer.
   b. Windows XP Professional computers can be less powerful than Windows XP servers.

   c. The requirements for Red Hat Linux workstations are the same as for its servers.
   d. Workstations with Windows XP Professional installed won't run unless the Microsoft recommended hardware minimums are met.

5. Performing which of the following component upgrades inside your computer's CPU will allow a more effective Windows XP Professional installation?
   a. Upgrading from a dual to a quad processor
   b. Increasing RAM from 16MB to 32MB
   c. Replacing an AMD K5 with an AMD K6 processor
   d. Increasing the size of the partition where the C:\WINNT folder is currently located from 500MB to 1.5GB

6. All of the following statements are true *except* which one?
   a. A list of incompatible items can be obtained by using AUTORUN and selecting Check My System Automatically on a Windows NT 4.0 workstation before upgrading to Windows XP Professional.
   b. Service packs must be installed on Windows 2000 Professional before upgrading to Windows XP Professional.
   c. Automatic system compatibility checks are not available when booting from the Windows XP installation CD.
   d. Service packs must be installed on Windows NT 4.0 servers before upgrading to Windows XP Professional.

7. Which of the following is *not* a valid method for checking your computer's conformance to the Windows XP Professional HCL?

   a. Searching for each of your computer's components in the HCL located on the installation CD in the Products folder

   b. Visiting Microsoft's catalog-like HCL web page and inspecting vendor equipment listings

   c. Downloading the text-based HCL from the Microsoft FTP site and checking each computer component

   d. Running Check My System Automatically

8. Which of the following is *not* required in order to perform a bootable Windows XP Professional installation?

   a. Either a bootable CD or set of bootable setup disks

   b. A mouse

   c. An SVGA display adapter that supports an 800 SYMBOL 180 \f "Symbol" \s 11 600 resolution

   d. At least 64MB of RAM

9. Which of the following is *not* true regarding Windows XP Professional boot setup disks?

   a. Boot setup disks are available only through Microsoft's web site.

   b. A complete set of boot setup disks contains six floppy disks.

   c. The bootable set of six setup disks can be created using your installation CD.

   d. A single file is used to create the complete set of boot setup disks.

10. Which of the following is true regarding Novell Client software?

   a. You must use the Novell Client software included on your NetWare 6 server installation CD.

   b. Novell Client software is available on a set of bootable floppy disks.

   c. Novell offers free downloads of its latest Novell Client software through its web site.

   d. Novell Client software must be loaded before installing a Windows operating system.

11. Of the following Windows operating systems, which cannot have Novell's latest client (4.83) installed?

   a. Windows XP

   b. Windows 2000

   c. Windows NT

   d. Windows 98

12. Which of the following statements is *not* true regarding Novell's client software?

   a. Novell Client is capable of creating a single-step login process, where you log in to multiple servers with one user name and password.

   b. Your NetWare 6 server must be operational prior to installing the latest version of Novell Client on a workstation running Windows XP Professional.

   c. Using the Novell Client software gives you the option of logging in to your workstation only.

   d. There are multiple versions of Novell's client software, and you should select the version applicable to your workstation's installed version of Windows.

13. Which of the following is the executable file used to install Novell Client software on your Windows XP Professional computer?

   a. setup.exe

   b. setupclient.exe

   c. setupnw.exe

   d. c483SP1e.exe

14. Which of the following is *not* true when logging on to your Windows XP Professional computer using Novell Client?

   a. On the NDS tab, you can use the Trees button to select your NDS tree.

   b. On the Windows tab, you can use the Servers button to select your Windows server.

   c. On the NDS tab, you can use the Servers button to select your Novell server.

   d. On the Windows tab, you can enter a local computer password different from the one used for your Novell login.

15. Which of the following is not a package that you can choose on the Package Group Selection window during a Red Hat Linux workstation installation?

    a. Videos and Games

    b. KDE

    c. GNOME

    d. Software Development

■ Essay Quiz

1. Describe the process that you would use when upgrading a Windows NT 4.0 server to Windows XP Professional.

2. Explain a major difference between using a workstation as a Novell client versus using one as a Microsoft client.

3. What must you do to log in to your computer when the Novell server is inoperative?

4. Describe the workstation you would see in front of you if you installed Windows XP Professional, Novell Client, and Red Hat Linux workstation, in that order, using each manufacturer's recommended installation techniques.

5. What is one major drawback of using Red Hat Linux on your workstation computer instead of Microsoft's Windows XP Professional?

Lab Projects

Time to roll up your sleeves and apply what you've learned. The following lab projects will enable you to practice the concepts discussed in this chapter.

• Lab Project 5.1

Your TEACH organization has just recently installed a NetWare 6 server, upgraded its workstations to Windows XP Professional, and installed Novell Client software on each of the workstations. Some of your users have suggested that the login procedures they use should not include logging them into the NetWare server unless they have business on that server. They have requested training from you showing them how to change whether they log in to the server and how to browse their Windows XP Professional workstations to verify their network connection.

You will need the following:

■ A lab computer with an operational NetWare 6 server

■ Networked workstation computers running Windows XP Professional and Novell Client

■ Access to the default administrator accounts on both the NetWare server and the local workstation

Then do the following:

1 Restart your workstation.

2 Press CTRL+ALT+DELETE at the Begin Login dialog box.

3 Observe the initial user name that is displayed. Unless your default configurations have been changed, the user name displayed should be the administrator account—admin.

4 Click the Workstation Only option. Notice that the user name changes to the one you use when logging in to your Windows workstation. If you are still using the default accounts, this will be administrator.

5 Enter your administrator password and click OK.

6 Click the Start button and select My Computer. Notice that no Novell connections are displayed, and then close the My Computer window. Click the Start button, click the Log Off button, and click the Log Off button in the Log Off Windows dialog box.

7 Press CTRL+ALT+DELETE at the Begin Login dialog box to log in again.

8 Observe the initial user name that is displayed. The user name displayed should still be the administrator account—admin.

9 Ensure the Workstation Only option is not selected.

10 Enter your administrator password and click OK. You should see the Novell login screens appear as they are invoked.

11 Click the Start button and select My Computer. Notice that two default Novell connections are now displayed—System and Public. Close the My Computer window, click the Start button, click the Log Off button, and click the Log Off button in the Log Off Windows dialog box.

• Lab Project 5.2

Part two of the training you put together for your coworkers in the TEACH organization will show them how to verify their network connections from the Novell Client perspective. They have also requested training from you about how to create their own Documents folder on the NetWare server, and they want an easy way to browse directly to that folder using the Novell Services icon in their taskbar's notification area.

You will need the following:

- A lab computer with an operational NetWare 6 server

- Networked workstation computers running Windows XP Professional and Novell Client

- Access to the default administrator accounts on both the NetWare server and the local workstation

Then do the following:

1 Restart your workstation.

2 Press CTRL+ALT+DELETE at the Begin Login dialog box.

3 Ensure the Workstation Only option is not selected.

4 Enter your administrator password and click OK.

5 Right-click the Novell Services icon (the red *N*) in the taskbar's configuration area, select Browse To, and select My Computer. Notice that the same My Computer window opens as when you use the Start button on the Windows XP taskbar. Notice also that the same two default Novell connections are displayed—System and Public. Close the My Computer window.

6 Double-click the Novell Services icon, and double-click the Novell Connections icon to display the Novell connection objects you logged in to—your server, context, and tree.

7 Double-click the server icon, double-click the SYS icon, and click the Make a New Folder option in the left panel of the SYS on NW6_ svr1 window (inserting your own server's name in place of "NW6_svr1"). Rename that new folder Rich_Documents (inserting your own name where I have placed mine). Close the window.

8 Right-click the Novell Services icon, select Browse To, and select Edit Browseable Path.

9 In the Edit Browseable Path dialog box, click the Browse button, and browse to the folder you just created, locating your server and SYS folder icons in the Network Resources window.

10 Highlight that new folder, click OK, click the Add button, and click the close button.

11 Verify your new browse path's location operates properly by right-clicking the Novell Services icon, selecting Browse To, and selecting your new location.

12 Close the window and log off your computer.

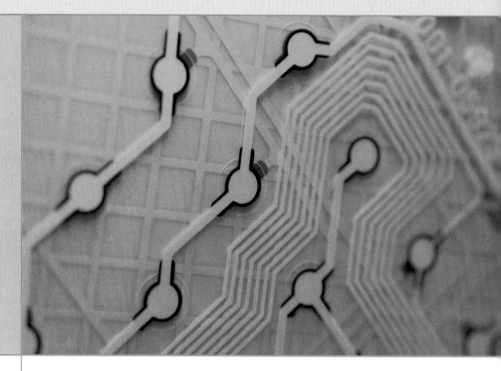

chapter 6 Building a Directory Service

"Whilst the rights of all as persons are equal, in virtue of their access to reason, their rights in property are very unequal. One man owns his clothes, and another owns a country."

—Ralph Waldo Emerson

In this chapter, you will learn how to:

- **Use Novell Directory Services**
- **Describe Windows 2000 Active Directory**
- **Expand your network's directories**

Since the beginning of this course, most of you have been logging on to your networks using the Administrator account. Now it is time to learn about creating your own server accounts. This will help you learn about the constraints that must be put on user accounts to limit their network access. You would never create users and leave them with the almost unlimited rights you have enjoyed while working with the network Administrator accounts. On the other hand, you still need that unlimited control because you are the network administrator.

In this chapter, you will create user and computer objects on your classroom network. You will first learn about Novell's method for storing and retrieving network information using Novell Directory Services (NDS). Next you will learn about the comparable system Microsoft uses in its Active Directory (AD). Then you will use both of these services as you add users and link them together to create single login capabilities for your network's users.

Understanding Novell Directory Services

Up to this point, whenever Ricky wanted his SinkRSwim Pools users to do anything with the Novell server, he has had to go to the users' locations, log in using his Admin account, perform the action for the users, and log back out. Ricky feels that he needs a little more knowledge about Novell's servers himself before he starts telling those users to explore more of the Novell network's features. Ricky decides that he would be better off starting with a basic understanding of the operating system's structure so that he can explain it to the other employees.

Inside Novell's network operating system (NetWare) is an integral database component called Novell Directory Services (NDS). It, combined with a NetWare Administrator component (called NWAdmin), provides the key to the way NetWare manages your Novell network. In Novell NetWare 6, NDS stores information about users, groups, and resources in a database called the **Directory**. Using NDS, you can manage the resources of your network by grouping similar objects together hierarchically and assigning **attributes**, which are descriptive pieces of information, to each of the objects, such as users, groups, and servers.

NDS then organizes the data about each of these objects, and it verifies assigned **access rights** (the permissions needed to use those items) to control whether the objects are made available to a user. Whether users are assigned those access rights depends on whether the users actually need specific objects, such as files or printers, to do their jobs. The access decision, therefore, is made by IT managers before granting or denying someone the ability to work with, or access, those networked resources.

NDS, through its Directory database, contains information about the location, characteristics, and authorized users for every resource on a NetWare network. NDS access rights determine who can use what on your network from the very point of initial access, as shown in the illustration.

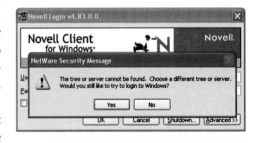

• NetWare controls access to your network from your initial login attempt.

Step-by-Step 6.01

Creating a NetWare Administrator Desktop Shortcut

Although your Novell network can be controlled from the server's console, much of the administration you will perform will be accomplished using Novell's NetWare Administrator from your workstation. It is handy to create an NWAdmin (as it is called) shortcut right on your workstation's desktop. In this exercise, you will locate the appropriate NetWare Administration application (nwadmn32) inside your NetWare 6 server, and you will create a shortcut icon on your workstation desktop that will facilitate easy access to this function.

To complete this exercise, you will need the following items:

- Operational NetWare 6 server
- Networked Windows XP Professional workstation with Novell Client installed

Step 1

As an administrative user, log in to your Windows XP Professional computer and your NetWare 6 server from your workstation.

Step 2

Right-click the NetWare Services icon in your taskbar's notification area, select Browse To, and then select My Computer.

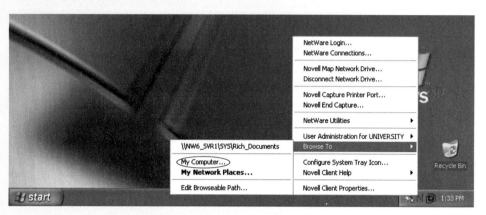

Step 3

Right-click the Public (Z:) drive and select Search.

Note: If the default selection for the Public drive (Z:), the location where Novell stores items for general use when logging in to the network, has been changed, you should request assistance from your instructor to help locate the Public drive on your NetWare 6 server.

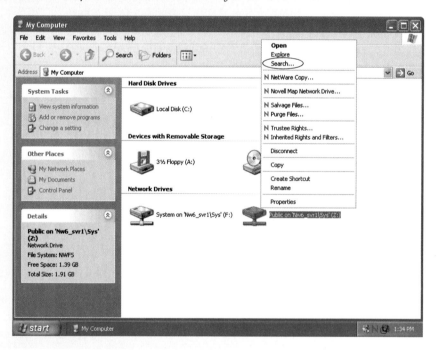

Step 4

In the All or Part of the File Name text box, type **nwadmn32**, and click the Search button to initiate the search.

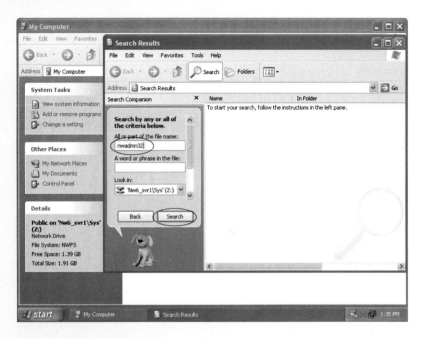

Step 5

Right-click the nwadmn32 icon in the right panel of your Search Results window, select Send To, and select Desktop (Create Shortcut).

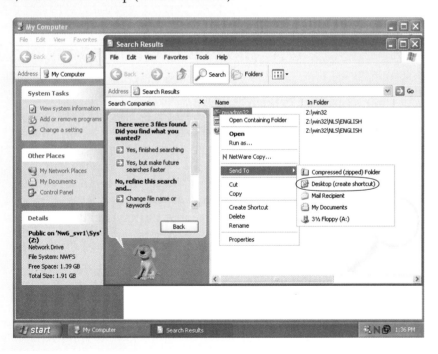

Close all open windows and confirm that you created a new icon named "Shortcut to nwadmn32" on your desktop, as shown here.

Novell Directory Services Structure

One of the most important services provided by NetWare through NDS is the ability to create a unified network with a single point for accessing and managing access to networked objects. For NDS to do this, every resource on the network must have a unique name. Users don't need to know where the resource is located on the network. Simply providing NDS with the resource's unique identifier is enough for it to locate any object.

Like the TEACH organizational chart from Chapter 1, the NDS structure resembles an inverted tree. In an organizational chart, the root of the upside-down tree is at the top, and the divisions within the tree structure usually represent its geographically (or sometimes functionally) separated company operations. As you descend through the typical organizational chart, the company's operational divisions, associated organizations, and departments fan out in a tree-like fashion. At the bottom of the upside-down tree is the lowest-level employee.

Novell Directory Services is also structured like an inverted tree with its [Root] object at the top. As you descend through a company's network in NDS, the tree-like structure of the Directory resembles that of a company's organizational chart.

Remember to use the square brackets when referring to the [Root] object in NDS. Their use is required to ensure that the proper NetWare component is being discussed. Without the brackets, the term *root* would be interpreted as the root directory, or the first directory on the hard disk drive, just like on Microsoft systems. There is definitely a difference between these two uses of the word *root* so you should be very careful.

NDS is extremely efficient because it can keep track of the many **objects** (network resources) it manages by subdividing the information that describes the objects into smaller pieces of data. The information NDS maintains on each resource or service it provides on the network is separated into **properties** and **values**. Properties are descriptive catagories, similar to the name you would give to a column where you would store object names or locations. NDS uses properties to describe all similar objects. Values are the individual pieces of information you store in each catagory for a particular object. Values are like the specific name you give to the object or the location you store to help find it. Because it can quickly process such information about the objects on your network, NDS easily facilitates client requests for the services of those objects. NDS locates network resources, validates client rights to those resources, and provides connections between those clients and the resources they need. These actions, performed by NDS, are some of the most important services Novell NetWare provides on a network.

Objects

The resources and services NDS makes available on the network are described by the pieces of information contained in the Directory about specific NDS objects. The NDS object descriptions resemble records used inside a typical database. The NetWare servers on the same network share the database of information they maintain about their own objects. This database includes information about users, the groups to which those users belong, workstations and servers, and all peripheral resources the users share (such as printers) that are connected to their network. This database of information is then combined with the information from all the other servers and forms the Directory.

Effective use of this shared information allows network managers to distribute administrative or security responsibilities for networked resources among themselves. For example, while the network will function the same way in any case, the decision can be made to assign all network security responsibility to a single administrator or to divide that responsibility among several administrators. The attributes assigned to individual user objects control the user's access to networked resources, so management-level users can have administrative attributes set that allow them to perform specific tasks on groups of objects. Such security decisions can be based upon on how much control (or how much distributed security) the company desires. Dispersing object administration is possible because objects, like users, are created only once, but all servers share the information about those objects.

Object Types   There are only three NDS object types, or classes of objects. Each NDS object can be classified as a [Root] object, a container object, or a leaf object, and each of these classes helps organize the objects in your NDS tree into logical groupings. One of the benefits of grouping objects is that you can create one login procedure and assign it to be used by large numbers of objects instead of creating and assigning a different one for each individual object.

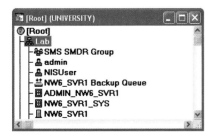

The [Root] is this NetWare network's placeholder, the Lab is an Organization container, and the other objects displayed here, including the NW6_SVR1 server, admin user, and NW6_SVR1_SYS volume, are all leaf objects.

[Root] Object The first object type, the [Root] object, is the highest object in the network's organization. An NDS Directory can have only one [Root] object and it can only be created during the original network software installation. The [Root] cannot be moved, renamed, or deleted, and if you right-click the [Root] to add a new object you will notice that the [Root] has no properties. In the menu provided you will see that the Details selection will be grayed out. Additionally, the [Root] object can have **trustees** (NDS objects with permission to perform specific actions on other objects) and can have **rights** (permission to perform actions) on other objects. Often, the [Root] and the tree name are the same, but this can lead to naming confusion, because the tree name can be changed later but the [Root] name cannot. The NDS [Root] object is similar to the root directory in DOS.

• Objects that make up the University tree

However, unlike the other two object types you will learn about (container and leaf objects), the [Root] object is a special object that marks the beginning of the network. Because the [Root] object is primarily just a placeholder, it does not contain the same information that is associated with most other NDS objects.

Beneath the [Root], a strict structure determines the network's tree-like organization. For instance, the [Root] object may not contain any object information but it must hold one or more of any of the following: Country objects, Alias objects (rarely used), or Organization objects, as shown here.

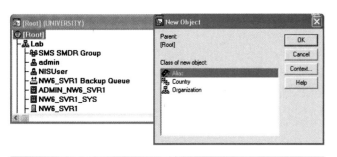

• Very few objects can be added to the [Root] object.

Container Objects Since NDS treats all networked resources (or services) as individual objects, keeping track of everything can quickly become an unruly management task. To assist you in organizing your Directory, NDS provides special storage locations, called *container objects*, in which other objects can be placed for administrative purposes. Just as you can organize a filing cabinet by storing documents inside folders, and grouping folders inside other folders, you organize the Directory by placing individual objects within these special container objects. The containers help group the resource objects (or other container objects) for access or for assigning rights.

A container object is referred to as a parent object if it contains other objects. A child object is one contained in a parent object. If you are familiar with Microsoft DOS, the use of NDS container objects is

Try This!

[Root] as a Placeholder

Confirm that the [Root] object is a placeholder. Try this:

1. Double-click the "Shortcut to nwadmn32" icon you created on your desktop.

2. If NetWare Administrator does not open in [Root], press the BACKSPACE key to go up one level at a time in your Directory's hierarchy. Depending on where your administrator user was created, you may have to press the BACKSPACE key more than once to arrive at the [Root] object.

3. Right-click the [Root] object.

4. Verify that the "Details" selection is grayed out, which means that it is not available.

5. Close your NetWare Administrator window.

similar to the DOS system of directories, where files are stored in a directory, which can then be stored inside another higher-level directory.

There are three special container objects that have specific uses:

- Country object
- Organization object
- Organizational Unit object

Country (C) Objects Some of the larger company structures may include use of the optional Country objects as dividing points under the [Root] object, especially when a company organizes itself by geographical location. Novell created Country container objects just to obtain higher industry-standard ratings (the X.500 directory specification certification requires their use), and Novell does not even recommend their use. In its documentation, Novell states, "… using the Country object might add an unnecessary level of complexity." If Country container objects are used, they will help organize your network's NDS tree by country. They can hold only a valid two-character country abbreviation and can exist only directly below the [Root] object.

Organization (O) Objects Another example of the strict structure requirements inside NDS is that each Directory tree must have at least one Organization (O) container object. Typically, this requirement is met by companies using an Organization object as the first object below the [Root] rather than a Country object. Unless a Country container (or locality container) is used, the Organization container object must be directly below the [Root] object.

Although it can hold additional container objects (Organizational Unit objects), the Organization container is the first level of container that can contain leaf objects (besides an Alias object representing an organization). Organization container objects usually designate companies, divisions of companies, and organizations with subordinate departments, or the departments themselves, depending on the desired NDS structure. Organization container objects cannot contain additional Organization container objects. The objects that can be contained in an Organization object are shown here.

In DOS, a major application's primary folder in either the root directory or the Windows Program Files folder, such as the MS Office folder, would be similar to an Organization container object. It is a major division of items, which helps organize and categorize all other items below it.

Organizational Unit (OU) Objects The use of the Organizational Unit (OU) container object is also optional, but it is the most commonly used container object. OUs help organize the lower levels of an organization. They can be used as lower-level containers themselves, or they can contain NDS objects directly. They are frequently used to designate business units within a company, departments within a larger entity, or separate projects within a department. When used, an OU must be placed directly below an Organization container object or another Organizational Unit container object.

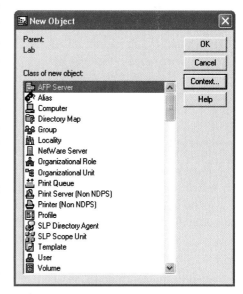

- New objects that can be added to an Organization container

Leaf Objects   With the Directory being similar to an inverted tree, the network's lowest-level resources and services themselves are referred to as **leaf objects**. As on a tree, a leaf in NDS is the final division and cannot contain any offshoot branches or include any other objects. A leaf object represents an individual resource or service that you make available on your network. You can find leaf objects in container objects. Leaf objects are similar to actual documents stored in a DOS directory.

Properties

NDS groups information stored about objects using categories, or properties. Properties are very similar to database fields. Think about searching for a student in a school as an example of using object properties. When a principal tries to find a specific student, she decides which properties will fully describe just that one student she is trying to locate. If those properties include the student's last name, his scheduled location during the period in question, and his class ranking, there may be multiple students fitting the description.

The more properties the principal adds when trying to narrow the choice of students, the more likely she will succeed in finding him. Successful searches can be ensured if the principal can identify a unique property that no other student could have, such as a social security number.

This example illustrates that some properties are more important than others. When logging on to a network, for example, the user name, **context** (location in the tree), and password properties are all vital pieces of information. The user's job title is not. Similarly, when looking for the student, his class ranking was not as important as his social security number.

Taken together as a set, the different properties associated with an object determine the **class** of that object. For instance, the properties of a user object and the values in those properties are different from the properties and values associated with a printer. They both may have a name and a unique network node number, but it is doubtful that the printer will have a telephone number or mother's last name for security reasons. NDS allows you to determine which properties each object should possess.

Values

Like the data in a database, the pieces of information within the property fields that describe an object make up the property, or values, of the object. For example, "Jones, room 105, junior" are the values the principal had in mind when specifying the "properties" she wanted searched when she was looking for a specific student. However, because names like Jones are common, there could be two of them in room 105. Worse, both of them could also be juniors. The principal would have increased her chances of finding the student if she had added more properties and their applicable values to her description.

Some properties can require that values be entered for all objects. For example, if the principal wants to find her students, she should require students to furnish their social security numbers before allowing them to enter the school, or she could issue them unique student numbers. In NDS, a last name is mandatory when creating a new user. Other properties may have optional multiple values. For example, when you enter a telephone number on different kinds of paperwork, you may write your cellular phone number, pager number, home phone number, parent's work number, guardian's phone number, nearest relative's phone number, or some other telephone number in that property's field. On the other hand, you could leave it blank.

Object Naming

If all objects on a network were stored in just one container and tracked on a single list within that container, finding a specific object would be a relatively simple, though time-consuming, task. But networks are no longer designed that way. For efficiency and ease of administration, network directories consist of multiple containers for various combinations of objects, based upon their function, geographic location, or other description of their use. It is no longer efficient for a server to search its entire database when seeking a particular object.

It is important to remember that NDS narrows the required search by relying on its own structure and avoids searching its entire database when locating resources or services. If users want access to something on the network, they simply provide NDS with a request that includes the correct object name for the item. When NDS receives the request, the server controlling that object checks its own copy of the Directory to determine whether the user object is valid, then it locates the requested object and verifies that the user has the **permission** (rights) to do what they are asking to do with that object. NDS inspects the property values of both the requested object and the user before providing or denying connection to the requested object. The key to the whole process is the object's name.

Object Name

Novell Directory Services keeps a name for every object in the Directory tree. Each object in the Directory has its own unique object name (the name value stored in its name property) that specifies its location in the Directory. You can access any object in the Directory simply by knowing its name. When properly formatted, the object name allows only one path to the named object from any other properly named resource on the network. If NDS knows a user's name and that of a networked resource, it can easily provide the user with access to the specific resource. Without those names, access cannot be provided. Precision naming is the key.

Common Name   Naming should be nothing new to you. We each have a name that we use to differentiate ourselves from others in various social situations. For example, when you are working with a small group of people you know well, you can usually just use each person's first name, called their given name, without confusion. However, in larger groups or situations where you need to know which family a group member belongs to, you have to add another name to more specifically identify each person. In this situation, adding the group member's last name, or surname, will help identify each individual.

Although this method of naming people is not a perfect system, it will help you understand the NDS naming scheme. In NDS, objects are also given a single name (like your user name) that doesn't give any reference to its position in your network's hierarchy. That single name is called an object's **common name** (CN). In NDS, the letters CN are called an attribute type abbreviation, depicted as the leaf name, and shown next to the leaf icon of an NDS object in the Directory.

For example, if a person's name is Herb Licon and his user name is HERBL, then an appropriate common name for Herb's user object would be HERBL. The designation CN=HERBL, as you will later learn, is also an appropriate method for specifying his user object's common name (using typeful notation).

However, recall the Daryl brothers of Chapter 3 and the problem of using first names in large group situations. Sometimes the common name is not enough to uniquely identify an object—two people can have the same first name. In a large group, simply adding last names to specify the family (like using an NDS container) will usually clear up any confusion encountered with identifying specific individuals. In NDS, you can also have two objects, such as users, with the same common name.

Unlike the situation with the Daryl brothers, however, those two identically named objects cannot be located in the same NDS container. In the previous example, if Herb Licon worked with Herb Little in the same office, the resulting HERBL user name could not be used for both Herbs—the naming convention you use would have to include another distinguishing identifier (such as a number or a letter). However, if the two Herbs worked in two different sections of the organization so that their user information would be stored in different portions of the Directory, the user names could both be HERBL. Therefore, in some cases you need to know the location of an object as well as its common name to uniquely identify it in NDS. This is done using the object's context.

Context   Just as adding your last name to your first name identifies you more specifically, an object's exact location in the NDS tree is specified by its context. The difference is that the context includes all the higher-level container information leading to the user name, and you end up with information resembling a genealogy chart that, in human terms, would trace the person's ancestors back to the family's root. Because you can designate an NDS object's location by fully describing the container in which the object resides, the context can also be considered the name of the parent container of the object. Therefore, when describing an object in the Directory, its context is a list of all the container objects leading from that object to the [Root] object.

Cross Check

TEACH Organizational Chart

The organizational chart you used for the TEACH organization in Chapter 1 used a naming convention to create user names for company employees. The employee's given name was followed by the first letter of the person's surname (resulting in user names like RichardM). Use that naming convention when answering the following questions.

1. Does the user name previously created for Herb Licon comply with the naming convention used in the TEACH organization?

2. Describe three problems that may be encountered when implementing the naming convention used in the TEACH organization.

(This is similar to the directory PATH statement in DOS.) While NDS allows multiple objects to have the same common name, it never allows them to occur in the same location, or in the same context.

NDS takes the idea of context a little bit further and tracks the location where an object is currently working, as in the case of a user who logs in to another server or through a different container object. (This is similar to using the change directory (CD) statement when you are working in DOS, and then typing DIR to list that directory's contents.) This location-based context is referred to as the user object's current context and is commonly called the **name context**. Users can locate (or use) an object in their current context by simply typing that object's common name. The current context is the default container (the first place) in which NDS looks for a resource if its full context is not specified, so a user's current location in the NDS tree affects the amount of detail required when seeking access to a resource. If everything a user needs is in the current context, then only common names are required. If not, additional context information is required for proper resource access.

Distinguished Name

When you refer to an object using only its common name, NDS uses your current context as its current context. If the object is elsewhere in the tree, you must provide more information about its actual context. One way of doing so is to provide the exact full context to identify the object. This full context is referred to as an object's **distinguished name** (or was called a *fully distinguished name* in previous versions of the software). A distinguished name starts with the object in question and identifies each of the container objects in the path to that object.

Let's look at an example. Suppose you had created your tree with a UNIVERSITY Organization container, a LAB Organizational Unit container, and you had used the user name convention of first name last initial). If HERBL were in your class under those circumstances, his distinguished name would be .HERBL.LAB.UNIVERSITY because that shows all the containers leading to his user object. Since NDS does not allow two objects to have the same distinguished name, this distinguished name completely identifies the user HERBL and ensures that NDS will not find two of the same users in the same location at the same time.

Note the use of the leading period in the previous distinguished name. A distinguished name always begins with a period. The format also requires periods to be used between each object's name, and for each successive container object going up the NDS tree to be listed to the right of the lower-level object it contains. Trailing periods (periods at the end of the name) are used in relative distinguished names but are not allowed in distinguished names. Although this distinguished name format is similar to the backslash used in DOS, the flow from the smaller to the larger object is the opposite of that used when locating DOS files.

Relative Distinguished Name   As you already learned in this chapter, NDS keeps track of an object's current location in the Directory, and NDS can use that information to help locate the resource a user seeks. An NDS **relative distinguished name** can be used to determine the location of an object relative to your current context. This is in contrast to identifying object locations relative to the [Root] object, as distinguished names do. As you just learned, distinguished names start with a period, so any name that starts without a period is considered to be a relative distinguished name.

Relative distinguished names list the path of all the objects leading from the object you seek to your current context. By default, then, common names are relative distinguished names. If the object is not in your current context, you can adjust the relative distinguished name by using a trailing period to indicate that you wish to move up one level in the Directory tree. For each trailing period that is added to a relative distinguished name, one object is removed from the left side of an object's current context. So, for example, if HERBL, located in the LAB Organizational Unit container mentioned earlier wants to use PRINTER1 in the UNIVERSITY Organization container, he would enter PRINTER1.UNIVERSITY. as its relative distinguished name. This feature is similar to the CD feature DOS uses when navigating its directory structure.

Typeful Names

As you saw briefly earlier, you can use the notation CN= with common names to create typeful names like this: CN=HERBL. You simply add the attribute type abbreviation with an equal sign to the common name. When you use typeful names, it helps NDS because you specify an object's location rather than requiring NDS to determine it for you, which means the access is faster. Typeful names tell NDS which of the different container types and leaf objects are being used, and they can be used in both distinguished and relative distinguished names.

Typeful names are optional, but they assist NDS in locating objects, and NDS works with typeful distinguished names whether you provide them or it has to calculate them itself. If you don't provide them, NDS will determine your current location and then append the rest of your typeful distinguished name so it can know precisely where you are and where the objects are that you are intending to access.

Returning to our earlier example, Herb Licon's typeful name would be the following more descriptive name: .CN=HERBL.OU=LAB.O=UNIVERSITY. Given that typeful name, NDS would not have to append any information.

Typeless Name   Using the typeful name for HERBL requires extra keystrokes that users don't always like to type in. Typeless names provide users the option of leaving those attribute type abbreviations off their entries, and this is the typical naming method employed by users. Typeless names do include the names of all the objects leading to the desired object, and they are in the proper sequence. They just don't include any of the object's attribute types.

When users employ typeless names, they take advantage of NDS's ability to calculate the missing attributes and add them to the name. It may take NDS a bit longer to make those calculations, but saving users the time it takes to key in those extra entries is sometimes more important. In rare instances, the utility used for this calculation makes a mistake, and the objects fail to communicate, but most users are willing to take that chance.

Installing Novell ConsoleOne

Another utility, similar to NetWare Administrator, that also gives you the ability to work from your workstation and conduct much of the Novell network's administration is Novell's ConsoleOne. Once you have installed ConsoleOne, it is handy to create a shortcut icon on your workstation's desktop for this application just like you did for NWAdmin. In this exercise, you will install Novell's ConsoleOne and then create a shortcut icon on your workstation desktop.

To complete this exercise, you will need the following items:

- Operational Novell NetWare 6 server

- Networked Windows XP Professional workstation with Novell Client installed

- ConsoleOne installation CD

| Step 1 | Log in to your Windows XP Professional computer and your NetWare 6 server from your workstation as an administrative user. |

| Step 2 | Insert the ConsoleOne CD into your CD drive, click the Start button and select My Computer, double-click the CD drive containing the ConsoleOne CD, and double-click the c1_nw_win.exe file to open the WinZip Self-Extractor. |  |

| Step 3 | Click the Setup button to extract the ConsoleOne files, and after reading the warning about closing all programs, click the ConsoleOne Installation window's Next button to begin the actual installation. | 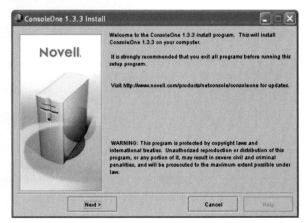 |

Step 4

Read the license agreement and click the Accept button (if you do agree to it). Click Next to accept the default installation path, and click Next again to install the default components.

Step 5

Select any additional languages to install and click Next. Read the JREPORT licensing agreement and accept it by clicking Next. Then click the Finish button to analyze the objects you selected and initiate the installation.

Step 6

Monitor the installation in the Progress dialog box, and click the Installation Complete dialog box's Close button when it finishes. Close the ConsoleOne window to return to your workstation's desktop. Notice that a shortcut icon, ConsoleOne, has been added to your desktop.

Step 7

In the Installation Complete dialog box, note whether the installation was successful. Click the Close button and then close the ConsoleOne window to return to your workstation's desktop.

Step 8

Ensure that ConsoleOne works properly by double-clicking the ConsoleOne shortcut icon. Watch the different screens during the application's loading process, and notice the Novell ConsoleOne window that appears in the background of the installation progress windows.

Tip: *If your desktop icon does not change from the generic icon to the ConsoleOne icon, you may have to right-click it and choose the correct icon before it will display properly.*

Step 9	Continue monitoring the loading screens and notice that the Novell ConsoleOne window includes an "Expanding NDS" box that begins with My World and includes an NDS icon.	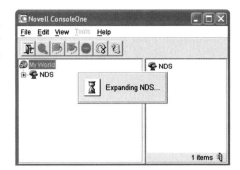

Step 10	After the Novell ConsoleOne window finishes its loading process confirm that it properly displays your UNIVERSITY tree.	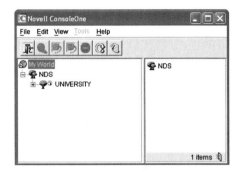

Step 11	In the left panel, click the plus sign (+) located to the left of your UNIVERSITY tree icon to display your Lab Organization container's icon. *Note: Notice that the information in the right panel of the Novell ConsoleOne window does not change as you expand the items in the left panel using the plus signs (or when you contract them using the minus signs).*	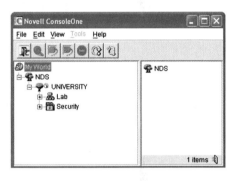

Step 12	In the left panel, double-click the plus sign (+) located to the left of your Lab Organization container icon to display the contents of your Lab Organization container in both the left and right panels, as shown here. *Note: Notice that the information in the right panel of the Novell ConsoleOne screen includes all icons in a container, whereas the left panel displays only specific container objects. If you need access to all leaf objects in a particular container, you must double-click on the container object in the left panel to display the contents in the right panel.*	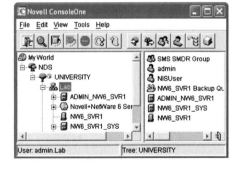

Step 13	Close the Novell ConsoleOne window to return to your desktop.

■ Describing Windows 2000 Active Directory (AD)

Lauren has decided that Ricky should also offer his SinkRSwim Pools users access to the features of the Windows 2000 Server installed on their network. She has informed Ricky that users are no longer to be allowed to log in to local computers and has directed him to convert everyone in the SinkRSwim Pools operation to domain users. She knows that Ricky has his hands full learning and experimenting with NDS, so she decides to help him by learning and implementing Active Directory herself. Since Ricky has had very good success learning and teaching NDS by first learning its structure, she decides to start by learning how Active Directory is structured.

With the release of Windows 2000, Microsoft added a directory services component that is somewhat comparable to Novell's NDS. That component, called Active Directory (AD), allows you to access or manage networks from a single logon. Like Novell's NDS, Microsoft's Active Directory in Windows 2000 includes the information normally expected in a directory (such as where things are), but AD also manages all the services that are involved in users gaining access to that information. You will later configure your server to include Active Directory as a networked service.

Active Directory Structure

When Active Directory is implemented, it keeps track of and provides access to all the resources on the network by using a database. This is just like Novell's NDS, and since the outcomes from both systems are basically the same—networked access to resources—it only makes sense that much of the structure for the AD component is similar to NDS's. However, since the two companies are also competitors, it also makes sense that there will be several differences too. In the sections that follow, you will learn some of the similarities and differences between the two database implementations.

Active Directory Schema

Like NDS, Active Directory is extremely efficient at tracking network resources and is theoretically capable of dealing with tens of millions of objects. And like NDS, AD also locates network resource objects by their distinct name and potential attributes. However, the term Microsoft uses for the whole set of database information (called *properties* and *values* in NDS) is the **schema**.

The Microsoft schema amounts to a list of what objects can be contained in the Active Directory and what information can be stored about each object. The schema, then, is itself another object, and as such it has attributes and can be administered like any other object on the network.

Schema Definition Objects   The network's overall schema, also called the **metadata**, is further broken into schema class objects and schema attribute objects, which are similar to what NDS calls a *leaf* and its *properties*, respectively. By default, your network includes a schema class object called User, and that object has several schema attributes, such as user logon name, first name, last name, and telephone number, to name but a few.

Microsoft has broken down the database into smaller units using the schema like Novell did with NDS in order to speed up data access and retrieval, with the ultimate goal of providing more efficient access to network resources. So, for example, a specific user with the name Sid Waqif would simply be one item listed in the schema class called Users. Sid's user object itself, sidw, would have the same types of attributes as all other user objects on the network, but Sid's would include the specific values that make his user object unique.

Containers

Since Active Directory treats networked resources (and services) as individual objects just as NDS does, the job of effectively managing these objects can also be a huge task on a Microsoft network. Active Directory is organized by by using container objects, in which other objects are placed for administrative purposes. These containers also help group network resource objects (or other container objects) in a hierarchical parent/child relationship that simplifies access and rights assignments.

Starting with an Organizational Unit (OU) container at the bottom, similar to the one Novell uses in NDS, Microsoft's next larger group is the domain. After that, it uses the tree, like NDS. Finally, Microsoft's largest container object is an extension to its own tree theme, called a forest.

The beginning of AD is actually a single server on which you have installed AD. This server is the first server in the root domain of the first (root) tree in the forest. In some cases, like your classroom configuration, it is all there—domain, tree, forest—represented in one computer

Forest Objects   Microsoft uses the term **forest** to describe the result of joining multiple domain trees together. Trees would join a forest to communicate or share networked resources with other related trees, but each tree in a forest remains an independent entity and is completely self-administered using its own naming convention. When the trees join the forest, a relationship is formed, and each tree in the forest employs the same schema where they all share information about their networked resources by using a **global catalog**.

A forest can thus be seen as the boundary of AD. All domain controllers within a forest share the same schema, configuration, and global catalog, but only domain controllers within the same domain replicate all domain objects and their attributes. A forest can contain a single domain and a single tree. If you add a domain, you choose to add it to the first tree of the forest or have it be the root domain in a new tree in the forest. Alternatively, you can create an additional forest!

Tree Objects   Microsoft uses the term *tree* to indicate a container object that contains multiple domains. Each domain is a distinct unit, but it joins the tree to communicate and share its networked resources with other domains. Each domain in a tree is itself an independent entity and can be completely self-administered using its own naming convention.

Domain Objects   The **domain** is the most important container object in Microsoft's hierarchical directory services structure because all Active Directory objects must be part of a domain. Each domain is capable of storing information about nearly ten million objects and of controlling the security and access to each of those objects separate from all other domains on the network. Microsoft indicates that the practical limit in each domain is closer to one million objects, but since few organizations would form a single domain with even that many objects, the theoretical upper limit is not really much of a constraint.

A domain begins by being controlled by a single server, called a domain controller. Although a domain controller is a single entity, do not get the impression that a domain is in any way physically confined. Domains can indeed be limited so that they include only physically contiguous computers (those close to each other). However, and just as likely, a domain can span a wide physical or geographical area when it is based on the logical relationships within a company. When this is the case, domains can and should have more than one server for redundancy, fault tolerance, availability, and performance. A company's operations, even though they may be spread across the country in various locations, can still be focused on only one mission, and thus can be logically represented by a single domain.

Organizational Unit (OU) Objects   Inside a Microsoft domain, the container object that helps structure the network to imitate the actual company's internal organization is the Organizational Unit (OU) container. As in NDS, Microsoft uses the OU to compartmentalize objects so they can be effectively administered and access to networked resources can better be controlled. In fact, much of the administrative organization of AD must be done with OUs and by creating appropriate user groups within OUs and by nesting OUs within one another. Inside a domain, OUs are where the real work of administering AD lies.

Step-by-Step 6.03

Installing Active Directory

The single login capability that is the real power of Windows 2000 is not available until Active Directory is installed on your server. Once you install your server and start it for the first time, the Configure Your Server window appears, and one of the options will install Active Directory. You could have elected, at that time, to install Active Directory, and the following information would apply. However, since you did not install Active Directory when you created your server, you will do so now. In this exercise, you will install Microsoft's Active Directory on your existing Windows 2000 Server.

To complete this exercise, you will need the following items:

- Operational Windows 2000 Server running DNS and with a minimum of 200MB of free disk space on the boot partition

- Networked Windows XP Professional workstation with Novell Client installed

- Windows 2000 Server installation CD

- The domain name provided by your instructor

- The Active Directory Restore password provided by your instructor

Step 1

Log in to your Windows 2000 Server as your Administrator user. In the Configure Your Server window, select the This Is the Only Server in My Network option, and click Next to restart your computer.

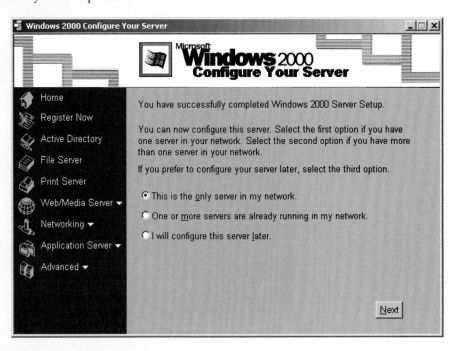

Step 2

Log back into your Windows 2000 Server and, in the Configure Your Server window click the Active Directory link in the dark blue panel at the left. This will open the Active Directory window.

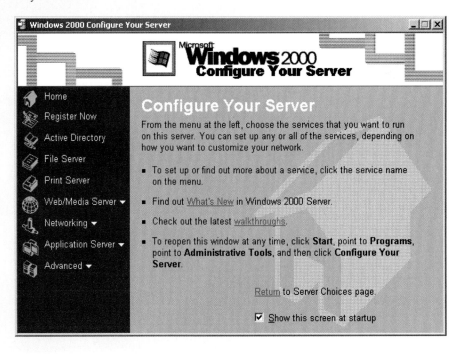

Step 3

In the Active Directory window, scroll down to the Start the Active Directory wizard link and click it.

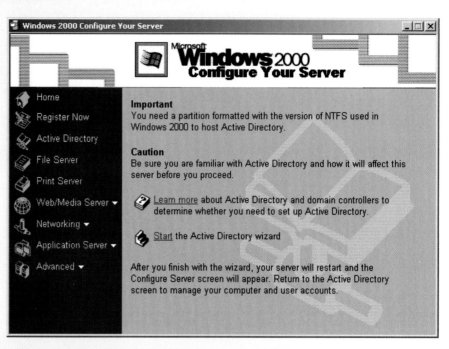

Step 4

Click Next in the Welcome to the Active Directory Installation Wizard window. In the Domain Controller Type window, select the Domain Controller for a New Domain option and click Next. In the Create Tree or Child Domain window, select the Create a New Domain Tree option and click Next. In the Create or Join Forest window, select the Create a New Forest of Domain Trees option and click Next.

Step 5

In the New Domain Name window, enter **School.net** (or the name provided by your instructor) as your new DNS name and click Next.

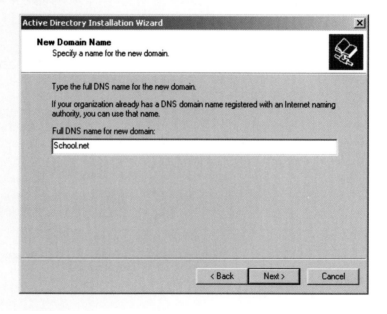

Step 6

Click Next to accept the suggested domain NetBIOS name. Click Next again to accept the database and log locations, and again to accept the folder location for the shared system volume. Click OK to confirm the need to configure a new DNS server.

Step 7

In the Configure DNS window, select the Yes, Install and Configure DNS on the Computer option and click Next. In the Permissions window, select the Permissions Compatible with Pre-Windows 2000 Servers option and click Next. Enter and confirm your Directory Services Restore Mode password, and then click Next.

Step 8

In the Summary window, review your selections and click Next. Click the Finish button to complete the Active Directory installation, and then click the Restart Now button to restart your server.

■ Expanding Your Network's Directories

The SinkRSwim Pools network is built around two servers that Lauren and Ricky have installed—the NetWare 6 server and the Windows 2000 Server. Other than adding the software for Novell Client and installing several Windows XP Professional computers as workstations around the company, neither Lauren nor Ricky has given much thought to how they were going to add the company's users to the network. Lauren has already decided to use the NetWare 6 server for logins, but nobody has mentioned where their users should be located or what specific network resources they need to perform their jobs effectively. Lauren, Ricky, and the company owner feel it is now time to expand the SinkRSwim Pools network and properly add the company's users so those users can start working with networked resources instead of relying on either Lauren or Ricky.

Although we'd all like to think that we are perfect, you will most likely have to add objects to your network after it is created, no matter how carefully you plan things during its creation. In fact, you already have added components, because after you created multiple servers, you were then instructed to add new clients and workstations. Both of these actions increased the number of objects on your network. Because you performed these actions as the network administrator, you had no difficulty at all. You created the network, and you controlled all access and granted yourself permission to do whatever you needed to do to your network once it was created. Now it is time to add additional users and assign them appropriate rights to their network objects.

Deciding on Initial Expansion

The first thing you need to do is develop a plan for where your network's resources are to be stored and how they will ultimately be managed. Normally, especially in a large company, this process would be a major concern, and it should be initiated early in your network's development. Your classroom lab is not such a large undertaking, but you should still develop a plan. Keep in mind that although the actual purpose of your network is to work with course materials in your classroom, you should plan your lab's network around your job position in the TEACH organization.

You already know that all users will be working on Windows XP workstations, you have decided that everyone will be logging in through the NetWare 6 server, and you know that the training center has requested that its trainers have access to files on the NetWare 6 server. The trainers need storage on the NetWare 6 server in addition to the space they need for files they store on the Windows 2000 Server. This gives you a good plan of attack, and the first step is to gather the information about the users and groups you need to add to your network. You will begin adding the users to the same server that your TEACH users will be using when they log into the network—the NetWare 6 server.

Administering Your NetWare 6 Server

NDS provides a global database that gives network administrators centralized access to networked information, resources, and services, and allows them to manage it. NDS standardizes the methods of managing, viewing, and accessing these items. It also logically organizes the network resources independent of the physical network configuration and it allows dynamic mapping between an object and its actual physical resource.

NDS makes it easy to administer the network. Users and other NDS objects are managed using either NetWare Administrator or ConsoleOne. Both are user-friendly GUI programs. The NetWare Administrator executable file is located on the server but it can be run either there or from the workstation, and ConsoleOne also runs either from the server's console or right at your workstation. In a small network, the network administration functions can all be accomplished by a central administrator, but in larger companies where additional administration is required, the tasks might be divided among various levels. The NDS Directory provides administrators with manageable groupings of objects that make network design and organization a logical process while providing greater security for the networked resources.

In addition, because the Directory (or pieces of it) is stored on numerous servers around the network, fault tolerance (the network's ability to withstand a failed component) is increased, and the inevitable loss of an occasional server becomes much less critical. In the event that a server does fail, the Directory information needed to make the network function again is available on more than one server, and any server's copy can be used to restore the Directory onto repaired or replaced servers.

Creating NetWare Users

You will decide on your own plan for storing and using resources on your servers, but since those decisions will be based on your actual classroom lab's organization, everyone will need a user on the NetWare 6 server and they will all likely be added to a single container. Since there are relatively few students in a typical class, this single-container method will not hamper your network's speed. However, if your network were large, putting all users in a single container would be like creating a single telephone book—resulting in a flat file, which is how servers used to be configured.

Consider how long it takes to find someone in a large phone book when you are not sure of how to spell his or her name. When you don't know what city he or she lives in, it becomes even more difficult. However, imagine the trouble you'd have if you were not sure of the name, did not know the city, and couldn't even find the phone book. Without the single-logon concept, that would basically be what you would have to go through when looking for users. You would have to remember what server they belonged to, where the resources they owned were located, and what their password was for the first server, your requested resource, and any servers you had to pass through to get to the resource or the user.

Creating a list of users in a single-logon environment and organizing them into hierarchical containers makes everyone's job much easier. It is easier on the administrator when creating or maintaining the network. It is easier for the user to work with networked resources. And finally, it is easier on the network itself, which makes it run faster.

Since the introduction of NetWare 4.0, all NetWare servers on the same network combine to form a large pool of services and they share the information about the resources available from any location with all users. This pool of services creates the NDS tree with its system of containers and leaf objects. Networks are now

Try This!

Obtain ConsoleOne Information

Novell has a significant amount of information available on its web site that will help you make use of all ConsoleOne's capabilities. For example, to find out why you should use ConsoleOne rather than what Novell calls its "legacy" NetWare Administrator application (the nwadmn32 application you installed earlier), try this:

1. Double-click your desktop's ConsoleOne icon.

2. Select Help | Contents from the menus.

3. Click the ConsoleOne User Guide link in the bottom section of the ConsoleOne Help window to open Novell's online version of its ConsoleOne User Guide. You can download a copy of the online ConsoleOne User Guide as a PDF file for local use or to print out as a reference guide. Simply clicking on the PDF link next to the Guide's name lets you either open the PDF or designate a location to save the file.

4. Click the Getting Started link in the User Guide's table of contents.

5. Click the Why Use ConsoleOne? link.

6. Read the information provided, which explains the advantages of using ConsoleOne.

network-centered, in that they now focus on providing unified access to all networked resources, rather than just those on a single server, which was the case when networks were server-centered. A single password allows users to access the entire network, and their security authorizations follow them throughout the entire network.

Step-by-Step 6.04

Creating NDS Objects

You now need to add users to your network. Novell provides you with two different applications you can use—NWAdmin and ConsoleOne—although we have already explained the reasons for using the newer ConsoleOne to perform this function. In this exercise, you will create a Users Organizational Unit container on your NetWare 6 server and add multiple users to that folder.

To complete this exercise, you will need the following items:

- Operational NetWare 6 server
- Networked Windows XP Professional workstation with Novell Client and ConsoleOne installed

Step 1

As an administrative user, log in to your Windows XP Professional computer (and your NetWare 6 server) from your workstation, right-click your NetWare Services icon in your taskbar's notification area, select Browse To, and then select My Computer.

Step 2

Double-click the "Public on NW6_SVR1\SYS (Z:)" icon. Then, click the Create New Folder link in the left panel and type the new folder name **Users** (as shown here), and press ENTER. Close all windows to return to your desktop.

Step 3

Double-click the ConsoleOne icon on your desktop to start ConsoleOne, and maximize your ConsoleOne window. Click the plus sign (+) to expand the UNIVERSITY tree, right-click the Lab Organization container, and select New | Organizational Unit.

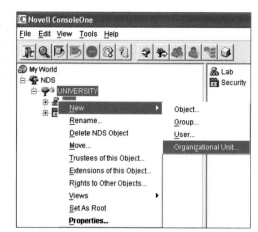

Step 4

In the New Organizational Unit dialog box, enter the container name **Students**, and click OK to create the container in the Lab container. Click the plus sign (+) to expand the Lab container.

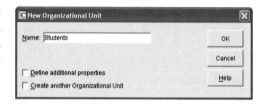

Step 5

Right-click the new Students Organizational Unit, and select New | Group. In the New Group dialog box, enter the group name **Managers**, and click OK.

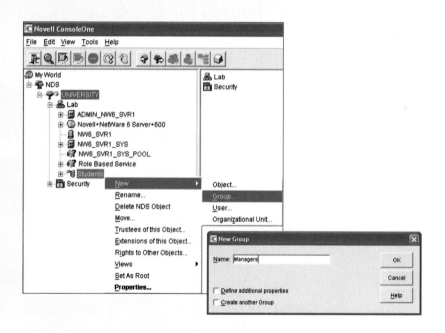

Step 6

Highlight the Students container, click the New User button, and click OK. In the New User dialog box, enter the name **MCepeda** (or an individual user name that you will create for yourself on the Windows XP Professional computer), type **Cepeda** as the surname, and click the Create Home Directory button. Click the Browse button to browse to the Users folder you created earlier in the Public folder, and click OK.

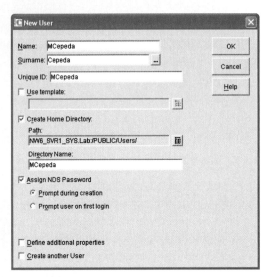

Step 7

Enter and confirm Marie's password, and click OK to create the new user. Right-click the new user object and select Properties, as shown here.

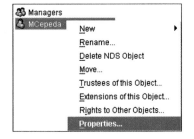

Step 8

Fill in the appropriate information on the General tab of the Properties of MCepeda dialog box, and click the Memberships tab.

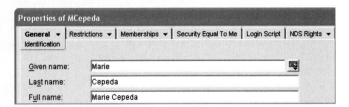

Step 9

Click the Add button, select the Managers group in the Select Objects dialog box (as shown), and click OK. Close the Properties of MCepeda dialog box, and then close ConsoleOne.

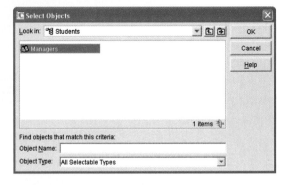

Joining a Domain

If you had trouble joining a domain when you installed Windows XP Professional, or for some other reason you have not already joined one, the next thing you need to do is add your Windows computers to your Windows 2000 School domain using an administrative account from the new network. After that, you can create the users and other objects on your network. Once you have done that, your users will have a single login networking capability and will be able to use your School domain and your University NDS tree.

Administering Your Windows 2000 Server

Microsoft, in its Active Directory, also provides network administrators with a global database for managing the networked information, resources, and services. Active Directory provides a different standardized method of managing, viewing, and accessing networked objects than you used with NetWare. Although it uses a schema that differs from Novell's NDS, AD also logically organizes networked resources independent of physical location. That is, physical location is not significant; a single domain can include computers and other resources that span several continents or can be completely contained in a single building.

Microsoft makes it easy to administer the network. Users and other networked objects are managed from the server's console or through remote administration capabilities. Both options use the familiar graphical Windows display. The server console runs its own copy of the Windows operating system and presents the user with a typical desktop that includes additional server features. Remote administration, which is not covered in this text, uses Terminal Services and any TCP/IP connection to facilitate administration from any client workstation. In small networks, the network administration functions are also typically performed by a single central administrator. In some companies with larger networks, administration duties can be divided among several administrators. In either case, a user sitting at a Windows 2000 or Windows XP computer can also install the Administrative tools

Try This!

The Microsoft Management Console (MMC)

Microsoft provides a tool that can be installed and used from Windows 2000 Professional or Windows XP Professional workstations as well as from your server, called the Microsoft Management Console (MMC). MMC hosts the various management functions. While this tool does not provide any management capabilities by itself, the MMC does consolidate preconfigured consoles as well as allow you to create and customize other consoles to fit your environment.

To access one of the preconfigured MMC consoles (which also works on your Windows XP Professional workstation), on your Windows 2000 Server try this:

1. Log in to your Windows 2000 Server as the administrative user.

2. Click the Start button, select Programs | Administrative Tools, and note the consoles displayed there. Your listing will include the default consoles used with the operating system and other consoles for custom features you installed during or after the system's original installation.

3. Select Active Directory Users and Computers. This Active Directory Users and Computers console will very likely be the one you use most frequently for your classroom activities.

4. Expand the Computers folder in the left panel and note which computers have already been added to your network. Close the Active Directory Users and Computers window to return to your desktop.

and, with the correct permissions, administer AD and the server through various consoles (such as Active directory Domains and Trusts, Active Directory Users and Computers, Active Directory Sites and Services).

A copy of Active Directory is sent (or replicated) to all domain controllers. This makes losing a server much less critical. In the event that a server does fail, the Active Directory information needed to make the network function again is available on more than one server, and any server's copy can be used to restore Active Directory onto repaired or replaced servers.

Creating Windows Users

In addition to the users you created on your NetWare 6 server, everyone in your class will also need a user on the Windows 2000 Server. Your network should not be slowed much by creating users for the relatively few students in your class. Having users in both networks will, however, provide you the opportunity of using a single login to access multiple server environments.

Step-by-Step 6.05

Creating AD Objects

Additional administrative features are available from the Windows 2000 Server that you will be using with your networked resources, so you now need to add users and computers to Active Directory to take advantage of those features. Although you can add workstations at the server console the same way you create users, they can also be created right from the workstation you are adding, itself. In this activity, you will add a computer to your Windows 2000 domain from its own desktop and then create

a domain user for yourself at the Windows 2000 Server console.

To complete this exercise, you will need the following items:

- Operational NetWare 6 server
- Operational Windows 2000 Server
- Networked Windows XP Professional workstation with Novell Client and ConsoleOne installed

---

Step 1

First, log in to a Windows XP Professional computer using the workstation's Administrator account. Click the Start button, right-click My Computer, select Properties, and click the Computer Name tab. Then click the Change button.

Step 2

In the Computer Name Changes dialog box, click the Domain option in the Member Of section, enter **School** in the Domain text entry box (or enter your domain name if it is different), and click OK.

Step 3

In the next Computer Name Changes dialog box, enter the name and password of the account you are using, which must have been allowed (or assigned the right) to join the domain, and click OK.

Step 4

Click OK to the "Welcome to the School domain" message in the next dialog box, and click OK to restart the computer so the changes can take effect.

Step 5

Click the Yes button to again acknowledge that the computer must be restarted for the changes to take effect and to confirm that you want to restart the computer now.

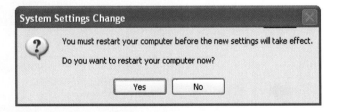

Step 6

Log in to your Windows 2000 domain controller as an administrative user, click the Start button, and select Administrative Tools | Active Directory Users and Computers.

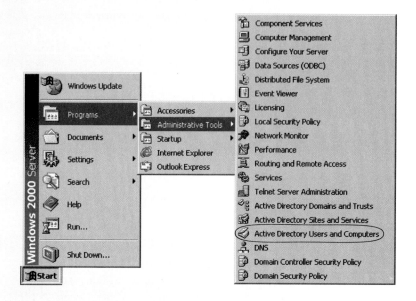

Step 7

In the left panel of the Active Directory Users and Computers window, click the Computers container and verify in the right panel that the computer you just added is listed (STUDENT01 in the example).

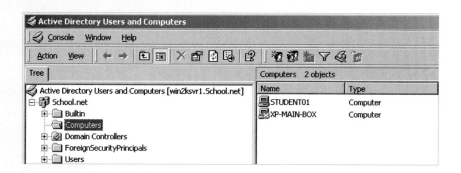

Step 8

In the left panel, click the Users container and verify in the right panel that the user you intend to add has not already been created.

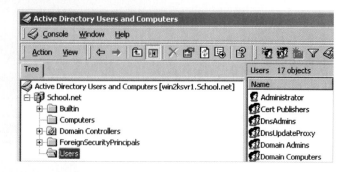

Step 9

Select Action | New | User, as shown here.

Step 10

In the New Object – User dialog box, enter Marie Cepeda's (or your own) user information, and click Next.

Note: Marie's user object was added earlier in the chapter to the NetWare server and is used here as an example. If you have already added your own user to the NetWare server, you could create an object on your Windows 2000 Server to match your own user instead of using Marie's information.

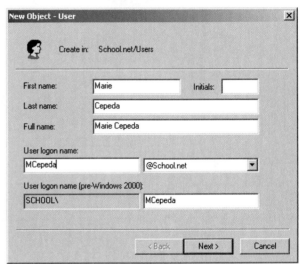

Step 11

In the next screen of the New Object – User dialog box, enter and confirm Marie's password, select the appropriate options concerning the user object's creation (Password Never Expires is selected as an example) and click Next.

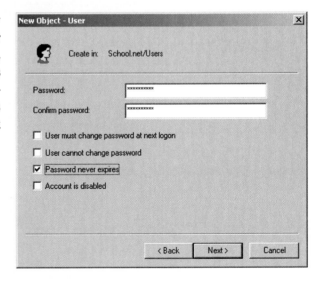

Step 12

In the next screen of the New Object – User dialog box, confirm the user's information, and click the Finish button to create Marie's Windows 2000 Server user object.

Double-click the new user object in the right panel of the Active Directory Users and Computers window to display the user Properties dialog box. Here you can update any user object values. Click OK when you are finished updating the user's information.

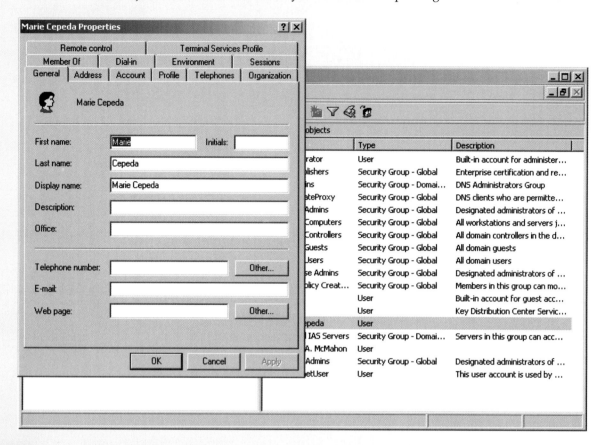

Close the Active Directory Users and Computers console to return to the server's desktop. Log in to the network from your Windows XP Professional computer using the new user object in both the NetWare section of your login and your Windows section as well.

Chapter 6 Review

■ Chapter Summary

After reading this chapter and completing the Step-by-Step tutorials and Try This! Exercises, you should understand the following facts about networking:

Use Novell Directory Services

- Novell Directory Services (NDS) is an integral database component of Novell's NetWare network operating system.

- NDS and ConsoleOne (or NWAdmin) help you manage your Novell network.

- Networked resource information is stored in NDS's database, which is called the Directory (capitalized to refer to the database component of NDS).

- NDS manages resources by allowing you to group similar objects together and assign attributes, and NDS then controls whether the resources are available to a user.

- NDS provides information about the location and characteristics of resources, and about authorized users.

- Your access rights are controlled by NDS right from your initial login.

- You can administer your network from the console or from the client using ConsoleOne or NWAdmin (nwadmn32).

- NetWare provides a single point for accessing and managing the network.

- NDS is structured like an inverted tree with its [Root] object at the top (brackets are required when referring to NetWare's [Root] object).

- NDS tracks objects by storing information in the form of properties and values.

- NDS servers share information about resources on their own portions of the network.

- In NDS there are three object types—[Root], container, and leaf objects.

- The [Root] object is a placeholder created during the initial installation, and it has no properties.

- Container objects are special storage locations for other objects, including other container objects.

- An object that contains other objects is referred to as a parent object.

- If used, a Country (C) container can only contain a two-letter country identifier and can only exist immediately below the [Root] object.

- A Directory tree must have at least one Organization (O) container, and it must be in either the Country container or immediately below the [Root] object.

- An Organizational Unit (OU) container is optional, but they are generally used to organize lower levels of the organization.

- The leaf objects are the lowest-level resources on a network, and they cannot contain any other objects.

- Properties help describe objects, and a set of properties determines the class of an object.

- The pieces of information within property fields that describe an object are called values.

- NDS narrows its search for an object by using a naming structure that results in each object in the Directory having its own totally distinct object name.

- An object's name without any reference to its position in the network is called its common name (CN).

- An object's context specifies its exact location in the NDS tree.

- A distinguished name starts with the object's common name and identifies each container object in a path to that object.

- Relative distinguished names locate objects based upon your current location in the NDS tree.

- Typeful names include attribute type abbreviations and an equal sign for each object in the path, whereas typeless names do not use the abbreviations.

Describe Windows 2000 Active Directory

- Microsoft added a directory services component (Active Directory) to its Windows 2000 operating system software, comparable to NDS.

- Active Directory keeps track of and provides access to all networked resources.

- Active Directory is a database similar to Novell's NDS.

- The properties and values for objects in the Active Directory database are combined and referred to as the schema.

- Schema class objects and schema attribute objects are similar to NDS leaf and properties, respectively.

- Microsoft's Active Directory breaks down the database into smaller units using the schema to speed up data access and retrieval.

- Active Directory is organized much like NDS, with Organizational Units and container objects.

- Microsoft uses the term forest when it joins multiple domain trees.

- A global catalog contains information shared by all trees in a forest.

- A tree contains multiple domains.

- A domain can contain multiple Organizational Units, and it is the most important container object in Microsoft's directory services structure.

Expand Your Network's Directories

- You should develop a plan describing where your network's resources will be stored and how they will be managed.

- You need to decide which NDS or AD server will be used for your primary login.

- NDS's standardized method for managing, viewing, and accessing objects makes it a good choice for your classroom network's login.

- NDS's Directory provides administrators with manageable groupings of objects that make network design and organization a logical process and offer greater security.

- In a small organization, all users can be kept in a single container, but in larger organizations they should be further divided.

- A single login environment with organized hierarchical containers makes administering and using the network easier.

- You can use NWAdmin or ConsoleOne to create NDS objects.

- Users created on a NetWare network start with limited access rights.

- Users created on a Microsoft network start with full access rights.

- You can join a domain from the workstation if you are logged in as a user with rights to join a network.

- Microsoft users can be managed from the Windows server console or by using remote administration capabilities.

- The Microsoft Management Console (MMC) is a tool used to host networking management functions.

■ Key Terms

access rights *(169)*	**domain** *(185)*	**permission** *(177)*
attributes *(169)*	**forest** *(185)*	**properties** *(173)*
class *(176)*	**global catalog** *(185)*	**relative distinguished name** *(179)*
common name *(178)*	**leaf objects** *(176)*	**rights** *(174)*
context *(176)*	**metadata** *(184)*	**schema** *(184)*
Directory *(169)*	**name context** *(179)*	**trustees** *(174)*
distinguished name *(179)*	**objects** *(173)*	**values** *(173)*

■ Key Term Quiz

Use the preceding vocabulary terms to complete the following sentences. Not all the terms will be used.

1. The integral database component of Novell's NetWare networking operating system is called the _____.

2. When grouping similar objects together hierarchically, such as users, groups, and servers, Novell's network operating system assigns descriptive pieces of information, called _____, to describe networked resources.

3. Novell's NetWare, before granting or denying someone the ability to work with networked resources, checks a user's _____, which are also called permissions.

4. In Novell's Directory, there are only three object types, each also called a(n) _____ of objects.

5. Novell [Root] _____ can only be created during the original NetWare software installation; they cannot be moved, renamed, or deleted, and they have no properties.

6. A Microsoft network's overall schema is also called the _____.

7. Microsoft uses the term *tree* to describe multiple instances of the _____, which is the most important container object in its hierarchical directory services structure.

8. When logging on to a network, the user name, _____, and password properties are vital pieces of information.

9. In NDS, the single name that does not give any reference to an object's position in the network is called the object's _____.

10. In NDS, the lowest-level resources and services are referred to as _____.

■ Multiple-Choice Quiz

1. Which of the following correctly identifies Novell's database that is used to store information about networked users, groups, and resources?

   a. NetWare's Directory Servers

   b. The Directory

   c. Novell Directory Servers

   d. The Metadata

2. Which of the following correctly identifies Novell's legacy application that can be used to control the network from your workstation?

   a. Client

   b. nwadmin32

   c. ConsoleOne

   d. NetWare Administrator

3. You can create an icon on your desktop to use Novell's legacy network administration application by searching which of the following?

   a. Public (Z:) drive

   b. System (F:) drive

   c. Your C: drive

   d. Novell Client

4. Every resource on a NetWare network must have which of the following?

   a. A container

   b. A leaf

   c. A unique name

   d. Its own [Root]

5. Which of the following is a Novell object class that can contain no additional objects?

   a. Container

   b. [Root]

   c. Tree

   d. Leaf

6. Which of the following is an example of a user object's properties?

   a. Name

   b. MCepeda

   c. Leaf

   d. Parent container

7. Which of the following is an example of a user object's values?

   a. Name

   b. MCepeda

   c. Leaf

   d. Parent container

8. Which of the following is *not* one of Novell NetWare's classes of objects?

   a. [Root] object

   b. Leaf object

   c. Country object

   d. Container object

9. Which of the following *cannot* have its name changed after it is initially created?

   a. [Root] object

   b. Leaf object

   c. Country object

   d. Container object

10. A container object is referred to as which of the following if it is contained within another container object?

    a. Parent object

    b. Country object

    c. [Root]

    d. Child object

11. Which of the following is used by both Novell and Microsoft in their network database?

    a. Organizational Unit

b. Organization

   c. objects

   d. values

12. Which of the following is the largest object grouping used by Microsoft in its directory services database?

   a. Domain

   b. Tree

   c. Global Catalog

   d. Forest

13. When domain controllers join Active Directory they employ the same schema because they share information about all networked resources as part of which of the following?

   a. Domain

   b. Tree

   c. Global Catalog

   d. Forest

14. Networks that focus on providing unified access to all networked resources rather than just those on a single server are referred to as which of the following?

   a. Server-centered

   b. Network-centered

   c. Metadata-oriented

   d. Network Directed Orientation

15. When you created a new user, that user was by default immediately granted all rights to the objects on the network. Which of the following represents an operating system that you did *not* use when creating that user?

   a. Novell Client

   b. Windows 2000 Server

   c. Windows XP

   d. NetWare 6

■ Essay Quiz

1. Explain the types of information NDS provides through its Directory database.

2. Explain why unique names are important to a network.

3. Differentiate between NDS properties and values.

4. Discuss the Microsoft Global Catalog.

5. What is the purpose of the MMC?

Lab Projects

Time to roll up your sleeves and apply what you've learned. The following lab projects will enable you to practice the concepts discussed in this chapter.

• Lab Project 6.1

You have been called to the TEACH training center. The training center manager has been requesting that the trainers all be added to the NetWare server and he wants to know why they are not yet available. You promised them weeks ago but have been unable to spend the time to create them until now. Your boss wants you to create the six users right away and then wants you to explain to the training center

manager how the new users can be used for single login capability.

You will need the following:

■ A networked lab computer with Windows XP Professional and Novell Client installed

■ An operational Novell NetWare 6 server

- The following information about the eight training center users:

Manager	Steve Ruhl
Trainer1	Ramon Carlos
Trainer2	Christopher Zvolensky
Trainer3	David Lopez
Trainer4	Jonathan Mendoza
Trainer5	David Rinaldi
Trainer6	Jeffry Roque
Trainer7	Milton Hardin
Trainer8	Larry Reichert

Then do the following:

1 Log in to your local Windows XP Professional workstation and your NetWare 6 server using your administrator user account.

2 Double-click the ConsoleOne shortcut icon that you created on your desktop.

3 Expand your University tree in the left panel.

4 Right-click your Lab Organization container, select New Object, select Organizational Unit, and click OK.

5 Enter **Training Center** as the new Organizational Unit's name.

6 Right-click your new Training Center Organizational Unit container and select New | User.

7 Enter **SRuhl** in the Name field, **Ruhl** in the Surname field, and **Steve Ruhl** in the Unique ID field. Click the Create Another User check box, and click OK.

8 Enter **networking** in the New Password entry box and again in the Retype Password entry box, and then click the Set Password button.

9 Repeat Steps 7 and 8 for each new user (making sure to use the different names of the different employees), and click the Cancel button after setting the last new user's password.

10 Close the ConsoleOne window to return to your desktop.

11 Right-click the NetWare Services icon in your taskbar's notification area, and select NetWare Login.

12 Click the Advanced button, click the Contexts button, click the Training Center container, and click OK.

13 Enter **sruhl** as the user name, enter **networking** as the password, and click OK.

14 Confirm your intent to log in as the new user.

• Lab Project 6.2

After creating the training center users on your network's NetWare 6 server, you discover that they are unable to log in to your network using these new user accounts without using an administrator account for the local workstation. You have been asked to create Windows users on your School workstation for each of the training center users.

You will need the following materials:

- A networked lab computer with Windows XP Professional and Novell Client installed
- An operational Novell NetWare 6 server
- An operational Windows 2000 domain controller with Active Directory installed
- The user information from Lab Project 6.1

Then do the following:

1 Log in to your Windows 2000 Server computer as the administrator user.

2 Click the Start button, select Administrative Tools, and select Active Directory Users and Computers.

3 Expand School.net, and right-click on the Users object in the left panel.

4 Select New | User.

5 Enter **Steve** in the First Name field and enter **Ruhl** in the Last Name field.

6 Enter **sruhl** in the User Logon Name field, and press Next.

7 Enter and confirm **networking** as the password, click the Password Never Expires option, and click Next.

8 Verify the information and click the Finish button if it is correct.

9 Repeat Steps 4 through 8 for each of the training center users, making sure to use each different name.

10 Close the Active Directory Users and Computers console.

11 Verify your ability to log in to your Windows XP Professional computer using your NetWare 6 user and your Windows 2000 Server user in the Novell Client login window.

Creating Network File Systems

chapter 7

"Early to bed, early to rise, work like hell and organize."
—AL GORE

In this chapter, you will learn how to:

- Use Novell's network file system
- Describe Windows file storage
- Utilize your network file systems

ecause this text has not yet discussed filing systems, most of you have probably been storing your files throughout the network. Now it's time to learn about creating a file system on your servers so you can have planned storage associated with the user accounts that you created in the last chapter. This will help you understand the reasons behind limiting where users store items on the network—until now, your users have had unlimited storage. Just as you now control the rights users have on your network, you should also control where they store objects on your network and how much storage space they use. To do this, you will need unlimited controls on your administrative account's access to the filing system, just as you did when working with the directory.

In this chapter, you will learn more about storing data and applications for users to share on your classroom network. You will first learn about Novell's method for storing and retrieving these items. Novell does not usually refer to the NetWare file system it uses as a **network file system (NFS)**, an industry standard for organizing network files that was originally proposed by Sun, but for the sake of simplicity, this text will. Novell's version of NFS helps you organize data access into a hierarchical system similar to the filing cabinet system used in typical offices, and it ends up being quite similar to MS-DOS's organizational structure. Next you will learn about the comparable filing system Microsoft uses in Active Directory (AD). Finally, you will use both of these filing systems to store items on your network.

Understanding Novell's Network File System

The SinkRSwim Pools users have been allowed to store things just about anywhere they wanted to on the network, and it is now time for Ricky to implement filing systems to better control, organize, and secure his users' file storage methods.

During the NetWare installation, some network files are created that are part of the operating system. These files can be configured by administrators and later employed by users. Other files created by users and stored on the NetWare servers can be shared with other users. Remember, sharing files with others was a main reason for creating networks in the first place.

The NetWare file system allows users to share their files. Users will join the network in order to gain access to the resources the network users share. They will then add more information to what already resides on the disk drives attached to the NetWare servers. The NetWare file system stores the network's data and facilitates sharing it with all the other NetWare network users. The NetWare file system also stores networked applications and shares them with network users.

NFS is on all NetWare servers. Its components include file servers, volumes, directories, subdirectories, and files. NFS provides centralized access to these components, and it coordinates efforts to share applications and data. The storage structure formed by these components is another example of NetWare's orientation toward a hierarchical filing system like that used in its implementation of NDS.

File Servers

Think of NetWare's file server as being similar in function to a typical filing cabinet. The file server, like the entire filing cabinet, is the highest level storage unit in the NFS structure. Inside the file server, all the other lower level components are organized. The file server's volumes are thus similar to the drawers used to separate stored items inside the filing cabinet. The volumes are then divided into directories, just as folders are used in the filing cabinet's drawers. Each directory can then be further divided into subdirectories, which would be similar to storing folders within other folders in the filing cabinet. Finally, stored inside those volumes, directories, or subdirectories are the files.

Volumes

A volume is a physical device used for storage and is either installed in or attached to the NetWare file server. A volume is commonly a hard disk drive, but it can also be a CD drive, a tape drive, or any other large storage device. Volumes are similar to DOS disk drives. As with DOS disks, NetWare volumes can be either entire hard drives or major subdivisions within a hard drive, divided to separate the information in one volume from everything else stored on the drive. This subdividing of a drive is similar to partitioning DOS disks with FDISK.

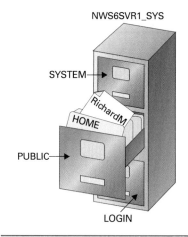

NWS6SVR1_SYS

SYSTEM

RichardM

HOME

PUBLIC

LOGIN

• A file server can be likened to a filing cabinet.

In Chapter 4, when you set up the DOS partition on your NetWare server, the remaining space was available for subdividing into NetWare volumes. During the NetWare installation, you were instructed to use the Express setup method and thus created only one volume for this course.

Typically, the SYS: volume is the place where only required system files are kept, while additional volumes are created for everything else.

Inside Information

Additional Volume Names

If you create additional volumes, your NetWare server automatically names them Vol1:, Vol2:, and so on unless you specify individual names during installation. You can change these default names later if you wish. To make them more understandable, you may name your additional volumes for geographical locations (lab 1:, Florida:, West Coast:, and so on), for different departments (finance, drafting, and so on), or using any other descriptor that will help clarify your structure.

Because your initial installation used the Express setup, which did not permit you to add a second volume on your server, this separation of information on various volumes is not yet important. If you use the Custom setup for your next installation, however, you can take this into account and create any additional volumes you need.

Your NetWare server initially boots up in the DOS partition that you created on your NetWare server—that partition contains the main server executable file (server.exe), which is the file that starts your NetWare operating system. The server.exe file loads some additional system files and then switches to the NetWare partition for all other operating system functions.

The first NetWare volume created on a server is always the SYS: volume. Each NetWare server must have at least one NetWare volume, the SYS: volume, where the operating system files that run the server are stored. Deleting or changing the name of this volume will cause the server to operate improperly and may prevent it from starting at all. Administrators should monitor the available disk space on the SYS: volume because if it becomes full, the server could crash (suffer a complete system failure), requiring the system to be rebooted and restarted.

Volumes are located on NetWare servers, and some servers may contain more than one volume. Unlike DOS drives configured using FDISK, however, a NetWare volume can span (be partially contained on) more than one physical hard drive while still being considered a single volume. The object used by NDS to represent a volume on NetWare networks is the volume object, and the system itself automatically gives the object its name. A volume object name, therefore, is a combination of the name of the server and the name of the volume, connected by an underscore.

For example, the volume object name for the volume you created in your NW6SVR1 server was NW6SVR1_SYS:, and an icon that looks like a filing cabinet represents your volume in the NDS tree. Because all servers have a SYS: volume, and, as we discussed in Chapter 4, all objects must have unique names in NetWare, using this naming scheme and storing all your items in the SYS: volume will ensure that those objects are assigned unique names.

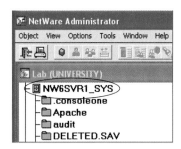

- The NetWare Administrator view of the filing cabinet icon next to the name of your NW6SVR1_SYS file server

The volume name is the highest level in NFS's directory structure on a server, much as the root directory designation is the highest storage level on DOS hard disk drives. Also, like the DOS file system structure, NetWare's file system directory structure is set up like a tree, with directories and subdirectories branching out from its root directory, and with its stored files being the lowest level object in the structure.

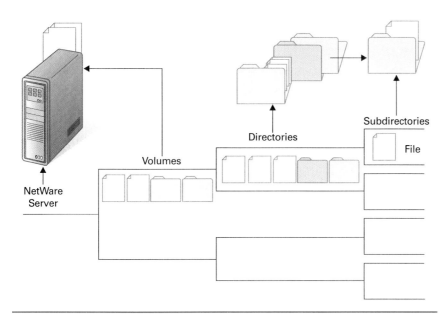

 Creating a folder in any one of the numerous versions of the Windows operating system is similar to creating a directory in NFS.

Subdirectories

File

Directories

Volumes

NetWare
Server

• The NetWare file server's NFS directory structure

Directories

A **directory** (with a small *d*) is an object representing an area on a NetWare volume where files or additional directories (called *subdirectories*) are stored.

The main reason for subdividing volumes is to increase network organization. The more you can subdivide volumes and group similar objects together, the more organized your network will be.

You can create optional directories yourself, and required directories are created for you. Both help you keep your system organized.

Optional Directories When you attempt to organize the information stored on the NetWare file server that you use in this course, you will likely find that this part of a network administrator's job often involves creating and working with optional directories (those directories that you can add as you like or as they are needed). Think about the filing cabinet described earlier. Although extra drawers may not be necessary, when you wish to store and later retrieve a

 Try This!

Verify Your Volume Object Name

The server name you used when you originally installed your NetWare 6 server should be the one displayed in your directory structure. Try this:

1. Log in to your Windows XP Professional workstation and to your NetWare 6 server as your administrative user.

2. Locate and double-click the ConsoleOne icon you created on your desktop in Chapter 6.

3. When ConsoleOne opens, expand NDS by clicking the small switch to the left of its icon name in the left pane. When you click the switch, its small line will point downward to expand (or open) the container object and reveal any additional container objects below it in the left pane. All of its contents (containers and files) will be displayed in the right pane.

4. Clicking the switch again will point the switch's small line to the right and collapse (or close) the container object and hide its container contents in the left pane.

5. Expand your University tree, then expand your Lab container, and verify the name of your server (NW6SVR1_SYS). Click its filing cabinet icon to display its contents in the right pane without expanding its containers in the left pane.

document easily, having things organized sufficiently by subdividing file folders makes it easier for you to locate the specific file (and then the document) you want. The same is true of your file server's storage system. In fact, most of the directories you will work with are those you or your classmates elect to create in an effort to keep your system organized. However, still other directories that you and your classmates will use are created on a server during the operating system's original installation.

Required Directories   Several required directories (directories that must be on the server) are always created when a NetWare operating system is installed. They help start you off in an organized fashion when you first begin using the new NetWare server. Following are some of the required directories that NetWare automatically installs (provided you are installing NetWare 4.0 or higher). You will be working with these directories frequently as you administer your class's NetWare 6.0 network.

- **SYSTEM**   The majority of the tasks you will perform on your NetWare server will use the operating system's NLM (or NetWare Loadable Module) configuration files and various other utilities that are contained in the SYSTEM directory (SYS). These items should be accessible only to those individuals designated as having administrative responsibility for the network. The majority of these files affect how your NetWare server functions, and they should be continually protected from access by unauthorized users.

- **PUBLIC**   The files and programs that you want available to all users after they have logged in can be placed in the PUBLIC directory. Many of the items stored there are needed by users when gaining access to or using specific network services. By default, all users on a NetWare network are granted Read access to the PUBLIC directory.

- **LOGIN**   The files located in the LOGIN directory are there to be accessed by all users prior to their logging in to the network. Merely connecting to the network gives any individual access to these files and programs. Users can see what servers are available for them to log on to and they can attempt to log on to any of those servers. Whether or not they are successful in their attempt determines whether they gain access to the network itself. Network administrators should be very careful when placing programs in the LOGIN directory because everyone (whether authorized or not) has access to those programs at all times.

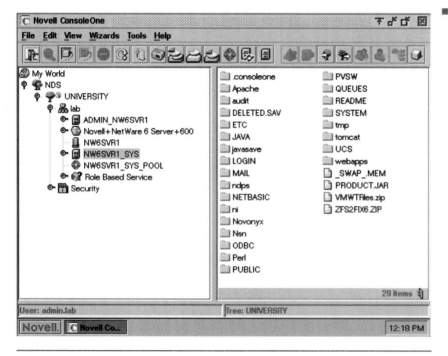

- The NW6SVR1_SYS server with two of the required directories displayed

Typical Directories In addition to the required directories just discussed, you will usually see several other typical directories (ones that are not required but nonetheless are used on the typical NetWare network). It may be your job, while administering the network, to create and maintain these supplementary directories.

- **APPLICATION** Applications that the network administrator determines should be available to multiple users over the network are placed in an APPLICATION directory (commonly named APPS). Within the APPLICATION directory, you should create a separate directory for each application. Separate storage space for each application allows you to segregate your most frequently accessed items from other files. In case of failure or data corruption, your more important application files are not affected (just as when you segregated your SYSTEM files from all others). All users authorized to log in to the network will generally have access to these applications.

- **USERS** Users will typically have files stored in a USERS directory that they wish to keep on the server so they can access that information from any workstation on the network. These files and the associated documents are customarily stored in each user's own HOME directory located inside the USERS directory. Think of it as the user's "home base," the location where the user gets to keep personal "possessions." When you created new users on your NW6SVR1 server, you were asked to designate their HOME directory, and you specified the USERS directory. Without creating a directory actually named HOME, the system created directories with the users' names instead.

  Therefore, all users you created on your NetWare network currently have what amounts to a HOME location (considered a HOME directory by the system, but named with the user's name instead) in your PUBLIC\USERS directory. This can get confusing. Typically, a directory actually named HOME is created, and the directory named with the user's name is placed inside this HOME directory, making things easier to follow. In any case, only the users themselves will be granted access to their own HOME directory (the one with their user name on it).

- **SHARED** Frequently, your users will also have shared files, perhaps a client database, that they wish to allow others to use over the network. Such items are usually stored in a SHARED directory created by the administrator. Users who are permitted to share all of the information in the directory should be granted access to the entire SHARED directory, while other users may be granted access to individual items stored in the SHARED directory instead.

Subdirectories

A subdirectory is merely a directory stored inside another directory. Some of the directories identified previously were actually subdirectories because they were stored within other directories. Even though their names indicate

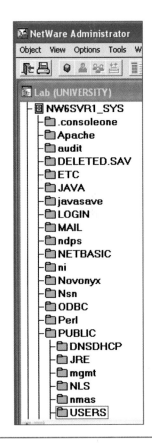

- The NetWare Administrator view of the more typical implementation for a user's HOME directory

Cross Check

Where's Home?

Refer back to "USERS" section in the previous discussion when answering the following questions:

1. What directory/subdirectory combination defines the location of your users' HOME directories?

2. What graphical user interface utilities can be used to alter the location where your users' HOME directories are located, and where are those utilities located?

that they are directories, they are actually classified as subdirectories. For example, the USERS directory you created on your NetWare server is actually a subdirectory within the PUBLIC directory on your NW6SVR1_SYS: volume. Furthermore, each of your users can have a HOME directory assigned that is actually a subdirectory of the USERS directory (or more correctly, of the USERS subdirectory).

It should be clear, then, that a subdirectory is simply a further subdivision of the information stored in its higher level directory object. In the USERS directory, for example, each user has a storage area on the network. Each user's storage area should be a separate folder within that USERS directory to separate each user's information from that of another user. Thus, each user has his or her own subdirectory within the USERS directory. As you can see, the terms *directory* and *subdirectory* are typically used interchangeably.

Step-by-Step 7.01

Changing a User's HOME Directory Location

You already created HOME directories for your network's users, but you want that location to be similar to what they will find on the typical network. You decide to create an additional subdirectory named HOME, in which you will put the system-created HOME directories (the ones with the users' names) to make the HOME directories easier to understand. In this exercise, you will use ConsoleOne first to create the new directory at your workstation, and then you will use ConsoleOne from your server to reassign that new directory as your users' new default file-storage area.

To complete this exercise, you will need the following items:

- Operational NetWare 6 server with the GUI operational and started

- Networked Windows XP Professional workstation with Novell Client installed

- ConsoleOne installed on your Windows XP Professional workstation

Step 1

Log in to your Windows XP Professional computer and your NetWare 6 server from your workstation as an administrative user.

Step 2

Double-click the ConsoleOne icon on your desktop. When ConsoleOne opens and displays the NDS and University icons, expand your University tree by clicking the plus sign (+) to the left of the icon, and then similarly expand your Lab container, NW6SVR1_SYS server, PUBLIC directory, and USERS subdirectory.

Introduction to Networking

Step 3

Right-click the USERS directory and select New | Object. Highlight the Directory folder, and click OK.

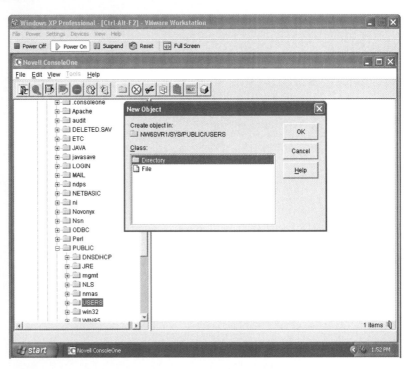

Step 4

Enter **HOME** as the directory's name, and click OK.

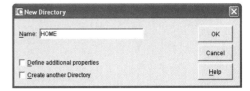

Step 5

Verify that the new HOME directory has been created in ConsoleOne's right pane.

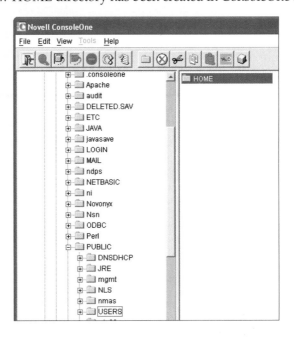

Step 6

From your server's GUI screen, click the Novell button and click ConsoleOne. When ConsoleOne starts, navigate in the left pane and highlight your LAB container object, to expand it.

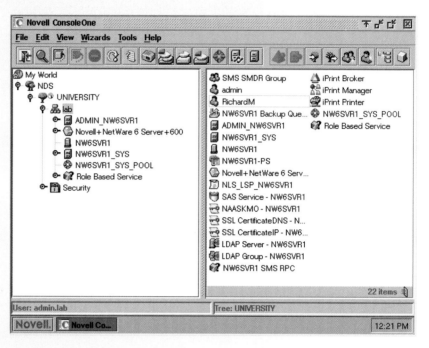

Step 7

Double-click the user object in the right pane whose HOME directory is to be changed (RichardM in this example) to open the Properties window. Click the General tab in the Properties window, and select Environment from the tab's drop-down selections. Use the browse button in the Home Directory section to locate your newly created HOME directory, and click the Apply button.

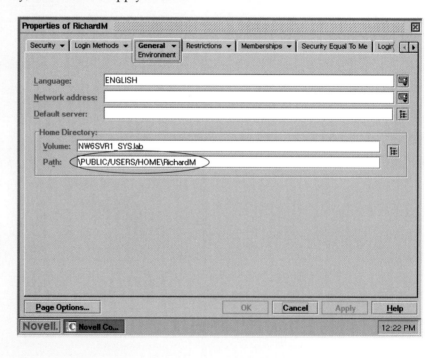

Return to ConsoleOne on your workstation, and double-click your new HOME directory. Verify that the new location is now being used for your user's HOME directory.

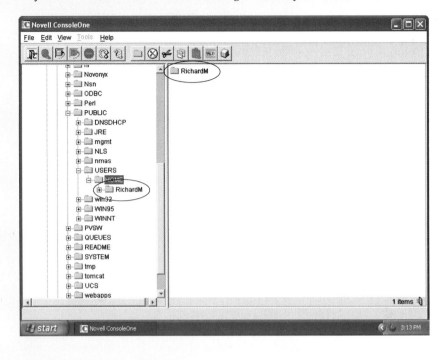

Files

Much like the documents stored in a filing cabinet, Novell uses the term file to represent a document (containing data) stored in NFS. Although files are at the end of the NFS description and may seem insignificant when viewed from that perspective, remember that the whole reason you developed your network in the first place was to allow you to share just such information (files consisting of data) with your classmates.

Files can be spreadsheets, PowerPoint presentations, Word documents, graphics files, or other individual data items. They can also be applications or any other blocks of data. You initially set out to develop a network to have somewhere to store your own files. Now, assuming you have sufficient space on your server, you have a place to store all the files you or your classmates create in this course.

Syntax

The normal **syntax** (or formatting structure) of the filename helps NFS locate your files. NFS requires a colon between the volume name and the directory and backslashes between subsequent directory, subdirectory, and filenames.

For example, your NetWare server and your PUBLIC directory would be identified as NW6SVR1_SYS:PUBLIC. Since the system is also aware that the NW6SVR1_SYS is the SYSTEM volume (or SYS), the same subdirectory can also be specified by the more simple name SYS:PUBLIC.

 On a network containing multiple servers, you may need to specify the full path from the specific server to the individual subdirectory when referring to those other servers. To do this, begin with the name of the server (NW6SVR1), followed with a slash (/), followed with the name of the volume (SYS), followed with a colon (:), and then followed with the normal directory syntax. RichardM's HOME directory on your NetWare server would be as follows: `NW6SVR1/SYS:PUBLIC\USERS\HOME\RichardM`.

Try This!

Map a Drive to and Create a File in Your HOME Directory

You want to be able to store files in your HOME directory from the workstation where you create them. To do so, you first need to **map a drive** (configure an object in such a way as to have the operating system recognize that object as a separate hard drive) to your HOME directory. Then you will navigate to and create your file in that new location using an application available to you on the workstation.

Try this:

1. At your Windows XP Professional workstation, log in to your Windows 2000 server and to your NetWare 6 server as a user (preferably not as an administrator).

2. Click the Start button and select My Computer. Double-click the Z: drive in the Network Drives section of the My Computer window, double-click the USERS folder, and double-click the HOME folder.

3. In the HOME folder, right-click the folder with your user name (your own HOME folder, or

directory), and select NetWare Map Network Drive to open the Map Drive dialog box.

4. Use the Choose the Drive Letter to Map drop-down list to select the H: drive, ensure the network path points to your own HOME folder (with your name displayed as the last item in the path), and enter your NetWare user name in the Enter Your Network User Name text box. Check the Check to Make Folder Appear at the Top Most Level check box, and check the Check to Always Map this Drive Letter When You Start Windows check box. Then click the Map button.

5. Inside your new H: window, select File | New | Wordpad Document, and rename your new file as **Added Document File**. Then close your H: drive's window.

6. Open ConsoleOne from your server, navigate to your user's HOME directory, and confirm that your Added Document File was correctly added.

A reference to a subdirectory within its parent directory looks like this:

```
SYS:PUBLIC\USERS\HOME\RichardM
```

This example identifies the RichardM user's directory in the HOME directory in your NetWare server.

RichardM's HOME directory location is shown in the following illustration, which also contains the correct syntax showing the server through file format:

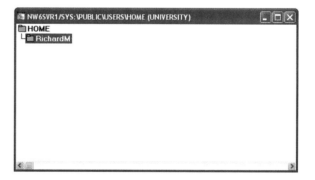

• The NetWare Administrator view of RichardM's new HOME directory showing the proper filename syntax

Describing Windows File Storage

Although the SinkRSwim Pools network does provide for some users to have storage on its Novell NetWare server, the majority of the network's users prefer sticking with what they are most familiar using—the Windows desktop. Ricky and Lauren are developing the company's network with that in mind and have installed all Windows operating systems with NTFS partitions. Therefore, Ricky needs to make sure every user understands how to store files within NTFS.

The Windows operating systems that you installed on your network, Windows 2000 Server and Windows XP Professional, each support the same several different Windows file systems. These include two read-only file systems used for CD-ROM support, the CD-ROM file system (CDFS) and the Universal Disk Format (UDF), and two other file systems that support read and write capability for file storage: FAT (file allocation table) and NTFS (NTFS file system). The latter two will be discussed in this section.

Before making the decision about which of those different Windows file systems you will use for your file system, however, you must decide which of the two storage types, basic or dynamic storage, will be used on your Windows systems. That principally decides whether the top component in your system is referred to as a *disk* or a *volume*, while the remainder of the structure involves folders, subfolders, and files. All these components can be compared to storage within a filing cabinet much as Novell's NFS components were earlier in the chapter.

Types of Windows Storage

Two types of storage are available on the disks you formatted that can be used by the Windows operating systems chosen for your network. The first storage type is the traditional one that has been available since the early implementations of Microsoft storage systems. This is basic storage, and it involves primary and extended partitions. The other storage type is available to you because you are using Windows 2000 or later versions of Windows, and it is dynamic storage, which involves the use of various Microsoft volumes.

In either case, you start by creating partitions during the original installation or by using the New Partition Wizard from the Computer Management snap-in in the Microsoft Management Console, as shown in Figure 7.1.

Basic Storage: Traditional

On Microsoft computer systems from early versions of MS-DOS up through those using Windows XP, the primary storage type has

Cross Check

Your Server's Partition Size

Go back to Chapter 4's Step-by-Step 4.04 (where you installed Windows 2000 Server) and answer the following questions:

1. What was the size of the partition that you used when creating your server?

2. In Step 4 of your server's installation (Step-by-Step 4.04), what would you have to do to create a partition of a particular size instead of installing (as you did) using all the remaining space?

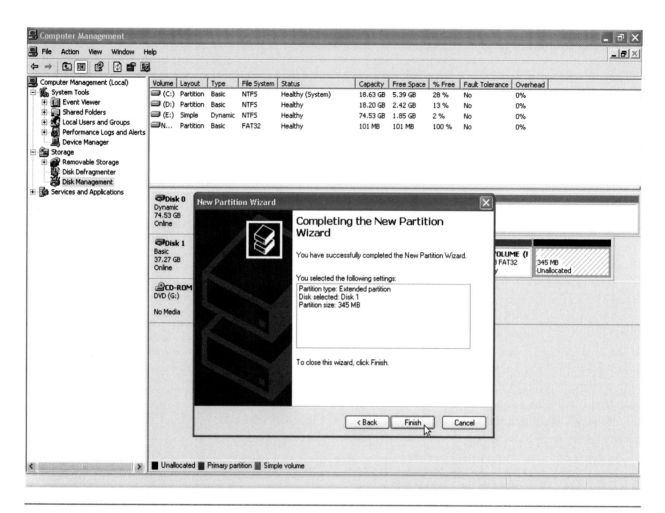

● **Figure 7.1**   The New Partition Wizard creates partitions from remaining space after the initial Windows installation.

been basic storage, which is the industry standard for disk storage. Basic storage involves using **basic disks**, which are disk drives formatted using primary partitions, extended partitions, and logical drives. Understanding these optional partitioning methods is important before trying to understand the benefits of upgrading storage to the newer alternative—dynamic storage.

Basic Disks   All disk drives partitioned using the default storage type are created using basic disks with basic storage. Basic disks are divided into partitions that act as independent storage devices even though they may only be part of the actual physical storage device. That means you can divide your hard drive into distinct areas where you can store separate items, possibly to provide a more secure area or to ensure one area is not affected if another is corrupted or fails. Up to four partitions can reside on each basic disk. Partitions can either be primary partitions or extended partitions. The four partitions can be either all be primary partitions or they can include one extended partition, as shown in Figure 7.2.

Introduction to Networking

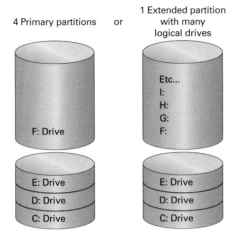

4 Primary partitions   or   1 Extended partition
with many
logical drives

F: Drive

Etc...
I:
H:
G:
F:

E: Drive
D: Drive
C: Drive

E: Drive
D: Drive
C: Drive

• **Figure 7.2**   Four basic storage areas can be all primary partitions or can include one extended partition.

Primary partitions can be used to store the files needed by the operating system when starting your computer. When you create a primary partition, you assign a drive letter and you format the drive. One of the four possible partitions can be created as an extended partition. **Extended partitions** can then be used when you need additional separate storage areas (more than the four available when using only primary partitions) created with their own drive letters on a single hard disk drive. Three primary partitions and one extended partition are being used in Figure 7.3 when dividing Disk 1 into storage areas. However, if you needed additional separate areas, the single extended partition could have been divided into 21 areas, which can each have its own drive letter. While this will not gain any additional space from the same physical drive's size, it does add the flexibility of more separate areas.

After creating a primary partition, your installation program stored the operating system's startup files (boot files) there and marked the primary partion as the active partition. The active partition is the primary partition that the system goes to when looking for the boot files. It is also called the **system partition**, because that is where the hardware-specific files necessary for starting the operating system are located. Notice that the C: drive, shown earlier in Figure 7.1, is the system partition and is marked with the word "System" in the partition's Status column. The operating system files themselves can be located in another primary partition or in an extended partition's logical drive, which is then called the boot partition. Only one partition can be declared as active on a particular physical hard disk drive. The system and boot partitions can both be located on the same partition,

Inside Information

Number of Drives

When you create an extended partition, you should assign any remaining drive space to it, but you do not have to format it or assign drive letters. Storage areas created on extended partitions are called logical drives, and each can be allocated up to the entire amount of remaining drive space and assigned its own drive letter before being formatted. Drive letters A: and B: are system-controlled drive letters, and C: is typically your active primary partition. You can usually create up to a maximum of 23 logical drives in your extended partition.

Cross Check

Your Server's Partition Indications

Refer to the corresponding section and Figure 7.3 when you answer the following questions:

1. What does the green highlighting around drives H:, I:, and J: indicate?

2. How many partitions are located on the basic disk named Disk 1?

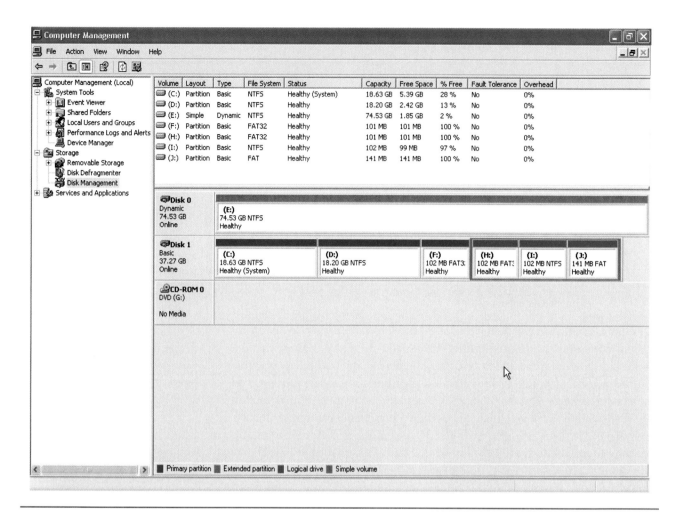

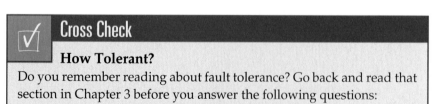

● **Figure 7.3**   Numerous partitions added to a computer's physical drives

as was the case when you installed your entire system in a single partition, but the system partition must be located on an active partition.

Dynamic Storage: NT-Based

The newer of the two alternatives, **dynamic storage**, is a storage type available on your installed systems that requires upgrading basic disks, and it allows you to use the additional capabilities of your newer NT-based operating systems. The benefits of using dynamic storage range from the storage devices being more efficient to providing fault-tolerant storage space.

Storage areas on dynamic disks are called volumes rather than partitions or sets, which were the terms MS used previously (primary partition, extended partition, mirrored sets, volume sets, and stripe sets).

Cross Check

How Tolerant?

Do you remember reading about fault tolerance? Go back and read that section in Chapter 3 before you answer the following questions:

1. What does fault tolerant mean?

2. Why is fault tolerance important to a system?

Volume Types   When working with dynamic storage devices, five different types of volumes are available, as shown in Figure 7.4. Which one you choose depends on what features you decide your system needs.

■   **Simple Volume**   A **simple volume** is a dynamic storage area that is located on one physical disk and uses all (or just part) of the disk's space for a single volume. When you created your Windows 2000 server and your Windows XP workstations, you built them using the entire drive for a single volume, so they were all simple volumes. While the name may seem to suggest how easy they are to create, it actually means that fewer complex features are available on this volume type than can be found on the other types. One of the features available on this type of storage is the ability to extend the volume to include more of the unused space on the physical drive.

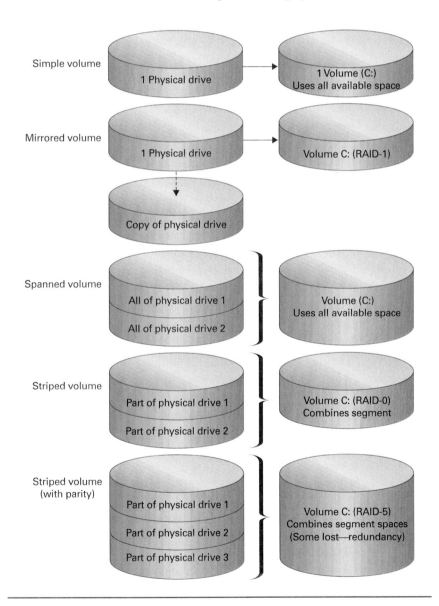

● **Figure 7.4**   The five different types of dynamic storage

Simple volumes are efficient to use because they use all the available space, but they do not provide any degree of fault tolerance. If a simple volume is extended, it actually becomes less fault tolerant because the information maintained on the individual segments that were combined provide additional points of failure. If any of those points fail, the entire volume fails and is unrecoverable. This makes them RAID-0 (no level of RAID).

- **Mirrored Volume** If you have two identical simple volumes on separate physical drives, and you use one to maintain an exact copy of the other on your Windows 2000 server, you would have what is called a **mirrored volume**. In the event that your working copy fails, you would still have a complete copy of that volume in the mirrored volume that you have been maintaining. By disconnecting that mirroring function and removing the failed copy, you **break the mirror**. Then, when you replace the failed hard drive with an operational one, you would **restore the mirror** (or reconnect it), create another exact copy, and then maintain the mirror once again. While you end up being able to use only half of your total available disk space (the other half being used for the mirror copy), you have the ability to restore your stored data in the event of a failure. This type of fault tolerance is called RAID-1, the first level of RAID.

- **Spanned Volume** Dynamic storage provides an efficient way to use numerous disk drives. Combining those multiple spaces—up to 32 individual disks—results in what is called a **spanned volume**. A spanned volume consists of multiple disks joined by setting up what are known as *pointers* that give the operating system directions on how to get from one disk to the next. Data is stored on the spanned volume by writing to the first available space and filling the rest of that disk before moving on to the next. Losing any one of the disks on a spanned volume results in total loss of all data stored on the entire volume. That data is unrecoverable using normal means. This means that spanned volumes do not provide any level of fault tolerance, making them RAID-0.

- **Striped Volume** A **striped volume** is somewhat similar to a spanned volume, because it provides an efficient way to use storage space in multiple locations. However, where spanned volumes use whole disks, striped volumes just use an equal amount of space (not necessarily the entire drive) from multiple disks. Like the spanned volume, the striped volume can use up to 32 disks to create its storage space.

  The striped volume creates no level of redundancy in the event of failure, so it creates the same problem of multiple points of failure encountered in an expanded disk as well as a spanned volume. Thus, the striped volume is also RAID-0—loss of any segment results in loss of all data on the volume. However, a benefit of using striped volumes is that the multiple heads on the multiple disks can be used simultaneously, and numerous reading or writing actions can take place at the same time, making data transfer faster. Striped volumes end up providing greater efficiency as a result of this ability.

- **Striped Volume with Parity** If, in addition to striping data on multiple disks, you duplicate the stripe by storing a piece of it on each of the striped disks and creating a duplicate copy of the volume, you would have efficiency as well as redundancy. A **striped volume with parity**, thus, is a fault-tolerant arrangement (RAID-5), and it produces redundant storage as a result. If one of the volumes fails, the extra stripe (the parity stripe) stored on the remaining disks is used to re-create the failed segment and keep the system in operation while the failed disk is replaced. Like mirroring, however, this level of RAID is not available to you on your network except for your Windows 2000 server. Remember, RAID levels 1 and 5 are not available on Windows XP.

Converting to a Volume You can convert from a basic disk to a dynamic one very easily, as shown in Figure 7.5. However, before performing that conversion, you should make sure that no computers running Windows operating systems other than the ones currently on your network—Windows 2000 Server and Windows XP Professional—will later need to read data on the converted disks. This is because the earlier Windows operating systems cannot read dynamic storage devices.

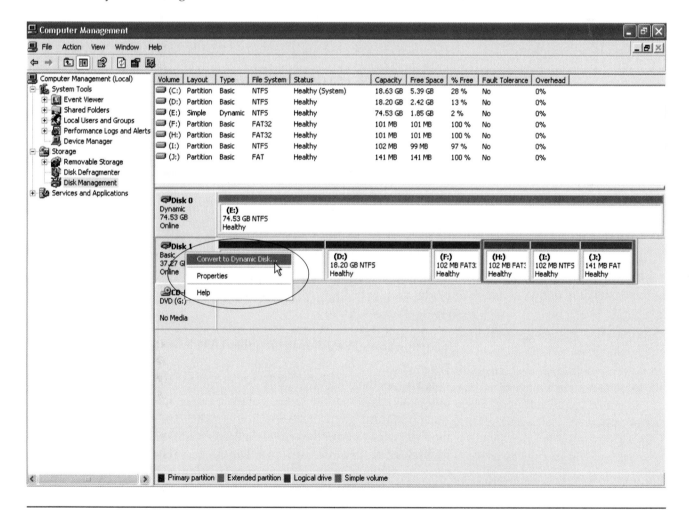

- **Figure 7.5** Use the Computer Management console to convert from basic disks to dynamic volumes.

Try This!

Convert to a Dynamic Volume

You have decided to convert one of your disks from basic to dynamic. Try this:

1. Log in to your Windows XP Professional workstation as an administrator.

2. Click the Start button, and select Control Panel | Performance and Maintenance | Administrative Tools.

3. Double-click the Computer Management icon, and then click Disk Management in the left pane.

4. At the left side of the bottom portion of the right pane, right-click the icon next to the drive you have decided to convert, and select Convert to Dynamic Disk. Drive H: shown in Figure 7.5 is used as an example.

5. Inside your new H: window, select File | New | Text Document, and rename your new file as **Added Document File**. Then close your H: drive's window.

6. Open ConsoleOne from your server, and navigate to your user's HOME directory. Confirm that your Added Document File was added correctly.

Once you decide to convert to a dynamic volume, you perform the conversion using the Computer Management console. Provided you have at least 1MB of unallocated space on the disk, you can click the Upgrade to Dynamic Disk option in the Computer Management console.

You should keep in mind, however, that this conversion is a one-way process that cannot be reversed without complete data loss. Once you convert a disk to be a dynamic volume, the only way to restore it to a basic configuration is to remove all volumes from the disk and use the Revert to Basic Disk option in the Computer Management console. This means that you can only use the Revert to Basic Disk command on entire disks and unallocated space, and any data that is stored there will be erased.

Windows File Systems

After you've decided how you would like to store your data, and you have created the storage devices for use on your Windows 2000 or Windows XP operating system, you will have to decide between Microsoft's two major file-system alternatives: FAT and NTFS. Although this decision was made for you when you installed your network's computers, you should be aware of and understand the differences between these two file systems. When you installed your OS, you chose to format the primary active partition as NTFS, but you may have computers with FAT partitions that were later added to your networks. You could also be using FAT partitions on computers in other locations, such as at home. You should be familiar with using NTFS and understand why the decision was made to format your network computers with NTFS.

The Windows File Allocation Table (FAT) File System

When Windows was initially created, MS-DOS (Microsoft's disk operating system) was the most commonly used operating system on personal computers, and its file system was called the **file allocation table (FAT)**. Early versions of Windows actually functioned as an overlay on top of DOS. As such, those versions of Windows simply incorporated what DOS was using as its file system, so they also used FAT. During that time, floppy disks were the common medium for storing information. Additionally, the file system used for hard disks was based on disk allocation (setting aside disk space) on very small (5MB to 10MB) hard drives, as well as on those small floppy disks.

Using FAT　When the FAT file system is used, a partition is divided into *sectors* (storage units each consisting of 512 bytes of space), where data is written in what are known as *clusters*. A cluster contains one or more sectors (usually many) and is the minimum amount of space used each time any amount of data is written to storage. Cluster size typically varies from 512 bytes to 64KB, depending on the size of the partition, but on larger disks the cluster size can even be 128KB or 256KB. Since the cluster is the smallest unit written to disk at a time, wasted space can result when larger cluster sizes are used and the amount of data written is smaller than a complete cluster. In other words, when you write a 1KB piece of information, 63KB of disk space would be wasted if the cluster size were 64KB. Remember, a complete cluster is used whether it is filled or not.

FAT Space Usage   When data is written to FAT storage, the system looks for the first empty cluster and begins writing. After that cluster is full, the system keeps writing if the adjacent space is available. If that adjacent space is already used, the system goes looking for another cluster where it can continue its writing action. This process continues until the complete file is written to storage. Whenever adjacent space, called **contiguous space**, is unavailable and space from another non-adjacent sector elsewhere on the disk, called **non-contiguous space**, is used to contain the completed file, the data on that disk is said to be **fragmented**.

You can defragment, or **defrag**, the data by using the Disk Defragmenter utility located in the System Tools folder in the Accessories folder of your Start menu. The Disk Defragmenter utility defragments your partition by relocating all the data stored there such that it ends up stored contiguously. That is, all data is stored from start to finish in clusters physically located next to each other. This often improves data storage and retrieval, which lets your computer operate faster.

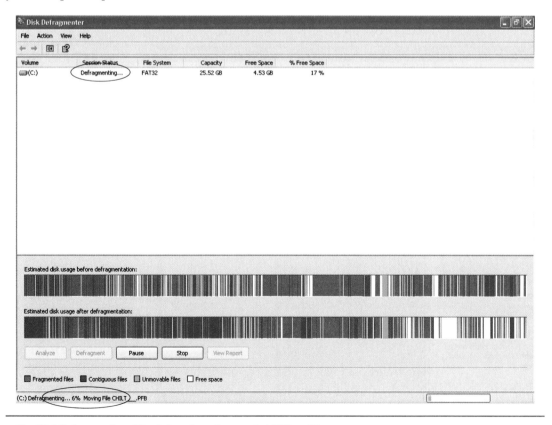

• The Disk Defragmenter utility defragging a fragmented FAT partition

Support for FAT   The FAT file system itself takes up very little storage space. The original FAT file system was an extremely efficient way of storing files on partitions whose size was less than 400MB, but its efficiency fell off rapidly when larger partitions were used. The largest partition reasonably maintained by the early version of FAT was 4GB, and its use on the smaller partitions ended up producing a speed advantage over the other possibilities available at the time. Although it was clearly not designed for use with the single partitions you likely have available in the computers on your network, FAT file systems are still supported by the operating systems you installed on those computers. Your Windows 2000 systems, therefore, offer support for both FAT16 (the file system for DOS, Windows 3*x*, and Windows 95) and FAT32 (the file system that has been available in Windows since Windows 95 OSR2). Your Windows XP systems offer that support and add additional FAT32 capability with what has come to be known as VFAT, or virtual file allocation table.

Widespread Use   The FAT file system is still the most widely used file system. In part, this is because of the added FAT32/VFAT support now available with Windows 2000 and Windows XP systems. That added support makes the speed advantage gained from using FAT techniques extend to partition sizes of 2GB or larger. However, the system's popularity is probably more the result of the fact that partitions using FAT are compatible with a wider range of operating systems. Not only can FAT partitions be accessed from computers running MS-DOS, OS/2, Windows 3*x*, and Windows 9*x*, but all the derivatives of Windows NT (NT, 2000, and XP) can also work with files stored using the FAT file system. Although speed may be an attractive benefit, the file system's compatibility with such a wide range of operating systems may be the most influential factor in its continued widespread use.

Drawbacks of Using FAT   The main detractors from using FAT file systems involve system capabilities. In fact, the best single word describing FAT file systems would have to be *inefficient*. In addition to the wasted space resulting from writing full clusters when only partial clusters are needed, the system's structure also adds to FAT inefficiencies. When you create your FAT partitions, they store their file allocation tables close to the volume's starting point and near the beginning of the root directory. These two must be located in very near proximity. The file allocation tables keep track of where items are stored on the disk and they must be constantly updated. Since they are at a fixed location near the start of the partition, frequent updates to those tables from distances much further than originally intended (on small storage partitions) waste significant time. The physical distance that the read/write head has to move from where it writes the data to where it must update the table is significantly increased on larger disks available now as compared to the original design intended when using only up to 400MB. Another detractor is that the FAT file system lacks the additional security features available with the NTFS system.

The Windows NTFS File System

The Windows **NTFS file system** is Microsoft's most capable file system, and it is more suited for use as a file system on a network than the FAT file system. In fact, when you installed your network's Windows 2000 server and your Windows XP Professional workstations following the instructions in this book, you chose the option to use NTFS. At the time, the choice was between using FAT and NTFS. You were instructed to choose NTFS because its added features will be more useful to you in this networking course. Let's take a look at some of the features available when you use the Windows NT file system.

The History of NTFS   The Windows, NTFS, first appeared in Windows NT 3.1 at a time when Windows 3.x was still being used and Microsoft was working with IBM's OS/2 operating system. What Microsoft referred to as the Windows "new technology" turned out to be a dramatic change from the operating systems in use at that time. Most were heavily dependent on the original FAT file system developed for use on small storage devices and intended for use with MS-DOS-like file storage. Windows NT, and its included NTFS, put added emphasis on the file system efficiency needed when using larger storage devices and on the growing use of networking.

Try This!

Format Using FAT

When viewing your disk drive usage, you notice that additional unallocated space is still available, and you decide to format it using a FAT partition. Try this:

1. Log in to your Windows XP Professional workstation as an administrator.
2. Click the Start button and select Control Panel | Performance and Maintenance | Administrative Tools.
3. Double-click the Computer Management shortcut icon to open the Computer Management console.
4. Click the Disk Management icon in the left pane to display your disk information in the right panes.
5. Right-click the space with the Unallocated annotation, and select New Partition to open the New Partition Wizard. Click Next, keep the default setting of Primary Partition, read the Description section describing Primary Partitions, and click Next.
6. Keep the default setting (using all available space) or configure the drive to your desired size in megabytes, and click Next. Accept the default drive letter by clicking Next.
7. In the Format Partition window, change the File System setting from the default of NTFS to FAT32, and click Next to begin formatting the partition.
8. Verify the completion, and close all windows to return to your desktop.

Since that somewhat disjointed initial attempt with Windows NT 3.1, Microsoft has added enhancements to NTFS with each new version of Windows NT. Its releases of NT 3.5 and NT 4.0 quickly made NTFS the most popular file system used on networked business computers. Although released with non-NT names, both Windows 2000 (originally developed as NT 5.0) and Windows XP both still use the NT architecture, and both new operating systems have added even more enhancements to the Windows NTFS capabilities.

NTFS Space Usage   One of the main goals when Microsoft developed Windows NT was more efficient use of disk storage space. FAT partitions were too inefficient in the way they used clusters to store files in a partition's sectors and in how they kept the file storage system, itself, updated. NTFS does store files using clusters, but it uses smaller cluster sizes and even

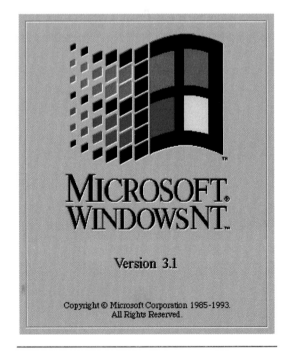

• The original Windows NT startup screen

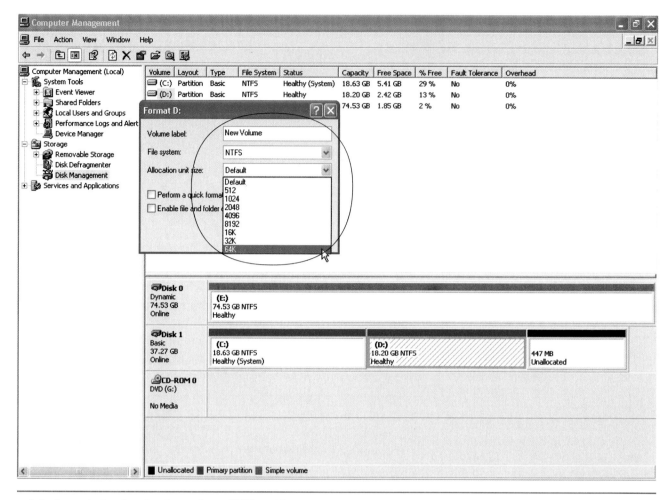

• Selecting a cluster size when formatting an NTFS partition

allows you to adjust the cluster size during partition formatting to better fit your storage needs.

NTFS uses file tables similar to FAT's tables. An NTFS table, called a Master File Table (MFT), like a FAT table, maintains a record of the information concerning the files stored on the NTFS formatted partition. Unlike the FAT table, however, NTFS makes use of the MFT space to store a sector map. With FAT file retrieval, pointers direct the retrieval mechanism (your disk drive's read head) to lists of sectors that have to be read prior to actually locating the desired files. By storing sector maps inside the MFT space, NTFS cuts down on the time spent locating files and therefore speeds up all file usage.

Systems Supported by NTFS   NTFS partitions are not as widely accessible as FAT partitions. This is the main drawback to using NTFS. Unfortunately, only systems running with the NT architecture can support, or access, data that is stored using all the features of NTFS, thus excluding any of the Windows 9x systems.

Benefits of Using NTFS   Unless you want the possibility of booting your computer using more than one of the additionally supported operating systems listed in the previous FAT section, a condition called dual-booting,

Microsoft recommends formatting all Windows 2000 and Windows XP partitions with NTFS. In addition to being more efficient, NTFS has other useful features. One of the most important is the file system's recoverability. NTFS stores a copy, or mirror, of its MFT in various locations within the partition itself. One of these mirrors is located in the logical center of the partition, along with a copy of the complete boot record. The mirror also stores a copy of the pointers to the original MFT. Combined, these features make NTFS recoverable—it is able to restore itself if it recognizes a recoverable failure.

In addition to storing mirror copies of the MFT, NTFS stores files intelligently. That is, smaller files are put closer to where the disk read head will normally travel. Since the read head has to go to the MFT when locating a file, the more files that are centrally stored near the start of that MFT, the faster those files can be retrieved. Larger files are automatically located further away from the start of the MFT so the head can more quickly locate the multiple smaller files that are located closer. This intelligent storage coupled with smaller cluster-size requirements results in significantly reduced retrieval times and a faster overall file system.

Furthermore, even though NTFS storage media are less likely to become fragmented than those using FAT, because NTFS uses intelligent storage, the Disk Defragmenter utility is also available in the Windows 2000 and Windows XP operating systems. This allows you to further reduce any tendency toward inefficient use of storage space. Although early versions of Windows NT did not include the defrag utility, both systems you installed on your Windows computers in this course offer that capability.

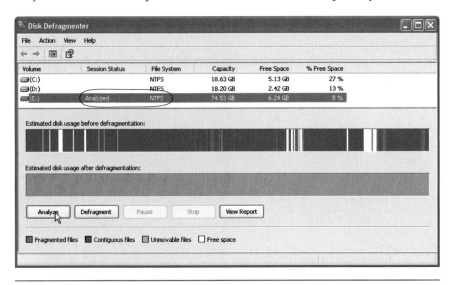

• Reduced fragmentation on NTFS partitions makes the defrag utility less important, but still handy.

Another important benefit to using NTFS is the addition of file system permissions, which enhance your ability to decide (and control) who sees or uses your stored objects. FAT storage is shared at the folder level, but NTFS storage can be controlled right down to the file level. You are, therefore, able to better control users' rights when they access your stored files. This is an extremely important benefit to material stored on networks. Furthermore, NTFS supports all Windows 2000 and Windows XP features, such as using Active Directory, file encryption, and file compression.

Convert a FAT Partition to NTFS

You can use the CONVERT command to convert a FAT partition into an NTFS partition at any time after its initial creation. However, this conversion is also a one-way process that cannot be reversed (or halted) once initiated, and the performance on the resulting partition is not quite as good as if the partitions were originally formatted with NTFS. In this exercise, you will use the FAT32 partition you created in the Try This! exercise "Format Using FAT".

To complete this exercise, you will need the following items:

- Operational Windows XP Professional workstation with the FAT32 partition you created earlier in this chapter

Step 1

Log in to your Windows XP Professional computer as an administrative user, click the Start button, and select Run.

Step 2

Type **cmd** (or **Command**) and click OK to open a Command Prompt window (the DOS-like simulator), where you can type in DOS commands that will be executed directly by your computer.

Step 3

To convert your F: drive to NTFS and have the computer provide you with all the messages during the conversion, type this command

```
convert f: /fs:ntfs /v
```

and then press ENTER.

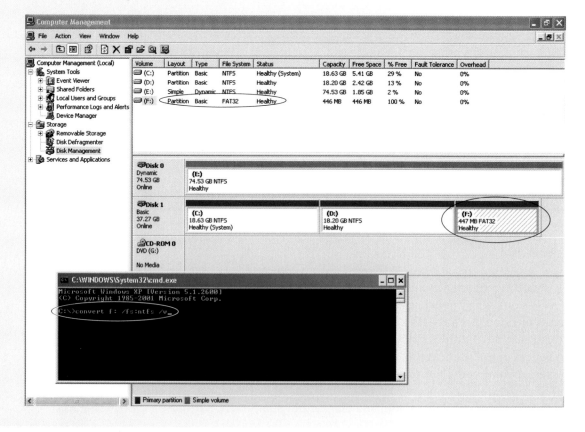

<table>
<tr><td>**Step 4**</td><td>Monitor your Command Prompt window and note the returned messages resulting from the conversion. You should see a note saying "Windows has checked the file system and found no problems."</td></tr>
</table>

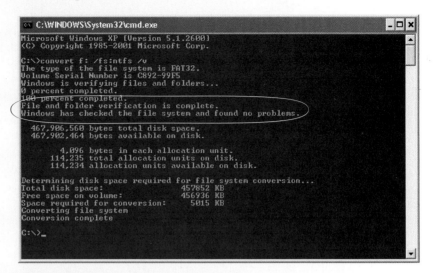

<table>
<tr><td>**Step 5**</td><td>Confirm that your drive has been converted and that it is reported as being "Healthy" in the Computer Management window. Then shut all windows to return to your desktop.</td></tr>
</table>

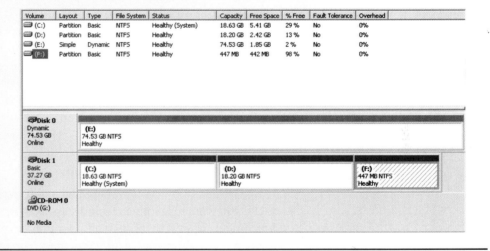

■ Utilizing Your Network File Systems

The users on the SinkRSwim Pools network have really started gathering files and trying to share them over the network. Ricky has noticed a huge increase in the number of complaints submitted by users who have shared files only to see them altered or totally disappear. Although everyone involved has the best intentions, but data has been lost and a downturn in employee productivity has started to impact the comfortable feeling that had surrounded network use up to this point. Lauren has approved additional training sessions for groups of employees to better teach them how to store and share their information.

Cross Check

Sharing Prerequisites?

Do you remember reading about sharing in this book? Go back and read Step-by-Step 2.02 to review the requirements that must be met before sharing can be implemented on your computer. Use that information to answer the following questions:

1. What piece of equipment must be installed before the Windows 98 or higher computer that you used in that exercise could share items on the network?

2. Once your computer recognized the piece of equipment in the previous question, what icon appeared on your Windows desktop?

3. What button did you later have to click to implement sharing on your computer?

Share-Level Permissions

Unless you share your files, nobody on the network can use them. How you share them depends on the system you install and its ability to allow you to grant others different levels of access. The following sections of this chapter will discuss the sorts of access control you can have over your files and will help you decide which type of storage system you will develop for your network.

As you have already learned, before you can do any sharing on your network, you need to install a network interface card, you need to be connected to the network, and you must have all the necessary software components installed to allow network functionality. Then you must run the Network Setup Wizard. The result on your current Windows network is that you have what used to be called a Network Neighborhood icon on your desktop. Now that icon is called My Network Places on both your Windows 2000 server and your Windows XP computers. This means you can share your information with other Windows networked users. Additionally, the files you store on your NetWare network can be shared only with other NetWare users, and only after you have installed the Novell Client.

Some of the decisions about the different levels at which sharing can occur on your network have already been made during the installation you already completed. However, because you can install additional computers and create them with different systems, you should know about these possibilities.

Sharing Options on FAT Partitions

FAT partitions allow you to share items only at the folder level. That means that if you want to let others have access to an individual file on a FAT partition, you must add that file to a folder you have already shared with them (or one that you will later let them share). Once users have access to that shared folder, they have access to any files that folder contains. You installed your network without using FAT partitions, but the fact that you, or someone else, could add them later makes it important for you to know their sharing abilities and limitations.

Workgroup Users   As a workgroup user (someone using a networked Windows computer as a member of a workgroup, rather than a domain) working on a FAT partition, you can decide either to keep the folder you share as a private folder (shared only with users on the local computer) or name it and share it over your network. If your decision is to share it, you can then decide whether or not to allow networked users to change your files. Those are the only decisions you get to make as a workgroup user on a FAT partition. Additionally, you have no control over what local users do with your

234

files. Anyone with local access to a computer with a FAT partition and who is operating as a workgroup member has full access to all files located on that computer.

Domain Users   If you are a user logged into a domain computer (a computer that is part of the domain) that stores files on a FAT partition, you have more control over your shared files, but not much more. Only three sharing permissions (plus an optional Deny permission), as shown in Figure 7.6, are available for files stored on FAT partitions of domain member computers.

Although your intent in using these three permissions is to control access to your files, the permissions can be assigned only to folders—they cannot be assigned to the files inside a folder. Permissions can, however, be assigned to folders such that they apply to either a domain's groups, its individual users, or both. All files inside a particular shared folder are shared using the share permissions applied to that folder.

The share permissions that are available to you are Read, Change, and Full Control. Additionally, you have the option to Deny these permissions either individually or collectively.

- **Read**   The Read permission really grants a user more than the name implies. Granting the Read permission first grants users permission to see the list of files stored on a partition and then allows them to read the information you have stored in the particular files they choose to view. Once this permission is applied to a folder, the permission is

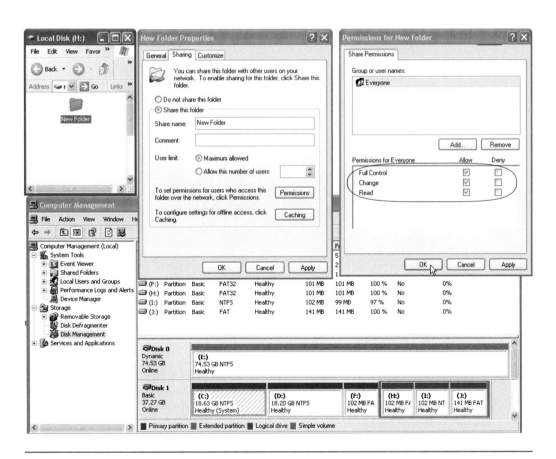

- **Figure 7.6**   You can either apply (or deny) any of the three share permissions to a new folder.

Granting permission to perform a particular task does not ensure that the user has the ability to ac-complish that task. Telling a two-year-old that he or she has your permission to fly a Lear jet from Houston to New York does not in and of itself give that child the capability of actually flying the jet. In the case of granting a user permission to access files, the ability to perform the permitted action depends on whether the user has the required application installed on his or her computer and the knowledge to use it.

applied to all files in that folder. Thus, users can see any file they choose as long as it happens to be stored in a folder to which they have the Read permission granted. They can read the file or the folder's attributes (the settings you have applied to either of these items), they can run any program files you have stored in the folder, and they can change any folders that are placed inside the folder to which they have been granted access.

- **Change**   Assigning the Change permission to a folder allows either the group or individual recipient to perform all the actions available to someone with the Read permission plus the option to alter the folder or its contents. Granting users the Change permission grants them permission to change everything in the folder and even to make changes to the original folder itself. Changing files or folders includes the option to create them, add more of them, append data to the ends of files, and change their attributes. Note that permission to change these items also includes the option to delete them completely.

- **Full Control**   The default share permission assigned to newly created share folders is the Full Control permission, and it is configured with the Read, Change, and Full Control options selected for the Everyone user, as shown in Figure 7.6. The Full Control permission grants users all the options they normally have available to them when they have the Read and Change permissions, plus they can change the folder's permissions and take ownership of the folder or its contents. You should not give out this permission freely if you are in charge of network security issues.

- **Deny**   You also have the ability to make sure users (or groups) do not access your files by using the Deny option. The Deny option refuses any applicable level of user access to the folder where the option is applied. It completely overrules any other comparable share permission's effect. That is, you decide the level of access that will be denied a user by choosing which of the three deny options, shown in Figure 7.6, you want to apply. Although the Deny option is not actually a share permission, because it does not grant any degree of file or folder access, it is another powerful option that is available to you when deciding share permissions.

Similar Sharing on NTFS Partitions

If the partition where you store your files is formatted with NTFS, and you want simply to share those files with other network users, you can set per-missions on folders whether you are logged into a workgroup or logged into a domain just as you can with FAT partitions. However, this ignores the ad-ditional capabilities you have available when using NTFS partitions. As you will learn in the next section, sharing materials on NTFS-formatted parti-tions affords you additional methods for controlling access to the items you wish to share over your network. Despite Microsoft's suggested use of the advanced capabilities of its NTFS access control, using network shares is the level of control that you should implement on your relatively small net-work. As you will learn later, additional control brings with it added complexity that is unnecessary in your class environment.

No Sharing on NetWare Partitions

While there is a Shared directory in NetWare's NFS, and network users are encouraged to place files and applications there that can be shared with other users, no equivalent to Microsoft's sharing capabilities is available on your installation of Novell's NetWare products—either server or client. In fact, the term "shareable" is used on Novell's NetWare networks, but it is not used for granting users access permissions. Rather, when it is used in NetWare, the term "shareable" designates a file that can be worked on by more than one person at the same time.

Although you can allow others access to your NetWare files, such access is available only to NetWare users. Furthermore, the users who do obtain access through the permissions you assign them do not get their access through share permissions they have available from the Microsoft portion of your network.

File-Level Permissions

If you want to implement control down to the file level, you must either store and share your files from within an NTFS partition or store and share them from a NetWare partition. Since no file-level permissions are available for files stored on FAT partitions, the following discussion will cover only NTFS and NetWare implementations of file-level permissions.

File-Level Permissions on NTFS Partitions

On NTFS partitions, in addition to the three permissions available for shared folders , you also have the ability to apply file-level permissions on files. That means that once your partition is formatted with NTFS, and you have files and folders on that partition, you can either use the shared permissions discussed previously or assign **file-level permissions** to your shared folders and to the files themselves.

Whether you are operating as a user logged in to a workgroup or in to a computer that is a member of a domain, Microsoft recommends that after creating and initially sharing a new folder, you should accept the default share permissions that are automatically assigned. Then you should use the Security tab, shown in Figure 7.7, and apply the additional file-level permissions that become available to you because you are using an NTFS partition.

In addition to the Full Control and Read permissions that are somewhat similar (although not the same) to the share permissions you have already seen, these new permissions include Modify, Read and Execute, List Folder Contents, Write, and special permissions. Each of these additional permissions is discussed, from the least restrictive to the most restrictive, in the following sections. To differentiate them from the share permissions discussed earlier, and from similar NetWare permissions that will be discussed later, *NTFS* will be included in their names for this discussion only.

NTFS Read   Unlike the share's Read permission, the NTFS Read permission does exactly what its name implies. That is, with the NTFS Read permission, the only action a user can perform is to read the contents of a folder or an applicable file. Any other action is prevented. Should additional access be required, additional permissions must be associated with this user.

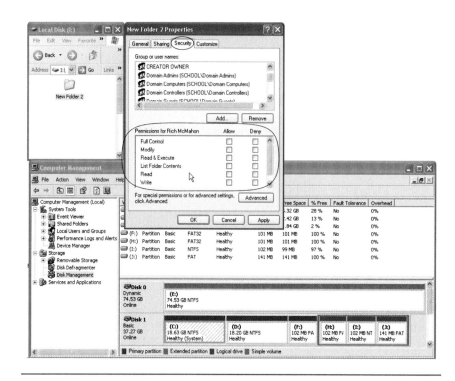

● **Figure 7.7** An additional Security tab is available in the Properties window for folders created on NTFS partitions.

NTFS List Folder Contents The NTFS List Folder Contents permission adds two actions to what a user can do with the NTFS Read permission. Those additional actions include the option to **traverse** a folder and to run an executable file (which is typically an associated application or some other program needed to interpret the file). Traversing a folder means navigating through a particular folder on the way to another file or folder that is contained either within or below the original folder. Being able to traverse a folder does not affect, nor is it affected by, any permissions applied or denied to the folders being traversed. This permission is not inherited by files created within the folders to which this permission is applied.

NTFS Read and Execute The NTFS Read and Execute permission applies the same permissions as those the NTFS List Folder Contents permission, with one exception: folders and files created within a folder with this permission inherit the same permission.

NTFS Write Assigning the NTFS Write permission simply allows a user to write information. Writing, in this7 case, includes creating new files (or folders) as well as writing changes to files (or folders) that already exist.

In keeping with its name, however, this permission does not allow the user to read the contents of a file or even to view the contents of a folder. Neither does the NTFS Write permission grant the user permission to traverse the folder in an effort to access another included file or folder. In order to perform any of these additional actions, one of the previously discussed permissions must be applied.

NTFS Modify Although the option to write to a file may seem as strong as modifying a file, the NTFS Modify permission does quite a bit more. In fact, the NTFS Modify permission combines all the previous permissions together and permits them all. This permission is second only to the most powerful NTFS Full Control permission.

NTFS Full Control   The NTFS Full Control permission grants authorization to all users to perform all actions permitted by the NTFS Modify permission, and adds the ability for those users to take ownership of a file or folder, as well as to change a file or folder's permissions. The NTFS Full Control permission is the default permission applied to all newly created files and folders.

File-Level Permissions on NetWare Partitions

Files stored on your NetWare server are kept on partitions that you formatted with Novell's NetWare operating system. You normally put them there so you can take advantage of (or, in this case, learn about) using its implementation of NFS, the file system discussed at the beginning of this chapter. NetWare also allows you to assign specific rights at the file level, somewhat like the NTFS permissions just discussed. However, since one of NetWare's main features is its ability to store and control enormous corporate-wide access to files using its implementation of an NFS, you can expect this system to be a bit more complicated than anything you have already seen. You will not, therefore, be expected to become an expert on using NFS just by reading this text. Neither will you be expected to convert your entire network storage over to Novell's NFS. Rather, you should strive to recognize the similarities between the two storage systems' capabilities and be able to apply what you learn to implementations of either system.

Eight different rights are assigned to both files and directories in Novell's implementation of its NFS. The eight file system rights are Supervisor, Read, Write, Create, Erase, Modify, File Scan, and Access Control. Although access to the files and the directories is controlled using these eight rights, you can set them independently of each other. Thus, you can set a user's rights to the files contained within a directory to be different from the rights on the directory itself.

Each of Novell's eight rights assignments will be discussed in the sections that follow. Their coverage here, however, will not take you from the least restrictive to the most restrictive as in the discussion of Microsoft's permissions. Rather, they will be discussed in the order listed previously, because that order better fits the mnemonic device almost all Novell NetWare administrators use to remember NFS rights: Some Rights Will Cause Extreme Mental Fatigue, Always.

These rights will include *NetWare* in their names during this discussion only. Each of the rights has a Novell-assigned name and a single-letter abbreviation that is used in Novell's system documentation as well as in the graphical depictions you will see on your server console and your workstation's client, as shown in Figure 7.8. Thus, the identifier is provided in the following discussions, along with a description of the capabilities of the user who is granted each specific right. Whenever speaking of NetWare rights, the names of the rights are always capitalized.

NetWare Supervisor (S)   The highest of the NetWare file system rights, the NetWare Supervisor right grants the user all rights to the applicable file system component (directory, subdirectory, and/or file) where the right is assigned. This right also grants the user all rights to any subcomponents below the file system component where the initial rights are assigned. This

Inside Information

NTFS and NFS: One Major Difference

One major difference between the NTFS and NFS implementations of permissions, in addition to using different terms, is that while Microsoft's default permission grants Full Control to all newly created files and folders, Novell's default settings grant absolutely no rights to anyone. The only time this absolute is violated is during network creation, when the administrator is granted the highest right (the Supervisor right) over everything on the network. Without that exception, after all, there would be nobody on the network to grant anyone rights in the first place. The administrator, therefore, had to be allowed in, but nobody else.

Typically, an individual's access rights to a NetWare directory and to the files within that directory are the same. The only time they might be set differently is in the case where an administrator wishes to limit access to certain files. Although this would not be the typical use of these rights, it is an alternative available to an administrator should the need arise.

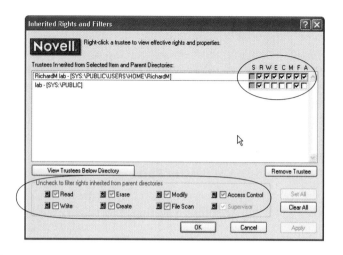

● Figure 7.8   Verifying a user's NetWare file system rights

is because the Supervisor right is the only right that cannot be blocked by an **Inherited Rights Filter (IRF)** (the method, discussed later, that NetWare uses to block the automatic transference of rights, called inheritance, down through the directory's hierarchy). A user with the Supervisor right also has the authority to grant rights to other users. The Supervisor right is the only right automatically assigned by the operating system itself—it is granted to the Admin user during system installation.

NetWare Read (R)   The NetWare Read right allows a user to open and read files stored in a directory. Assigning this right also allows a user to run programs stored within the directory where this right is assigned.

NetWare Write (W)   The NetWare Write right allows the user to open and change or add data to the contents of the directory where the user has this right assigned.

NetWare Create (C)   The NetWare Create right allows the user to create new files and subdirectories inside the applicable directory.

NetWare Erase (E)   The NetWare Erase right allows the user to delete the applicable directory and/or any files or subdirectories contained inside the directory where the right applies.

NetWare Modify (M)   The NetWare Modify right allows the user to change the name of a file, directory, or subdirectory, or to change the attributes associated with any of those applicable objects. It does not allow a user the right to modify the contents of the file, directory, or subdirectory where the right applies.

NetWare File Scan (F)   In order to work with files, you must be able to see them, and with NetWare this means that you must be able to scan files. The NetWare File Scan right allows a user to scan and see directory listings. This includes the right to see the names of files, directories, and subdirectories available on the portion of the NetWare network where the rights apply.

NetWare Access Control (A)   The NetWare Access Control right allows the user to grant another user the right to access a file, directory, or subdirectory or to remove that user's access to those affected objects. The NetWare Access Control right also allows the user to change all applicable IRF and trustee assignments. However, remember that you cannot make any changes to the Supervisor right by altering or setting any IRF, so a user applying this right cannot cause this to occur either.

Effective Permissions

Determining whether a user has the resulting permission (called effective permission) to access a file seems like it would be a pretty simple decision. After all, if that user is granted the permission to perform a particular action on a file or folder, shouldn't that be the action that the system allows the user to perform? Well, it's not quite that simple.

What Are the Causes of the Effective Permissions?

The difficulty in determining actual permissions comes from the fact that user objects are rarely as simple as they look. Frequently, a user object is a member of multiple groups and can therefore have different levels of access coming from different permissions that have been granted to any of its multiple groups.

Determining effective rights on both Microsoft and NetWare networks has always been a difficult task. In the past, painstaking detail and lengthy hierarchical charts were helpful tools for keeping track of network users' effective rights. The combined effects of inheritance and permissions were so involved that even the slightest change could throw off any determination

 Try This!

Check Your Inheritances

You want to check a Microsoft folder for its current inheritance configuration and then check the effective permissions your user has been granted to that folder. Try this:

1. Log in to your Windows XP Professional workstation and your NetWare 6 server as a non-administrator user.

2. Click the Start button and select My Computer. Double-click one of the NTFS drives that you created in Step-by-Step 7.02, earlier in this chapter.

3. Right-click inside the drive's window and select New | Folder. Name the newly created folder **New Folder 2**.

4. Right-click New Folder 2 and select Properties. Highlight your user's name in the Group or User Names section, and scroll to view your permissions in the Permissions For section.

Verify that Special Permissions is dimmed, shown by being gray-checked (meaning that it is inherited), and click the Advanced button.

5. Select the In Permissions tab in the Advanced Security Settings dialog box, and verify that the first Inherit from Parent option in the bottom section is selected.

6. Click the Effective Permissions tab, and click the Select button to open the Select User, Computer, or Group dialog box. Have the system search for your full user name by entering at least part of your name in the Enter the Object Name to Select field, and click the Check Names button. Select your returned user name, and click OK. Your effective permissions will be displayed.

7. Close all open dialog boxes and windows to return to your desktop.

that seemed like it could be logically explained. There was no easy method for calculating these rights. However, with the latest releases of both companies' network operating systems, what used to be a never-ending quest for determining rights has turned into quite a simple process.

Inheritance   In both Microsoft and Novell file systems, rights (or permissions) flow downward. That is, when a user is granted access to a NetWare directory or a Microsoft folder, the same access flows downward and applies to any subdirectory or subfolder.

In either operating system, this downward flow can also be interrupted. With NetWare rights, you can implement an Inherited Rights Filter (IRF) that stops the flow, and with Microsoft permissions, you can change the default setting that configures files and folders for inheritance.

Combining Permissions   On networks, the matter of determining permissions (or rights) gets confusing because the intended controls on the user's access come from numerous sources. To determine their overall effect (commonly called *effective permissions* or *effective rights*), you must have a method of combining the controls and seeing the result.

- **Share Combinations**   When deciding the final share permission a user really has when there are multiple sources for permission, you have to combine all the shared permissions attributable to that user (including those obtained through membership in any group). When they are combined, the least restrictive permission is the resultant share permission.

- **File-Level Combinations**   Similarly, when deciding the final file-level permission a user ends up with when there are multiple sources for permission, you again have to combine all of that type of permission attributable to the user and also include any file-level permissions obtained through membership in any group. When they are combined, the least restrictive permission is again the resultant file-level permission.

- **Combined Combinations**   If your files are stored on an NTFS partition and you happened to have combined share permissions with file-level permissions, the least restrictive of each is taken from the two possibilities. Then the two are combined, and the more restrictive of the two is taken as the final permission.

- **Denied Access**   Although it is very simple to use, the Microsoft option to deny someone's user object the permission necessary to access another networked object is actually quite powerful. No matter how many of the seemingly more powerful granting options have been exercised, the application of just one deny option overrides them all.

Step-by-Step 7.03

Check the NetWare Rights to the HOME Directory

You have several options when it comes to working with assigned rights to particular objects on the Novell NetWare portion of your network, some of which can be exercised at the workstation while others must be exercised at the server console. In this exercise, you will use the functionality available at your workstation to verify a user's rights to your network's HOME directory. Then, you will log on as an administrative user to check the rights to that same directory and see if that is how you intended them to be configured.

To complete this exercise, you will need the following items:

- Operational networked Windows XP Professional workstation
- Operational networked NetWare 6 server
- Network user login information
- Administrative user login information

Step 1

Log in to your Windows XP Professional computer and your NetWare 6 server as a non-administrative user. Right-click the NetWare Services icon in your taskbar's notification area, and select Browse To | My Computer.

Step 2

Scroll through your PUBLIC\SYS drive (Z:) to the HOME directory that you created earlier in this chapter. Your HOME directory should be located inside Z:\USERS\HOME\, it should be identified by your user name, and you should notice at this point that you can see the other users' HOME directories.

Step 3

Right-click an empty space in your HOME directory's window, and select New | Folder. Name the newly created folder **New Folder N**.

Note: You are working from a Microsoft Windows workstation using folder terminology. However, remember that you are working in NetWare, so you are actually creating subdirectories according to Novell terminology.

Step 4

Right-click your New Folder N folder and select Trustee Rights to open the NetWare Services dialog box, which depicts the rights your user currently has assigned to it, relative to the newly created folder.

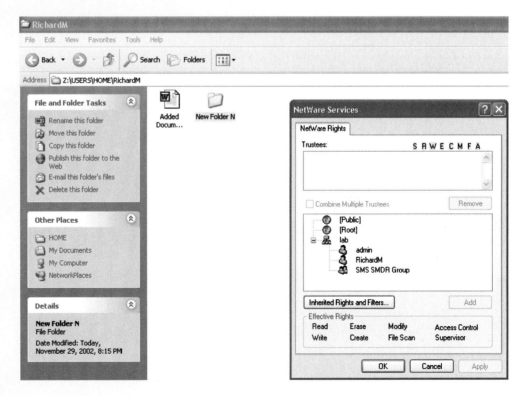

Tip: A similar dialog box can be opened by selecting Properties instead of Trustee Rights. (The dialog box's name is New Folder N Properties, much like other Windows Properties dialog boxes.)

Step 5

Click the Inherited Rights and Filters button, and verify your user's inherited rights. The current configuration of your IRFs at the bottom of the dialog box should look like what was shown earlier in Figure 7.8.

Step 6

At your NetWare 6 server's graphical console screen, click the Novell button, select ConsoleOne, and expand the University tree. Log in as your administrative user (if required), navigate in the left pane to the HOME directory, right-click the HOME directory, and select Properties.

Step 7

In the Trustees tab of the Properties of HOME window, click the Effective Rights button. In the Effective Rights dialog box, click the Browse button to the right of the Trustee field, and browse to and select your user object in the Lab Container. Click OK in the select object window, and notice the Effective Rights section of the Effective Rights window. This means that you (and any other users) have the right to scan and read anything in anybody's HOME folder.

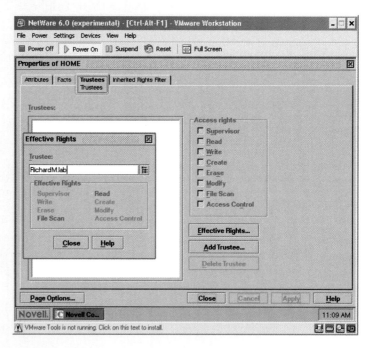

Step 8

Close all windows and dialog boxes and return to your desktop at your workstation. Click the Close button two times at your server console to return to the GUI startup screen.

Chapter 7 Review

■ Chapter Summary

After reading this chapter and completing the Step-by-Step tutorials and Try This! exercises, you should understand the following facts about network file systems:

Use Novell's Network File System

- When the NetWare operating system is installed, some of the file system is created, and it gets configured by administrators and employed by users so they can share their files.

- Accessing networked resources becomes a reason other users join the network.

- The NetWare file system also stores and shares networked applications.

- All NetWare servers contain NFS components, which include file servers, volumes, directories, subdirectories, and files, that together provide centralized access and coordinated sharing for users.

- Names within NFS have to be unique to allow the system to find the files; the names cannot include any reserved characters.

- A volume is a physical storage device and is similar to a DOS disk drive.

- The first volume created on a NetWare network is the SYS: volume, where the operating system files are stored.

- Although they are automatically named by the system, you can change additional volumes' names during installation or later to help clarify your system's structure.

- NFS is another tree-like hierarchical structure similar to NDS.

- Inside NFS are required directories, such as SYS, PUBLIC, and LOGIN, as well as optional directories, such as USERS, HOME, and APPS.

- Mapping a drive tells the operating system to treat the newly mapped object as a separate hard drive.

- Filename syntax is a formatting structure that helps NFS locate your files.

Describe Windows File Storage

- Your network's Windows 2000 and Windows XP Professional computers both support several different file systems, such as CDFS, UDF, FAT, and NTFS, and they use two storage types: basic and dynamic.

- The Windows file storage structural components can also be likened to the way a filing cabinet is organized.

- The primary storage type is basic storage on basic disks formatted using primary partitions.

- Basic disks can have up to four primary partitions, with one of them being an extended partition with logical drives that extend the number of divisions allowed on the disk.

- The active partition is the primary partition that the system uses when looking for boot files; it is called the system partition.

- The operating system files can be located in a primary or an extended partition, called the boot partition, and they do not have to be on the system partition.

- You can upgrade, or convert, basic storage to the newer dynamic storage for increased efficiency and fault tolerance.

- Five levels of RAID (redundant array of independent disks) have different volume types and varying redundancy (the ability to be recovered after failure), commonly called fault tolerance.

- Dynamic storage includes the following volume types: simple, mirrored, spanned, striped, and striped with parity.

- Your Windows file system partitions are formatted as FAT or NTFS partitions.

- The file allocation table (FAT) system was designed when file systems were small; FAT is inefficient with newer, larger systems.

- The NTFS file system is more efficient than FAT and handles larger file systems.

- FAT files have a greater tendency to be stored in non-contiguous space and therefore become fragmented, but the FAT file system is still the file support system most widely used with Windows.

- FAT partitions waste space, are inefficient, and do not offer the additional security available with NTFS partitions.

- NTFS uses a smaller cluster size than FAT, it is more efficient, it uses a Master File Table (MFT), it is more recoverable, and it includes added security features that make storage at the file level possible.

Utilize Your Network File Systems

- One of the main purposes of your network is to share files, and you have to decide how much control you need over that process—folder-level or file-level permissions.

- You must run the Network Setup Wizard on your network to enable networking functionality before you can do any sharing.

- Network resources stored on your NetWare servers are available only to users with the NetWare Client installed.

- Different sharing options are available for workgroup and domain users on FAT partitions and NTFS partitions.

- FAT storage can be shared at the folder level, whereas NTFS storage can set permissions down to the file level.

- Access control for shares on FAT partitions is limited to Read, Change, or Full Control, but NTFS has all those and the file-level controls available.

- The Deny option can negate any access permission.

- Access control at the file level on NTFS partitions can include the NTFS Read, List Folder Contents, Read and Execute, Write, Modify, and Full Control permissions.

- NetWare controls access at the file level using rights that are similar to the Microsoft file-level permissions.

- Microsoft's default permission is Full Control, whereas Novell's default is to assign no rights to the user.

- Novell capitalizes its NFS rights names, and they include Supervisor, Read, Write, Create, Erase, Modify, File Scan, and Access Control.

- An Inherited Rights Filter (IRF) blocks (or allows) NetWare's rights to flow downward through the file system's hierarchical structure from parent containers to their contents.

- The NetWare Supervisor right cannot be blocked by an IRF.

- The effective permissions reflect the actual access granted as a result of combining all permissions or rights granted to a user.

- When evaluating share permissions from multiple sources, all are combined and the least restrictive is used as the effective permission.

- When evaluating file-level permissions from multiple sources, all are combined and the least restrictive is used as the effective permission.

- When combining share permissions with file-level permissions, the two are combined and the most restrictive of the two becomes the effective permission.

Key Terms

basic disks *(220)*
break the mirror *(224)*
contiguous space *(227)*
defrag *(227)*
directory *(211)*
dynamic storage *(222)*
effective permissions *(242)*
effective rights *(242)*
extended partitions *(221)*
file allocation table (FAT) *(226)*

file-level permissions *(237)*
fragmented *(227)*
Inherited Rights Filter (IRF) *(240)*
map a drive *(218)*
mirrored volume *(224)*
network file system (NFS) *(208)*
non-contiguous space *(227)*
NTFS file system *(228)*
primary partitions *(221)*

RAID *(223)*
restore the mirror *(224)*
simple volume *(223)*
spanned volume *(224)*
striped volume *(224)*
striped volume with parity *(225)*
syntax *(217)*
system partition *(221)*
traverse *(238)*

Key Term Quiz

Use the preceding vocabulary terms to complete the following sentences. Not all the terms will be used.

1. The highest-level storage unit in the _____ structure is called the file server.

2. On a Windows NT–based network, the dynamic storage area that is located on one physical disk and uses all of the disk's space for a single volume is called a(n) _____.

3. A(n) _____ is an object representing an area on a NetWare physical network storage device where files are stored.

4. User files and associated documents are usually stored in their own HOME _____.

5. Only one of the four possible partitions on a basic disk can be created as a(n) _____.

6. The active partition, also called the _____, is the primary partition that the system goes to when looking for the boot files.

7. One of the benefits of using _____ is fault-tolerant storage space.

8. If, after a single point failure, an entire volume fails and is not recoverable, this lack of redundancy is described as being the lowest level (level 0) of _____.

9. Combining multiple dynamic storage disks results in what is called a(n) _____.

10. Adjacent storage space on a disk drive is called _____.

Multiple-Choice Quiz

1. Which of the following correctly identifies Novell's official designation for the file system in use on NetWare 6 operating systems?

   a. NetWare's File Directory Servers

   b. NetWare File Service

   c. Novell File Servers

   d. None of the above

2. Which of the following is not a component of the file system used on NetWare 6 networks?

   a. File servers

   b. Folders

   c. Files

   d. Volumes

3. When comparing the filing cabinet to the file system used on NetWare 6 networks, which of the following components would be most like the filing cabinet's drawers?

   a. File

   b. Folder

   c. Volume

   d. Subdirectory

4. All of the following are reserved characters that cannot be used to name NetWare file system objects except which one?

   a. = < >

   b. ? " *

   c. + , :

   d. - . $

5. All of the following are required in the NetWare 6 operating system except which one?

   a. APPLICATION

   b. SYSTEM

   c. PUBLIC

   d. LOGIN

6. Basic storage involves the use of disk drives that can be formatted using all of the following except which one?

   a. Primary partitions

   b. Logical drives

   c. Volumes

   d. Extended partitions

7. If your disk is divided into two basic partitions and an extended partition, what is the maximum number of logical drives that you can use on that disk drive?

   a. 32

   b. 22

   c. 4

   d. 1

8. Which of the following does not describe the basic disk's partition where you store the operating system's startup files?

   a. Primary partition

   b. System partition

   c. Active partition

   d. Boot partition

9. When you upgrade basic storage devices to be dynamic storage devices, the disk drives themselves are then called which of the following?

   a. Volumes

   b. Directories

   c. Folders

   d. Dynamic drives

10. When you extend a simple volume, what is the effect on the fault tolerance of that storage device?

    a. It goes from RAID-1 to RAID-0.

    b. It goes from RAID-0 to RAID-1.

    c. It is reduced.

    d. It is increased.

11. Which of the following represents the most correct initial action that you should take in the event that your mirrored volume fails?

    a. Restore the mirror.

    b. Break the mirror.

    c. Remove the failed copy.

    d. Create another copy.

12. If a disk on a spanned volume using 32 individual but identical disks fails, how many of the remaining disks have recoverable data?

    a. 3

    b. 0

    c. 31

    d. 4

13. Which of the following is the most likely to be formatted using NTFS?

   a. Permissions granted to the root directory

   b. Storage using share permissions

   c. Storage using file-level permissions

   d. Storage using folder-level permissions

14. File tables are used in which of the following?

   a. FAT32

   b. FAT

   c. NTFS

   d. All of the above

15. None of the following has any impact on the effective access a Microsoft user has to a file stored in a folder on a FAT partition, with the exception of which one?

   a. The Share This Folder option is deselected, but the user still has access to it anyway.

   b. The default sharing option is altered in the file's Properties dialog box.

   c. The user has Full Control permission assigned to the file.

   d. The user has Deny permissions assigned at the file level.

■ Essay Quiz

1. Explain the comparison between an office filing cabinet and the Novell and Microsoft network file systems.

2. Explain why a filename's syntax is important on a network.

3. Differentiate between initial access that is granted a user to a file on a Microsoft network versus that which is initially granted on a NetWare network.

4. How is the Microsoft Deny permission option similar to Novell's use of IRFs?

5. What is the purpose of mapping a drive?

Lab Projects

Time to roll up your sleeves and apply what you've learned. The following lab projects will enable you to practice the concepts discussed in this chapter.

• Lab Project 7.1

Everyone at the TEACH training center is furious. Suddenly, you are being asked to secure files and folders on your Novell NetWare 6 server. The whole thing started when you demonstrated how users could verify the effective rights to objects on a

NetWare network and you used the HOME folder as your example. During that demonstration, users learned that they all had the Read and File Scan rights to each other's stored information. Right after the briefing you gave, Lauren logged everyone off the Novell portion of the network and called you into her office and presented you with a new HOME directory configuration. Nobody (except the administrator) should even see anyone else's HOME folder, let alone be able to read what is kept there. You are to fix the problem immediately.

You will need the following:

- A networked lab computer with Windows XP Professional and Novell Client installed

- A networked operational Novell NetWare 6 server

- A non-administrative network user's login information

- Administrative user login information

Then do the following:

1. At your NetWare 6 server's graphical console, click the Novell button, select ConsoleOne, and navigate in the left pane (including logging in if required) to the HOME directory.

2. Right-click the HOME directory icon, select Properties, and click the Inherited Rights Filter tab in the Properties of HOME window. Verify the configuration of the IRFs. Remember, the

Supervisor right cannot be blocked by adding or deleting an IRF, and its icon is grayed out because the right is inherited.

3. If the IRFs have already been cleared, skip to Step 5 of this exercise; otherwise, clear all the IRFs displayed. Notice that the arrow on the left of each right changes from its pass-through form to one indicating that it is blocked. This indicates that the right is now filtered.

4. Click the Apply button.

5. As your non-administrative user, log in to your Windows XP Professional workstation, click the Start button, select My Computer, and navigate using your Z: drive to your network's HOME directory.

6. Verify that you can no longer view the other users' HOME directories and that only your HOME directory (the one you created with your own user name) can now be viewed.

7. Close all windows to return to your desktop on your workstation and the GUI startup screen on your server.

• Lab Project 7.2

Apparently, the training center users have been bragging to other network users about the HOME directories you configured for them on their NetWare server. Now, everyone on the network has suddenly started requesting a similar configuration on the Windows 2000 server. You have been asked to configure the server and provide the Windows users on your network with storage space in a HOME directory similar to what the NetWare users have.

You will need the following:

- A networked lab computer running Windows XP Professional

- An networked operational server acting as a Windows 2000 domain controller with Active Directory installed

- Your user information

Then do the following:

1. Log in to your Windows 2000 server computer as your administrative user.

2. Double-click the My Computer icon on your desktop, and if multiple disks are attached to your server, decide which will be used for the HOME directory storage. Then double-click that disk's icon.

3. Click the blank space in your drive's opened window, select New | Folder, and rename the newly created folder **HOME**.

4. Right-click your new HOME folder, and select Sharing | Share This Folder.

5. Click the Permissions button and deselect the Full Control and Change permissions on the Everyone group. Click the Add button and scroll to and select the Users group. Click Add and click OK.

6 Select the newly inserted Users group, select the Full Control permission, and click OK.

7 Click the Security tab and deselect the Full Control permission on the Everyone group. Click the Add button, scroll to and select the Users group, click Add, and click OK.

8 Select the newly inserted Users group, select the Full Control permission, and click OK once and then again.

9 Click the Start button and select Programs | Administrative Tools | Active Directory Users and Computers.

10 Expand Users in the left pane, and double-click your user in the right pane.

11 Click the Profile tab of your user's Properties dialog box, click the Connect option, and scroll to drive letter H in the drop-down selection box. Enter the following in the To field and then click OK:

```
\\Win2kSvr1\HOME\%username%
```

12 Check that the HOME directory is working properly by logging into your Windows XP Professional computer and the Windows 2000 server using your domain user account information. Click the Start button and select My Computer. Verify the presence of the H: drive.

13 Right-click your H: drive and select Properties, click the Security tab, and verify that your Full Control permissions are configured. Click the Advanced button, click the Effective Permissions tab on the Advanced Security Settings dialog box, and click the Select button.

14 In the Enter the Object Name to Select field, type another user's name, click the Check Names button, select the correct returned name, and click OK.

15 Verify that none of the effective permissions are selected in the Effective Permissions section of the Advanced Security Settings dialog box.

16 Close all server and workstation dialog boxes and windows, and return to your desktop.

chapter
8
Printing Over a Network

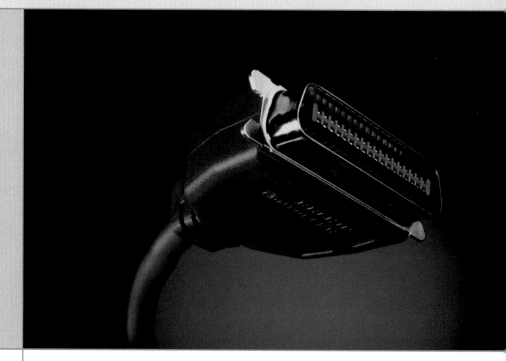

"If sharing a thing in no way diminishes it, it is not rightly owned if it is not shared."

—St. Augustine

In this chapter, you will learn how to:

- **Explain network printing concepts**
- **Describe Windows network printing**
- **Explain NetWare network printing**

One of the main reasons that most schools (and home users) create small networks is to gain the economic advantage of sharing printers. When printers are shared over a network, individual printers for each computer are not needed, and this can result in significant savings. Users can also get the added benefit of having more choices about which type of printer they want to use if there is more than one attached to the network. Although you probably started this course with a network that already had computers and printers attached and running, it is time, now, to learn about installing and using printers on your network.

In this chapter, you will learn about network printing, and you will create local printers and access those printers over the network. Then you will start sharing your printers, and you will take a look at Microsoft's printer-sharing techniques. Finally, you will learn about the complex system Novell uses with its NetWare operating system. You will add Novell's new iPrint optional feature, which uses the Novell Distributed Print Services. You will use your Internet browser to put this complex service together. Then you will install the iPrint client on your Windows workstation.

Understand Network Printing Concepts

Lately, Ricky has been receiving almost constant complaints about the inconveniences of printing at SinkRSwim Pools. When the network was first created, there were only a few users, and each computer had its own printer. That is no longer the case. All of the company's employees are now on their own computers, but several do not have locally attached printers. Those employees are getting around this lack of equipment by transferring their print requests to computers with attached printers and having their work printed at that different location. This is causing frustration and unnecessary delays. Ricky explained to Lauren that he thought it was time to configure the network for shared printing, and to provide the added convenience of network printing to all the company's users.

There are three basic printing configurations that can be used when designing a network and configuring printing equipment for users. If there are enough printers to allow each user to have his or her own, then configuring everyone with separate local printers (also called print devices) is the first option. Since that is not very likely to happen, even in your classroom labs, any computers that have their own printers can be configured so that the printers can be shared with other network users. Those computers then offer their printing capability to others on the network and effectively become **print servers**. Finally, many printers can be directly attached to the network, and all networked users can print to them from anywhere on the network. The three basic printing configurations are shown in Figure 8.1.

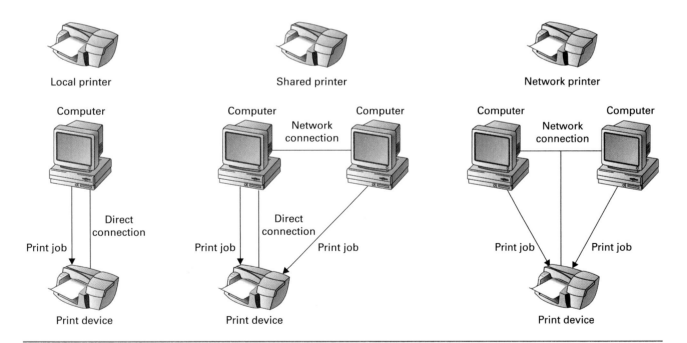

• **Figure 8.1** There are three basic printing configurations for networked computers.

You may have to visit your print device vendor's web site to download updated drivers for your print device.

Locally Connected Print Devices

Probably the most convenient way to print from a workstation computer is to have a **local print device**—a physical printer directly connected to the computer itself. This is how you would set up your own computer for printing if neither your computer nor your printer were attached to a network. In that case, your print device would be located near your computer, and it would be plugged into one of the computer's **output ports** (connections for parallel, serial, USB, SCSI, or other output).

The Windows operating systems that you are working with in this textbook are all capable of recognizing most of the printers that you can connect to the workstations or servers on your network. When Windows recognizes that you have connected a print device, it installs the **drivers** (the software programs that run that print device). Whenever local users want to print materials from that workstation, they simply send their work as **output** to the locally connected print device.

Although simply clicking an application's Print button easily sets in motion the functions necessary for sending the output to the printer, the process is nowhere near as simple as it appears. First of all, you should notice in the previous paragraph that what the typical user knows as a printer is actually a *print device* in Microsoft terms. Print devices are simply machines that are capable of creating printed output.

However, those devices can't work without the software that connects them to the applications on the computer. The software (or more precisely, the software interface) is actually what Microsoft considers to be the **printer**. When you send your intended output to that software, it determines where and when your output will be sent. Even if there is only one print device connected to a computer, that printer (the software that controls the printing process) has choices of where to send the output. It can go to the local print device or it can go to some other output device, such as an output file or even the computer screen.

Setting Up a Local Print Device

One of the principal methods for printing output from your computer is to connect a print device directly to your computer and send print jobs to it locally. Once you have the print device connected to one of the local ports on your workstation computer, it is an easy matter to set your Windows operating system to print your output to that device. In this exercise, you will connect a print device to your workstation, ensure a local printer is loaded on your computer, and end the installation by sending a print job to your print device so you can test its local connection.

To complete this exercise, you will need the following items:

- Print device suitable for connecting locally to your computer
- Windows XP Professional workstation

Step 1	Start your Windows XP Professional workstation and log in as your administrative user.
Step 2	Click the Start button, select Printers and Faxes, and confirm that there are no printers currently installed on your computer, as shown here. Remove any that are currently installed.

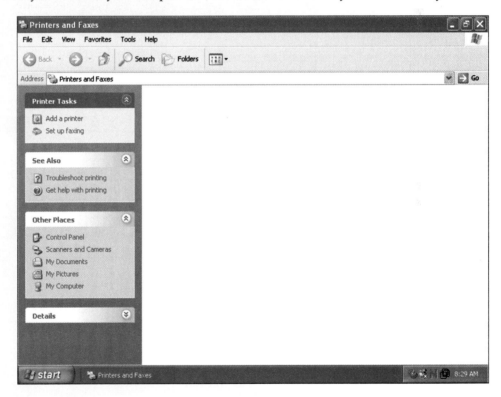

Step 3

In the left panel, click the Add a Printer option to open the Add Printer Wizard. Read the information about automatically detecting attached printers, as shown in the illustration. Connect your print device to your computer, and then plug it in and turn its power switch to the on position. If it is automatically detected by your computer, follow the instructions to configure your particular print device. Otherwise, click Next to continue with the manual setup.

Step 4

Select the Local Printer Attached to This Computer option, ensure that the Automatically Detect and Install My Plug and Play Printer option is selected, and click Next.

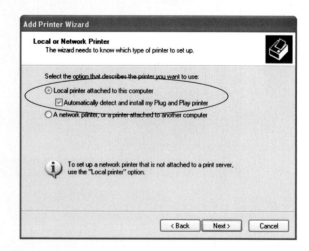

Step 5

If the wizard finds your printer, confirm the selection by clicking OK. Otherwise, continue with the manual installation by clicking Next.

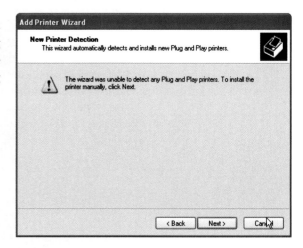

Step 6

Ensure the Use the Following Port option is selected and that the drop-down box is set to LPT1: (Recommended Printer Port). Read the note in the middle of the Select a Printer Port dialog box for information about the printer port and its connector, and click Next.

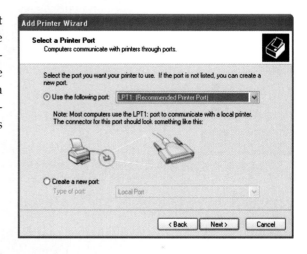

Step 7

The wizard will look for printer driver information and display any recommended drivers in the Install Printer Software dialog box. Ensure that the correct print device is selected. If the Windows recommendation is not correct, scroll to and select the proper printer.

Tip: If you have printer installation diskettes or have printer drivers that you downloaded from your printer manufacturer's web site, you can click the Have Disk button and navigate to your file location to install your printer using the updated drivers.

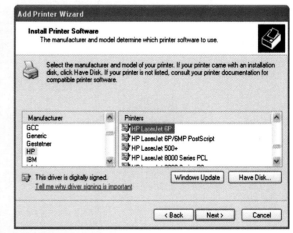

Step 8

If your computer finds existing drivers already loaded, you may be asked whether you want to keep the existing drivers or install new ones. Click Next after making your choice. Otherwise, enter the name you would like to use for your printer, as shown in the illustration, and click Next.

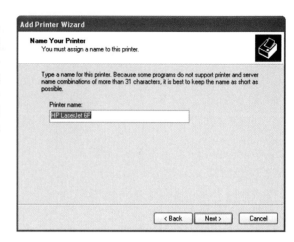

Step 9

Select the Do Not Share This Printer option, and click Next. Later in this chapter you will learn about sharing printers.

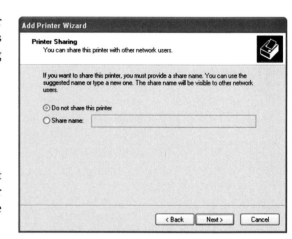

Step 10

Select the Yes option to print a test page, and click Next. Confirm your printer's information, and click the Finish button.

Step 11

Click OK after confirming that your test output page was printed properly. This will close the Add Printer Wizard and return you to your Printers and Faxes window, where you should see your new printer's icon, as shown here.

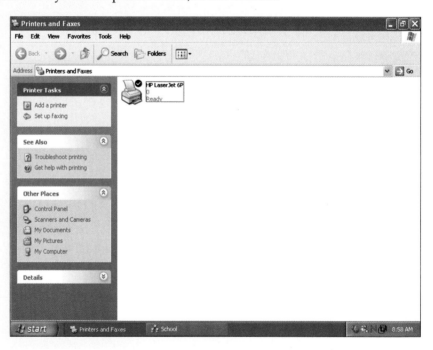

*Note: Notice the small black circle with the check mark in the upper-right corner of your print device icon. That check mark indicates that this is the **default printer**—the print device that your output will be sent to unless you specify otherwise. Since you only have one print device installed, it is automatically marked as the default printer. Otherwise, you would be asked whether the printer you were installing was to be used as your default printer.*

Step 12 | Close the Printers and Faxes window and return to your desktop.

Shared Print Devices

Sharing print devices is really at the heart of what **network printing** (producing printed materials using networked resources) is all about. Such sharing, after all, is what ends up saving money, which may be the most important reason for network printing in the first place. There are two ways print devices can be shared—they can be locally connected to a computer or directly connected to the network.

The first option involves configuring locally installed print devices so that others can use them whenever the need arises. This configuration allows users to decide which print devices to use. It puts a burden on the computer that is directly connected to the print device when it handles the additional workload, and that computer's user will be interrupted when printed output is retrieved. However, most computer network designs do not include installation of print devices at each workstation or let you choose to use any shared printer you'd like, so these first two configurations may still not include printing capability for all users.

More often, networks are configured so that a high-speed print device is centrally located on the network to give multiple users convenient access. Such a configuration means that users can send their own work to print devices, and they can retrieve their printouts themselves. Such device sharing saves money because it decreases the number of print devices that have to be purchased, installed, and maintained. Convenient central access also decreases the number of support personnel required to distribute the printed output.

Sharing Locally Attached Print Devices

You can share locally installed print devices like the one you installed in Step-by-Step 8.01. Sometimes older computers can be dedicated solely to printing when using this setup. More likely, however, individual users appreciate having their own print devices as a matter of convenience. This is the most likely reason for sharing locally installed print devices. When users share their attached devices, they make them available to multiple users on the network.

Even in circumstances where several (if not all) workstations have their own locally attached print devices, it is still beneficial to share them. If the user's local print device fails, the output can still be printed on another device. Additionally, those other shared devices may have features (such as color or higher quality paper stock) that specific print jobs may need. If all print devices are shared, the user can choose from every print capability

Try This!

Sharing an Existing Locally Attached Print Device

You have the existing locally attached print device that you added in Step-by-Step 8.01, and now you want to share it over your network. Try this:

Note that in the following exercise you will notice the use of a List In Directory option check box. Since you are logged into a workstation that is part of a Windows 2000 domain with Active Directory running, your printers are automatically added to Active Directory. If you wish, for some reason, not to **publish** this information to the directory (releasing the printer information such as name, type, and location to all domain users), you can deselect this check box.

1. Log in to your local workstation as your administrator user.

2. Click the Start button and select Printers and Faxes.

3. Right-click your newly added print device icon, and select Sharing.

4. Click the Share This Printer option, enter the name you wish to use, and click OK. If you are informed that your name may not be viewable by some MS-DOS workstations, click the Yes button.

5. Notice the small hand below your printer icon signaling that the object, your print device in this case, is being shared. Close your Printers and Faxes window to return to your desktop.

available on the network and can simply send the output to the appropriate print device.

There are some drawbacks to sharing locally attached devices. In many cases, repeated interruptions from multiple users retrieving printed output may be a distraction and affect the workstation user's productivity. Additionally, that workstation's capability may be affected. Whenever print jobs are sent to locally connected print devices, the workstation's resources are employed to produce the output. During that time, the local user may detect a noticeable reduction in speed and response times. These may even occur during what may possibly be higher priority job functions than those of the printing users.

Sharing Print Devices Directly Connected to the Network

The second method for sharing print devices is available when those devices can be connected directly to the network. Usually this involves high-speed (and therefore higher-priced) print devices that have their own network connections. A print device may have an internal network interface card that provides it with its own recognized network identification. It may also have an externally configured networking capability that can result in the same individual network recognition as if it were internally configured. Connecting a properly configured **network print device** (also called a network-interface print device) to the network, and turning its power switch to the on position, announces its presence to everyone on the network. It can then be used to print output just as if it were actually connected to a networked computer.

■ Describe Windows Network Printing

Lauren now has most of the networked users printing to the various print devices situated around the SinkRSwim Pools facilities. However, when those print devices were installed, they were not configured as shared devices, so not all users are able to print their own output. Many of the users have to send files to the workstations with print devices attached and go there to print their output. Several complaints have been heard as the users of this new network become more aware of the network's capabilities.

Lauren recently instructed Ricky to configure all of SinkRSwim Pools' print devices so they are shared by all users attached to the network.

As you learned in the previous section, the Windows printing operations on your network will come from both the Windows 2000 Server and Windows XP Professional workstations. Active Directory (AD) can be used when configuring your network printing capabilities on both of these operating systems. Using this AD option effectively, however, involves understanding some additional terminology. Although the distinction between printers and print devices explained earlier in this chapter may have been difficult to follow, understanding this distinction makes further discussions about Microsoft printing a bit simpler.

Add Printer Wizard

Whether networks are as small as your classroom lab or they grow to include thousands of computers with hundreds of print devices, you can still use the same Add Printer Wizard that you learned about in Step-by-Step 8.01. In fact, although you were already connected to your School domain when you used the wizard earlier, you would use that same interface if you were part of a workgroup adding either local or shared print devices.

The main difference between local and shared print devices is where the information about those print devices gets distributed. When you are connected to a workgroup and add a shared print device, the printer's attributes are only stored locally on the computer where you added the shared object. However, when you are part of a domain, the print device's information is automatically entered into Active Directory and is available to all other networked users.

Workgroup Printing

Although your network for this text has been installed as a domain, network administrators sometimes find their users inadvertently transferred over to a workgroup. When this happens, there are visual indicators that you can watch for that help identify what your users might otherwise think is a network problem. Additionally, you may also have a smaller network at home and will likely configure workgroup sharing there if you attempt to share your printers.

If your computer is part of the domain when you add a shared print device to a Windows 2000 network, that print device's information gets added to the Windows Active Directory. If your computer is on a workgroup, it is not added to Active Directory. In fact, information can be gathered over the network for non-domain Windows XP computers by a new operating system feature called **NetCrawler**, which searches for and automatically adds all available shared network objects.

Cross Check

Printing with Active Directory

Use the information you learned about Microsoft's Active Directory in Chapter 6 and your experience sharing print devices in this chapter when answering the following questions.

1. Explain how a service such as Active Directory can assist a networked user when printing.

2. What indication do you have when sharing printers that Active Directory is available?

• **Figure 8.2**   Domain printers—These two printers were added when logged in to a domain.

When you log in to your workgroup computer and refresh your network connection, or simply refresh your Printers and Faxes window, NetCrawler searches the network and updates your display so that it shows all available networked resources. This includes those resources added through other workgroup computers, like the one you are logged in to.

The examples here demonstrate what you will see from a computer named Student02 that was removed from the School domain and then added to the MSHOME workgroup. A printer named "HP LaserJet 6P" was created and not shared. (You do not need to configure your computers like that unless you want to.)

In Figure 8.2, two print devices have been added to a domain computer and shared in Active Directory. Notice that both print devices are shown using the **shared indicator** (the small upward-facing hand below the print device's icon), and one is depicted with the **default printer indicator** (the small check mark in the upper right).

The networked printers accessible from a computer belonging to a workgroup, as shown in Figure 8.3, include the two print devices that were added to the domain (shown in Figure 8.2) along with another local printer shared from the Student02 workgroup computer. That local printer is designated as the default printer for Student02. Notice the addition of the word Auto in front of the domain-named printers signifying that they were indeed identified by NetCrawler and then automatically added to the workgroup computer's available print devices.

One thing you should watch out for is that NetCrawler simply locates shared devices and automatically adds them using the information it found in its search. Although you may have added the print device and specified a different share name for the print device, as shown in Figure 8.4, NetCrawler does not report that name on the device it locates. NetCrawler located the share and reported it as HPLASERJET6P instead of using the share name of LocalHPLJ6P that you assigned that print device. NetCrawler does add the location (on Student02, in this case) to the end of the located devices, which may help you isolate any problems your users encounter as a result of misnamed print devices.

• **Figure 8.3**   Workgroup view of printers—The two domain printers viewed from a workgroup computer

Active Directory Printing

Your classroom computers are members of a domain with Active Directory installed (if you followed the procedures outlined in this book). When adding print devices, you have already seen that you use the same Add Printer Wizard whether you are working on a stand-alone computer, a computer that is part of a workgroup, or one where you are logged in to a domain. Even though you are on a computer that is part of a domain, if you elect not to share your print device during installation, its information will not be added to Active Directory or shared with other domain members. Therefore, the majority of your printing in this course will utilize shared print devices that are either connected to local computers or connected directly to the network.

Active Directory and Shared Local Print Devices The same method that was used for adding print devices to workgroup members is used for adding local print devices to members of domains. You have seen that the same procedures were used in the Add Printer Wizard to share the domain print devices. However, print devices added locally to domain-member computers have their print device information listed in Active Directory by the Add Printer Wizard.

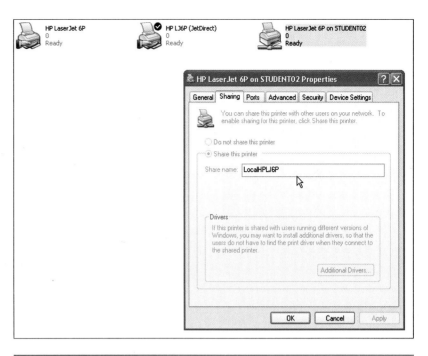

• **Figure 8.4** Misnamed print device—The NetCrawler name on a shared print device is not the shared name it was given.

Active Directory and Shared Network Print Devices The Add Printer Wizard is also used when adding network-capable print devices directly to the network. **Network-capable print devices**, commonly called network printers, are print devices that are connected directly to the networking medium, avoiding the need to be connected to a workstation. Such print devices provide their own network identities. However, even though these print devices have an identity, they must still be contacted by computers on the network. In fact, your use of these network-capable print devices should help clarify the new printing terminology you have been forced to adopt when printing on Microsoft networks.

Notice the absence of the List In Directory check box that you previously used on the Sharing tab of your printer's Properties dialog box. This indicates that you are not actively connected to a Windows 2000 domain with AD activated, but rather are part of a workgroup instead. Another indicator can be found by selecting Search from the Start menu and noting whether it gives you the ability to search for Printers, Computers, or People (connected to AD) or just Computers or People (not connected to AD).

Cross Check

Basic Networking Requirements for Printing

Use the information you learned in Chapter 2 about basic networking requirements when answering the following questions.

1. If you wanted to add a print device to your network, such that it was not directly connected to any computer, what basic network requirements would you have to make sure were available for the print device?

2. What kind of address will be required (and where will it come from) if you want to directly connect a network print device to your network so that you can print output from your Microsoft Windows 2000 Servers and Windows XP Professional workstations?

A network-capable print device is one that can be connected directly to the network so that it receives instructions and produces your printed materials from anywhere on the network. However, none of the computers on your network can do anything with that capability until at least one of them locates and announces your print device's capabilities to the network's members. To make that announcement, you use the same Add Printer Wizard that you used earlier in this chapter, but you go a little further with identifying the print device.

Using the wizard, you identify a port on your computer so that it correctly routes your output whenever you direct it to. In order to do that, you must know each network-capable printer's network address. You obtain

---

Try This!

Installing, Sharing, and Verifying a Domain Print Device

You have recently attached a print device directly to your computer that is a member of the School domain, and you want to share it with the rest of the domain users on your network. Try this:

1. Log in to a Windows XP Professional workstation as your administrator user. Click the Start button and select Printers and Faxes.

2. In the left panel, click the Add a Printer option, and click Next.

3. Click the Local Printer Attached to This Computer option, deselect the Automatically Detect and Install My Plug and Play Printer option, and click Next.

4. Use the recommended port in the Use the Following Port selection, and click Next.

5. Select your print device's manufacturer and your printer in the Install Printer Software window, and click Next. If the Use Existing Driver window appears, click Next.

6. Select and copy the printer name displayed in the Name Your Printer window, and click Next to accept the printer name.

7. Ensure that the Share Name option is selected, select the name provided in the text box and paste the name you copied in Step 6, and click Next.

8. Click Yes if cautioned about not seeing your share name from MS-DOS–based computers.

9. Enter a location in the Location text box, enter your workstation computer's name in the Comments text box, and click Next.

10. Select No for the test page option (unless you want to print another test page), and click Next. Confirm the information provided, and click the Finish button.

11. Right-click your new print device icon and select Sharing. Confirm that the List In Directory option is selected, and close the printer's Properties dialog box. Close the Printers and Faxes window to return to your desktop.

that address from the print device's configuration when adding the device. Each device has its own interface, where you perform a network setup and obtain its address. From there, you tie your output port to that address and add a new print device using the Add Printer Wizard.

Cross Check

Microsoft Printing Terminology

Recall the discussion earlier in this chapter about Microsoft printing terminology when answering the following questions.

1. What are the three print-related items you need when printing on a Microsoft network?

2. Describe the Microsoft process for producing printouts of your work.

Step-by-Step 8.02

Installing and Configuring a Network-Capable Print Device

Print devices capable of handling heavy loads are now typically network-capable devices that you can connect directly to your network. Once you install one of these print devices, all users on your network can access and print their output using this device. In this exercise, you will configure your workstation to print to an already-installed network-capable print device.

To complete this exercise, you will need the following items:

- Operational Windows 2000 Server with AD installed and running

- Networked Windows XP Professional workstation

- Network-capable print device or suitable substitute (such as the Jet Direct device used in this example)

Step 1

Log in to your Windows XP Professional workstation computer as your administrative user. Click the Start button and select Control Panel | Printers and Other Hardware | View Installed Printers or Fax Printers. Select and delete any print devices that are currently installed.

Step 2

Click the Add a Printer option in the left panel, and click Next to continue with a manual setup.

Step 3

Click the Local Printer Attached to This Computer option, and read the informational note at the bottom of the Local or Network Printer window. Deselect the Automatically Detect and Install My Plug and Play Printer option, and click Next.

Step 4

Click the Create a New Port option, click the Type of Port drop-down list, and select Standard TCP/IP Port. Click Next.

Step 5

Read and perform the two steps listed on the first page of the Add Standard TCP/IP Printer Port Wizard, and click Next.

Step 6

Enter the print device's IP address in the Printer Name or IP Address text box, and click Next.

Step 7

The wizard will look for the print device at the IP address you provided. If it requests additional information concerning ports or print device setup, provide the necessary information and click Next.

Step 8

Confirm the information provided in the Completing the Add Standard TCP/IP Printer Port Wizard window, and click the Finish button to continue with the Add Printer Wizard.

Step 9

Select the print device's manufacturer and printer type, and then click Next. Then select the Keep the Existing Driver option, and click Next.

Step 10

Click the Share Name option, and enter the name you wish to use as the print device's share name in the text box. Click Next. Click Yes if cautioned about your share name not being viewable from MS-DOS workstations.

Step 11

Enter your Location and Comment information, and click Next.

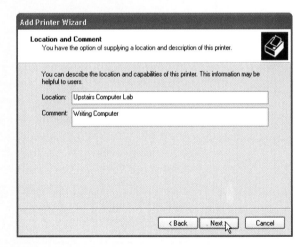

Step 12	Click Yes to print a test page, and click Next. Confirm the information and click OK if your test page prints properly.

Step 13	Close the Printers and Faxes window to return to your desktop.

■ Explain NetWare Network Printing

Lauren and Ricky have been discussing the SinkRSwim Pools network's printing requirements. Since the print device information was added to the Windows 2000 Server's Active Directory, user printing has nearly doubled. Ricky is trying to convince Lauren that it is now time to implement a more capable printing system. Lauren liked the relative simplicity of adding print devices to their mostly Microsoft Windows network, but Ricky's explanation of Novell's print job handling has won her over. Now Lauren is willing to invest the time required to initially configure NetWare printing so the network can benefit from the added control and smooth operation Novell's Distributed Print Services promises.

The extra effort you spent learning the new terminology necessary for a thorough understanding of Microsoft's printing process will help you understand Novell printing. You will draw heavily on the concept of separate and distinct printing components as you now learn what may be the most capable of the printing systems we will discuss in this text. Novell takes what you learned for Microsoft printing (three printing components: the printer, the print job, and the print device) to an even more detailed level. The highest-capability Novell printing option available for use with your NetWare 6 server is Novell Distributed Print Services (NDPS). You will learn how to configure and use NDPS while also learning the newest of Novell's printing options, called iPrint.

iPrint Components

NetWare printing services are not installed by default. You must intentionally install them (either during your initial server's installation or as an add-in later) and execute an extensive setup process to piece together the necessary service components. The Novell NetWare 6 operating system's printing service that you end up installing includes a new printing service, called **iPrint**.

The iPrint service is Internet-based, it uses Novell's strongest print option (Novell Distributed Print Services), and it makes printing available from any computer with an installed Internet browser using the simple Internet Printing Protocol (IPP), the printing protocol used on the Internet. Novell has included NDPS with its operating systems since NetWare 5 and it effectively combined its older print components (printer, print queue, and print server) into one print object called the Printer Agent. NDPS focuses on the printer, and manages its configuration and use through Novell Directory Services (NDS). NDPS handles the drivers used at the workstations, with the result that print drivers are no longer stored at a user's location. Instead, they are downloaded to the workstation by NDPS before printing.

The goal behind IPP is to make it possible to print anywhere, and Novell's iPrint service uses IPP to get closer to this goal. In fact, Novell refers to its new iPrint service as the next generation of printing software.

With the proper authentication credentials assigned to user accounts, network users can simply browse to the location where they want to print, and then send their output on its way. As you will see, setting up this service is a bit cumbersome and initially difficult to master. However, once you get used to it, this service is well worth the added effort. This will also help you understand Microsoft's use of Internet Printing (using IPP) which they have supported since Windows 2000. Both companies' implementations are intended for use on an intranet or the Internet.

Novell's iPrint offers users tremendous printing capability from any computer with an Internet browser installed. In order for iPrint to do this, though, NDPS must be installed so it can distribute the print process to all networked users. This distribution aspect of NDPS also allows the administrator to assign the burden of the print process to the most capable computers that are available on the network. Although this may sound similar to the Microsoft printing system, Novell takes printing control and information availability to a more detailed level. In addition, some significant speed increases are available when using NDPS as opposed to using Windows printing.

When using iPrint, the NDPS components that you must learn and be proficient with are the Broker, the Manager, the Gateway, and the Printer.

Cross Check

Server Console Review

It has been a while since you had to work from your Novell server's console. Think back to the NetWare 6 installation processes in Chapter 4 when answering the following questions.

1. What is the name of the Novell graphical user interface available at either the console or at a workstation that has Novell Client installed?

2. Explain how you get to the Novell graphical user interface from the server console if it has not yet been started.

3. Suppose the Novell graphical user interface has already been started, but when you arrive at your server you see another screen (such as the Logger screen). Explain how to change from one screen to another so you can view the GUI screen.

Adding the iPrint Service to the NetWare Server

To add the iPrint service (and NDPS) to your NetWare 6 server, try this:

1. At your NetWare 6 server, insert the NetWare 6 operating system installation CD. From the server console's System Console screen, type **LOAD CDROM**, the NetWare command for adding the CD as a NetWare volume, and then type the command **StartX** to start the Novell graphical user interface.

2. Press the CTRL and ESC keys, and select the X – Server – Graphical Console screen.

3. Click the Novell button, and select Install to open the Installed Products window. Scroll through the installed products and ensure that iPrint/NDPS has not yet been installed. If iPrint/NDPS is already installed, skip the remainder of this exercise.

4. Click the Add button to open the Source Path window, and click the browse button.

5. In the left panel of the Source Path window (with path browsing open), double-click on your NetWare 6 CD-ROM volume and notice that the item PRODUCT.NI appears in the right panel.

6. Click OK to accept the NetWare 6 path to PRODUCT.NI, and click OK again to first copy the file and then start the Installation Wizard. In the Components window, click the Clear All button, scroll to and select the iPrint/NDPS option, and then click Next to validate your selected components.

7. Provide the administrator user's information and click OK to log in and again validate your selected components and installation authorization. Accept the default LDAP port information, select the Allow Clear Text Passwords option, and click Next.

8. Click the Finish button to complete the installation, and click the Close button on the Installation Complete window to close the installation files and return to your server console's GUI interface.

The Broker

The **Broker** is one of the iPrint components and it is essential to the proper operation of Novell's print process using iPrint or NDPS. The Broker connects the printing process to various services on the NetWare server, and it should be invisible to the user. Each time the server starts, the NDPS Broker logs in and authenticates itself for each of the following three services it provides:

■ **Service Registry Services (SRS)** The Broker is responsible for registering the information and services provided by printers that advertise this information for network users. Specific information, such as type, name, address, and model number, can be registered for each printer, and this provides a mechanism for locating printers when requesting their services.

■ **Event Notification Services (ENS)** The Broker is responsible for hosting the event notification from each printer. That is, when print jobs finish or the status of the printer (or the print job) changes, the server is notified. It is the Broker that makes that notification possible.

■ **Resource Management Services (RMS)** When clients attempt to print using networked printers, and they need the proper drivers or other items such as additional printer fonts, the Broker supplies these components. The Broker is thus a central repository for these necessary additional items and is responsible for storing them.

Creating a NetWare iPrint Broker

You will start activating iPrint by creating an iPrint Broker. In this activity, you will use iManage, Novell's Internet management feature, and create an iPrint Broker on your NetWare 6 server.

To complete this exercise, you will need the following items:

- Operational NetWare 6 server with iPrint and NDPS installed
- Networked Windows XP Professional workstation with Novell Client and ConsoleOne installed

Step 1

Log in to your Windows XP Professional computer and your NetWare 6 server from your workstation as an administrative user. Click the Start button, and select Internet to start your web browser (Internet Explorer, by default).

Step 2

Enter **https://**, followed by the IP address of your server, followed by **:2200** (https://192.168.0.91:2200 in this example) in the address bar of your browser, and click the Go button (or press the ENTER key) to browse to your NetWare server's Web Manager.

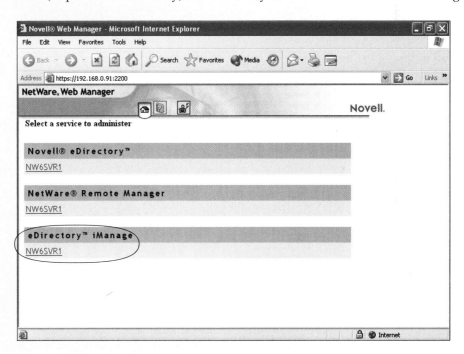

Step 3

Click Yes if you receive a Security Alert dialog box, and click your server's eDirectory iManage link (NW6SVR1 in the example). Enter your administrator user information and click the Login button to log in to iManage.

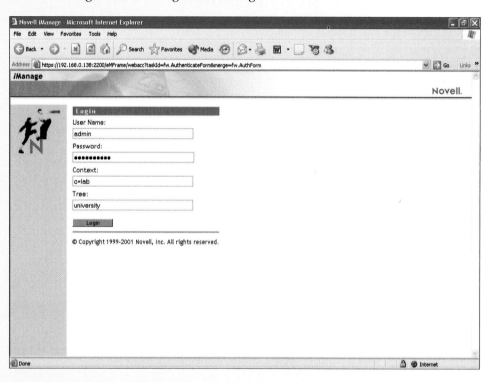

Step 4

In the left panel of the iManage window, click the plus sign (+) next to the iPrint Management item, to display the iPrint Management options.

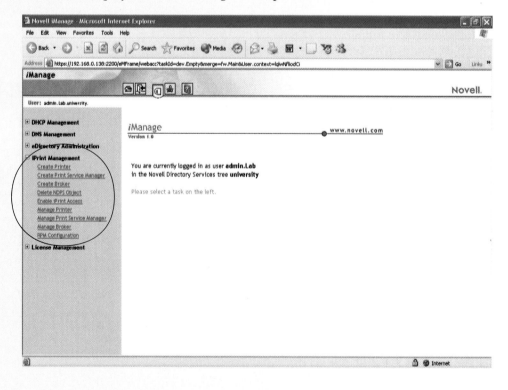

Step 5

Click the Create Broker link. Type **iPrint Broker** as the Broker name and use the browse button to locate your Lab container. For the Resource Management Service option, use the browse button to locate your SYS volume as the RMS volume. Click OK to continue.

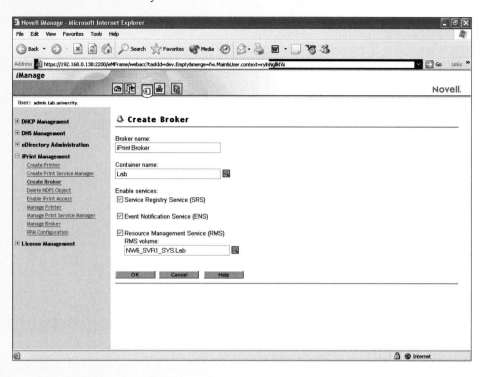

Step 6

If this is the first time iPrint is being used on your workstation, you will need to install the iPrint client by clicking the OK button, as shown in the following illustration, and then clicking the Open button to initiate the installation. Otherwise, skip to Step 9 of this exercise to continue creating your Broker.

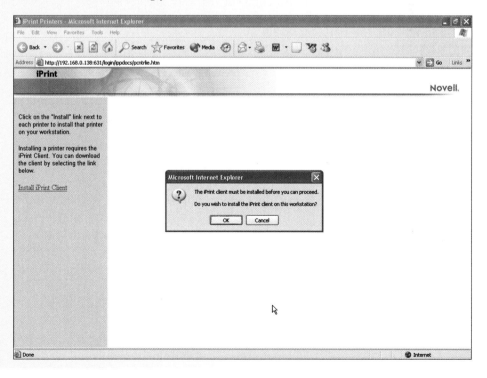

Click OK after choosing your setup language. The Novell iPrint Client Setup window will open. Click Next to view the License Agreement, and click Yes to agree to it.

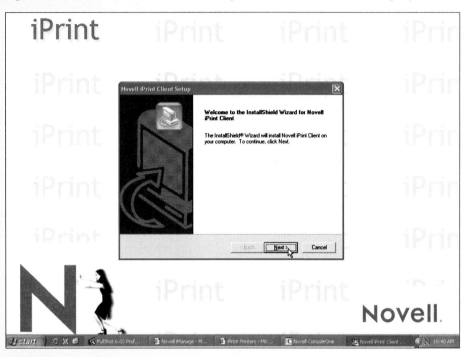

Click Next in the Select Program Folder window, select the Yes I Want to Restart My Computer Now option, and click the Finish button to complete the client's installation.

Continue your Broker's installation and return to the iManage window by clicking the OK button in the Create Broker Request Successful window. Leave the iManage window open for use in the next Try This! exercise.

At your NetWare 6 server's System Console screen, type the command **BROKER**, after the NDS Broker loads. Select your iPrint Broker from the Contents list, and press ENTER. When the Supported Services screen opens, press the CTRL and ESC keys, and select System Console screen.

The Manager

The NDPS Manager (NDPSM) provides a location to store information about your network's print devices. The NDPSM is an object created in your NDS tree, and it must be present there prior to the installation of any Printer Agents that will be supported by iPrint using the NDPSM.

NDPS focuses on the printer and manages its configuration and use through Novell's Directory Service (NDS). NDPS handles the drivers used at the workstations, with the result that printer drivers are no longer stored at a user's location. Instead, they are downloaded to the workstation by NDPS before printing.

The information stored in NDPSM is used to manage the Printers operating from a particular server. A specific NDPSM can only reside on one server, and each server can house separate NDPSMs. Further, each NDPSM can represent more than one Printer. If NDPSM is not running when you create the first Printer Agent, NetWare will ask you if you want it loaded.

You will install Novell print devices as Printers in the next section.

Additionally, typing the command **NDPSM** at the server console activates NDPSM.NLM (a NetWare Loadable Module), which implements the Manager. Some Manager configuration is then available through your server console, but as you have already noticed, most management configuration is performed through the browser-based iManage tool.

The Printer

With Novell's printing configuration, each physical printer (the print device in Microsoft) is represented by a **Printer Agent (PA)**, commonly called the Printer or Printer object. The Printer Agent represents Novell's efforts at focusing on printing by centering attention on the printer. Printer Agents can be software items running on a server that represent printers attached directly to the network, to servers, or to workstations. They also can be embedded in the printer attached directly to the network.

Try This!

Creating a NetWare iPrint Manager

The next object you need to create is your iPrint Manager, and doing so involves almost the same procedures employed to create your iPrint Broker. To create an iPrint Manager, try this:

1. Return to your still-open iManage screen from the previous Try This! exercise, or use your browser and return to `https://192.168.0.91:2200` (substituting your server's IP address), log in to iManage with your administrator user information, and open the iPrint Management listing in the left panel.

2. Click the Create Print Service Manager link, and enter **iPrint Manager** in the Manager Name field. For the Container Name field, browse to your Lab container. For the Database Volume field, browse to your SYS volume. Then click OK.

3. At the Create Manager Request Succeeded window, click OK to return to the iManage window.

4. At your NetWare server System Console screen, enter the command **NDPSM**.

5. In the Contents of Current Context section of the NDPS Manager window, select iPrint Manager, and press ENTER.

6. At the Printer Agent List (which should return an empty list), press ALT+ESC repeatedly to cycle through the available console screens, and return to the System Console screen.

Before any output can be sent to the physical printer, you must create a separate PA for that printer on the server and store it in that server's NDPSM. Each PA can only represent a single physical printer.

The Printer objects serve multiple functions. They manage the printing process for their respective physical printers, they answer any client-generated queries for print job information or printer attributes, and they provide the server with event-notification information about the printers they manage, including information about print job status, error notification, or print job and printer status changes.

Printer agents manage the processing of the print job. They also manage many of the printer's own internal functions, and they respond to network clients' requests for information about their print job status or about the capabilities of the printer. Events can be set up so that the relevant individuals are notified when print jobs finish, when problems are encountered, or when a job's status changes.

The new Printer Agent allows printing to a wider range of printers than it did in the past. Printer Agents also ensure the scalability of the printing environment when changing from LAN to WAN or even to Enterprise situations because fewer changes are necessary during an expansion.

The Gateway

For printers whose agent is not hardware-embedded and thus not labeled "NDPS-aware" right out of the box, Novell has created the **Gateway**. Gateways are information objects that are configured to provide printer specifics over the network. They translate requests sent to the printers into **printer-recognizable machine code,** (computer code that runs the printer).

The Gateways allow non-NDPS-aware printers to receive print jobs over the network and facilitate their management and use.

Novell NetWare 6 includes Gateways that provide access to printers that are not NDPS-aware. Specific examples you should be aware of are the Hewlett Packard, Xerox, and Novell Gateways. The first two are company-specific and provide detailed information on those company's printers for use on NDPS networks. Novell's Gateway is for printers with neither NDPS nor a specific company gateway.

The Client

Finally, in order to use an iPrint printer and the NDPS printing service from your network's workstations, you must add a small piece of software called the iPrint client. The client is installed on the workstation used to configure iPrint initially, but it is also required on each workstation where Novell network printing will be used.

The iPrint client is located by using your web browser to reach your iPrint Printer. When you first use any iPrint service, you will be prompted to install the iPrint client. Additionally, the first screen in the iPrint service's web page (`http://192.168.0.91:631/ipp`, with your own server's IP address substituted) offers you a link to download the iPrint client to your workstation. You must restart your computer after installing the iPrint client.

 **Try This!**

Creating and Enabling a NetWare iPrint Printer

The next object you need to create is your iPrint Printer, and doing so involves basically the same procedures employed to create your iPrint Broker and Manager. To create an iPrint Printer, try this:

1. Return to your still-open iManage screen from the previous Try This! exercise, or use your browser and return to `https://192.168.0.91:2200` (substituting your server's IP address), log in to iManage with your administrator user information, and open the iPrint Management listing in the left panel.

2. Click the Create Printer link, and enter **iPrint Printer** in the Printer Name field. For the Container Name field, browse to your Lab container. For the Manager Name field, browse to your iPrint Manager. Leave the default Gateway type, and click Next.

3. In the URL field, enter something like **ipp:// 192.168.0.6/ipp/iPrintPrinter**, but substitute the IP address of the network-capable print device you used earlier in this chapter.

4. Scroll to and select the correct drivers for your print device in the Select Default Drivers for Printer iPrint Printer window, and click Next.

5. At the Create Printer Request Succeeded window, click OK to return to the iManage window.

6. Click the Enable iPrint Access link, and in the Enable iPrint Access window, browse to iPrint Manager in the NDPS Manager field. Click OK.

7. At the Printer Agents window, press ALT+ESC, click the Enabled box on your iPrint Printer's line entry, and click OK.

8. At the Enable iPrint Access Results window showing Success for your iPrint Printer, click OK to return to the iManage window.

9. At your NetWare 6 server, press CTRL+ESC and select your NDPS Manager screen, which should show the error message "Not Bound."

10. Select your iPrint Printer and press ENTER, select Configuration and press ENTER, and select Configuration Utilities and press ENTER.

11. Change the Gateway Type to Hewlett Packard IP/IPX Printer Gateway and press ENTER. Press ENTER again to accept the Automatically Search IP Printers default setting, and press ENTER again to accept the Enable DNS Lookups default.

12. Select your located print device, and press ENTER.

13. Scroll to the Printer Definition Type and press ENTER. Select your printer from the Printer Definition List, press ENTER, press CTRL+ESC, and return to the System Console screen.

Installing and Configuring a NetWare iPrint Client

You already loaded the iPrint client during your iPrint installation. However, you will need to install the client on all other workstations where you intend to allow users to print using iPrint. In this activity, you will add the iPrint client to a Windows XP workstation and then connect to and print to your iPrint Printer.

To complete this exercise, you will need the following items:

- Operational NetWare 6 server with iPrint installed and configured
- Networked Windows XP Professional workstation with Novell Client and ConsoleOne installed

Step 1
Log in to a Windows XP Professional computer using your administrator account. Click the Start button and select Internet.

Step 2
Enter **http://192.168.0.91:631/ipp** in your browser's address bar (but substitute your server's IP address) and click the Go button.

Step 3
If this is the first time iPrint is being used on your workstation, you must install the client by clicking OK and clicking the Open button to initiate the installation. Otherwise, skip to Step 6 of this exercise to continue configuring your iPrint Printer.

Step 4
Choose your setup language and click OK to open the Novell iPrint Client Setup window. Click Next to view the License Agreement, and click Yes to agree to it.

Step 5
Click Next in the Select Program Folder window, and then select the Yes I Want to Restart My Computer Now option, and click the Finish button to complete the client's installation.

Step 6
After restarting your computer, logging back in, and restarting your browser, go back to http://192.168.0.91:631/ipp (substituting your server's IP address) to display your iPrint Printer, and click the Install link.

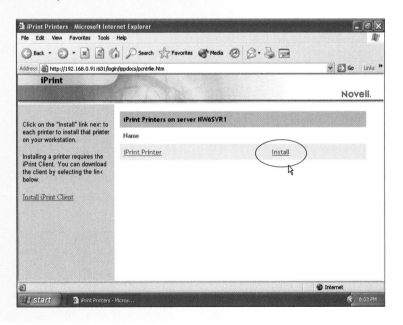

Step 7

Monitor the installation, and click OK when you are informed that your printer was installed successfully.

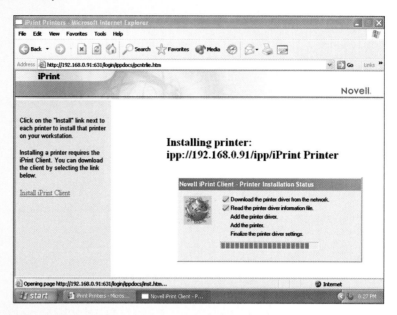

Step 8

Click your workstation's Start button, select Printers and Faxes, and verify the existence of your iPrint Printer.

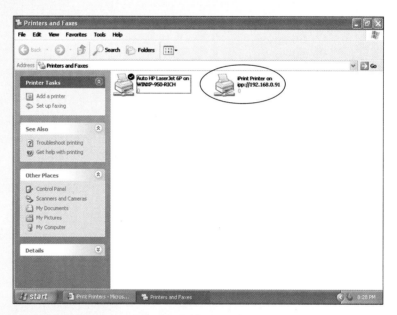

Step 9

Right-click your new iPrint Printer icon, select Properties, and click the Print Test Page button to test your newly installed printer.

Step 10

Close the Printers and Faxes window to return to your desktop.

■ Chapter Summary

After reading this chapter and completing the Step-by-Step tutorials and Try This! exercises, you should understand the following facts about network printing:

Explain Network Printing Concepts

- The three basic printing configurations available when designing a network and configuring printing equipment are local printers, print servers, and network-capable printers.

- A printer connected to a computer is a local print device.

- Computers offering their printing services to others on the network are print servers.

- Printers connected directly to the network are network print devices.

- Print devices are connected to the computer's output ports.

- Software programs that run print devices and convert digital output to the printed format are called drivers.

- Microsoft checks driver software and adds a digital signature or embedded secret code to verify that the drivers you install have not been tampered with since they were certified.

- Microsoft uses the term *printer* to refer to the software interface between an application and the print device.

- The default printer is identified by a small black circle with a check mark inside, at the upper-right corner of the print device icon.

- Sharing print devices on a network saves money.

- A print device can be locally connected to a computer and be accessed by other users.

- Print devices can be directly connected to the network where multiple users have convenient access.

- Drawbacks to shared print devices include employee interruptions on the computer connected to the print device, and reduced computing capacity.

- A network print device is also known as a network-interface print device.

Describe Windows Network Printing

- Active Directory can be used on Windows 2000 and Windows XP systems.

- The Add Printer Wizard is used to add information about print devices into Active Directory when you are part of a domain.

- Information about shared workgroup print devices is not added to Active Directory.

- NetCrawler is a Windows XP feature that searches and automatically lists all network objects that are able to be shared.

- The indicator that a printer is shared is the small upward-facing hand below a print device's icon.

- The Add Printer Wizard is used when adding local print devices and network-capable print devices.

- There are visual indicators available to let you know if Active Directory is activated.

- A network-capable print device is one that can be connected directly to the network.

Explain NetWare Network Printing

- The highest-capability Novell printing option for use with the NetWare 6 server is Novell Distributed Print Services (NDPS).

- Novell's newest printing option is an Internet-based service called iPrint, which requires NDPS and uses the simple Internet Printing Protocol (IPP).

- The administrator can assign the printing process to the most capable computers on the network.

- NDPS focuses on the printer and its components, which are the Broker, the Manager, the Gateway, and the Printer.

- Novell refers to its new iPrint service as the next generation of printing software.

- The Broker provides Service Registry Services, Event Notification Services, and Resource Management Services.

- The Manager provides a location for storing information about the network's print devices and must be created before the first Printer Agent is created.
- Each physical printer is represented by a Printer Agent, usually called the Printer or Printer object.
- Printer Agents can be software items running on a server or embedded in a printer attached directly to a network.
- The Printer Agent allows printing to a wide range of printers.
- Gateways are information objects that allow non-NDPS-aware printers to receive print jobs over a network.
- In order to use an iPrint printer and the NDPS printing service from your network workstation, you must install the iPrint client.

■ Key Terms

Broker *(270)*
default printer *(259)*
default printer indicator *(262)*
drivers *(254)*
Gateway *(275)*
iPrint *(269)*
LOAD CDROM *(270)*

local print device *(254)*
NetCrawler *(261)*
network-capable print device *(263)*
network print device *(260)*
network printing *(259)*
output *(254)*
output ports *(254)*

print servers *(253)*
printer *(254)*
Printer Agent (PA) *(275)*
printer-recognizable machine code *(275)*
publish *(260)*
shared indicator *(262)*

■ Key Term Quiz

Use the preceding vocabulary terms to complete the following sentences. Not all the terms will be used.

1. NDPS-aware printers use an information object, called a(n) _____, that is configured to provide printer specifics over the network.

2. Small pieces of software that run print devices and convert the digital output from an application during printing are called _____.

3. A small black circle with a check mark inside at the upper-right corner of a print device's icon indicates that the printer will be used as the _____.

4. In Active Directory, you can elect not to _____, or release, printer information to domain users.

5. In non-domain Windows XP computers, _____ searches for and automatically lists all available shared network objects, such as print devices.

6. When you share a print device, you can verify this shared status by ensuring the device's icon is shown with the _____ (a small hand below the icon).

7. A computer can have a printer connected to one of its parallel, serial, USB, or SCSI connections. These outbound connections are called the computer's _____.

8. The command line entry used at the NetWare 6 server to add a CD as a volume is _____.

9. Each time it starts, the NDPS _____ logs in and authenticates itself for several NetWare server services.

10. The _____ represents Novell's efforts at focusing on printing by centering attention on the printer.

■ Multiple-Choice Quiz

1. Which of the following most correctly identifies a print device directly attached to a computer and not shared with other network users?

   a. Local printer

   b. Print server

   c. Novell Distributed Print Service

   d. Active Directory printer

2. Which of the following correctly identifies a type of output port that you can plug a printer into when directly connecting a print device?

   a. Parallel

   b. Serial

   c. USB

   d. All of the above

3. When installing new drivers on your computer, Microsoft recommends which of the following?

   a. Check for the Certificate of Authenticity.

   b. Read and accept the EULA.

   c. Verify the existence of the digital signature.

   d. Look for the presence of the authorized hologram.

4. When adding a print device to your local computer, which option do you select from the Printers and Faxes window to initiate the installation process?

   a. Add Printer Wizard

   b. Add a Printer

   c. Look for Printer

   d. Search

5. Which of the following options would be incorrectly configured if you were trying to create a shared print device connected to a non-domain computer?

   a. Do Not Share This Printer: deselected

   b. Use the Following Port: selected

   c. Publish in Directory: selected

   d. Local Printer Attached to This Computer: selected

6. When installing a print device on your computer using the Add Printer Wizard, which of the following shows the correct response necessary to print a test page?

   a. Click the Yes button.

   b. Click the Print Test Page button.

   c. Click the Print Test button.

   d. Click the Print Test Now button.

7. Which of the following is *not* necessarily present when a shared print device is being used as the default printer?

   a. A print device icon in the Printers and Faxes window

   b. A small black circle with a check mark at the upper-right corner of the printer icon

   c. A small upward-facing hand underneath the printer icon

   d. A print device listing in Active Directory

8. Which of the following does *not* identify an area of potential savings from sharing print devices on a network?

   a. Decreased number of support personnel

   b. Decreased amount of network traffic

   c. Decreased number of purchased devices

   d. Decreased number of installed devices

9. Which of the following *cannot* be used to search for print devices in Active Directory?

   a. A user on a Windows XP Professional workstation logged in to a Windows 2000 domain

   b. A user logged in locally to a Windows 2000 Server

   c. A domain administrator working on a Windows 95 computer, which is a member of a Windows 2000 domain

   d. A computer whose Search option on the Start menu returns the ability to search for Printers, Computers, or People

10. Which of the following *cannot* be determined by searching Active Directory?

    a. Whether an unshared print device is idle

    b. A print device's name

c. The type of print device attached to a computer

d. A network computer's IP address

11. Which of the following configuration settings for a shared print device that is directly connected to the network is correctly set?

   a. Local Printer Attached to This Computer: deselected

   b. Automatically Detect and Install My Plug and Play Printer: deselected

   c. Create a New Port: deselected

   d. Share Name: deselected

12. Which of the following is used with iPrint?

   a. NDPSN

   b. NDF

   c. IPP

   d. ConsoleOne

13. iPrint focuses on which of the following?

   a. The workstation

   b. The services

   c. The drivers

   d. The printer

14. Which of the following correctly identifies the service connected with the Broker?

   a. Service Registry Services (SRS)

   b. Service Registration System (SRS)

   c. System Registry Services (SRS)

   d. System Registration Service (SRS)

15. Which of the following must be present prior to installing any Printer Agents?

   a. A Broker

   b. A Manager

   c. The iPrint client

   d. A Gateway

■ Essay Quiz

1. Explain the need for network printing.

2. Compare the printing environment of Microsoft print services to Novell print services.

3. Describe the typical printing environment.

4. How is network printing similar to taking a print job to a printing company?

5. Fully explain the four main components of the NDPS printing environment?

Lab Projects

Time to roll up your sleeves and apply what you've learned. The following lab projects will enable you to practice the concepts discussed in this chapter.

• Lab Project 8.1

Lately you have been working quite frequently in the TEACH training center. The personnel there have been asking for an easier way to add printers. You have been busy performing repairs and have so far been unable to spend the time necessary to explain the process. The training manager has asked you to schedule some time to explain printer configuration.

To locate and add an Active Directory print device, you will need the following:

■ A networked lab computer with Windows XP Professional

■ A Windows 2000 Server with Active Directory installed and operational

Then do the following:

① Log in to your domain through a Windows XP Professional workstation using your administrator user account.

② Click the Start button and select Printers and Faxes | Add a Printer. Click Next to continue.

③ Select the A Network Printer, or a Printer Attached to Another Computer option, and click Next.

④ Select the Find a Printer in the Directory option, and click Next.

⑤ Leave the default setting for the In field set to Entire Directory. Enter a segment of an Active Directory printer's name (such as HP, if you know at least one print device has those letters in its name), and click the Find Now button.

⑥ Select the print device's name in the bottom panel, and click OK. If no print devices were returned, continue your search using additional information about the print device.

⑦ In the Default Printer dialog box, select the Yes option and click Next.

⑧ Verify that the information is correct in the Completing the Add Printer Wizard dialog box, and click the Finish button.

⑨ Confirm that your new print device's icon has been added to the Printers and Faxes window.

⑩ Close your Printers and Faxes window to return to your desktop.

• Lab Project 8.2

After creating the iPrint components on your network's NetWare 6 server, you decide that you want the graphical user interface and the iPrint components all to start automatically each time your server reboots. You would like to add the correct commands to your server's AUTOEXEC.NCF file so that the GUI and the primary iPrint components are automatically loaded.

You will need the following materials:

■ An operational Novell NetWare 6 server with iPrint already loaded and configured

Then do the following:

① At your NetWare 6 server, press ALT+ESC and select the System Console screen.

② At the System Console screen, type the command **EDIT AUTOEXEC.NCF**.

③ In the AUTOEXEC.NCF file, scroll down to the bottom of the file and type the new command line entry **STARTX** and press the ENTER key.

④ Type the new command line entry **LOAD BROKER** and press the ENTER key.

⑤ Type the new command line entry **LOAD NDPSM** and press the ENTER key.

⑥ Press the ESC key and click Yes to save your changes.

⑦ Press the CTRL+ESC keys.

Securing a Network

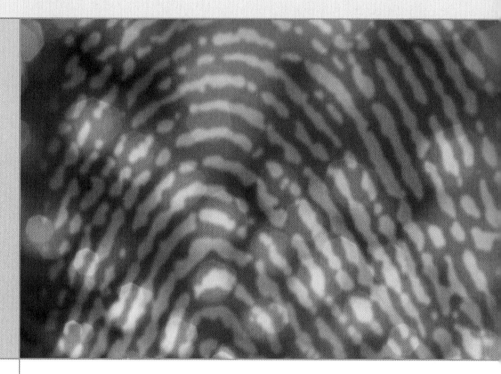

"Security gives way to conspiracy."
—WILLIAM SHAKESPEARE
IN *JULIUS CAESAR*

In this chapter, you will learn how to:

▪ **Identify threats to your network**
▪ **Plan for a secure network**

When we speak of security, the first image that usually comes to mind is one of door locks and alarm systems. In the physical world, these controls, in addition to armed guards and TV cameras, are very evident aspects of our security. These are things that protect and deter. Some controls protect our possessions by preventing the thief from stealing them, and other controls deter the thief because of the likelihood of being apprehended, convicted, and punished.

In the same manner, we must place controls on our computer networks. We use network controls, such as passwords, access control, firewalls, and antivirus software, to protect our networks from various malicious activity. The same devices may deter people from intruding on a network.

Unfortunately, it is impossible to protect networks completely. As with all sorts of security precautions, it comes down to cost and usefulness. Spending more money on a myriad of security devices may make a network more difficult to damage, but it may be unaffordable and may make the network too hard to use. Thus, security is a constant balancing of risk and cost. **Risk** is the likelihood that damage or injury may occur, and we can limit risk only to the extent that we can afford to do so.

Identifying Threats to Networking Security

Threats to the security of a network can come from inside the network as well as outside. Generally, a **threat** is someone or something that could inflict damage or injury. More specifically, for a threat to be worth our attention, the potential attacker requires motive, means, and opportunity. This means that there has to be a reason for the attack and that there must be some way for the attacker to make the attack (means and opportunity).

Who has the most knowledge and access to the systems and network of any company? The employees and other authorized users, of course. This means that internal threats are potentially the most common and the most dangerous.

Of course, you cannot ignore the external threats. **Hackers**, individuals who use their knowledge of computers to do harm, often just for fun, are a threat to any network. When you speak of securing a network, you must pay attention to both types of threats.

Internal Threats

All right, you already know that there are insiders who may seek to do harm to computer networks. Keep in mind that not all insider security issues are malicious. It is just as possible, and more likely, that an insider will cause a security problem by accident. Think of the employee who accidentally deletes an important file. The file may be critical to the operation of the company, but it is now gone. The employee did not intend to cause harm but, for whatever reason, managed to destroy the file.

In comparison, it might have been infinitely more difficult for an outsider to delete that important file. The file was likely on an internal server (with the appropriate security in place) and on the network. The outsider would have needed a lot of information, and possibly even some help, to gain access to the file. However, the employee, due to his or her trusted status in the organization, was able to delete the file accidentally.

Any security strategy designed to combat internal threats is comprised of three primary components:

- Account security
- File and directory permissions
- Practices and user education

The following sections detail how each of these components can be used to secure key systems and the network itself.

Account Security

Maintaining account security means preventing unauthorized individuals from gaining access to an account on the computer or network. The primary defensive measure, in this case, is **identification and authentication** (I&A). I&A is the security mechanism that allows a computer to uniquely identify the person who is attempting to log on or perform an action.

It is often difficult to specifically identify threats to an organization. This is because people who wish to cause harm also try to hide their intent and their actions. In most circumstances, it is sufficient to know that there are bad people in the world and that having a business or even just an Internet connection can make you a target of such individuals.

Some controls (like locks on doors) are expected to be there. Other controls are not expected, but certain conditions in the system or network may require them. As you go through this chapter, think about which controls fall into the "expected" category and which do not.

Methods of Authentication   As it turns out, identifying a person is the easy part—you just assign user IDs and names to each person on your system. The harder part is providing a mechanism for the user to prove that she is who she claims to be.

A person can prove his or her identity in three ways:

- By something the person knows
- By something the person has
- By something the person is

The first option, something a person knows, usually involves a password or personal identification number (PIN). To prove his or her identity, the person tells the computer system the password. Since only one person is supposed to know the password, the computer authenticates the person and allows access. This is the cheapest and easiest method of authentication and is also the most widely used.

The second option, something a person has, can be as simple as a credit card or driver's license. For very sensitive computer systems and networks, a smart card is used. These cards have computer chips in them that allow information to be stored. Since only one person should have the card, the person is authenticated because he or she possesses the card. This type of mechanism can be stronger than the use of passwords, but it also tends to be expensive, as each card costs between $25 and $100. If you think about organizations with tens of thousands of employees, you can see how quickly the cost skyrockets.

Biometrics involves using unique human characteristics for authentication—something the person is. The following characteristics can be used for authentication:

- Fingerprints
- Hand geometry
- Retina scans
- Facial geometry
- Voice prints

Figure 9.1 shows a picture of a hand geometry device (commonly called a *palm scanner*) that is used to grant access to a data center. The unique hand geometry of authorized individuals is recorded ahead of time. When a person requires access to the data center, the system compares the person's hand that is placed on the scanner with the record of authorized hands in the database. If the hand matches, the individual is allowed into the room.

Biometrics are expensive and there is some resistance to their use by employees (placing your head into a device and having a laser look at your eye is not the most comfortable feeling). They are also inappropriate for use in situations where the organization cannot physically control access (such as when a person makes a purchase across the Internet).

If you have the option, it is best to combine mechanisms, such as combining the use of a password and a smart card. This way, if the smart card is

Some people and civil rights groups have objected to the use of some types of biometrics, including fingerprints. Before you introduce such a system into your environment, make sure you understand the objections that may be raised.

● Figure 9.1   Hand geometry is one form of biometrics that is commonly used for physical access.

Introduction to Networking

lost or stolen, an intruder with the card would still not know the password and could not get into the system.

Strong Passwords   Since passwords are by far the most common type of authentication mechanism, it is worth taking a few minutes to look at how to choose a strong password. First off, passwords provide good authentication when they are kept secret. This means that they should not be written down or shared with coworkers. Sharing passwords is hard to prevent, but there are things that can be done (see the "File and Directory Permissions" section that follows).

Preventing employees from writing down passwords involves a combination of education and having the employees select easy-to-remember passwords. Do not fall into the trap that says easy-to-remember passwords are also weak passwords. This is not the case, as you will see in a minute.

Strong passwords have the following characteristics:

- They are hard to guess even if the person knows you.

- They are hard to discover using brute force.

If a person chooses a password that has something to do with himself or herself, it may be easy to guess. Thus, choosing the names of family members or pets, or the name of an interest, are generally not good choices for passwords. Likewise, passwords that are short or that can be found in a dictionary can be easily discovered using brute force (which will be explained shortly).

So how can you choose strong passwords? In reality, this is an easy thing to do. Passwords should be at least eight characters in length and contain a mixture of uppercase and lowercase letters, numbers, and special characters.

Of course, passwords should also be easy to remember so people don't write them down. Stringing multiple words together and substituting numbers for letters can help users create good passwords that are easy to remember, like these:

- Time4Lunch

- Itsmy1ife (note that the letter *L* is replaced with the number *1*)

Strong passwords can also be created by choosing the first letter of an easy-to-remember phrase:

- TbontbtitQ (To be or not to be, that is the question)

- oibLTibs (One if by land, two if by sea)

Breaking Passwords   Passwords are not so much broken as discovered. As was stated, strong passwords are hard to guess and hard to discover by brute force. Weak passwords are often discovered through simple guessing at the password prompt. Of course, this type of activity can be prevented through the use of **password lockouts**. Most computer systems allow administrators to set the maximum number of failed password attempts that are to be allowed. After this number, the computer system locks the account so that no further attempts can be made.

Inside Information

I&A Touches Everyone
The choice of I&A mechanisms will touch every user in the organization. It also becomes a very personal issue with employees. The choice of the mechanism and the restrictions placed on how the mechanism is used (such as the length of passwords) can cause all sorts of reactions from employees. Changes to I&A systems must be coordinated with education campaigns and with the organization's help desk. If this is not done, extensive problems will arise.

Unix systems generally limit passwords to 8 characters in length by truncating the password after 8 characters. Windows systems allow longer passwords (up to 14 characters).

If you need to see how well your users understand the use of strong but easy-to-remember passwords, walk around your office area and look for yellow post-it notes on monitors or under keyboards. Don't forget to look at the ceiling above the desks. Some enterprising users may write their passwords on the tiles above their chairs!

Setting the Password Lockouts on Windows 2000

Setting the password lockouts on Windows 2000 is a good practice as it prevents password-guessing attacks. In the following steps, you will use the Windows 2000 Administrative Tools to set the password lockout for the system.

To complete this exercise, you will need the following items:

- A computer running Windows 2000
- An account with administrator access to the system

Step 1

Log in to the system using the administrator account or another account with administrator access.

Step 2

Click the Start button and select Settings | Control Panel.

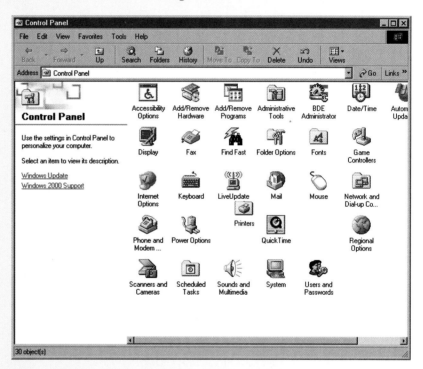

Step 3

Double-click the Administrative Tools icon.

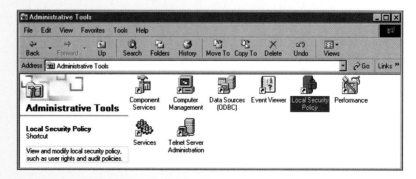

Step 4

Double-click the Local Security Policy icon, and select the Account Lockout Policy option under Account Policies.

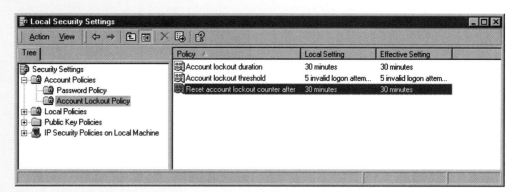

Step 5

Set the Account Lockout Duration by double-clicking the Account Lockout Duration item in the right panel. The lockout duration is the amount of time (measured in minutes) that the account will be locked out after some number of failed login attempts has been detected. The duration can be set as high as 99,999 minutes. Setting the duration to zero minutes will lock the account until it is reset by the system administrator.

Step 6

The Account Lockout Threshold option sets the number of failed login attempts that will be allowed before the lockout occurs. A number between three and five is usually appropriate for most environments.

Step 7	The last configuration item to set is Reset Account Lockout Counter After _____ Minutes. This item tells the system how long to track the failed login attempts. For example, setting this value to 30 minutes means that the system will count failed logins within a 30-minute window in order to lock the account. If the lockout threshold is not reached during that time frame, the lockout will not occur.

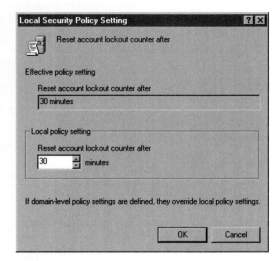

Step 8	Close all of the windows by choosing Cancel.

Passwords are normally stored in an encrypted format on computer systems. The encryption system used is one-way, so that you cannot get back to the original password by knowing the encrypted version. This is to prevent anyone who might see the password file from discovering a password.

Passwords that are difficult to guess can be discovered through a brute force attack. A **brute force attack** means that the attacker tries every possible combination of letters, numbers, and special characters to obtain a password. This may be done one of two ways: The attacker tries to log in with every possible combination of passwords (which would presumably be defeated by the account lockouts) or the attacker obtains the password file or copies of the encrypted passwords. The attacker encrypts each potential combination in the same manner as the system normally does and compares the results to the encrypted password. If the two match, the attacker has the correct password.

Clearly, this type of attack would be very time consuming and tedious to do by hand. To overcome this difficulty, several password-cracking programs have been developed. If the attacker can obtain the password file (called passwd, or the shadow password file—usually called shadow—on Unix, or the SAM file on Windows), the password-cracking program can be used to try to discover the passwords by brute force.

Figure 9.2 shows the results screen of L0phtCrack. (Note that the second character is a zero, not the letter *O*). This is one of the better programs for cracking passwords, and it can be obtained from `http://www.atstake.com/research/lc/index.html`. With such a program, it is possible to attempt every possible combination of letters, numbers, and special characters. Obviously, the more combinations that are attempted, the longer it takes to run, but the more complete the results will be. Once the attacker has the password file, it is impossible to prevent him or her from obtaining the passwords.

It is also possible to obtain encrypted passwords from the network as they are communicated between systems. This activity is called **sniffing** the wire. Often the passwords will not be encrypted here, and no cracking is necessary. Windows passwords are encrypted as they cross the network, however.

Even the administrators of the system cannot look up passwords. If a password is lost or stolen, the administrator must change the user's password to something like "password" and set the account to require the user to change the password on the next login.

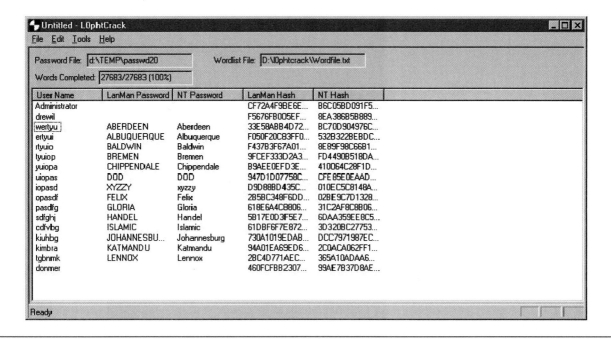

Figure 9.2 The main L0phtCrack screen

File and Directory Permissions

File and directory permissions (part of what is called *authorization* in many systems) allow the computer to identify which user IDs have access to what files. This is also called **access control**. Access control can be very granular, thus allowing only certain individual users access to a particular file or directory, or they can be established for groups of users.

Access control is a mechanism that is used to restrict what authorized users can do on a computer system. Establishing proper access controls can prevent users who do not have access rights to a file or folder from accidentally destroying or disclosing information and files. However, access control will not prevent an authorized user from disseminating information to others.

Windows Systems Windows has the ability to set access control permissions at a very detailed level. Figure 9.3 shows the permissions that are available. As you can see, for each individual user or group in the domain, you can set any number of permissions on each directory or folder.

In normal circumstances, permissions are set on directories. The groups of users that need to have access to the files in the directory are identified, and only these groups are given access. Some groups may be given read-write or full control, while others may be given only read access.

Linux Systems Linux systems (like most Unix systems) do not have the granularity of access controls that are found on a Windows system. On Linux systems, permissions can be set for the owner of the file, for the group, and for the world. For each of these three, read, write, and execute permissions can be granted.

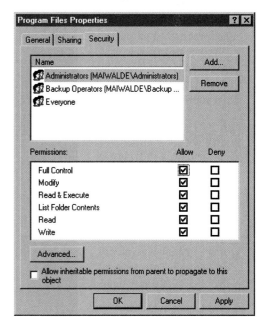

Figure 9.3 Windows allows significant flexibility in access control configurations.

To see the permissions on a file, issue the command `ls -l`, and you will see something like this:

```
-rw-------  1 emaiwald  ppp        0 Nov 22 15:49 test.file
```

The permissions on `test.file` allow the owner read and write access. You can see this by the first set of characters. For this exercise, ignore the first hyphen (-). Positions 2–4 indicate the permissions for the file owner. In this case, `rw-` means that the owner has read and write permissions. If the owner had execute permissions, the fourth space would have an *x*. Positions 5–7 show the permissions for the group, and positions 8–10 indicate the permissions for everyone on the system or the world.

To change the permissions, you use the command `chmod` followed by the type of access and the category of access. For example:

```
$chmod 777 test.file
```

This command grants read, write, and execute privileges to all three categories (owner, group, and world). The three 7s represents the type of access to grant to each category based on this system: 4 gives read access, 2 gives write access, and 1 gives execute access. The number entered in the command is the sum of the access to be granted. Therefore, 7 means that read, write, and execute is granted (4 + 2 + 1 = 7). If only read and write access were to be granted, the number would be 6(4 + 2).

Practices and User Education

Technical security controls, such as password configurations and access control, can help an organization manage the security of its networks. However, such technical security controls can only go so far. These controls are based on the expertise and diligence of the system and network administrators, and because administrators are human, something likely will be forgotten or missed at some point that will open the computer systems and network to compromise.

Security Policies An organization's security **policies** define the expected level of security that is to be configured. These policies also define acceptable behavior for employees and users of the computer systems and networks.

Policies come in all shapes and sizes (some organizations do have one-page policies) and must be tailored to the culture of the organization. The following is a list of the areas that should be covered in an organization's network security policies:

- System configuration
- User authentication (such as passwords)

 Try This!

Setting Permissions on a Folder

It is important to know how to set permissions on files and folders in Windows 2000. Try this:

1. Log in to the computer with a regular account that can create files on the local system.

2. Use My Computer to bring up the list of files and folders on your system.

3. Create a new folder for this exercise. (Don't change something on the system that might cause it to malfunction!)

4. Select and right-click the new folder. Select Properties from the list, and you will see a dialog box that provides general properties for the folder.

5. Click the Security tab and you will see who has what rights or permissions on the folder.

6. By adding individuals or groups to the list, you can establish the permissions that each group or user has to the folder.

Introduction to Networking

- Access control configurations

- Network connectivity (how the internal network can be connected to the Internet)

- Computer and Internet use

- E-mail use

- Incident response (what to do when someone breaks into your systems)

- Disaster recovery (what to do when very bad things happen)

Overall, these policies provide the basic instructions for the administrators to do their jobs.

Security Awareness   As mentioned earlier, it is very important to explain the need for security to your employees. Changing the password requirements without teaching your employees about the new requirements is a sure recipe for disaster.

When most people think of security awareness, they think of long, boring, required training classes. While classes are certainly part of it, they are not the only part, and they do not need to be long and boring. A good length for a basic class is less than one hour. Ideally, this would occur over lunch and would include videos as well as a presentation.

In addition to training classes, the awareness program should also include posters, newsletter articles, and e-mail reminders. The choice of how to use these parts of the program depend upon your organization. Get human resources or your public relations departments involved!

Audit Trails   It is considered good practice for each server to keep an **audit trail**. An audit trail is a log that records certain security-related events that occur on a computer system. These events may include logins and logouts, system shutdowns and reboots, or even access to certain files. The audit log can be very useful in reconstructing events after a problem or concern has been identified. Keep in mind, however, that auditing can also generate a vast amount of information. Auditing every file access on a system is usually a bad idea, but auditing access to a file full of very sensitive information may give you an idea of who was trying to access the file.

It is good practice to record the following events in the audit trail:

- Successful logins

- Failed logins

- Successful logouts

- Failed logouts

- Successful management actions

- Failed management actions

- System events

- Failed access attempts

If your organization does not have policies of this sort, don't just buy a book and copy the policies. Policies must be tailored to the organization.

Commonwealth Films (`http://www.commonwealthfilms.com`) sells a large number of training videos. Many of them are useful for security-awareness training classes.

Try This!

Turning on Audit Trails in Windows 2000

It's important to know how to turn on audit trails in Windows 2000. Try this:

1. Log in to a Windows 2000 system as administrator or as a user with administrator access.

2. Click the Start button and select Settings | Control Panel.

3. Double-click the Administrative Tools icon.

4. Double-click the Local Security Policy icon.

5. In the left panel, expand the Local Policies item and select Audit Policy. Look at the list that is displayed in the right panel.

6. Double-click any of the items and you will be presented with a screen that allows you to configure the auditing for this type of event.

7. Go through the list and turn on the audit for the events that you would like to log.

8. Close the audit configuration screen.

9. Open your Event Viewer by clicking Start, Settings | Control Panel. Then choose Administrative Tools and double-click Event Viewer.

10. Choose Security Events in the left pane and you will see the events you turned on being logged.

The exact events that are tracked should be defined by the security policy and reflect information that is important for the organization.

It is also good practice to review your audit trails periodically. Unfortunately, audit trails that are generated by computers are not the easiest things to read. Creating or finding a tool that will automate the review of audit trails is best.

External Threats

Internal threats may be more dangerous, but, luckily, few insiders are likely to do malicious harm. External threats are more numerous, and hackers tend to attempt to cause harm when they are able to compromise a system. The good news is that external threats tend not to have the necessary access to compromise the system. Thus, they must somehow first gain access.

Front Door Attacks

The most common type of external attack is for a hacker to identify vulnerabilities on any of the organization's systems that are on the Internet. These systems may include mail servers and web servers, as well as network devices such as routers. We will call these types of attacks *front door* attacks because they attempt to exploit vulnerabilities in the organization's public face.

The Hacker's Attack   A hacker looking for a system to compromise is likely to search large portions of the Internet. This means that port scans will be used to find vulnerable systems. A **port scan** is a probe used to identify systems that are running services that may be vulnerable to attack. For example, if the hacker is looking for web servers to attack, he or she will search for systems that respond on port 80 (HTTP). Once these systems are found, the hacker will attempt to identify whether the system is vulnerable to attack. This may be done by simply issuing a bogus command across the connection. The web server at the other end will (in most cases) helpfully identify itself.

When a potentially vulnerable system is located, the hacker will launch an attack, with several potential outcomes:

- A web server might be defaced (the hacker changes the home page of the system).

- The system might be compromised so that the hacker is able to log in to the system.

- A service running on the system may cease to function.

Any combination of these things may occur, as they are not mutually exclusive. If the hacker is able to log in to the system, it is likely that he or she will drop what is called a **rootkit** on it. A rootkit is a set of programs that will aid the hacker in returning to the system and hiding his or her presence. Once a rootkit is on a system, it is very difficult to completely remove it. Usually it is best to rebuild the system from scratch.

Network Protections Protecting a network from external threats means that you must start with proper network architecture. Figure 9.4 shows a basic network layout. The router and firewall can both help protect the web server and the internal network. The router is a network device that is designed to pass traffic, but it is possible to configure access control lists on the router so that certain unwanted traffic is blocked or dropped rather than passed on. The access control lists could drop such things as inbound telnet traffic or traffic that is targeted at ports that are not used.

The **firewall** is a network security device that can be configured to allow certain traffic through. Firewalls will drop all traffic by default—they must be configured to pass traffic that is necessary for

Try This!

Determining Which Web Server Is Running

Techniques such as determining which web server is running can be very useful for debugging as well as for gathering information. This exercise shows how easy it is to gather such information. Try this:

1. Log in to your system as a normal user.

2. Find a local web server or one on the Internet. You can do this by looking for a system named *www.<your domain name>*. Most companies use *www* as the name of their web servers.

3. Choose Start and Run. Type **cmd** when the computer asks you what you want to run. This will bring up a command prompt window.

4. Type the following:
   ```
   $telnet <web server> 80
   ```
   Telnet is used to establish an interactive session with a system. The *80* at the end of the command tells the telnet client to connect to port 80 on the web server. Replace *<web server>* in the command with the name of the web server that you have located.

5. Once the client connects, type the following:
   ```
   http /1.0 Get
   ```
   Then press ENTER two times. In most cases, you will get back some text that indicates a bad page request. Embedded in the response, though, may be some information about the web server in use. For example:
   ```
   HTTP/1.1 400 Bad Request
   Date: Mon, 25 Nov 2002 19:49:34 GMT
   Server: Apache/1.3.27
   Connection: close
   Content-Type: text/html; charset=iso-8859-1
   ```
   In this case, the web server is running Apache version 1.3.27. See what you can find.

business. In Figure 9.4, HTTP traffic must get to the web server so that the information on the web server can be made available to the Internet. E-mail must also get to the mail server so that the organization can receive mail. The firewall would be configured to allow this traffic. However, traffic to other ports would be blocked, since there is no reason for anyone on the Internet to connect to ports other than ports 25 and 80. Similarly, all traffic bound for the internal network would be blocked, as there is absolutely no reason to allow external systems to connect to sensitive, internal systems.

Through the use of basic security tools, such as firewalls and router access control lists, you can prevent hackers from targeting vulnerabilities that may exist in services that people on the Internet do not need to access.

Patching Vulnerabilities Perhaps the most important thing you can do to a network or system to protect it from hackers is update vulnerable software.

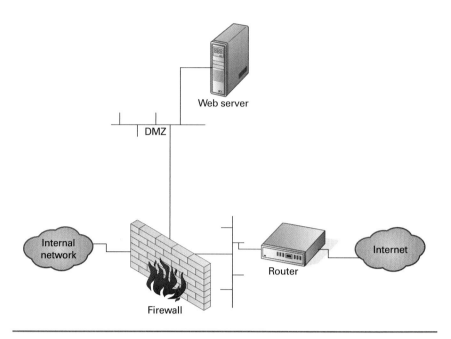

• **Figure 9.4** Basic external network security protections

Today, software has become so complex that it appears to be impossible to eliminate programming errors completely, and some of these errors lead to security vulnerabilities that could allow a hacker to take control of the system. The only defense is to stay up to date on the vulnerabilities and patches, and update the system on a regular basis.

Many sources can provide information on vulnerabilities and patches. In fact, the manufacturers of operating systems and software usually provide mailing lists to keep you updated. Other organizations also provide this information. These are two of the major ones:

- Computer Emergency Response Team (CERT)—Provides a mailing list on major vulnerabilities and patches (`http://www.cert.org`)

- Security Focus (now part of Symantec)—Provides several mailing lists on software vulnerabilities (bugtraq), computer incidents (incidents), and others (`http://www.securityfocus.com`)

Patching systems can take time, but the protection that it affords the organization is well worth the effort.

Step-by-Step 9.02

Upgrading a Windows 2000 System

Microsoft has provided an easy-to-use web site where you can upgrade the software of any Windows system, including Windows 95, 98, 2000, and XP. The procedure is very simple, and the web site walks you through all of the necessary steps.

To complete this exercise, you will need the following items:

- A Windows computer (either 95, 98, 2000, or XP)
- An administrator login to the system

Step 1	Log in to your computer as an administrator or equivalent.
Step 2	Start Internet Explorer, enter **http://windowsupdate.Microsoft.com** in the Address field, and click the Go button. Note that you will have to allow Internet Explorer to run ActiveX scripts for this site to work properly.
Step 3	Click the Scan for Updates link and wait as the scripts identify the necessary upgrades for your system.

Step 4	Click the Review and Install Updates link so that you can choose which updates to install.

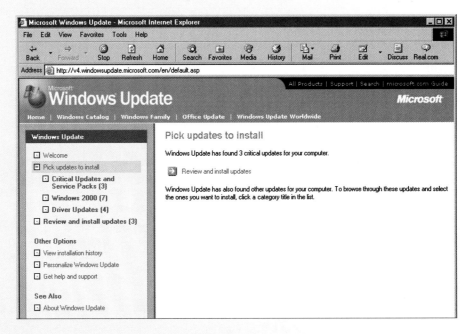

Step 5	Carefully review the list of updates that you can download and install. Some of them may have to be downloaded and installed separately. This information will be included

in the descriptions. Also be aware that some of the updates can be rather large. If you have a slow connection, you may need to download one or two updates at a time. After you make your choices, click the Install Now button to begin the installation.

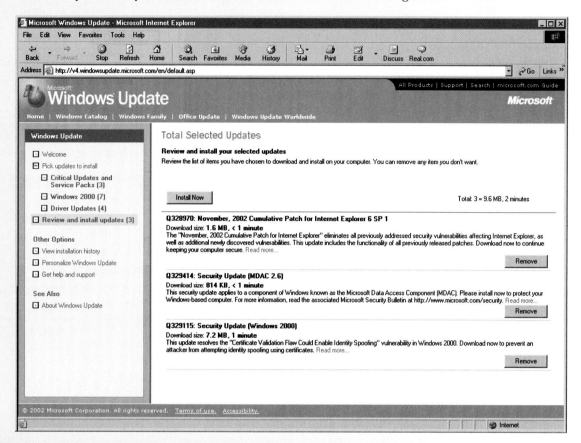

Step 6

After installation, it may be necessary to reboot your system for the updates to take effect.

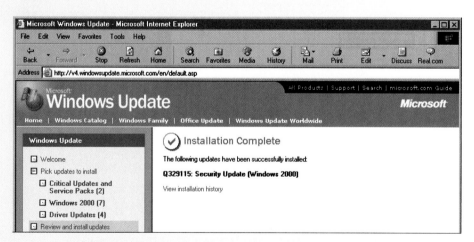

Back Door Attacks

We have talked about hackers coming through the front door. While this is one way in for hackers, it is not the only one. Keep in mind that hackers want to gain as much access as they can while hiding their true identities. Often, the best way to do this is to come in the back door—there are ways to get information or access to computer systems other than just attacking the security of the computer system. Here are some back door approaches:

- Physically breaking into the facility
- Using a remote access connection
- Using a wireless network access point
- Using social engineering to trick an employee into giving out information

Physical Security   The longer a person works with computers, the clearer it becomes that physical access to a system is a key component of security. If a hacker can gain physical access to a system, it is likely that he or she will be able to take control of the system. Therefore, the physical security that is provided around your organization's computer systems is as important, if not more so, than the network security.

In real life, physical security measures are fairly simple:

- Locate sensitive systems in a data center that has good physical access controls.
- Limit the access outsiders have to the organization's facilities so that they cannot use employee computers or attach their own systems to the network.

Following these basic principles will prevent the majority of physical access threats to your systems.

Remote Access Security   In an effort to allow remote or traveling employees to access internal resources, many organizations have implemented some type of remote access solution. Whether this is a dial-up solution or a virtual private network (VPN) over the Internet depends on the particular situation of the organization.

If these access points are properly secured—meaning that appropriate care has been taken to use strong authentication systems—there is usually little additional risk to the organization. However, sometimes remote access via dial-up phone line is not centrally controlled by the organization, and departments or individual employees establish their own remote access points. Too often, this is simply a single phone line into a single computer running pcAnywhere with no authentication. A configuration such as this allows anyone who finds out about the phone number to take control of the computer and act like a legitimate user of the organization's network.

One of the security tests that Lauren ordered performed against the SinkRSwim Pools network is called a **penetration test**. This is a test that looks for vulnerabilities in the computer and network systems of an organization. In some cases, the organization actually asks the testers to exploit a vulnerability to gain access to sensitive information. Ricky was part of a team that was testing the organization. Lauren gave Ricky the address of the firewall and web servers to try to penetrate, and he performed basic tests against these systems and found no obvious vulnerabilities. However, further examination of the web page showed fax and phone numbers.

Using the phone numbers, Ricky proceeded to **war-dial** approximately 1,000 phone numbers similar to them. War-dialing is an attempt to find

Inside Information

Updating Linux

Updating Linux systems is not as easy as updating Windows systems because there are many flavors of Linux, and each system may include software from several other vendors. It is usually best to periodically visit the web sites of the distribution you are using. For example, http://www.redhat.com will provide updates and patches for the Red Hat Linux distributions. These updates will usually cover any software that is included in the original distribution.

Once you have found the updates you want, you will need to download them and install them. Keep in mind that some vendors (such as Red Hat) also provide utilities to help you through the process. The Red Hat utility is called up2date, and it will start an interactive session that will walk you through the update process.

phone lines that are being answered by computers. Any time a computer answers a phone, a note is made of the number and attempts can then be made to gain access. Usually, automated programs are used to dial huge groups of numbers.

The next morning Ricky came in to find that the computer had found four numbers that responded with modem carriers. He tested each and found that one was a computer with pcAnywhere running and no password. From there it took the team only a quick five minutes to access the computers on SinkRSwim's internal network that contained the organization's most sensitive information.

Wireless Networks   In the past, controlling physical access to the office space of the organization usually controlled the physical access threat. Unfortunately, wireless technology now allows the organization's network to leak outside of the physical office space. The installation of a wireless hub may allow access to the network from outside the building or on other floors of the same building.

If wireless technology is installed, tests should be performed to determine exactly how far the signals travel. Be sure to check parking lots and other floors in the building. Unfortunately, the existing security measures associated with wireless networks have proven to be less than effective, allowing outsiders to gain access to internal networks. Figure 9.5 illustrates two of the potential dangers.

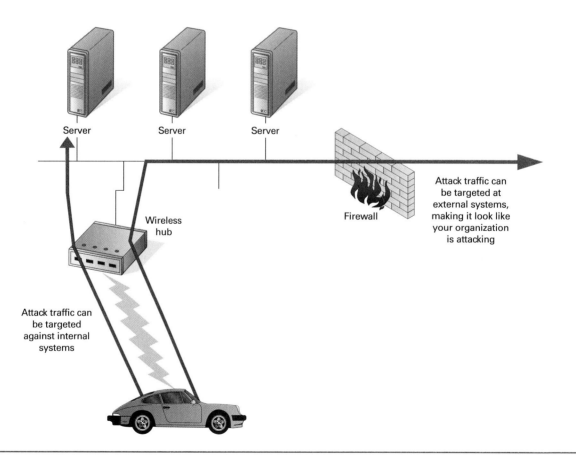

• **Figure 9.5**   Wireless security dangers

At the very least, if wireless networks are to be used, they should be segregated from the main internal network by a firewall and should require strong authentication. Also, try to keep track of how far your wireless network travels, as it may go farther than the parking lot!

Here are some other recommendations for using wireless networks:

- Monitor internal systems just as you monitor external systems, and use internal Intrusion Detection System (IDS) if possible.

- Understand the range and security features of your wireless systems.

- Use a VPN on your wireless networks.

- Use a firewall to limit access from your wireless networks to your internal networks.

- Identify valid MAC addresses and exclude all others from your wireless networks.

Social Engineering   **Social engineering** can be used to to gain unauthorized access to computer systems through non-technical means. A hacker may use lies and deceit to gain passwords or other information about the network. Consider the following conversation:

Hacker	"Hi, my name is John and I am with the Help desk. I am calling to solve a little problem with your computer."
Employee	"Gee, what kind of problem?"
Hacker	"Oh, nothing serious. Just a little unnecessary traffic. I just need your password so I can clear it up."
Employee	"OK, my password is g34hjuk8."
Hacker	"Thanks. I will take care of it and call you back in a few minutes to reboot your system."

Based on this conversation, how many of your employees will provide their passwords? Normally, the answer is about 60 percent (or even more!). The hacker may also take the role of an employee who needs remote access—the hacker tries to convince the help desk that he needs to provide a password or change an existing password. Remember that help desk employees are trained to be helpful.

The only way to combat this type of attack is by educating the users and help desk staff. Make sure that scenarios like this are included in the awareness training. A key point to make to employees is that the help desk will never ask for their passwords, since they already have all the access they need.

Denial of Service

A **denial of service (DOS) attack** is an attempt to prevent the legitimate use of a resource. This type of attack can be carried out with a pair of wire cutters or a backhoe, or it can be a sophisticated network-flooding attack. Most of the DOS attacks today take the form of some type of data flood on a network. This attack uses up all of the available bandwidth on a network and thus prevents legitimate traffic from reaching the computers on the network. The end result of this type of attack is that the legitimate users of the server cannot reach it, and it therefore appears to be down.

Have a help desk staff person participate in the awareness training program. This way he or she can relate firsthand what types of questions the help desk might have.

More recently, hackers have used large numbers of compromised servers connected to the Internet in what is called a **distributed denial of service (DDOS) attack**. The DDOS attack makes use of the compromised systems to increase the amount of traffic in the flood and thus take down larger connections or even multiple systems (see Figure 9.6).

DOS attacks do not have to be made against bandwidth. Attacks are also made against particular services (such as the web server or mail server). These types of attacks can be just as devastating as a bandwidth attack.

You can employ few methods to protect against DOS attacks. A DOS vulnerability that is caused by a software problem can be patched, but an attack against bandwidth is impossible to prevent. Any response by the victim also requires assistance from their Internet service provider (ISP) and the upstream providers. Even then, it may not be possible to stop the attack.

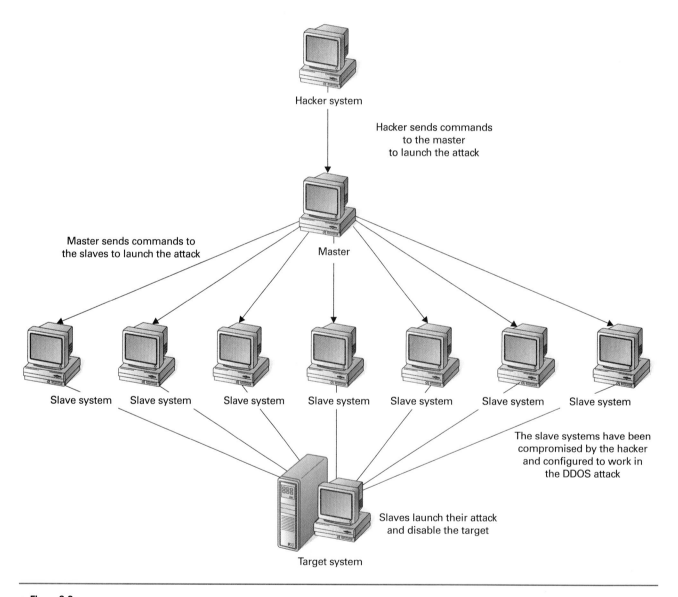

• **Figure 9.6**   A distributed denial of service attack

Viruses, Worms, and Other Malicious Code

Malicious programs are a significant security issue to all organizations. At the very least, these programs eat up staff time. At the other end of the spectrum, these programs can be very destructive or they can be used by hackers to gain entry into an organization's computer systems. Two useful sites that offer information about these malicious programs are McAfee Security at `http://www.mcafee.com` (makers of antivirus products) and Symantec at `http://www.Symantec.com` (makers of Norton AntiVirus). Both sites have searchable archives of malicious programs, where you can find fixes and the characteristics of the programs.

Types of Malicious Programs

There are three general types of malicious code: viruses, worms, and Trojan horses. Each has its own characteristics.

Viruses A **virus** is a program that piggybacks on another program—viruses are not programs that exist on a system by themselves. By attaching themselves to another program and hiding there in spaces not used by the original program, they cause themselves to be run anytime the infected file runs. Macro viruses attach themselves to word processor documents and files for other programs with macro programming capabilities.

Viruses propagate through the sharing of files—executable files (.com or .exe files) or, in the case of macro viruses, document files. They can be shared through FTP sites or web sites, or simply by transferring disks between computers. These types of programs can be destructive or passive. Examples of viruses include Michelangelo and Melissa.

Worms **Worms** are programs that execute on their own and use their own code to propagate. Generally, worms are programmed to exploit vulnerabilities on computer systems. Depending on the sophistication of the worm, it may do any of the following:

- Choose targets randomly or from a predefined list.

- Examine the target by searching for particular programs or vulnerabilities, or just attempt to exploit the vulnerability no matter what the target is.

- Send messages back to its creator about a system that has been compromised.

In effect, worms are automated forms of hacking, and they can compromise many systems in a very short period of time. Examples of worms are CodeRed and SaAdmind.

Trojan Horses A **Trojan horse** is a program that pretends to be something it is not. Normally, the Trojan horse program is accompanied by some type of social engineering that attempts to make the recipient execute the program. If you look back at two recent Trojan horse programs, you can see how this was done:

- **ILOVEYOU** The ILOVEYOU Trojan horse came as an e-mail message from someone that you knew. It pretended to be some type of love message, and that was a sufficient enticement to cause many people to open the file. Opening the file caused the script to run and propagate itself.

- **AnnaKornikova**   The same method was used with this Trojan horse, but instead of pretending to be a love message, the e-mail indicated that it was a nude picture of the tennis star Anna Kournikova.

Preventing Infections

It shouldn't surprise anyone that the most important way to prevent malicious code infections is to have proper antivirus software installed and configured. However, user education is also important. Users need to be taught that e-mails with unexpected attachments should be treated with suspicion and not opened immediately. With that said, the following sections offer some recommendations for dealing with malicious code at various points in the infrastructure of an organization.

Servers   Servers, especially file servers, should have antivirus software installed. This software should be configured to examine the entire file system for malicious code on a daily basis. It is best to configure these scans to begin in the off hours, as the scans can use a fair amount of the system's processing power.

Desktop Computers   Desktop computers are the most likely location for a malicious code infection to begin, so the installation of antivirus software here is more critical than on the servers. Periodic checking of desktop computers can be difficult, since many employees turn their systems off when they go home for the night. Instead, all desktop systems should be configured to scan files as they are opened. This will allow the antivirus software to identify malicious code even if the employee disregards your recommendations and opens the e-mail attachment. This configuration will also catch files that are moved between work and home.

E-Mail   E-mail is increasingly the medium of choice for spreading malicious code, which means you can watch for it and stop it before it gets to the desktop computers. Several products are on the market that will scan all incoming (and outgoing) e-mail messages for malicious code as they move through the e-mail server. If any is found, the e-mail is quarantined and not passed on to the destination without first being cleaned. It is usually easier to keep one antivirus installation configured and up to date than to try to keep every desktop properly configured and maintained.

Try This!

Checking Your Antivirus Configuration

Checking your antivirus configuration is a useful exercise, because an appropriate configuration can save you much time and aggravation. Try this:

1. Log in to your computer as administrator.

2. From the Start | Programs menu locate your antivirus program and start it up. This will bring up your user interface.

3. Look for a setting called "Realtime protection" or something close to that.

4. Check to make sure that the software is checking for malicious code in real time.

5. Once you have determined this, check to see what types of files are being checked. Many antivirus packages will default to checking only executable files, such as those with .com and .exe extensions. This configuration will not catch macro viruses. To catch macro viruses and other such malicious code, make sure the software checks all files.

Updating Antivirus Databases   No matter which antivirus software an organization purchases, the antivirus database must be kept up to date. Every major antivirus vendor provides a mechanism to update the databases with the latest information. It should be noted that if the latest information is not installed with the software, the software will not detect the most recent malicious code.

Do no rely on employees and administrators remembering to update their own databases. Even the most well-intentioned employees will forget from time to time. Instead, configure the antivirus software to check for updates automatically and install them if an update is found. Make sure the software does this at least once per day.

▣ Planning a Secure Network

As you might imagine, creating a secure network is not a five-minute task—it takes planning, testing, and constant awareness. A secure network begins with a definition of the security requirements, and it continues with the development of policies and awareness training of employees. Even if you have a good plan, though, bad things can still happen, and you must be prepared to deal with them.

Identifying Requirements

When developing a secure network, you must begin with security requirements. Security requirements fall into four basic areas:

- **Confidentiality**   What information must be kept from unauthorized individuals? This requirement will affect the need for network security devices, as well as access control on files.

- **Integrity**   What information must be protected from unauthorized changes? This requirement will affect the need for network security devices, as well as access control on files.

- **Availability**   What information, systems, or capabilities must be ready for use? This requirement will affect the need for redundant systems and communications, as well as backups and alternative locations for disaster recovery.

- **Accountability**   What information do you need to have about what has happened? This requirement will affect the need for authentication (so you know who was there) and audit logs (so you know what they did).

Together, the requirements in these four areas will drive the design of your network and the configuration of your systems.

Planning for Disaster

Planning for a disaster is a necessary part of building and maintaining a secure network. Disasters are events that cause massive damage to the organization's infrastructure. In most situations, this means that the organization's primary data center or site is no longer usable for business. When such a situation occurs, it is madness to expect employees to respond without a previously developed and tested **disaster recovery plan (DRP)**.

A complete DRP should take into account everything from the computer equipment and communications needs of the organization to where the employees will sit and work. This is not to say that every organization requires a backup site that can come online in minutes. Depending on the requirements for availability, the organization may not require such a response.

Meeting the availability requirements is often very expensive, as it may require duplicate equipment and an alternative location. These are costs that your organization may not wish to incur.

When developing the DRP, make sure that the organization understands who has the authority to initiate the plan. In most cases, this is obvious. In others, it is not. For example, a few years ago there was a major ice storm in the northeastern United States and eastern Canada. Many electric towers were taken down, and power to Montreal was cut. One organization in the city had a backup generator all set and ready to go. However, the managers of the organization were concerned about the supply of diesel fuel. They considered initiating a disaster response and contacted their hot site vendor. Unfortunately, they had not kept the configurations at the vendor up to date, and thus they could initiate the DRP only with the loss of some services. Clearly, the decision to initiate the DRP in this case needed to be made at a very high level in the organization.

This example also points out the need for testing the DRP. If the DRP had been tested on a regular basis, this problem could have been identified and corrected before a real disaster occurred.

Step-by-Step 9.03

Creating a DRP

Look around at your classroom configuration, or choose another network you know. You will use that network in this exercise.

To complete this exercise, you will need the following items:

- A pad of paper and a pencil

Step 1

Identify the components of the network. List the number and types of servers, desktop computers, routers, firewalls, printers—everything you can see. Be sure to note the make and model of the servers and the amount of memory and disk space. Also identify the operating system and the applications that run on each system.

Step 2

Try to prioritize the systems that you have listed. Take into account the use of each system and the dependencies. For example, a web server may be the most critical item because people on the Internet must have access to it. In this case, the network connections are also critical, because without them no one will be able to reach the server.

As part of this prioritization, identify how long each system can be down before it impacts business or operations.

Step 3

Find an alternative location for your computer systems. Ideally, your organization will have a facility that is somewhat remote from the current facility, and perhaps it can be an alternative location for the computer equipment. Remember that the site must have adequate space, power, climate control, physical security, and communications in order to work well as an alternative site.

Step 4

Develop a plan for getting the network back into operation at the new site. Take into account the amount of time each system can be down. Do you purchase duplicate equipment to keep at the alternative location, or will you try to procure this equipment after the disaster has occurred? This choice will depend on how quickly the systems must be returned to service and on your budget. Develop plans based on an unlimited budget and also on a very small budget. What is the smallest budget you can get away with?

Step 5

You have identified what you will do and how much it will cost. What do you need to do on a regular basis to make sure your plan stays up to date? If the network changes—if a new server or device is added, for example—what has to happen to the plan?

Which members of the staff must know about the plan? How will you keep these employees involved in the plan so that they will remember what to do next year?

Backing Up the Network

Small disasters are likely to occur more frequently than big ones. Small disasters include hard drive failures, accidental file deletions, and system crashes. In these cases, restoring a single file or an entire drive is required, rather than declaring a disaster and moving to an alternative location.

File backups are an important part of managing the security of a network. However, these can also become prohibitively expensive if not done properly. At the high end of the cost spectrum, each server could be configured with backup drives in a RAID (redundant array of independent disks) configuration. There are five levels of RAID (levels 2 and 4 are not used, however), and each provides advantages for protecting data. However, while RAID protects against the loss of data resulting from a disk failure, it is expensive (additional disks must be purchased, along with a RAID controller) and it does not prevent the accidental deletion of files.

The alternative to RAID for protection from disk failure is to back up the files onto tape or another disk. This has the added advantage of protecting files from accidental deletion (since they can be restored from tape). Tapes also tend to be less expensive than RAID configurations.

The schedule of backups needs to be well thought out. In most cases, a full backup (meaning that every file is written to tape) occurs once a week, and incremental backups (which record only the changes since the last backup) occur every day.

Tapes need to be stored in a secure location because if something were to happen to the data center, the information on the tapes would be needed to rebuild operations. Therefore, you should normally move tapes offsite as soon as possible. Some organizations provide offsite storage and pick up and deliver tapes, allowing you to rotate the tapes on a daily basis.

 Inside Information

Computing Backup Requirements

In most cases, organizations will take incremental backups on a daily basis and full backups weekly. Examine your servers and estimate the tape requirements for this backup schedule.

Now consider that you will want to keep some of the tapes offsite, following a regular rotation. A standard procedure is something like this:

■ *One weekly set of backups is kept offsite at all times and rotated weekly.*
■ *At the end of every month, a full backup is retained for a year.*
■ *At the end of every year, a full backup is retained for a year (or more, depending on legal requirements).*

Now, how many backup tapes will you need?

Chapter 9 Review

■ Chapter Summary

After reading this chapter and completing the Step-by-Step tutorials and Try This! exercises, you should be able to do the following regarding security in your network:

Identify Threats to Your Network

- Threats require motive, means, and opportunity.
- Employees or insiders are the most dangerous threats because they have means and opportunity.
- Hackers have sufficient means and motivation to attack your network. The only thing they may lack is the opportunity.
- User authentication must use at least one of the following: something known, something possessed, or a personal characteristic.
- Strong passwords can be constructed by using combinations of uppercase and lowercase letters, numbers, and special characters.
- Passwords are normally discovered through the use of a brute force attack.
- Access control mechanisms can be used to limit access to sensitive files.
- Technical security is not sufficient to protect a network. You must also have a security policy and educate users.
- Audit trails can be used to reconstruct events and thus can help in investigating security incidents.
- Hackers usually attempt to identify systems, services, and software before attacking.
- Once a vulnerability is identified, a hacker will exploit it and place a rootkit on the system.
- Firewalls are a basic component of a security architecture.
- Patching vulnerabilities is an important part of overall security.
- Physical security is necessary to protect overall computer security.

- Remote access via dial-up phone lines or a VPN can also be used by hackers to attack a network. Make sure such systems are protected by appropriate authentication.
- Wireless networks can extend beyond the physical confines of the building and can provide another means for hackers to gain access to your network.
- Hackers may use social engineering techniques to trick your employees out of information such as passwords.
- Denial of service attacks can take many forms, but all of them deny access to important systems or information.
- Malicious code often costs organizations significant time to clean up and remove.
- Antivirus software on desktop computers, servers, and e-mail systems is the best defense against malicious code.
- Antivirus signatures must be updated on a regular basis to make the antivirus software effective.

Plan for a Secure Network

- Requirements must be identified in the areas of confidentiality, integrity, availability, and accountability before a secure network can be constructed.
- Disaster planning is important for the availability of the network and systems.
- Proper disaster planning must include all key systems and information.
- Disaster planning is not a one-time exercise but must be updated every time a new system is added to the network.
- Backups are a necessary part of network security.
- Backups are used to reconstruct files after a disk failure or unintentional deletion.

■ Key Terms

access control *(291)*
audit trail *(293)*
biometrics *(286)*
brute force attack *(290)*
denial of service (DOS) attack *(301)*
disaster recovery plan *(306)*

distributed denial of service (DDOS) attack *(302)*
firewall *(295)*
hackers *(285)*
identification and authentication *(285)*
password lockouts *(287)*

penetration test *(299)*
policies *(292)*
port scan *(294)*
risk *(284)*
rootkit *(295)*
sniffing *(290)*
social engineering *(301)*
threat *(285)*

Trojan horse *(303)*
virus *(303)*
war-dial *(299)*
worms *(303)*

Key Term Quiz

1. _____ is dialing a large set of phone numbers in order to find computers that answer.

2. An attack that seeks to render systems or information unavailable is a(n) _____.

3. The starting point for a good security program is _____, which determines how systems will be configured.

4. A security device that is used for network access control is a(n) _____.

5. A(n) _____ is an individual with motive, means, and opportunity.

6. _____ is used to prove to the computer who you are.

7. A program that piggybacks on another program is called a(n) _____.

8. Listening in to a network to gather passwords is called _____ the network.

9. A security test that is used to identify security vulnerabilities is called a(n) _____.

10. The most effective way to discover passwords is through a(n) _____.

Multiple-Choice Quiz

1. What are the primary impediments to complete network security? Choose all that apply.
   a. Cost
   b. Usability
   c. Hackers
   d. Risk
   e. Threats

2. To be credible, a threat must posses motive, means, and
   a. Knowledge
   b. A computer
   c. Hacking tools
   d. Opportunity
   e. A vulnerability

3. Internal threats are dangerous because
   a. They are employees.
   b. They posses knowledge of which systems are most important.
   c. They posses motivation.
   d. They possess unauthorized access.
   e. They can be compromised.

4. The three types of authentication information are
   a. Something a person knows
   b. Something a person is
   c. Something a person wears
   d. Something a person does
   e. Something a person has

5. Which of the following is not a type of biometric system?
   a. Fingerprints
   b. Retina scan
   c. Voice print
   d. Facial geometry
   e. Password

6. Which of the following is the most widely used form of authentication?
   a. Fingerprints
   b. Smart cards
   c. Passwords
   d. User IDs
   e. Retina scans

7. Two characteristics of good passwords are that they are hard to guess and
   a. They are hard to discover using brute force.
   b. They are eight characters in length.
   c. They change every 45 days.
   d. They are made up of uppercase and lowercase letters.
   e. They include numbers and special characters.

8. Access control is used to
   a. Prevent hackers from gaining control of a system
   b. Prevent legitimate users from looking at files they are not authorized to see

c. Preventing employees from crashing systems

d. Preventing unauthorized users from conducting a port scan

e. Preventing users from encrypting files

9. Audit trails should be

   a. Deleted weekly

   b. Stored with other files

   c. Reviewed regularly

   d. Held for evidence

   e. Not created

10. Before attacking, a hacker will look for signs of

    a. A vulnerability

    b. A web server

    c. A port scan

    d. An employee

    e. Sensitive information

11. The most critical task that can be performed on a network to prevent a hacker from gaining access to a system is

    a. Creating a firewall

    b. Patching systems

    c. Educating users

    d. Creating policy

    e. Capturing audit trails

12. Wireless networks can cause problems in securing networks because

    a. Existing wireless security features are better than the rest of the network.

    b. VPNs are not used.

c. War-dialing can find the wireless nodes.

d. Many wireless networks are unpatched.

e. They extend the network outside of the physical building.

13. Which is the most effective means of preventing virus infections?

    a. User education

    b. Patching systems

    c. Using antivirus software

    d. Creating appropriate policies

    e. Conducting penetration tests

14. Security requirements should be identified in which of the following areas?

    a. Confidentiality

    b. Integrity

    c. Availability

    d. Accountability

    e. All of the above

15. Backups are needed in addition to disaster recovery plans because

    a. Tapes are included in disaster recovery plans.

    b. The recovery of a single file is a less frequent requirement than the move to an alternative site.

    c. Disaster plans re-create sites, while backups assist in the recovery of files.

    d. Disaster recovery plans may not work.

    e. Disaster plans must be constantly updated.

■ Essay Quiz

1. Compare and contrast the inside versus outside threats. List two ways in which inside threats can be thwarted. List two ways outside threats can be thwarted. Describe the similarities and differences between the two types of threats and the ways in which you can defend against them.

2. Using Amazon.com as an example, describe which security requirements you feel are most important and explain why. Think of the information that they must have to accept an order, the requirements on the information as it goes through their system, the ability to know

who ordered what, and the need for the site to be responsive to customers.

3. Describe the requirements that must be examined when choosing an identification and authentication system. In your discussion of the issues, be sure to include the level of trust, the cost, and other logistical issues.

4. Access control systems can become unmanageable if not used properly. The most common concern with access control is providing individual access (or denying individual access) to each file. Propose a policy for managing access to files across an

organization that is both easy to manage and appropriate from a security point of view.

5. In a certain organization, the security director determined that it was very important to track how administrators were using their access to systems. He decided to implement an audit policy to do this. Describe the events that should be audited in such a situation and what information each type of event will provide to the security director.

Lab Projects

Time to roll up your sleeves and apply what you've learned. The following lab projects will enable you to practice the concepts discussed in this chapter.

• Lab Project 9.1

Security awareness is an important part of any good security program. The most important part of awareness is getting the information to the employees in a meaningful manner. You have been given the job of creating a security awareness program for your organization, which is an online retailer selling outdoor apparel. Outside of the shipping and warehouse staff, the majority of employees use computers on a daily basis. These employees include office staff, customer service representatives, buyers, and IT staff members.

To complete this exercise, you will need the following items:

- Your networked Windows XP Professional workstation
- Sketch pad and pencil

1 Identify the parts of the awareness program (that is, what you will use to get your message of security across to the employees in each group).

2 Determine the material to be covered in each part of the program.

3 Outline how the material will be presented for each group.

• Lab Project 9.2

Your organization is investigating wireless technology. As part of the investigation, you have been asked to identify security issues. One issue that you identified was that the signal may be available outside of the facility. In order to provide hard data to management, you establish a wireless hub and use a wireless interface card in your laptop to check the range of the device.

To complete this exercise, you will need the following items:

- A computer running Windows 2000 XP Professional with a wireless NIC
- A wireless hub

1 Check the ability to connect to the network both inside the building and outside.

2 Record your results and present the results to management.

3 Identify and test protective measures to limit who can access the wireless network.

4 Present these measures as recommendations on how wireless technology may be used.

Managing a Network

> *"So much of what we call management consists in making it difficult for people to work."*
>
> —Peter Drucker

In this chapter, you will learn how to:

■ **Describe Windows network management tools**

■ **Implement Windows and NetWare network management**

Building a network can be likened to initiating a project. You try to efficiently complete a project such that the initial and adjusted goals are met using limited resources (and budget). This is true for the network you created, and it is now time for the next step—ensuring that your network's users can continue to use the network. This means you need to manage the network. Management, in the business sense, involves continuing to meet a set of refinable goals using a company's physical, intellectual, and human resources. Your goal now is to manage your network, whether you continue in a technical direction or apply these basics in a more managerial role.

In this chapter, you will learn more about managing your classroom network. You will first learn about tools available on your Windows workstation computers, and also about some available on your server. You will learn how users can help manage their own computers by running utilities that check their disks or defragment their storage, backing up their own files, and viewing their active tasks using Task Manager. On your server, you will learn about using the Simple Network Management Protocol (SNMP), Performance console, and Network Monitor. You will also learn about the compression and quota-management tools available on NTFS volumes. Then, you will learn to use Novell's text-based commands and NetWare Loadable Modules at the NetWare server console. Finally, you will examine some of the features of specific NetWare utilities, such as MONITOR, DSREPAIR, and NWCONFIG.

■ Describing Windows Network Management Tools

Your network, like that of SinkRSwim Pools, is centered around the main network operating system server you installed—the Windows 2000 Server—and the computer users access its resources through Windows XP Professional workstations connected to the network. The SinkRSwim Pool workers throughout the company have gradually become accustomed to using their newfound network resources. What's more, they have quickly become dependent upon those networked resources to get their day-to-day jobs done more effectively. Whenever the network is down, the SinkRSwim network community complains loudly that they want their network back. Ricky is only too glad to learn more about keeping the company's network healthy and being able to monitor it for signs that problems may be building so he can head them off before the network fails—even for a moment.

You have seen throughout this course that there are many complicated components associated with today's corporate-sized network operating systems and the advanced workstation computers where their networking services are employed. If any piece at either end, or anywhere in between, breaks down or stops communicating with the other pieces, whoever is managing the network will be expected to know how to fix the problem, and quickly. Therefore, the more you know about networks, the better you will be able to perform network support.

Some things can be managed by the users at their own workstations, but these things will only help support the network, not relieve anyone of the responsibility for keeping the whole system working. Therefore, now that your network is installed and operational, you should learn as much about these components as possible so you can keep them working and know how to get your system, itself, to help maintain your network.

Windows XP Professional Workstation Tools

The heart of most people's work on a network is their workstations. In addition to this being where users perform their work, the remote access that servers allow is fast becoming the most common way to manage a network, from anywhere inside (and oftentimes outside) the company. It is essential, therefore, for workstations to operate properly. The failure of a workstation obviously has an adverse effect on that particular user's network capability. Should that workstation also house additional networked resources, such as shares, other users' capabilities may also be affected.

To make troubleshooting a little complicated, what initially may appear to a user to be a networking failure quite frequently turns out to be a failure somewhere on the user's own workstation (in the workstation's internal hardware or something else locally installed) that requires a technician's intervention. As a networking specialist, you will probably not be making this type of workstation repair, but you should keep in mind that users will often blame the person maintaining the network first, and ultimately the network itself. Additionally, it may be your responsibility to differentiate between network troubles and a hardware problem that gets passed to the technician.

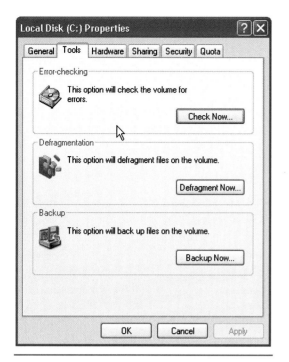

Local Disk (C:) Properties

| General | Tools | Hardware | Sharing | Security | Quota |

Error-checking

This option will check the volume for errors.

Check Now...

Defragmentation

This option will defragment files on the volume.

Defragment Now...

Backup

This option will back up files on the volume.

Backup Now...

OK   Cancel   Apply

• The three disk drive tools available to users

Error-checking

This option will check the volume for errors.

Check Now...

• The Check Now option

Many of the tools and techniques covered in the next sections can be used through your users' workstations. Although all the tools discussed here are intended for server management, four can also be used when troubleshooting local components. Making sure your users know how to use some of these tools will help you keep networked resources and the users themselves online, but you will have to decide which of the tools you want them using.

The four tools discussed here can be helpful if used on the workstation by the users themselves. You should think about teaching your users how to use all four so they can perform some local machine management themselves. Three of the tools are available through the disk drive itself, and the other can be reached through the taskbar.

Tools for Use on Local Disks

Three very powerful management tools are available on all your networked computers: the Error-Checking, Defragmentation, and Backup utilities. These tools can be reached by your users through the Properties dialog box by right-clicking on any hard disk attached to their computers.

Error-Checking Tool   The first tool listed on the Tools tab of a workstation's hard disk drive's Properties window is the Error- Checking tool, which, as its name implies, checks your drive for errors—it is also called the Check Disk tool. Clicking the Check Now button starts this tool. Frequent use of the Error-Checking tool lets users scan their hard disk drives and verify whether any operating system or filing system errors have occurred. If such errors exist, it gives them options for fixing those errors.

After clicking the Check Now button, the Check Now window for the local disk appears, displaying the two option boxes that control which function is to be completed by the Error-Checking tool. Clicking OK at this point, with the default settings (neither option selected), will simply scan the disk and return any errors. No repair actions will be performed, and this scan is accomplished very quickly. However, the typical use of the Error-Checking tool involves clicking the first option box so that the Error-Checking tool automatically fixes any file system errors that are identified in the repair process. When the tool makes those repairs, the process takes a bit longer, but it is still relatively fast.

You can also run the Error-Checking utility immediately through a DOS command by typing **chkdsk** in the Run dialog box (accessed through the Start menu). This will run the tool but not make any corrections. Typing **chkdsk /f** will run the tool and make corrections (the /f switch tells it to fix any problems it finds), but it will only run upon restart if the disk drive being tested is currently being used.

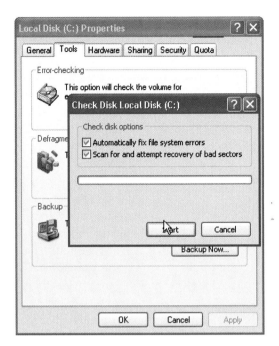

Inside Information

How Often Is Enough?

Users will often ask how often they should perform the maintenance techniques you show them or run tools similar to those discussed in this section. You should temper your immediate response—that they cannot be run enough—with the realization that users have varying levels of both technical ability and computer use. For both reasons, users may not need to maintain their systems as diligently as you would consider normal.

Rather, your response to them should be to tell them that the three tools should be performed on a monthly, weekly, daily, or hourly basis depending on the numbers and types of files they use and how easily they can get along without those files. A user working with a lot of client financial records that simply cannot be lost should use management tools more often than someone working with relatively few files that are easily re-created.

A better solution would be to recommend the weekly use of these tools by your users. You, yourself, may be performing them on a less frequent basis but you could instruct your users to increase or decrease the frequency of these tests by doing their own tests. You should tell them that a good way to decide how often they should conduct their own use of these management tools should be based on how difficult it would be to work without the material contained on their computer.

The other option available in the Check Now window allows users to scan for and attempt to recover bad sectors on the hard disk itself (or multiple hard disks if so equipped). While this is normally a fast process, simply because finding errors is rare, this option can take a long time if errors are located. If the tool does find errors and repairs them, you should then run the Defragmentation tool to relocate the information that was moved from the bad sectors so that it is stored contiguously. You should also give serious thought to replacing the disk drive, or at least backing up the information on the drive to another location, and doing so more often.

The hard disk being inspected by the Error-Checking tool must not be in use. If that hard disk's system files or any of its stored files or applications are currently being used, the tool notifies the user that the system cannot be checked without restarting the computer. It also asks whether the user wants the system to be checked when the computer is next started. Upon restart, the system's files are checked before being put into use. Additionally, when the Error-Checking tool is used on NTFS volumes, all actions taken during the repair process are tracked, any bad clusters are repaired automatically, and important information on all files is copied and stored on the disk.

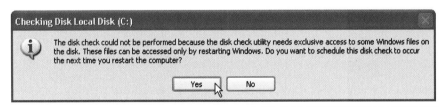

- You can schedule the disk to be checked the next time you restart your computer.

Defragmentation Tool You have already learned about defragmenting your hard disks in Chapter 7 of this text. However, the convenience of having the Defragmentation tool in the same location as the Error-Checking and Backup tools makes it easy for your users. When you explain how they can help with their own workstation management, it is better to show them that the tool is easy to use and easy to find as well. Clicking the Defragment Now button will start the same Disk Defragmenter that you studied in Chapter 7, and the procedures for its use are the same when it is started from the Properties dialog box.

The Defragmentation tool uses the Disk Defragmenter window. Along the top of the window are the menus and toolbars, which are like those on Microsoft Management Console. The section shown here lists pertinent information about each of the computer's volumes. To select a drive to defragment, just click on it.

Immediately below the volume-identification section are two horizontal bars where graphic depictions of your disk drive will be displayed. Click the Analyze button to allow the tool to check the drive to see if the data stored there is fragmented. The top bar will show the estimated disk usage before defragmentation.

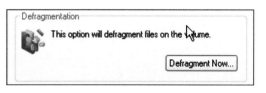

• The Defragmentation tool

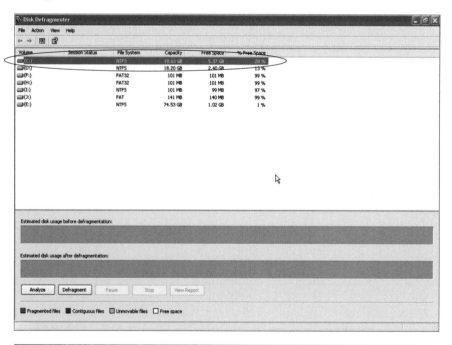

• The Disk Defragmenter window

Clicking the Defragment button also displays the "before defragmentation" depiction, but it does so as a reference point, since the program also begins to actually defragment your drive. The Estimated Disk Usage After Defragmentation bar provides a dynamically updated representation of the defrag process in action. You can actually watch your disk's information being moved from location to location as pieces are joined back together.

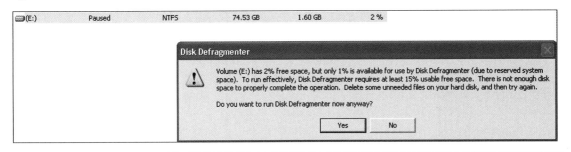

• Your computer will let you know whether you have enough free space for efficient defrag performance.

When the defrag operation is complete, you will be notified and can use the color codes in the fourth section (under the row of buttons below the two rows of graphical information) to determine the status of each identified area on the disk. You also have the option of either reviewing the tool's report to see a listing of files that could not be moved, or clicking the Close button to return to the Disk Defragmenter, where you can select another volume to defragment.

For effective operation, the Defragmentation tool requires that 15 percent of the total space available on your volume be available as free space that can be used when moving files. However, if you don't have that much free space, you can still conduct the defrag operation if you don't mind spending a bit more time completing the process.

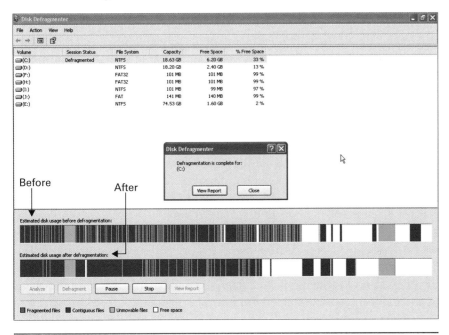

• The Defragmentation tool displays "before" and "after" depictions of your data.

Try This!

Defragmenting Your C: Drive

Use the Defragmentation tool to defrag your hard disk. Try this:

1. Click the Start button, select My Computer, right-click your C: drive, and select Properties. Your drive's Properties dialog box will open.

2. Click the Tools tab, and click the Defragment Now button.

3. Click the Analyze button, and note whether the system suggests that you conduct a defrag operation.

4. Click the Defragment button to initiate the defrag operation, and observe the two graphical depictions of your disk's information.

5. Click OK when the defragmentation is complete.

Remember, no matter how you get to the utility, defragmentation is a matter of taking noncontiguous or fragmented information and relocating its many pieces such that they are side by side (contiguous). Reading from or writing to contiguous data is much faster than doing either with noncontiguous information—storing or retrieving a file's information can be done in one continuous action on contiguous information. Otherwise, with noncontiguous data, your computer has to read or write a section, pick up the disk's head, look for the next segment, and then similarly continue to read or write additional sections until the file is complete.

Furthermore, after defragmentation is complete, the likelihood of new files being stored in noncontiguous space is lessened. This is because the Defragmentation tool, in putting your files back together, also joins your empty disk spaces together as well. Any new files written to your computer can thus be located in the newly recombined contiguous empty space. Since contiguous space is read and written to more efficiently, your computer can be noticeably faster after a defragmentation operation has been completed.

Backup Tool In Chapters 1 and 9, you learned about the importance of making backups. The Backup tool is another conveniently located management tool that can help your users help you maintain their systems. In this instance, as long as users have the proper permissions to access and use the files they wish to maintain copies of, they can easily use the Backup tool to keep their information backed up and accessible. While there are numerous third-party backup utilities available that you can choose from, simply clicking the Backup Now button in the disk drive's Properties dialog box initiates the Microsoft version of the Backup tool.

As long as users are working with their own files, or they have the Read, Read and Execute, Modify, or Full Control permission to the files, they can perform backup operations on the data. On the opposite end of the process, however, if restoring the data is necessary, users must have either the Write, Modify, or Full Control permission on the original files to overwrite them. Since users have these permissions on their own data, teaching them to use the Backup tool to keep an extra copy of their own data will help them maintain their own working environment.

In practice, the Backup tool is woefully overlooked at the local workstation. You can save yourself some headaches if you get in the habit of using this tool and make sure your users understand that it is available and how it works. Users all too often rely on the administrator's system-wide backups when they need to restore copies of their lost files—no matter why they were lost. Effective use of the Backup tool may let users restore some of their own lost files.

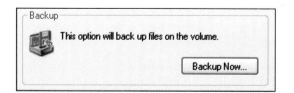

• The Backup tool

If the workstations have excess storage space on their own local drives or are equipped with external storage devices, such as floppy disk drives, Zip drives, or read-write CD drives, you may simply need to instruct users how to use the Backup tool. If users periodically perform a backup operation and save an extra copy of their own data somewhere on their local workstation, administrators called upon to restore a missing file may use these individualized backups to help a user quickly restore the occasional misplaced file or accidentally erased directory when it happens. Thus, restoring a single file from a small backup would likely be much easier than searching for that same file from a company-wide backup that an administrator would normally create.

Task Manager: A Tool on the Taskbar Itself

Many users know next to nothing about a very handy tool that is available to them through their taskbar. The **Task Manager** provides them with a means to not only gather information about their computer but also to start or stop most of their own applications. To access the Task Manager, right-click a blank space on the taskbar and select Task Manager.

If you make the decision to let your users help manage their own workstations, they should be taught about using the Task Manager tool which operates in the Windows Task Manager window.

Backup Progress   ?   X

Cancel

Drive:	C:
Label:	Backup.bkf created 12/8/2002 at 2:44 PM
Status:	Backing up files from your computer...
Progress:	▮▮▮▮▮▮▮▮

	Elapsed:	Estimated remaining:
Time:	3 min., 49 sec.	9 min., 14 sec.

Processing:	C:\...\Content.IE5\DHPWDAU7\serve_mail[13]

	Processed:	Estimated:
Files:	7,511	11,277
Bytes:	305,137,201	1,043,720,054

• The Backup operation in progress

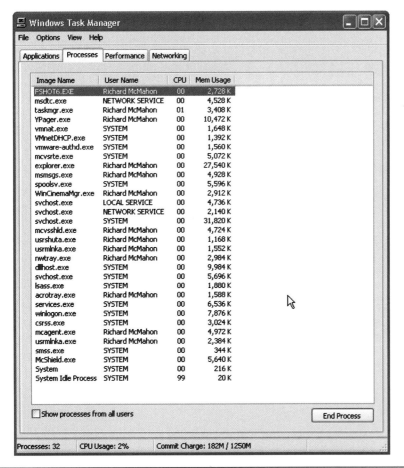

• The Task Manager

You can also open the Task Manager tool with what is affectionately called the Microsoft three-finger salute (CTRL+ALT+DELETE) and then clicking the Task Manager button, or by typing **taskmgr** in the Open field in the Run window, reached through the Start menu.

Try This!

Using the Local Workstation's Backup Tool

Use the local workstation's Backup tool to back up a user's information. Try this:

1. On your Windows XP Professional workstation, click the Start button and select My Computer. Right-click your C: drive and select Properties to open your drive's Properties dialog box.

2. Click the Tools tab and click the Backup Now button to start the Backup or Restore Wizard.

3. Click Next to accept the default backup settings, click Next again to accept the Back Up Files and Settings option, and click Next again to accept the default My Documents and Settings option.

4. Click the Browse button to select where you want to save your backup.

5. The default location for this save action is the floppy diskette. Click the Save button if you intend to save to a floppy diskette in the A: drive. Otherwise, click the Cancel button, click the Desktop button in the left panel of the Save As window, and click the Save button to designate the desktop as the place to save your backup file.

   Keep in mind that clicking the Browse button starts with the default intent of sending a backup to the A: drive, and it will probably take a lot of floppy diskettes to create even a moderately sized backup of your C: drive. If a diskette is not installed in that drive, the Backup tool will instruct you to insert a diskette, and the save action continues trying to save the data there. As indicated in Step 5, you must click the Cancel button if you intend to save data to any other location besides the A: drive.

6. Either accept the default "Backup" name for this backup or enter another name of your choosing.

7. Click Next, confirm the displayed information, and click the Finish button to initiate the backup operation.

When you open Task Manager, the tab that will be displayed is the same tab that was in view the last time the tool was closed, and the same settings will be in place too. On your Windows 2000 Server, there are three tabs available in the Windows Task Manager window: Applications, Processes, and Performance. Your Windows XP workstations will have a new Networking tab.

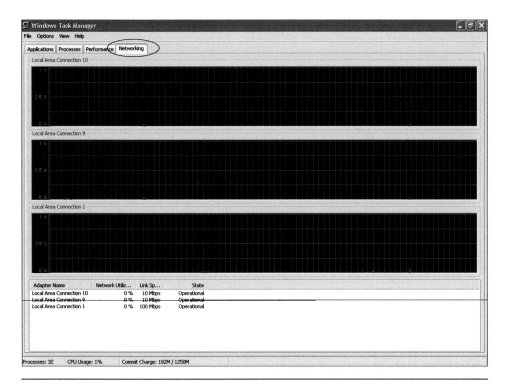

- Windows XP includes a new Networking tab in its Task Manager tool.

Many of the Task Manager's menu options for configuring settings change depending on which of the tabs you have open at the time. Some of the tabs have elaborate settings, and you may want to go through the menu bar options and configure your Task Manager to best suit your needs.

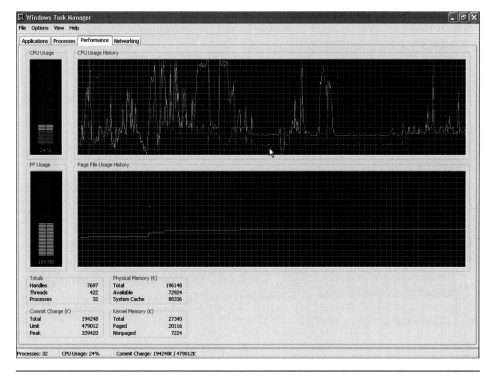

- You can configure the Task Manager to show the information you want.

Touring the Task Manager Tool

Use the local workstation's Task Manager tool to view information about your computer.

To complete this exercise, you will need the following item:

■ An operational networked Windows XP workstation or Windows 2000 Server

Step 1

At your Windows workstation or server desktop, right-click an empty space on the taskbar and select Task Manager. If you are working on your server, notice that there are only three tabs, which means you will not be able to view your networking information.

Step 2

Click the Applications tab to see the applications currently running on that computer. Choose View and select Details, and notice that the status is given for each application. Click the New Task button, notice that the Create New Task window that appears is similar to the Run window accessed through your Start menu, and click the Cancel button to return to the Applications tab.

Step 3

Click the Processes tab to see the processes currently running. Choose View and select Select Columns to view additional columns that are available, and then click the Cancel button to return to the Processes tab. Right-click a process and notice that you have the option to stop either the process itself (End Process) or the process and all other associated processes as well (End Process Tree). Note, though, that the system will not let you end a process that is critical to the system's continued operation.

Caution: You should not make any alterations to the Set Priority option available when right-clicking a process. Doing so may affect your computer's proper operation. You should also make sure to point out to your users that they should not make any such changes either.

Step 4

Click the Performance tab and note the graphs that provide dynamic information on your CPU and your **page file** (a temporary work space in memory). Click View and select Show Kernel Times to add another line (red) to the CPU Usage History graph depicting how much of the CPU usage was needed by the heart of the operating system—the **kernel**.

Step 5

If you are working on your Windows XP workstation, you can click the Networking tab to view activity to or from each of your own computer's network connections. Choose View, select Network Adapter History, and add either the Bytes Sent or Bytes Received lines to the default Bytes Total displayed in the graphs. The information listed at the bottom of the screen includes the link speed and the **link state** (or operational status) for each connection.

Step 6

Close the Task Manager to return to your desktop.

Windows 2000 Server Tools

Each of the tools discussed in the previous section is also available on your Windows 2000 Server, and you should use all of them as you monitor and manage the health of your server and workstations. However, there are other tools available at the server that will help you even more than the general tools found on the workstations. Three of these tools are the Simple Network Management Protocol (SNMP) service, the Performance console, and Network Monitor.

Simple Network Management Protocol (SNMP) Service

The Simple Network Management Protocol (**SNMP**) is an Internet-standard protocol (one that is widely accepted for use on the Internet) that facilitates monitoring the system and sending status updates to a central location called the network management system (**NMS**), which is also called the host or the **SNMP manager**. The SNMP service can be started or stopped through the Windows Components Wizard.

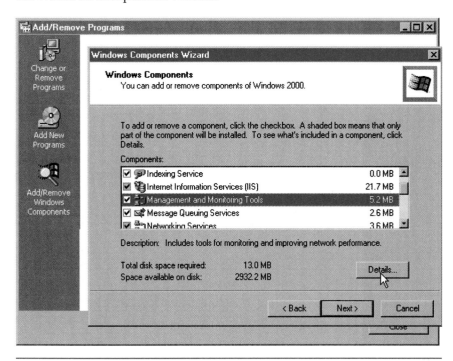

• Start or stop the SNMP service through your Windows Components Wizard.

The objects on your network, such as servers, workstations, printers, hubs, switches, and routers, are called **nodes**. These nodes can be monitored by SNMP and can send status updates to the SNMP manager. Once a network node is monitored by SNMP and managed by the SNMP manager, that node is referred to as an **agent**. Agents, the SNMP service itself, and all its other components are configured through the Services and Applications section of your Computer Management console. Agents normally just respond to queries about their status, but they can also send an alarm message, called a **trap message**, when they are configured to look for specific events (like login failures or other unauthorized access) and report their occurrence.

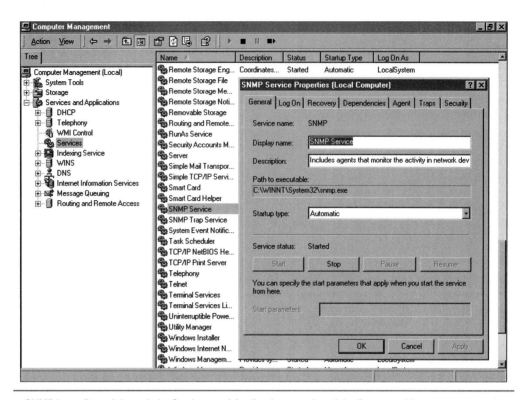

- SNMP is configured through the Services and Applications section of the Computer Management console.

The SNMP manager uses installed network management software (software not included with Windows but purchased from separate vendors) as it performs the monitoring and management duties it has been configured for. It creates and maintains a Management Information Base (**MIB**) that lists the information on each node that should be monitored at the agent and

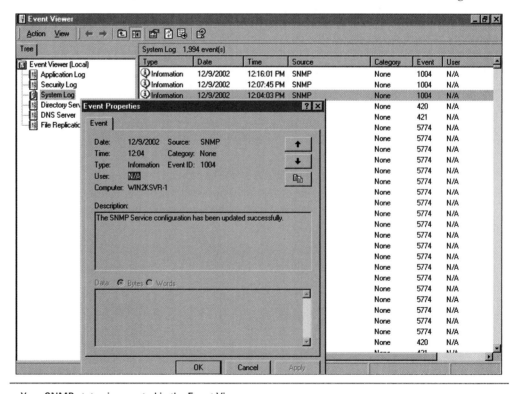

- Your SNMP status is reported in the Event Viewer.

reported back to the manager. You must configure at least one NMS if you intend to use the information that can be collected by SNMP on your system. The information collected can include things such as network performance, security breaches or similar alarmed events, and network auditing.

Although you don't get the true benefit of having SNMP configured on your network without having the third-party network management software installed, larger networks will typically employ this service, and you should know how to configure it. You can verify that the service was updated properly by reviewing the messages in your Event Viewer. You can get to the Event Viewer through Administrative Tools in your Control Panel.

Performance Console

Both Windows 2000 Server and Windows XP Professional provide you with the **Performance console**, a utility program that lets you collect data about your system's performance. Performance console comes preinstalled on both of your network's Windows operating systems and is accessed through Administrative Tools by selecting the Performance option. The Performance console actually provides you with two useful utilities that will help you monitor and analyze your system's health: System Monitor and Performance Logs and Alerts.

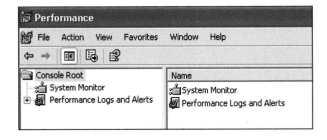

• Performance console opened showing its two utilities

System Monitor   The **System Monitor** portion of your Performance console utility allows you to view either current system activities or those you recorded using Performance Logs and Alerts (discussed in the next section). There are three different views available in System Monitor: graph, histogram, and report. Although the default System Monitor view displays data on three specific items in the graph view, you can select the items you want displayed from a large list and can easily change to either of the other two views.

- **Graph view**   The **graph view** plots the data for each item you are tracking along two axes: time along the horizontal axis and amplitude along the vertical axis. Different colors can be selected for each item being tracked, and the line width and style can also be changed. Items whose amplitude would create large numbers can be displayed by using different scales. Even the scale displayed on the axes can be changed, have text added, or a background added.

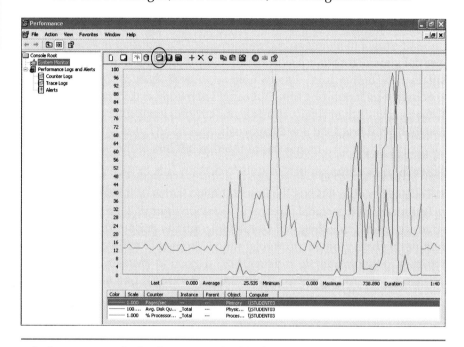

• Performance console showing an example of the System Monitor's data in graph format

- **Histogram view**   The **histogram view** displays the data for each item being tracked along the same two axes, time and amplitude, but does so with bars showing totals for different items. All the changes that can be made to the graph view can similarly be made to the histogram view. The type of data being viewed can also switch between current, minimum, average, or maximum values.

- **Report view**   The **report view** displays the data for each item being tracked in summary format only. Many of the same changes available in displaying the other views are available in the report view, such as different backgrounds, additional items tracked, and the four types of data to display. The graphical changes, however, are obviously not available in this view.

Introduction to Networking

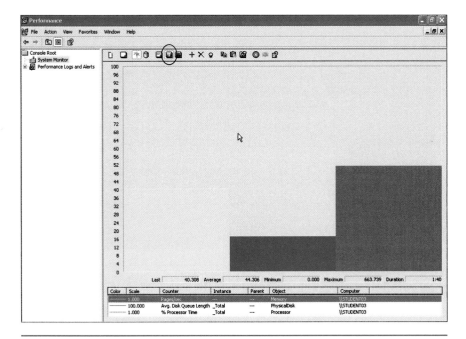

• Performance console showing an example of the System Monitor's data in histogram format

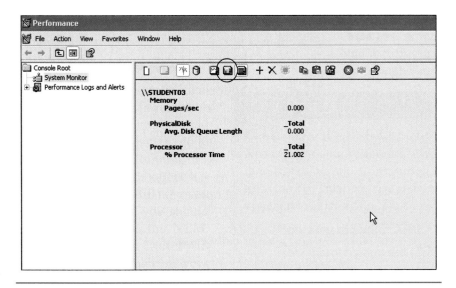

• Performance console showing an example of the System Monitor's data in report format

Performance Logs and Alerts   The Performance Logs and Alerts portion of the Performance console allows you to configure and record the sampled data that is displayed in the System Monitor. You can select the items you want sampled, schedule a time for the sample to be made, and save the information as a log in the default storage location, the Perflogs folder on your C: drive, or change it to another location, as you can see in the following illustration. You can create Performance logs manually when you want one or they can be done automatically at a preset time. Alerts can be configured to send their information when a predetermined condition occurs, such as low drive space or high processor use.

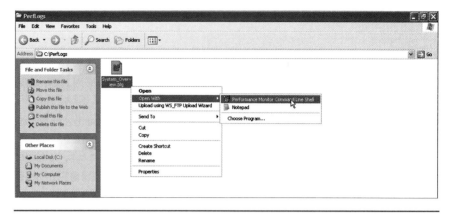

• You can open a Performance Log in the Perflogs folder.

Step-by-Step 10.02

Recording and Viewing a Performance Log

You want to use a System Monitor performance log to capture information on the three default items displayed in Performance Logs and Alerts. Then you want to view the log and check its information.

To complete this exercise, you will need the following item:

■ A Windows XP Professional workstation computer

Step 1

On a Windows XP workstation, click the Start button and select Administrative Tools | Performance.

Step 2

In the Performance window's left pane, expand Performance Logs and Alerts, and select Counter Logs to display the default System Overview log. In the right pane, right-click the System Overview log and select Properties. View the information on the General, Log Files, and Schedule tabs of the Properties dialog box. Pay particular attention to (and write down) the current log filename shown on the General tab.

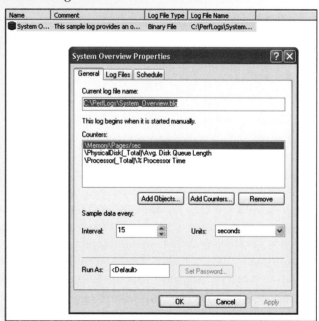

Introduction to Networking

Step 3

Close the Properties dialog box and select the System Overview log. Select Action | Start to start the System Overview log. This begins recording the information that you viewed in Step 2.

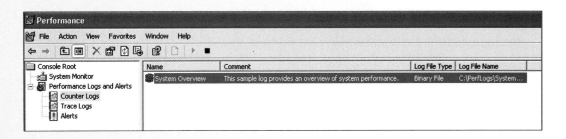

Step 4

After approximately two or three minutes, select Action | Stop to stop recording, and your system will automatically save the log file with the name and in the location that you viewed in Step 2. In the Performance window's left pane, click on System Monitor.

Step 5

At the top of the right pane, pause your mouse pointer over each of the buttons to view its function. Click the second button from the left to clear the display, and then click the View Graph button, and click the View Log Data button. On the Source tab of the System Monitor Properties dialog box, choose the Log Files option and click the Add button. Browse to the location you wrote down in Step 2, and double-click your log file in the Perflog folder.

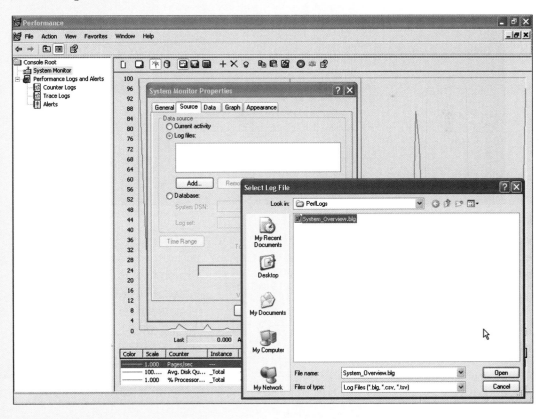

Step 6

Click the Apply button. Notice that your System Monitor now displays the data stored in the log file in the Perflog folder.

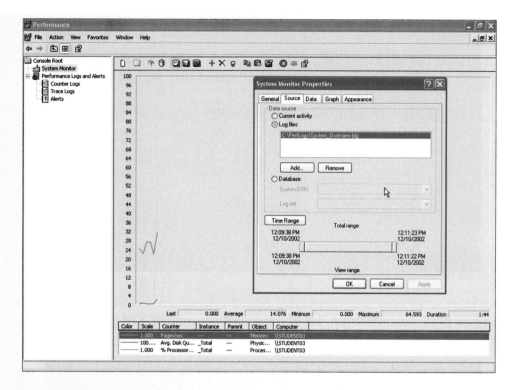

Step 7

Use the different tabs of your System Monitor Properties dialog box to change the appearance of the information in your log as you review the data you recorded. Click OK after returning to the graph view. Select one of the recorded items for emphasis by clicking on the item in the bottom section of the graph view (such as the yellow line in the previous illustration) and clicking the Highlight button. As you can see here, the selected item is highlighted in black.

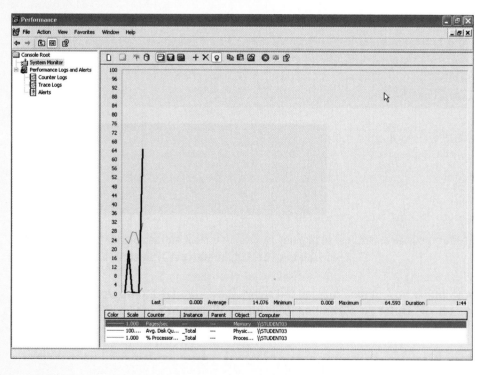

Step 8

Close all windows when you are finished checking your data.

Network Monitor

Network Monitor is another utility available on your Windows 2000 Server that is similar to the Performance console but is intended to provide you with information about the health of your network. Earlier in this chapter you learned how to show your users a similar function on their Windows XP Professional workstations—on the Networking tab of their Task Manager. However, the Network Monitor utility on your server is much more powerful and provides you with considerably more information about your local network than you can obtain using Windows XP's limited version. Network Monitor is not installed automatically on your server. You must install it like you installed SNMP—through the Windows Components Wizard.

Try This!

Installing Network Monitor

You want to install and configure Network Monitor on your network. Try this:

1. On your Windows 2000 Server, click the Start button and select Settings | Control Panel. Double-click Add/Remove Programs.

2. Select Add/Remove Windows Components to start the Windows Components Wizard.

3. Select Management and Monitoring Tools and click the Details button to see the tools available.

4. Select the Network Monitor Tools option, click OK, click Next, and then click the Finish button to implement your changes. Note that your computer may have to be restarted after configuring Network Monitor Tools.

When in use, the Network Monitor utility actually records a copy of the data flowing between the computers on your network and your server. Like a tape recording of a telephone conversation, this monitoring utility does not disturb the conversation but merely records a copy of it. Also, like the tape of that conversation, the recorded network session can be copied, reviewed, sent for analysis, or otherwise broken down and *listened to*. Thus, having Network Monitor running on a network can pose a serious security concern. Someone with the right equipment could interpret much of what goes on over your network. If the network information is not otherwise encoded or protected, it can be understood from the data recorded using Network Monitor.

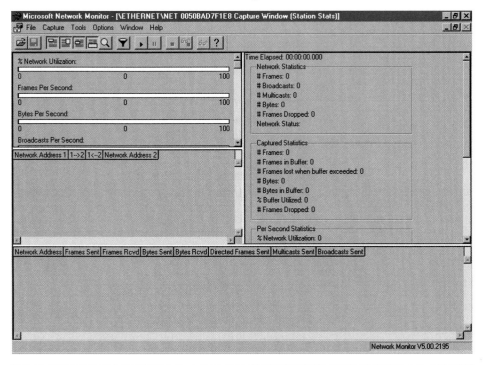

• The Microsoft Network Monitor utility.

You can obtain more information about SMS through the Microsoft SMS web site at `http://www.microsoft.com/smserver/default.asp`.

After installing Network Monitor on your server, you are asked which network you want monitored. As powerful as Network Monitor is, it is limited to monitoring a single network as mentioned previously, and it can only monitor traffic flowing to or from your local machine—your server. This is for security reasons. Even more powerful network monitoring is available with Microsoft's Systems Management Server (SMS) or applications from other third-party vendors if you need additional capturing capability.

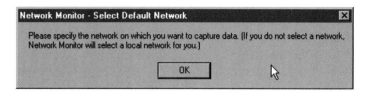

Network Monitor - Select Default Network

Please specify the network on which you want to capture data. (If you do not select a network, Network Monitor will select a local network for you.)

OK

• Tell Network Monitor which network to monitor.

Network Monitor will detect and alert you to any additional instances of Network Monitor running on your network. This ensures that nobody else is capturing traffic using Network Monitor as it comes from your server.

To use Network Monitor, you simply click the toolbar's Start Capture button. When you feel you have captured enough data to perform your analysis, you just click the Stop Capture button on the toolbar. If you want to pause your capturing for a short time, there is a Pause/Continue Capture button on the toolbar. After stopping your capture, you can then click the toolbar's Display Capture button to see the results. If you want to stop an ongoing capture and immediately view its contents, there is even a Stop and View Capture button that you can use.

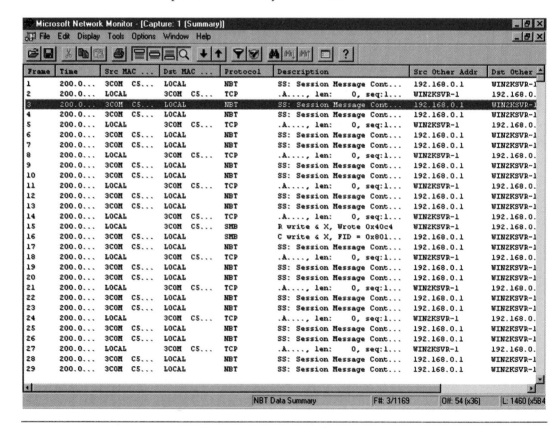

• Significant amounts of data are recorded when using Network Monitor.

Introduction to Networking

While this course is not intended to make you an analysis expert, able to decode captured network messages, it is good practice to know how to use the tool and understand the way it works. The data is extremely overwhelming to someone viewing real network traffic for the first time without serious additional training, and it may still be overwhelming to long-time networking specialists. When you make your first captures, remember that they record extremely high levels of data. Each frame recorded can be further broken down into all of its individual elements, and each character can be decoded to some level. Don't waste a lot of storage by unnecessarily recording more than you need to get a feeling for what is being monitored.

■ Implementing Windows and NetWare Network Management

How you manage your network, and how the network's users employ the resources entrusted to them determines the overall value of the network. If you don't properly maintain the network, the effort required to create it in the first place goes to waste.

Studying the network components discussed in the previous section will help you ensure your network's success. Regardless of the size of your network, many of the administrative responsibilities will involve managing networking functions. A healthy network's use will tend to increase rapidly, and the better your networking management skills, the better you will be able to maintain your network.

Windows Networks

When your network is operational and you are using many of the features discussed earlier in this chapter, it will become evident that the amount of storage space needed by your users seems to be ever-increasing. Microsoft makes two additional features available that will help you on the Windows portion of the network. The first, compression, helps reduce the amount of space needed for the data stored on your network. The second, quotas, lets you limit the amount of network storage space your users are authorized to use.

Compressing Data

Because you created your server and all your workstations using NTFS, you can use the Windows advanced storage feature that helps extend your network's existing storage capacity—**compression**. Compressing data reduces the size of a file so that it takes up less storage space. If you have a lot of data stored on your network, and you implement compression, you can store more in the same amount of space, making your network that much more valuable to the users without spending any money on additional storage space.

Compression is not quite as simple as it sounds—there are some trade-offs. For example, when copying a file to a compressed volume, NTFS reserves space for that file to be uncompressed, so if there is enough space for the compressed file but not enough to uncompress the file, the copy action will be disallowed. Furthermore, there is a slight decrease in performance due to the requirement to decompress a file before use.

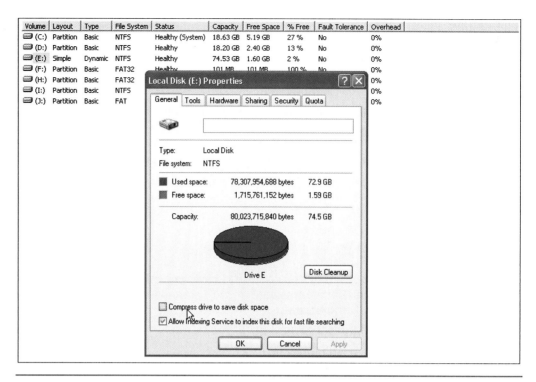

Volume	Layout	Type	File System	Status	Capacity	Free Space	% Free	Fault Tolerance	Overhead
(C:)	Partition	Basic	NTFS	Healthy (System)	18.63 GB	5.19 GB	27 %	No	0%
(D:)	Partition	Basic	NTFS	Healthy	18.20 GB	2.40 GB	13 %	No	0%
(E:)	Simple	Dynamic	NTFS	Healthy	74.53 GB	1.60 GB	2 %	No	0%
(F:)	Partition	Basic	FAT32	Healthy	101 MB	101 MB	100 %	No	0%
(H:)	Partition	Basic	FAT32						0%
(I:)	Partition	Basic	NTFS						0%
(J:)	Partition	Basic	FAT						0%

- This volume is an excellent candidate for implementing compression.

Compression Levels   Compression can either be initiated at the volume level, which compresses everything on the disk drive, or at the file level. At the file level, you can select individual files you want compressed, while leaving everything else uncompressed. Compression at the file level is implemented using the object's Properties dialog box. At the bottom of the General tab, you simply click the Advanced button and in the bottom section of the Advanced Attributes dialog box select the Compress Contents to Save Disk Space option.

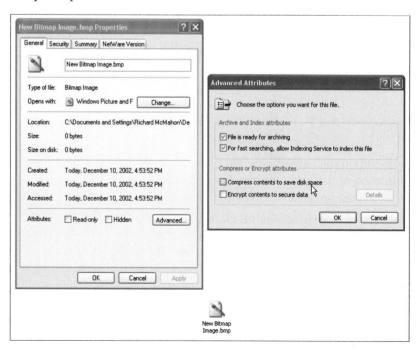

- File-level compression

At the volume level, this is reversed, and everything is compressed with the exception that you can selectively uncompress individual files. When compressing volumes, you again use the object's Properties dialog box, and at the bottom left of the General tab, select the Compress Drive to Save Disk Space option.

Compression on NTFS Volumes Only   Windows 2000 and Windows XP Professional only support compression on NTFS volumes. Whether you set compression to be employed at the file and folder level or at the entire volume level, each file on the volume has its own compressed or uncompressed condition attribute (which, when applied, results in a file's compression state). Applications using compressed files check the compression state and simply uncompress any applicable files prior to using them. All DOS- and Windows-based applications can thus use compressed files. When an application is done with a previously compressed file, or you initiate a save action, NTFS compresses the file once again.

Compression Rules   There is a general rule (with one exception) that helps explain compression attributes: A file, whether copied or moved, will inherit the compression attribute of the new folder it is being copied or moved into. The one exception is that a "move" within the same volume (partition) will not inherit the new folder's compression attribute. The reason for this exception is that the file is not actually being moved from the point of view of the operating system—only a pointer is moved, "pointing" to the original location.

An example will help explain. If you move a file from one location on an NTFS volume to another location on the same volume, the file retains its original compression state in its new location. If you copy that file from the same NTFS volume just discussed to the same new location, though, the new file acquires the compression state of the new location while the old file still remains in the original location with the same compression state.

The rule changes when using FAT partitions. When you copy or move a file from an NTFS volume to a FAT partition, the file is uncompressed first and then copied so that it matches the normally uncompressed level of the FAT partition.

When you implement compression at the directory (folder or above) level, you are given the option of leaving the object's contents in their present compression state (whether compressed or uncompressed) or imposing compression on all its contents. Additionally, once that directory-level object is marked as being in the compressed state, all objects subsequently added are immediately compressed.

 When deciding whether to use compression or encryption, which is the other option in the Advanced Attributes dialog box, you should be aware that they are exclusive of one another at whatever level they are incorporated (file/folder or volume). Selecting one means you can't select the other at the same level.

Setting Quotas

A second Windows advanced storage feature that you can use on your NTFS computers allows you to share what storage you have with as many users as possible—this involves the use of quotas. Providing users a specific **quota**, or an assigned limit on the amount of network storage space they can use, helps ensure an equitable distribution when such networked resources are limited. The use of quotas is implemented through the Properties dialog box on each disk drive formatted with NTFS. Microsoft's quotas feature is not available on FAT partitions.

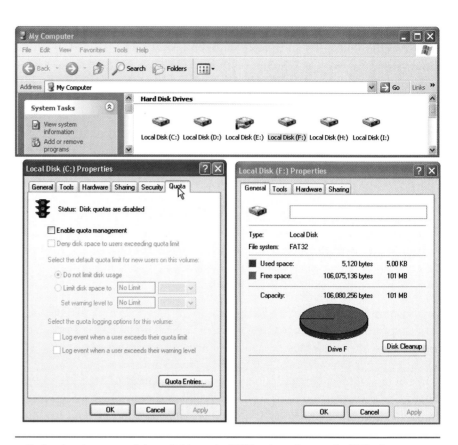

• Notice that the quota tab is available on the NTFS volume, but not the FAT volume.

Equal Access But No Limits   Typically, when networks are first created, storage space appears unlimited and users are granted storage privileges on a first-come-first-served basis. That is, everyone has equal access to the storage, but there are no limits. What frequently happens is that some users quickly take up all the space, and those users with little (or no) space on the disks complain that such a system is not fair. If all was fair, and everyone on your network was to have equal availability for storing their files, then your network's total storage capacity would have to be calculated and divided such that all users get an equal share. Keeping track of such an equitable storage solution at the network level would be burdensome.

Equal Access with Limits   All is not fair, and everyone on your network does not really need an equal amount of the total storage you have available. Nor should network management be unnecessarily burdensome. Rather, Microsoft's implementation of disk quotas lets you assign users limited storage on specified volumes anywhere on your network. The limits you place can be general, so that all users with access to a particular volume have the same amount, or they can be specific, so that some users have a higher storage limit. Thus, storage is divided at the NTFS volume level.

Setting Limits   You set limits on disk space use by implementing quotas on your NTFS volumes. After imposing the quotas, you have the choice of either enforcing their use or simply monitoring users for compliance. In addition to setting a limit on storage, you can give users a warning whenever they go beyond another, lesser, amount that you can also set. This warns users that they are running out of space and might encourage them to delete some files that they don't need to keep but haven't yet needed to delete.

You have the option of configuring quota management to halt further storage attempts when the quota is reached, or you can then have it simply send a notice to a predetermined recipient that the quota has been exceeded (usually an administrator or manager) who could then take the appropriate action—either increasing storage facilities or requesting compliance with the quota.

Another option you have when setting enforced limits is to reconfigure specific users separately. Some users may really need additional storage space, and you can increase the limits for those users on a case-by-case basis.

 Quota use on compressed volumes is calculated based on the uncompressed size of all stored files, regardless of file type. Although it may look like space remains available, users could still be prevented from saving more files on those volumes.

Step-by-Step 10.03

Implementing Quota Management

Your network storage capacity has been left open for users to store as much as they want on any of the storage devices. You decide to start monitoring potential misuse of this privilege by implementing quota management, and you want to practice on one of your network's NTFS volumes.

To complete this exercise, you will need the following:

- A Windows XP Professional workstation computer formatted using NTFS

Step 1

Log in to a Windows XP workstation as the administrative user, click the Start button and select Administrative Tools | Computer Management. Expand the Storage item in the left pane and select Disk Management. In the lower section of the right pane, right-click the icon of the disk that houses the volume where you will be implementing quotas, and select Properties.

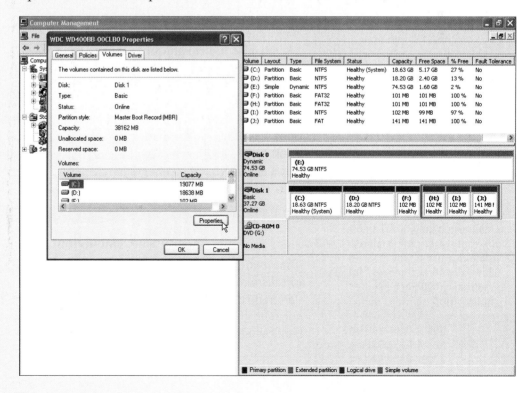

Step 2

In the Properties dialog box, click the Volumes tab and notice that you have access to all the volumes on your selected disk. In the Volumes section, scroll to and select the volume where you want quotas implemented, then click the Properties button.

Note: Accessing the entire disk drive's Properties dialog box gives you an alternative route to the Properties dialog boxes of all the volumes on that disk drive. If you are only configuring one volume, you can go directly to that volume's Properties dialog box through the My Computer window.

Step 3

In the resulting Properties dialog box, click the Quota tab, and check the Enable Quota Management check box. Select the Limit Disk Space To option and set both the limit and the warning levels. Select both logging options, and click the Apply button.

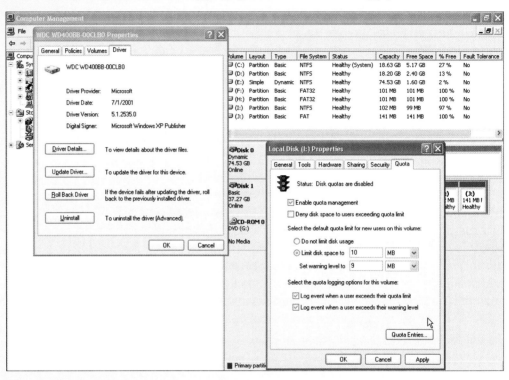

Note: If it is the first time quota management has been implemented on the volume, click the OK button on the Disk Quota window to enable the quota system.

Step 4

Click the Quota Entries button and observe the storage allocations currently set on the disk. In the Quota Entries window, notice that there are no imposed limits on any of the users. No limits are imposed unless you deny users additional space for exceeding their limit.

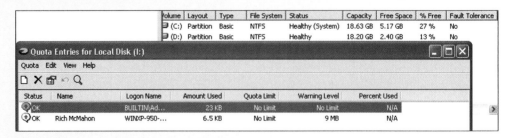

Step 5

Close all windows and dialog boxes to return to your desktop.

NetWare Networks

When it comes to managing your network components, you should consider the NetWare portion entirely on its own. This is true even though, as you have seen throughout this course, the majority of what you have done so far with your NetWare server has been accomplished from your Windows XP Professional workstation's desktop (and possibly from your Windows 2000 Server's desktop). Your NetWare 6 server offers its own, extremely detailed and oftentimes complex network management components. This course is not intended to prepare you to the point where you are an expert with these tools. Rather, the introductory nature of this course is intended to provide you with an understanding of some of the basic tools available and show you some that are comparable to those you learned about for managing the Windows portion of your network.

Using the Server Console

On large networks using most of NetWare's server capabilities, server management involves extensive communication between the administrator and the server's network operating system. This communication primarily takes the form of text-based commands and NetWare Loadable Modules (NLMs), and the majority of these are still entered or loaded by administrators using the server console. The ConsoleOne and Internet-based administration techniques, such as iManage, used in the Novell portions of this text are gaining more and more acceptance, but, for now, entering text-based commands at your NetWare server's console is still the most widely used management technique.

Entering Text-Based Commands at the Console   The NetWare operating system includes numerous commands that operators use when they interface with the file server's hardware and software. The commands are part of the operating system, just as DOS commands are part of the disk operating system (DOS) or Microsoft's utilities that are built into Windows. You must be just as careful when using NetWare commands as when working with DOS commands or Windows utilities. They will act immediately upon whatever part of the server you specify, and they will do whatever you ask of them. Some are stand-alone commands, in that they are used without any command **arguments** (parts of the command that usually tell the system what to execute the command upon). Other commands, such as the LOAD command, will not work unless the arguments are there.

If your syntax (the format of the command) is incorrect, the command may not be understood at all, or it may be misunderstood and performed by the software, returning either an error or the wrong result. On the other hand, if your syntax is correct but your command is for the wrong function, you could affect your server's health. Furthermore, in actual operation, many commands are interpreted by the system even if they are omitted. The command NAME.NLM could be executed at the console by typing **LOAD NAME.NLM** or by simply typing **NAME**. In the second instance, the system assumes you want it to LOAD an NLM and interprets your command appropriately. Therefore, typing **NAME** at the console would be an example of properly using a NetWare text-based command.

The results of using the commands are pretty easy to predict if they are used properly. The NAME command simply returns the server's name. Misspell it as NAM, however, and the system looks for a file named NAM to load.

Similarly, entering the TIME command at the server console returns the system time, and entering MEMORY returns the server's total memory; on the other hand, entering the misspelled TIM looks for a file named TIM to load. Not all commands are that easily interpreted, however, and depending on how bad your misspelling is, the system could end up doing something entirely different from what you intended.

```
NW6SVR1:name
This is server NW6SVR1
NW6SVR1:time
  Time zone string: "CST6CDT"
  DST status:  OFF
  DST start:    Sunday, April 6, 2003   2:00:00 am CST
  DST end:      Sunday, October 26, 2003   2:00:00 am CDT
  Time synchronization is active.
  Time is synchronized to the network.
Wednesday, December 11, 2002   9:02:15 pm UTC
Wednesday, December 11, 2002   3:02:15 pm CST
NW6SVR1:memory
Total server memory: 261,758 Kilobytes
NW6SVR1:_
```

• Three NetWare text-based commands entered at the server console, and their results

Table 10.1 lists some commonly used commands.

Using NetWare Loadable Modules Unlike console commands, NetWare Loadable Modules (NLMs) are commands stored in locations outside the operating system. NLMs add functionality to the operating system's core capabilities, and an operator must load the NLMs into the server's memory to use them. Performing a LOAD action tells the server to read the particular module into its memory from the default SYS:SYSTEM location (unless

Table 10.1	Common NetWare Text Commands
Command	**Description**
LOAD <NLM>	Reads the applicable NLM into the server's RAM
UNLOAD <NLM>	Removes the applicable NLM from the server's RAM
DOWN	Closes all open files/volumes and shuts down the server
SECURE CONSOLE	Removes DOS from the server; also allows loading NLMs only from SYS:SYSTEM
MODULES	Displays currently loaded NLMs
CONFIG	Displays server's network interface card information
DISPLAY NETWORKS	Displays all networks to which the server has access
DISPLAY SERVERS	Displays all servers on which the server has information
SET TIME	Allows changing of the current system date and time
SEND	Allows transmitting message to currently logged on users

Introduction to Networking

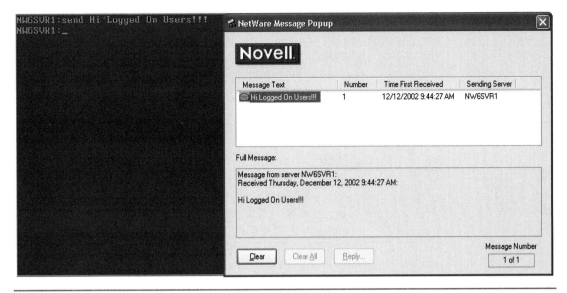

- The SEND command entered at the server console and its resulting message at the users' workstations

another path is specified), and to then execute (or run) the module. The added functionality then remains in the server, provided the server continues to run, or until the operator decides to UNLOAD the NLM.

At the console prompt, type **CDROM.NLM** to prepare the server to operate the CD drive. The NLM must be loaded before running the MOUNT command when working with CDs. The MOUNT command makes a volume available for users, and it is run only once after the server is started. The MOUNT command then stays in memory until the DISMOUNT command is run (making the volume unavailable) or you DOWN the server. The NLM can be added to the startup commands so that it loads automatically whenever the server is started.

Although many of the common NLMs have a .NLM extension following the command's name, there are other extensions available such as .DSK and .LAN as shown in Table 10.2. Table 10.3 lists some commonly used NLM modules.

Using the MONITOR NLM

MONITOR is an important NLM that you will likely use very often. If you are responsible for the overall health of your network, you will probably spend a great deal of your time reviewing the MONITOR.NLM's statistics. The server's performance and operating statistics, as well as information about the connections made to the server, can be accessed by using MONITOR at your server console.

Table 10.2	NLM Types
NLM Types	**Description**
.DSK	Provides direct control of server drives (located in the DOS partition)
.LAN	Provides control drivers for network interface cards
.NLM	Adds general purpose capabilities to the server

Table 10.3	Common NLMs
Common NLMs	Description
MONITOR.NLM	Provides general performance information on the server
NWCONFIG.NLM	Provides the main functions used for server configuration
CDROM.NLM	Adds CD support to the server
DSREPAIR.NLM	Allows repairs to NDS
VREPAIR.NLM	Allows repairs to specified volumes
REMOTE.NLM	Allows server operation (with password) at workstation
3C509.LAN	An example of a control driver (3Com network card)

Running MONITOR   Typing **LOAD MONITOR** (or just **MONITOR**) at the console prompt and pressing the ENTER key will give you a screen containing several pieces of information about your server, as shown in Figure 10.1.

If nothing else is entered through the console for approximately ten seconds after loading MONITOR.NLM, the General Information part of the screen opens further, as shown in Figure 10.2, and additional information is displayed. This additional information is also available in the initial screen if you press the TAB key. The TAB key also toggles you back and forth between the expanded window and the reduced initial screen.

Quick Snapshot   Sometimes a quick snapshot of a network's traffic flow while the network is in actual operation will tell you if a problem exists. For example, if the total number of **cache buffers** (available working memory) in the General Information window falls below half of the original cache buffers, this indicates that the server is running low on memory, and you should either increase memory or decrease the demands on the amount of memory you have. Either add RAM or UNLOAD NLMs.

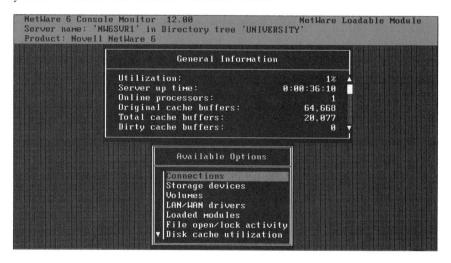

• **Figure 10.1**   The initial results of running the LOAD MONITOR command at your server console

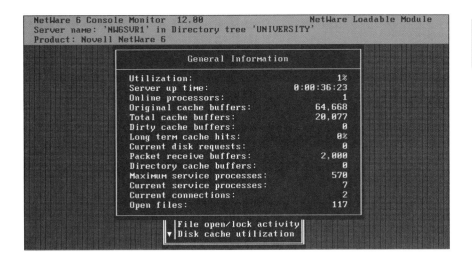

```
NetWare 6 Console Monitor  12.00               NetWare Loadable Module
Server name: 'NW6SVR1' in Directory tree 'UNIVERSITY'
Product: Novell NetWare 6

                         General Information
          Utilization:                         1%
          Server up time:              0:00:36:23
          Online processors:                    1
          Original cache buffers:          64,668
          Total cache buffers:             20,077
          Dirty cache buffers:                  0
          Long term cache hits:                0%
          Current disk requests:                0
          Packet receive buffers:           2,000
          Directory cache buffers:              0
          Maximum service processes:          570
          Current service processes:            7
          Current connections:                  2
          Open files:                         117

               ▲ File open/lock activity
               ▼ Disk cache utilization
```

● **Figure 10.2**   After ten seconds of inactivity, the General Information section expands.

This course is not intended to give you a complete understanding of each of the preceding items. The goal at this introductory level is to show you where to go should you need to locate such information in times of crisis. Keeping track of the information here also lets you record trends that can help you spot potential problems as they develop.

Using the DSREPAIR NLM

Hopefully, you will not *need* to repair your NDS tree. If you must repair it, though, you should have some idea of where to go to initiate the repairs. Running the DSREPAIR NLM will help you.

You used DSREPAIR after you built your server, so you should know a little about the NLM. Occasionally running DSREPAIR will help remove small network problems before they progress any further.

Copies of NDS are located on other servers in various locations around the network, and this makes the timing of updates critical. If you are wondering whether errors in timing, and the fact that NDS is spread over several locations can cause NDS to become disjointed at times, it can. That is when DSREPAIR really comes in handy.

NDS Replicas

In larger networks with multiple file servers, NDS stores duplicate pieces of the Directory, called **replicas***, on many of the servers around the network. Replicas provide fault tolerance and backup capability. The servers communicate with each other, sharing updates to the Directory as needed. Whether these updates are passed on to the next recipient is determined by the time stamp placed on them by the servers. If the recipient server has data with a newer time stamp, that update is determined to be unnecessary and is therefore ignored. The time-stamp system depends entirely on all servers knowing exactly what time it is, and this is accomplished through a centralized time-allocation system. For successful replica operation, one main server is responsible for providing accurate time to all the other servers working together.*

You should try to activate any repair process, such as DSREPAIR, during the network's idle times. Otherwise, users will be disrupted because the Directory is locked during the entire procedure. Additionally, any repairs made during the repair process will most likely create incorrect time stamps that occurr while your system is offline and you should allow your system time to synchronize after repairs are completed.

Unattended Full Repair You should recall that selecting the Unattended Full Repair option in DSREPAIR and pressing ENTER immediately initiates the repair action. Depending on the size of your network, this could take some time to complete. On a small network, such as yours, the process should take only a few seconds to complete.

When the repair action is completed, a window is displayed informing you that "All automatic repair operations have been completed." It also tells you the number of errors and the total amount of repair time the operation required. It is not uncommon for DSREPAIR to uncover numerous insignificant errors, so occasionally running DSREPAIR will help keep your network operating properly. You may need to run it several times when removing errors. Provided you have the network idle time available to you, rerun the process until zero errors are found by DSREPAIR.

Advanced Options Menu Selecting the Advanced Options Menu and pressing ENTER provides the following additional DSREPAIR options:

- **Log File and Login Configuration** Configures options for the DSREPAIR log file. Logging in to the Directory Services tree is required by some operations.

- **Repair Local DS Database** Repairs the Directory Services database files stored on this server.

- **Servers Known to This Database** Shows the names of the servers that have performed the following operations to this server's database: time synchronization, network addresses, and server information.

- **Replica and Partition Operations** Provides functions to repair replicas, replica rings, and server objects. This option also dynamically displays each server's last synchronization time.

- **Check Volume Objects and Trustees** Checks all mounted volumes for valid volume objects and valid trustees on the volumes.

- **Check External References** Checks for illegal external references.

- **Security Equivalence Synchronization** Allows users to synchronize security equivalence attributes throughout the tree.

- **Global Schema Operations** Provides functions to update the schema in the tree.

- **View Repair Log File** Allows you to edit the log file, which is optionally created when repair operations are performed.

- **Create a Database Dump File** Copies the Directory Services database files to disk in compressed format, to be used for offline repairs and diagnostics. This is not to be used as a backup method.

- **Return to Main Menu** Exits this menu and returns to the main list.

You will probably be interested in running only the Repair Local DS Database and the Check Volume Objects and Trustees options. The first will behave in the same way as the unattended option that you ran earlier, and the second will require that your fully distinguished administrator user name and password be used for authorization. It is useful to use both of these options on an occasional basis. They should not return major errors unless there is a significant problem.

Using NWCONFIG

You should become familiar with another frequently used NLM—the NWCONFIG NLM. This is the NLM that you will use to accomplish most of the configuration options needed on your NetWare server.

To complete this exercise, you will need the following items:

- An operational NetWare 6 server
- Your administrative user information (if not already logged in to the server)

Step 1

From your NetWare 6 server's GUI desktop, press CTRL+ESC to go to the Current Screens window. Enter the selection number for the System Console.

Step 2

Type **NWCONFIG** at the server console, and press ENTER to view the options available.

Note: Most of the options listed are self-explanatory. Several options have additional features when selected, but three, Legacy Disk Options, NSS Disk Options, and License Options, tell you that they no longer work through NWCONFIG when you select them and press ENTER.

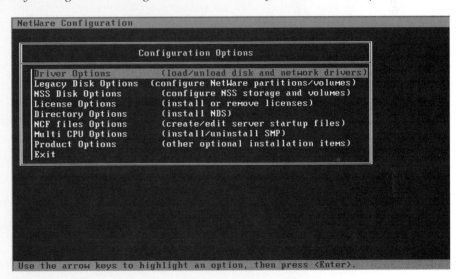

```
NetWare Configuration

                        Configuration Options
    Driver Options          (load/unload disk and network drivers)
    Legacy Disk Options     (configure NetWare partitions/volumes)
    NSS Disk Options        (configure NSS storage and volumes)
    License Options         (install or remove licenses)
    Directory Options       (install NDS)
    NCF files Options       (create/edit server startup files)
    Multi CPU Options       (install/uninstall SMP)
    Product Options         (other optional installation items)
    Exit

Use the arrow keys to highlight an option, then press <Enter>.
```

Step 3

Select Driver Options, press ENTER, and press ENTER again to view the disk drivers currently loaded on your server. You could press ENTER yet again to either search for additional drivers or load new drivers on your server. Press the ESC key twice to return to the initial NWCONFIG screen.

Step 4

Select Directory Options, press ENTER, and notice the important actions available to you here, such as installing or removing Directory Services, creating Directory backups, or extending the schema.

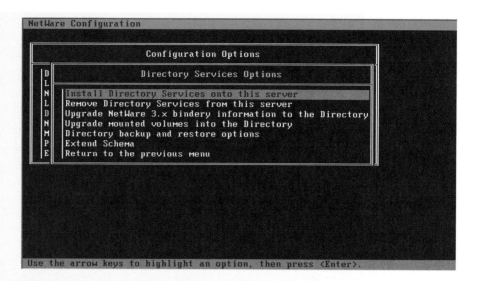

Step 5

Select Directory Backup and Restore Options, press ENTER, and press ENTER again to select the Save Local NDS Information Before Hardware Upgrade option. Read the notice that comes up on your computer screen.

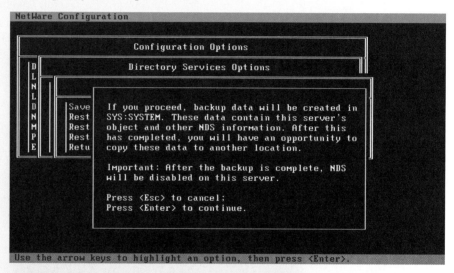

Note: If you do ever have to use this backup technique, you will be required to use your fully qualified administrative user name (CN=Admin.O=LAB) and password.

Step 6

Click Cancel so you do not actually implement the backup action. You could damage your copy of NDS in the process. Press the ESC key twice to return to the initial NWCONFIG screen.

Step 7

Look through the remaining options without implementing any changes (use the same general procedures as in Steps 3 through 6). From the initial NWCONFIG screen, press the ESC key again when you are finished, and select Yes and press ENTER to exit NWCONFIG.

Chapter 10 Review

■ Chapter Summary

After reading this chapter and completing the Step-by-Step tutorials and Try This! exercises, you should understand the following facts about network management:

Describe Windows Network Management Tools

- Access to the server through your workstation is becoming the most common way to manage your network.

- No matter what the problem is with a user's computer, they usually blame the network technicians first and then the network itself.

- Management tools, such as the Error-Checking, Defragmentation, and Backup utilities, are available on Windows workstations.

- The Error-Checking tool is also called the Check Disk tool, and it can be initiated with a DOS command by typing **chkdsk** in the RUN dialog box.

- The defragmentation window includes graphic depictions of your current and projected disk fragmentation.

- The Defragmentation tool requires 15 percent of the total disk space available on the disk to be empty in order to run properly, but it will run with less.

- The Backup tool can be used to keep users' information accessible because users can restore some of their own files if they keep their own backups.

- To initiate a backup, users must be working with their own files or they must have the Read, Read and Execute, Modify, or Full Control permission to the files.

- To restore from a backup, users must have the Write, Modify, or Full Control permission to the backed up files.

- The Task Manager is started by right-clicking the taskbar or using CTRL+ALT+DELETE and selecting Task Manager.

- Windows XP Professional adds a Networking tab to the Applications, Processes, and Performance tabs found on the Windows 2000 Server's Task Manager window.

- SNMP is an Internet-standard protocol that facilitates monitoring the system and sending status updates to a central location.

- SNMP nodes send messages when queried by the manager, but they can also send alarm messages on their own when properly configured.

- Performance console lets you collect data about your system's performance.

- System Monitor is a part of the Performance console that lets you view current or recorded information about your system.

- The different views in System Monitor are graph, histogram, and report.

- The Performance Logs and Alerts section of the Performance console records its data in the Perflogs folder on your hard disk drive.

- Network Monitor provides you with information regarding your network's health.

- Network Monitor actually records the data flowing between the computers on your network and your server.

Implement Windows and NetWare Network Management

- Improperly maintaining networks wastes the effort required to create them.

- A healthy network's use will tend to increase rapidly.

- Compression reduces the size of files so they take up less storage space.

- Having smaller files that contain the same data means that you can store more valuable information on your network without increasing storage space.

- Compression can only be implemented on NTFS volumes.

- Compression can be implemented at the volume level with everything on that volume being stored in the compressed state, or at the file level where only specific files are compressed.

- Compression and encryption are mutually exclusive.

- Applications using compressed files check the compression state and uncompress applicable files prior to use.

- Except for FAT partitions (which are always uncompressed), moving a compressed file from one location on a volume to another location on the same volume has that file retain its original compression state, whereas copying that file to another location on the same volume has the file acquire the compression state of the receiving location.

- When implementing compression, you have the option of leaving an object's contents as they are or compressing them.

- Quota management assigns a limit on the amount of space users can use for storage on specific volumes.

- Quota management is available only on NTFS volumes.

- Quotas can be implemented as mandatory, in which case they are enforced, or as informational, which means compliance is simply monitored.

- Quota use on compressed volumes is calculated based on the uncompressed size of the stored files.

- NetWare 6 has extremely detailed, and sometimes complex, network management components.

- The NetWare server console's text-based commands are still the most widely used management technique.

- Some NetWare commands are stand-alone commands, and others require arguments.

- There are hundreds of commands available for use at the NetWare server console, and you can get information about their use by using the HELP command.

- NLMs are commands stored in locations outside the operating system.

- The NetWare MONITOR NLM is a tool for gathering and monitoring information about your network's health.

- Periodically running DSREPAIR helps maintain your system.

- NWCONFIG is another important utility used to obtain and update information about your network.

■ Key Terms

agent (323)	**MIB** (324)	**report view** (326)
arguments (339)	**Network Monitor** (331)	**SNMP** (323)
cache buffers (342)	**NMS** (323)	**SNMP manager** (323)
compression (333)	**nodes** (323)	**state** (322)
graph view (326)	**page file** (322)	**System Monitor** (326)
histogram view (326)	**Performance console** (325)	**Task Manager** (319)
kernel (322)	**quota** (335)	**trap message** (323)
link state (322)	**replicas** (344)	

■ Key Term Quiz

Use the preceding vocabulary terms to complete the following sentences. Not all the terms will be used.

1. An alarm message sent by an SNMP agent is also called a(n) _____.

2. When running MONITOR on a NetWare 6 server, if the available memory, also called _____, falls below half of its original amount, a remedy could be to add RAM or UNLOAD NLMs.

3. An assigned limit on the amount of network storage a user can use is called a(n) _____.

4. The name of the tool that includes a Networking tab in its Windows XP implementation is the

   _____.

5. By clicking the Performance tab on the tool that can be entered using the Microsoft three-finger salute, you can view graphical screens showing dynamic information on your CPU and your

   _____.

6. Once a network node is monitored by SNMP and managed by SNMP manager, it is referred to as a(n) _____.

7. The Internet-standard protocol that facilitates monitoring the system and communicating status updates is called the _____.

8. The _____ portion of your Performance console utility provides you with optional viewing configurations.

9. The _____ utility records a copy of the data flowing between other computers and your server.

10. The Windows advanced storage feature that helps extend your network's storage capacity by reducing the size of files is called _____.

■ Multiple-Choice Quiz

1. Which of the following tools is not located on the hard disk drive's Properties dialog box?
   a. Backup
   b. Error-Checking
   c. Defragmentation
   d. Task Manager

2. Which of the following can be initiated using the RUN dialog box, accessed through the Start menu, with the *fix* switch?
   a. Backup
   b. Error-Checking
   c. Defragmentation
   d. Task Manager

3. Which of the following makes use of an Analyze button?
   a. Backup
   b. Error-Checking
   c. Defragmentation
   d. Task Manager

4. All of the following are associated with SNMP except:
   a. host
   b. nodes
   c. agents
   d. players

5. Inside the Windows Components Wizard window, you will see all of the following options or features except:
   a. The Add/Remove Programs option

   b. The Management and Monitoring Tools component
   c. A Details button
   d. Selection boxes

6. Which of the following is the default permission for SNMP service community names?
   a. Full Control
   b. Read Only
   c. Write
   d. Read/Write

7. Which of the following views in System Monitor allow(s) you to change the view's background?
   a. graph
   b. histogram
   c. report
   d. All of the above

8. Which of the following is listed in the Name column for the default Counter Log used in the Performance Logs and Alerts section of the Performance window?
   a. System Log
   b. System Overview
   c. System_Overview.blg
   d. C:\System Log

9. Which of the following is a true statement regarding Network Monitor?
   a. It records all network traffic on your network.
   b. Network traffic is only recorded when it is going to the local computer where Network Monitor is configured.

c. Network traffic can only be recorded at the local computer where Network Monitor is configured.

d. Network traffic is only recorded when it is going from the local computer where Network Monitor is configured.

10. When you copy a compressed 10MB file to a volume with 19MB of available space, which of the following will be true?

a. The copy action will be disallowed and the file will remain compressed.

b. The copy action will be allowed and the file will be uncompressed.

c. The copy action will be allowed and the file will be compressed.

d. The copy action will be disallowed and the file will remain uncompressed.

11. If you were to copy a compressed 10MB file from one volume to another volume that is not using compression, which of the following would be true?

a. The copy action will be disallowed and the file will remain compressed.

b. The copy action will be allowed and the file will be uncompressed.

c. The copy action will be allowed and the file will remain compressed.

d. The copy action will be disallowed and the file will be uncompressed.

12. Two users have 500MB quotas on a particular volume where they each have 550MB of information stored. The administrator then implements compression that reduces all files in storage by an average of 50 percent. Which of the following is/are definitely true?

a. Both users have to have specific quotas set on that volume.

b. Both users will still be over their quotas.

c. They each can store at least another 225MB.

d. Quota management is not being enforced.

13. Which of the following deals with NetWare NLMs?

a. MODULES

b. CONFIG

c. DISPLAY

d. All of the above

14. Which of the following is true when your NetWare 6 server's cache buffers fall below 25 percent of the original cache buffers?

a. You should decrease memory demand.

b. You should add RAM.

c. This is an acceptable condition.

d. None of the above.

15. Which of the following is/are true about DSREPAIR:

a. Running DSREPAIR locks the Directory during the entire procedure.

b. You should run DSREPAIR when user impact would be lessened.

c. Repairs made will likely have an incorrect time stamp.

d. All of the above.

■ Essay Quiz

1. How can this course help prepare you to become a better network administrator?

2. Why are network technicians blamed when network workstations malfunction?

3. Explain the benefits of having users involved in managing their own workstations.

4. When considering whether to use compression on your network servers, why is it important that you find out if encryption is being used?

5. What is the main difference between NetWare console commands and NLMs?

Lab Projects

Time to roll up your sleeves and apply what you've learned. The following lab projects will enable you to practice the concepts discussed in this chapter.

• Lab Project 10.1

The data in storage at the TEACH training center has recently been compressed. Your network's users are confused about which files are compressed and which are not. You decide to configure their computers so that the compressed files show up as a different color than those that are uncompressed. You now want to configure their computers to display this information.

You will need the following:

- A networked lab computer with Windows XP Professional

- Administrative user login information

Then do the following:

1. At your workstation computer, log in locally as your administrative user.

2. Click the Start button and select My Documents | Tools | Folder Options.

3. Click the View tab, and in the Advanced Settings section, scroll to and select the Show Encrypted or Compressed NTFS Files in Color option. (Note that this only allows you to employ the system-provided "different" colors, not to choose your own colors.)

4. Click OK and close all windows to return to the desktop.

• Lab Project 10.2

You implemented quota management on your TEACH volumes, but users are still storing as much as they want on all of the storage devices because the quotas are not being enforced. You decide to stop this misuse of storage by changing the quota management such that it is enforced, and users are not allowed to exceed their limit.

You will need the following materials:

- A networked lab computer with Windows XP Professional, formatted using NTFS

- Your administrative user's information

Then do the following:

1. Log in to a Windows XP workstation (where network storage is allowed) as the administrative user. Click the Start button and select My Computer. Right-click the volume you wish to change, and select Properties.

2. Click the dialog box's Quota tab and ensure the Enable Quota Management option is selected. Select the Deny Disk Space to Users Exceeding Quota Limit option, and adjust the Limit Disk Space To options as desired. Ensure that both logging options are selected, and click the Apply button.

3. Click the Quota Entries button and observe the storage allocations and limits imposed on users with storage on the disk.

4. Right-click a listed user (not the administrator) and select Properties. Notice the newly imposed limits on the user.

   Note: If the user's limits have not been updated to reflect your changes, simply click the Do Not Limit Disk Use option, and then click the Limit Disk Space To option again, and click the Apply button.

5. Close all windows and dialog boxes to return to your desktop.

Network+ Certification Path

appendix

A

Networking has become almost a necessity for businesses, and the demand for networking skills is growing at a phenomenal pace worldwide. Therefore, becoming a certified networking specialist, or going beyond that and certifying as a network administrator, can yield significant benefits and career opportunities. Either route requires a substantial investment of time, money, and effort, but both are well worth it.

■ Network Professional Certification

By completing this course, you have started on the road to official recognition as a qualified network administrator. The benefits of networks make network administrators almost mandatory for the typical business, so the demand for networking skills is high and will likely continue to grow around the world. Employers need trained network administrators capable of maintaining their networks.

Because it is important to standardize what "qualified" means, the major network software providers have developed their own certification programs, and additional "vendor-neutral" certification programs have been developed as well. Graduates of these programs (certificate holders) are highly qualified and capable of performing the duties commensurate with their level of certification. Certification is the employers' assurance that they are hiring a trained professional to whom they can entrust their network. Companies are increasingly using a combination of operating systems to run their networks and becoming certified on each of these multiple systems may be required of those who wish to manage them.

Novell determined that there was a need for certification standardization and developed its own industry-standard product training and certification. In 1986, Novell began the first professional Information Services/Information Technology (IS/IT) training program in the world. Novell's certification program provides a means for aspiring network professionals to demonstrate a high level of proficiency with network administration, even before being hired. Novell has issued more than 200,000 certificates since their Certified Novell Administrator (CNA) program was started in 1992 (CNA originally meant "Certified NetWare Administrator"). Novell began the program to establish performance standards for network administrators throughout the world, and it has helped standardize industry expectations regarding the capabilities and duties of those who will administer networks. The rigors of CNA training, and of its certification exam, assure employers that certificate holders are capable of creating and administrating an efficient and secure network.

Microsoft was one of the next companies to recognize the value of certifying its computer technicians. The Microsoft certification lineup now begins with the candidate becoming a Microsoft Certified Professional and then branching out into one of the various specialized tracks available. These tracks include the Microsoft Certified Systems Engineer (MCSE), the Microsoft Certified Systems Developer (MCSD), and the Microsoft Certified Systems Administrator (MCSA).

CompTIA was formed in 1982 by four companies under the name Association of Better Computer Dealers (ABCD). CompTIA now has over 10,000 corporations and 10,500 individuals as members. CompTIA's original intent was directed toward ensuring quality resellers and solution providers, but in the early 1990s, it began offering computer-oriented certifications with the added plus of not tying those certifications to any particular vendor's product lines.

Why Certify?

You have already taken an important first step toward becoming certified under CompTIA's certification program. You may even have decided to continue with a Novell, a Microsoft, or another certification program. The fact that you have selected this course and have made it this far into the textbook demonstrates a large measure of determination on your part. Your networking potential will be determined by the extent to which you have applied yourself so far, and by how much you apply yourself in the future. The process of CompTIA certification is devised to ensure that the same standard is applied to every certificate holder.

Once you make the commitment to work diligently toward obtaining CompTIA's N+ certification, the process is relatively simple.

1. Prepare adequately for the course using whatever means you choose. There are several methods available for accomplishing this step:

    ■ Attend an independent, non-approved course that includes CompTIA's network training (this course is a good example, if it is being taught at a school that is not affiliated with CompTIA).

    ■ Attend a training program at an educational facility affiliated with CompTIA Education. Usually the facility becomes a CompTIA Partner. Secondary and post-secondary schools are eligible for this partnership agreement.

    ■ Go to the bookstore, purchase CompTIA-oriented preparation guides, study the material, take whatever practice tests you can find, and prepare yourself at your own pace.

    ■ Get a job working with computing products and acquire, over several years, the technical experience necessary to pass the certification exam.

2. Register to take the exam at an approved testing facility, take the exam, and achieve a passing grade for the certification test of your chosen track.

Participating in instructor-led courses is the preferred method of preparing for almost any certification exams. Intensive courses of a relatively short duration are available through training centers worldwide. Your local CompTIA Authorized Service Center can help your company design a curriculum that meets its needs. Many schools and universities also offer CompTIA authorized training.

Benefits of Certification for Individuals

Each company that certifies technical specialists developed their own certification program to help their students demonstrate network administrator qualifications to potential employers. The benefits of hiring certified networking specialists are now universally recognized. Having a certification when applying for a position in a firm distinguishes you from non-certified individuals.

Inside Information

What Network Administrators Do

Network administrators provide direct administrative support for networked users and find themselves in work environments ranging from large office buildings to small businesses, and from single departments to entire corporate Information Services (IS) or Information Technology (IT) divisions. Certificate holders are expected to handle the day-to-day operation of any installed networking products. The CompTIA Network+ (commonly referred to as N+) certification is typically expected of anyone wishing to specialize in networked products. The N+ certification is recognized worldwide.

As a network specialist, you could find yourself

■ *setting up workstations, servers, and printers.*

■ *managing parts of or the entire network environment.*

■ *installing applications and sharing them as networked resources.*

■ *customizing and automating login capability for the network.*

■ *determining desktop configurations for all users.*

■ *monitoring network performance.*

Most self-study products are available through participating Authorized Service Centers and authorized CompTIA-affiliated product resellers. For more information on such courseware, contact CBT Systems (1-800-929-9050 or 1-415-614-5900), Gartner Group Learning Corporation (1-800-532-7672 or 1-612-930-0330), or NETG (1-800-265-1900 or 1-630-369-3000).

When companies decide to offer additional certification training to their employees, they know that the benefits of such training will be worth the investment. Employees perform well at the training sessions because they are aware of the personal benefits that the certification will provide.

Once you are certified, the certifying companies usually grant you access to the secure portions of their web sites, where you can obtain up-to-date information that helps you keep abreast of the rapid changes in network operating systems and software. You can also keep track of your personal certification information, update it as necessary, and track your progress toward additional certifications. Certificate holders are also authorized to use the logo associated with the certificates they have achieved. Often the vendor web sites also provide access to up-to-date product and technical information on networking patches, fixes, and press releases, along with updates to support publications.

The N+ certificate program starts you on the path toward advanced and more specialized certifications focusing on your desired track or a specific operating system you want to know more about. Each class you take, and each exam you pass in the track leading toward an advanced certification, builds upon what you have learned in the other networking classes you have taken. Combined, all your classes help prepare you for career progress in the networking community.

Benefits of Certification for Companies

Most companies are aware that employees with industry-standard certifications perform better than non-certified employees. They seek out certified individuals because they know those employees do a better job.

Companies also know that employees with certifications are more productive, which translates into a financial benefit. Certified employees save the company money because they accomplish more work in less time and perform their tasks well the first time they do them. Training needs for certificate holders are low, system downtime is reduced, and overall support quality is enhanced. Customer support is improved because of better employee morale.

■ The Basics of Certification

First, study, study again, and then study some more. Acquire whatever learning materials you can for the appropriate vendor's networks, and accumulate as much networking knowledge as you can. Many of the certifying companies have designed their testing databases to simulate on-the-job experience as much as possible. Additionally, their course materials often try to focus on the experiences of real administrators.

Next, work with networks. Get as much hands-on network experience as you possibly can. You should spend as much time working with the products you will be tested on as possible. Get lots of experience adding users, and then change every configuration setting you can find regarding the users you added. Understand all the steps you take, and know what effect your actions have on users.

Know What Will Be Required of You

Training specifically targeting the operating system you have chosen ensures that you know what will be required of you before you take that certifying company's test. Each vendor's web site, however, also clearly lists the objectives they will cover in their proficiency exams. If your method of study does not list these objectives, you can search the appropriate vendor's web site and request a list of the objectives for your specific exam. You should obtain this information for whichever test you plan to take. The objectives for the N+ certification are available in PDF format through CompTIA's web page: `http://www.comptia.org/`.

Test Taking

Although it is not a substitute for proper study habits, taking practice tests on a frequent basis will help you prepare for the actual exam. Your study guide includes some written practice exams. Take them *often*! They should also be completed right before you take the actual proficiency test. Used correctly, the practice tests can indicate whether you are prepared well enough to attempt the test or not. *Successful completion of the practice exams does not guarantee that you will pass the actual proficiency test, but they are a valuable test-preparation aid.*

Register for the Test

When you think you are ready to take the proficiency test, call the CompTIA testing center to select a location and date. Thomson Prometric and Virtual University Enterprises (VUE) are the companies CompTIA uses to conduct their certification testing. You may also decide to test at one of the many training centers that have a testing facility at their own locations.

Before choosing a test date, you must call a testing provider to verify site availability. Do not call to register until you are ready to take the exam. Also, do not skimp on studying or try to cram your studies into the night before the test, because you will almost certainly fail the test.

The toll-free number to register for Prometric N+ testing in the United States and Canada is 1-888-895-6116. You must tell them that you wish to check the locations available to take your N+ exam. They will ask you to confirm which test you plan to take, your present location's ZIP code (or postal code), and possibly your telephone number, in order to find the testing facilities nearest you.

Remember that you are planning to take the N+ (Network+) exam, and you should ask for any information that they may have available on that test. Sometimes newly released information about the test you will be taking can be obtained by asking that simple question. Do not forget to ask.

Make sure to record the letter identifiers they give you, as well as the address and telephone number of the testing facility. Request the testing center's hours, and the days that they offer testing. Also, ask for information regarding the type of test you will be taking, the duration of the test, and whether or not you will be allowed to review and change your answers. Some of this information changes occasionally, but the information they tell you when you register will be the latest. You might check the CompTIA web site for information about frequently asked questions about their test or search the site for helpful hints like "test fundamentals."

You may even decide to call at an early phase in your test preparation period to request a list of testing sites in your area. There may be several, so make a list and scout them out. Look for a testing location where you will be comfortable while taking the test. If you have a choice of locations, choose one that is quiet. Go there before your test date to make sure that it pleases you. The day of the test is not the time to be wondering what the facility is like. Take care of as many small details as you can before testing day so that you will be able to concentrate on taking the test.

After you have chosen where you will take the test, get back to test preparation. You will have eliminated one of the major test-taking nuisances, but the test is still your primary concern. Do not let up on your studying. Keep taking the practice tests, reading any textbooks you have, and studying the online documentation that came with your operating system software.

When you are ready to register for the exam, you must call Prometric again to tell them where you wish to take your exam. They will ask which test you plan to take, which testing facility you have chosen, and the day and time you would like them to reserve for you. Tell them both the location's name and the letter identifier that you received when you called earlier to verify locations.

Once you have given them this information, you will need to tell them how you plan to pay for the test. If you have discount coupons, you should inform them that you will be using a coupon, and tell them its registration number. If you intend to register by telephone, any remaining balance must be paid by credit card. Before you hang up, have them read back the information about the test for which you just registered. Confirm that the test number, the date, the time, and the test center are what you requested. Ask them to confirm the type of test, the number of questions, and ask if there are any special requirements. Make sure you add the date and time of the test, the center's identifying code, its phone number, and its address.

The Day of the Test

You should sleep at least eight hours the night before the test. Eat a good breakfast, and try to test early enough in the day so that you are still wide awake and alert. If you are not a "morning person," target noon as your testing period and prepare yourself in the same way.

The testing centers require that you show up early for your exam. You are required to be present 15 minutes before the exam begins—20 minutes early is typical, but arriving even a half hour before the exam is not too early. The testing facility personnel use this time to check you in for the test. They must verify your identification before allowing you to take your test. You must present an official current photo ID, such as your driver's license or passport. School photos are not accepted. You will also have to show one other piece of identification, such as a credit card, with both your name and signature on it. These identification requirements verify that you are the person who is registered to take the test.

If the two signatures on the two pieces of identification do not match, or if they do not look the *same* as your signature on the sign-in sheet at the test center, you will not be allowed to test. Furthermore, if the test center does not allow you to test because you could not verify your identification (even if you innocently left your wallet at home), they will *not* reimburse the testing fees. It is your job to provide that proof. If you are not sure whether your identification items are sufficient, it may be worth your while to have them verified ahead of time at the testing facility.

Once your identification is verified, you will sign for your test, and the test center personnel will upload the appropriate test (sent to them by the certifying company) into the computer located in the test booth where you will be working. Do not allow the test center personnel to rush you into the booth. Complete the check-in process, but then sit back down and refocus on your studies. Find a place where you can go over those last items that you want to have fresh in your memory when you start the exam. If you invented "memory joggers" to help you remember such things as rights assignments, OSI layers, or any other such things, take time to review them. Commit them to short-term memory.

Test centers electronically download the next day's tests on the night before your appointment. Your test is brought up on the monitor at your booth, and you will be asked to verify your identification again from the login screen. This time, you confirm to the computer scoring system that you are the person scheduled to take this exam, and that the exam is the one for which you registered. After you log in, the computer will offer you a sample test to practice on before your test starts. You can go through it if you wish, to verify that the computer works properly. You will then be asked if you are ready to begin. If anything is wrong at this point, get it corrected. It is *very* difficult to have any problems corrected after you have started the test.

When you go into your booth, you will have only a pencil and the paper that the center provides. Some centers will furnish dry erase markers and plastic-coated work sheets. These materials are only for your scratch work. Nothing written on them will be calculated into your test score—only the answers you enter into the computer will count. You will turn in all of the materials used in the booth at the end of the test, and the test center personnel will erase or destroy them.

Remember that your test does not start until after you sign in and either go through the practice test or decline it. Entering the booth does not automatically start the exam. Use this to your advantage. As soon as you sit in your booth, write down everything you have in your short-term memory. Write out as much information as you think you will need later. Provided you write it down after you enter the booth, you can use the information during the test. In this way, you will not have to rely entirely on your memory during the test. Spread out the sheets for easy retrieval when a question requires that material. Start your test only when you are completely ready to begin. Relax. Take a deep breath. Then start your test.

On most tests you must finish the test *before* time runs out. If you do not, you automatically fail regardless of your score up to that point. You are required to finish. Be careful—the questions remaining could be easy multiple-choice questions, but they could also be multi-step situational performance questions. Remember that if your test is adaptive (discussed on the next page), both types of questions will be asked until you pass or fail. This means that you could receive as few as 15 and as many as 25 questions in the same amount of time. Plan accordingly.

At the end of your test, it will be scored immediately, and any review items will appear on the screen at your booth. You will know immediately whether you passed. Your score report will appear on your monitor, and you will receive a printed copy of the score report. The printed copy will be waiting for you outside your booth. The report gives you your score, the score necessary to pass (the cutoff score), the pass/fail decision, and a list of objectives for further review. This is an important document—keep it. If you did not pass, review the list of objectives on your report before retaking the test. If you passed, celebrate, because you achieved something you can be very proud of.

Multiple-Choice Tests   All certification tests begin as multiple-choice objective tests. Unlike most multiple-choice questions you might be accustomed to, more than one answer may be correct. A question may state "Choose the four steps in …," and you must know all four answers to answer correctly. When using this method, most tests incorporate the Microsoft Windows convention that changes the selection radio buttons (small circles that you click to select and fill in when choosing that option) to square check boxes to provide a visual cue that more information is needed.

Some tests also use questions that have more than one correct answer, but you get credit for selecting any subset of the correct answers. For example, there may be a list of ten items with five of them being correct responses. You could then be asked to choose three of the ten items. Any three of the five correct responses would be acceptable, and you cannot select more than three. Most tests avoid ambiguous questions that require you to select "all that apply" without telling you how many do apply. Recently, tests have also moved away from using multiple graphics in test questions because of the difficulty displaying the screens together on the testing center's equipment. Older tests may still contain multiple graphics, but newly created tests should not.

Adaptive Tests   The certifying companies have also developed what is called an *adaptive* testing model. Most of these companies have found that traditional paper-and-pencil and computerized tests that ask the same set of questions of everyone, regardless of their level of knowledge and proficiency, are not the most accurate way to measure knowledge and skills. An adaptive test is designed to function like an oral test.

Adaptive tests begin with a moderately difficult question. Your response is scored and your probable ability level is calculated based on the information tracked about that particular question. The test then uses that probable ability level to select the next question. The test then calculates a new probable ability level based on your answer to that question, and again uses it to select another question. The testing software continues this loop, revising your probable ability level as you answer the questions it selects for you. With the statistics from each answer you give, the accuracy of the probable ability level increases. After the minimum number of questions have been asked, and before the maximum number, the software will determine whether your skill level is greater or less than the minimum level needed to pass the exam, and your test ends. You pass or fail based on that probable ability level.

Test objectives are subject to change without notice.

Certification Test Objectives   Studying test objectives can help you prepare for certification tests. Certifying companies offer their own authorized student kits that contain the material from which their test objectives and test questions are taken. They are the best resources for test preparation.

GLOSSARY

The number in parentheses that follows each definition cites the chapter number in which the key term is first mentioned and explained.

access control   The process of using permissions or authorization to identify who (which user IDs) has access to specific securable objects (files, network shares, printers, etc.) and what each user is permitted to do with those objects. (9)

access rights   The permissions attached to a securable object that define what actions users and groups may perform on those objects. (6)

active partition   The primary partition that the system goes to when looking for the boot files during startup. (4)

administrator password   The password used by the administrator to access the administrator account—the most powerful account on the system. (4)

agent   A network node that is monitored by SNMP and managed by the SNMP manager. (10)

alphanumeric   A set of characters that can contain letters, numbers, or both. (3)

analog   A type of signal that has an infinite number of points along a gradual transition from one state to another. (3)

applications   Computer programs that make a user's computer do what the user needs done, such as writing a report or calculating a budget. (1)

arguments   Parts of a command that usually control how the command functions. (10)

ARPANET   The original name for what has become known as the Internet, the Advanced Research Projects Agency Network. (3)

ASCII   The most accepted character set—American Standard Code for Information Interchange. (3)

attenuation   The weakening of a transmitted signal over a distance. (2)

attributes   Descriptive pieces of information about network objects that get stored as settings. These attributes become components of the objects and are used to determine how an operating system handles those objects. (6)

audit trail   A log that records events (often security-related) that occur on a computer system. (9)

AutoRun   A feature that enables Windows to automatically find and run the program needed to open and run a CD or other application. (5)

backbone   Another name for a bus. (3)

backups   Saved extra copies of the files on a computer. (1)

base 16   A numbering system that uses 16 alphanumeric characters instead of the customary 10—the letters A through F are added after 0 through 9. (3)

basic disks   Beginning with Windows 2000, the term for disk drives used for basic storage and formatted using primary partitions, extended partitions, and logical drives. (7)

binary   A numbering system that uses only the numbers 0 and 1. (3)

biometrics   A system that involves using measurable unique human characteristics for authentication. (9)

bit   The single instance of a digital signal, and the smallest unit of storage (on disk or in memory). A single bit is like a light switch: it is either on or off. On represents 1, and off represents 0. (3)

BNC connector   A twisting barrel-like connection found at the ends of thinnet coaxial cables. (2)

boot partition   The name of the separate section on the hard drive that contains operating system startup files. (4)

break the mirror   On a mirrored volume, the act of disconnecting that mirroring function and removing the failed copy. (7)

bridge   A network concentrator device that connects similar or dissimilar networks. (2)

Broker   One of the iPrint components, essential to the proper operation of Novell's print process using iPrint or NDPS. The Broker connects the printing process to various services on the NetWare server, and it should be invisible to the user. (8)

brute force attack   An attack on a network where the attacker tries every possible combination of letters, numbers, and special characters to obtain a password. (9)

bus   A common conductor for signals between two or more devices. (3)

bus topology   Describes a network in which all computers are physically attached to and listen for communication over what amounts to a single wire. (3)

byte   A group of eight bits. A single byte can represent a character, like the letter *A*, or a very simple command, like "move down one line." (3)

cache buffers   Available working memory. (10)

Cat-5   The most prevalent type of standardized network cabling currently in use. (2)

central processing unit (CPU)   An essential electronic integrated circuit (chip) which performs the calculations, or processing, for a computer. (2)

class   A category of objects identified in the directory by their common properties and values. (6)

client   In general, a customer who requests services of a server. In networks, software components on a computer that access services of a network server are called *clients*. (1)

client-based networks   A further refinement to the concept of a server-based network that relieves the heavy burden on the network's capacity resulting from frequent server-performed transactions. (1)

coaxial cable   A type of network cabling similar to wiring used for cable TV. (2)

cold start   A method of starting up a computer by turning the power switch off (if it is not off already) and then back on. Also called *cold boot*. (4)

collaboration   The act of sharing information between coworkers so that they can discuss each other's work or possibly exchange opinions about what other users created. (1)

common name   An NDS object's single name, excluding any reference to its position in the network's hierarchy. (6)

communication medium   The physical path between networked resources. (2)

compression   Reducing the size of a file so that it takes up less storage space. (10)

computer network   Two or more computing devices that are connected in order to share the components of a network (the resources) and the information stored there. (1)

concentrator   A network device that allows multiple cables to be connected together for access to networked resources. (2)

connectionless   An unreliable protocol that neither establishes a connection between the sending and receiving ends of network communication nor ensures that data is received and properly resequenced. It sends the transmission without concern for whether or not it is received. (3)

connection-oriented   A reliable protocol that establishes a connection between the sending and receiving ends of network communication and ensures that data is received and properly resequenced. (3)

context   An object's location in the NDS tree. (6)

contiguous space   Adjacent disk drive storage (located immediately next to another storage area). (7)

continuity tester   A device used to check the capability for signal flow over network cabling. (2)

crimping tool   A device used to fasten networking connectors to the networking cable. (2)

crossover network cable   A type of networking medium used to connect two computers or two hubs directly. (2)

daisy chaining   Computers or devices connected in a line from one to another. (2)

data   A piece or pieces of information. (1)

dedicated server   A computer that operates solely as a server. (1)

default printer   The print device that your output will be sent to unless you specify otherwise. (8)

default printer indicator   A small check mark in the upper-right corner of a printer icon. (8)

defrag   The act of using special software to rearrange the pieces of files that the file system has scattered in various places on a disk. (7)

demodulate   The process a modem uses to convert a transmitted signal for the receiving computer from analog to digital. (3)

denial of service (DOS) attack   An attempt to prevent the legitimate use of a resource by causing the system to become busy, usually by causing it to respond to a huge volume of otherwise normal requests. (9)

destination address   The destination address for transmitted packets over a network. (3)

DHCP   An acronym for Dynamic Host Configuration Protocol. DHCP allows computers to effectively lease IP addresses when needed. (3)

dialog box   A graphical window that allows a user to select and enter settings and options. (2)

digital   A type of signal with discrete or distinct states. (3)

Directory (capital D)   The database where NDS stores information about users, groups, and resources. (6)

directory (lowercase d)   When referring to Microsoft file systems, this is an older term for a type of file that can contain other directories as well as files; the newer term is *folder*. On Novell systems, this is an object representing an area on a NetWare volume where files or additional directories (called *subdirectories*) are stored. (7)

disaster recovery plan (DRP)   A formal document spelling out the planned activities that will occur in the event of an unexpected network failure. (9)

distinguished name   The Novell Directory Services (NDS) name that starts with the object in question and identifies each of the container objects in the path to that object. (6)

distributed denial of service (DDOS) attack   An attack that makes use of compromised systems on the Internet to increase the amount of traffic directed to specific destinations. This flood of traffic initiated simultaneously from multiple (hundreds or thousands) remotely controlled computers can prevent normal use of larger Internet connections or even multiple systems. (9)

DNS   An acronym for Domain Name Service. This is a method of locating resources on the Internet. (3)

domain   The most important container object in Microsoft's hierarchical directory services structure—all Active Directory objects must be part of a domain. A Microsoft domain is a collection of accounts representing network computers, users, and groups of users, all maintained in a distributed security-accounts database for ease of administration. (6)

drivers   The software programs that run devices, such as print devices. (8)

DSREPAIR   The Novell NetWare 6 command for initiating the directory services repair utility. (4)

DVD   A removable storage medium like a CD, but with higher capacity. (5)

dynamic addressing   A system whereby IP addresses are automatically assigned and configured. (3)

dynamic storage   Beginning with Windows 2000, a storage type option that requires upgrading basic disks, and that allows you to use the additional capabilities of your newer NT-based operating systems. (7)

EBCDIC   A character set developed by IBM—Extended Binary Coded Decimal Interchange Code. (3)

economies of scale   Savings brought on by buying more similar items (such as computers) and obtaining a lower per-unit cost. (1)

effective permissions   The permissions (or rights) that result after combining permissions from all sources. (7)

effective rights   *See* effective permissions. (7)

electromagnetic interference (EMI)   A degradation to networked message traffic caused by electrical signals radiating outward as the traffic travels through wires. (2)

e-mail   An electronic means of communicating that is similar to mail but written using computer applications and sent over networks, usually over the Internet. (1)

Ethernet   The most commonly used local area networking (LAN) architecture. (2)

executable   A program with an .exe filename extension that you can run, or execute, to perform a task. (4)

extended partitions   Areas on a disk drive used when you need additional separate storage areas, beyond the four available when using only primary partitions, created with their own drive letters on a single hard disk drive. (7)

extranet Two or more intranets networked to allow collaboration between two or more different organizations (like a manufacturer and supplier). (3)

FAT Acronym for file allocation table. (4)

fault intolerant Describes a system that stops functioning completely when a single component fails. (3)

fault tolerant Describes a system that can withstand the failure of one or more components and still operate, even if at some lesser degree of total capacity. (3)

FDISK A DOS command used to work with fixed disks or hard drives to create, delete, and examine partitions. (4)

fiber-optic cabling A type of network cabling composed of insulated glass or hard plastic fibers through which light passes and transfers data. (2)

file allocation table (FAT) The component of the FAT file system that an operating system uses to remember where your files reside on disk. Fragmentation causes a file to be divided into many sections that are scattered around the disk. The FAT keeps track of all these pieces. (7)

file-level permissions A security system allowing access control over objects down to the file level instead of just at the share level. (7)

File Transfer Protocol (FTP) This is a special-purpose networking protocol for the purpose of transferring files. (3)

finite Countable; having a measurable limit. (3)

firewall A network security device (hardware or software) that prevents unauthorized access to computers and data on a network. Firewalls are usually placed at the point where a private network (or group of networks) connects to a public untrusted network, like the Internet. (9)

fixed disks A computer's hard disk drives. (4)

forest Typically the result of joining multiple domain trees together. However, according to Microsoft, a single Active Directory tree can act as a forest. (6)

format The act of combining or arranging characters in a standard order or some other specific manner such that messages can be exchanged from sender to receiver. (1)

fragmented A condition that exists when individual files are stored in multiple non-contiguous storage areas. (7)

Gateway A Novell information object that is configured to provide printer specifics over the network. (8)

global catalog The location where all trees that join a forest (forming a relationship and employing the same schema) share information about their networked resources. Its primary purpose is assisting with Active Directory object searches. Users (and applications) can find objects in any Active Directory domain if they know at least one searchable attribute (such as the user name) of the target object. (6)

GNOME The name of a Linux GUI environment. (4)

graph view The System Monitor view that plots the data for each item you are tracking as a line graph, with time along the horizontal axis and amplitude along the vertical axis. (10)

hackers Individuals who use their knowledge of computers to do harm to other networked computers—usually over the Internet and often just for fun. (9)

hardware address Yet another name for the physical address, or the Media Access Control (MAC) address. (3)

HCL Short for Hardware Compatibility List, a list of hardware supported by the operating system. (4)

hexadecimal notation A numbering system that uses base 16 instead of base 10. (3)

hierarchy of information A method of organizing information such that the most detailed information is found at the top and the more general, less secure information is located at the bottom. For instance, a single document is less important and should have fewer security measures placed upon it than a whole file full of related documents. (1)

histogram view The System Monitor view that displays the data for each item being tracked along two axes, time and amplitude, with bars showing totals for different items. (10)

hub A type of network concentrator that each computer connects to. A hub repeats any signal to every connection equally. (2)

identification and authentication The security mechanism that allows a computer to uniquely identify the person or computer attempting to log on or perform an action. (9)

IEEE The networking industry's standards generating organization—the Institute of Electrical and Electronics Engineers. (3)

IMAP Acronym for Internet Message Access Protocol, a protocol used to retrieve e-mail from servers. (3)

infinite Unlimited; not countable. (3)

Inherited Rights Filter (IRF) The method that NetWare uses to block the automatic transference of rights, called *inheritance*, down through the directory's hierarchy. (7)

input Entering, or sending, something into the computer. Entering information via the keyboard or having your word processing program read a file from disk are examples of input. (2)

intranet Private networks that use Internet technologies (such as TCP/IP, e-mail, and web pages) without necessarily being connected to the Internet. (3)

iPrint The Novell NetWare 6 printing service that facilitates Internet-based printing. (8)

ISO The International Organization for Standardization that recommended the use of a standard layered model to explain network communication. (3)

KDE The name of a Linux GUI environment. (4)

kernel The core of the operating system. It contains all of the programs needed to manage the user's interaction (through loaded applications or other computer programs) with the computer using the operating system's basic operations. (10)

keyboard A mechanical means of communicating with the computer whereby a user presses keys to enter commands. (2)

Knowledge Base A database created by Microsoft Support Services containing articles on problems and solutions relating to Microsoft products. (5)

leading zeros The zeroes to the left of a number. (3)

leaf objects A network's lowest-level resources or services in NDS. Leaf objects represent the final division of objects and cannot contain any offshoot branches or include any other objects. A leaf object represents an individual resource or service that is available on a network. (6)

link state The operational status of a network connection. (10)

LOAD CDROM The NetWare command for adding the CD as a NetWare volume. (8)

local area network (LAN) A network that is contained within a relatively small area, such as a classroom, school, or single building. (1)

local computer The computer currently being operated by a user. This is a relative term—each computer user will consider their own computer to be the local computer. (1)

local print device A physical printer directly connected to the local computer. (8)

MAC address The Media Access Control address, which is another name for the physical address. (3)

map a drive The assignment of a local, unused drive letter to point to a share on a network, providing a logical connection to that share. It configures the resulting object in such a way as to have the operating system recognize that object as a separate logical drive. (7)

message traffic Network communication. (2)

metadata Information about data. The schema class and attribute objects are part of the metadata within a Microsoft network's overall schema that describes the network objects. (6)

metropolitan area network (MAN) A network that spans the distances involved in a typical metropolitan city. (1)

MIB Acronym for Management Information Base, which lists the information on each node that should be monitored by the agent and reported back to the manager. (10)

mirrored volume The use of two identical simple volumes on separate physical drives, with one volume maintaining an exact copy of the other. (7)

modem The device that modulates and demodulates digital computer signals so they can travel over analog media, such as telephone wires. (3)

modulate The process a modem uses to convert the sending computer's digital signal to an analog signal. (3)

monitor A video display that gives the computer a way to communicate with the user. (2)

mouse A method of communicating with the computer that is sometimes more convenient than using a keyboard when working in a GUI. Mouse movement is translated into cursor movement on the display screen. (2)

name context   A user object's context based upon its current location, also referred to as the user object's *current context*. Although a user object's context (where the object was originally created in the NDS tree) may be one location, the current location where that user object may be located will likely be different. (6)

NDOS   The name of the special version of DOS that Novell includes with its installation software package. (4)

NetBEUI   A non-routable networking protocol that can be used by Microsoft operating systems and is fast and easy to configure. It includes support for the NetBIOS name resolution. (2)

NetBIOS   An early session-layer networking protocol, short for Network Basic Input/Output System. It includes support for the NetBIOS name resolution used on Microsoft networks. NetBIOS is being replaced with DNS name resolution. (3)

NetCrawler   A new Windows operating system feature that searches for and automatically adds all available shared network objects to user workstations. (8)

network   Two or more entities sharing resources and information. (1)

network address   The combination of node address (if there is one) and MAC address. (3)

network-capable print devices   Print devices that connect directly to the network, avoiding the need to be connected to a workstation but still requiring driver software to be loaded on a print server computer. (8)

network client   A device (hardware or software) on a computer network that requests services or resources from a server. (2)

network data   Information shared over networked computers. (2)

network file system (NFS)   An industry standard for organizing network files that was originally proposed by Sun Microsystems. (7)

networking medium   The connection between each of the computers involved in a network. (2)

network interface card (NIC)   An integrated circuit card designed to interact with certain protocols and media (such as Ethernet or Token Ring) and to be a networking connection point, usually plugged directly into the computer's system unit. (2)

Network Monitor   A utility available on a Windows 2000 Server that is intended to provide information about the health of the network. (10)

Network Neighborhood icon   A graphical item displayed on the desktop in some versions of Windows that can be used to browse network resources and access network configuration settings. (2)

network plan   A formally created schematic that shows all the network's components and the planned connections between them. (1)

network print device   A print device with an internal network interface card that provides the print device with its own recognized network identification such that computers can send their materials to be printed directly to the printer and not require a separate print server. (8)

network printing   Producing printed materials using networked resources. (8)

network server   A computer that offers services and resources to clients, workstations, and other servers over a computer network. Commonly just called a *server*. (2)

NLM   Acronym for NetWare Loadable Module. (4)

NMS   Acronym for network management system, which is also referred to as the *host* or the *SNMP manager*. (10)

node address   A network address number that is required by some network operating systems (Novell in particular) to identify each node in the network. (3)

nodes   The term used for objects (such as computers) connected to a network. (10)

non-contiguous space   Storage areas that are not located immediately next to each other. (7)

Novell Client   Novell software that runs on Windows workstations and allows them to operate as Novell clients and connect to NetWare servers. (5)

Novell Services icon   A red *N* in the taskbar's notification area. (5)

NTFS   NTFS is the shortened name used when referring to the NTFS file system. Although this use appears to be redundant, Microsoft discourages using the term "NT file system." (4)

NTFS file system A Microsoft file system with features to improve reliability over the FAT file system, such as transaction logs to help recover from disk failures. This file system also allows controlled file access by setting permissions for directories and/or individual files. (7)

objects Entities with discrete sets of attributes. There are objects stored in a directory service, such as users, groups, and computers, and there are objects stored in a file system, such as files and folders. (6)

one-step login Requiring only a single set of user name and password entries to log in for all network access. (5)

operating systems Collections of software programs that provide a computer with basic functionality, such as the user interface, management of hardware and software, and ways of creating, managing, and using files. (1)

OSI Open Systems Interconnection, the name of the ISO's reference model. (3)

output Work sent from a computer to a device such as a printer. (8)

output ports Computer connections for parallel, serial, USB, SCSI, and other output. (8)

page file A temporary disk work space that is used as memory, with working items being moved in and out of the space as necessary. (10)

partitions Separate areas on a physical hard disk that are used for storage. (4)

password lockout An option that allows administrators to set the maximum number of failed password attempts that are to be allowed. (9)

password synchronization An option offered by Novell Client to change your Windows password so that it matches your Novell password. (5)

peer-to-peer network A type of networking that is not centrally administered, where all computers are considered equals, and where each computer can act as a file or print server to its peers. (1)

penetration test A test that looks for vulnerabilities in the computer and network systems of an organization. (9)

Performance console A utility program that lets you collect data about your system's performance. (10)

peripherals A very broad term, most often used to refer to nonessential add-on computer components, such as printers, scanners, and speakers, to expand the computer's use. (1)

permission A type of protection for files, folders, and other objects. Permissions define what a user or group can do with an object. (6)

physical address The element in a computer's network address that gets assigned to the network interface card (NIC) by its manufacturer. The physical address is also called the *MAC address*. (3)

policy One of a set of rules. In Windows, policies define the expected level of security that is to be configured, and specify acceptable computer behavior for employees and users of the computer systems and networks. (9)

POP An acronym for the Post Office Protocol, which is used to retrieve text messages on a computer so users can read them. (3)

ports Networking connection points. (2)

port scan A probe used to identify systems that are running services that may be vulnerable to attack. (9)

primary DOS partitions A primary partition created for the DOS operating system. (4)

primary partitions A type of operating system–partitioning that segments an area on the hard disk. (7)

printer In Microsoft terms, the software interface that facilitates printing computer output. Microsoft refers to the physical device that does the printing as the *print device*. (8)

printer agent (PA) The object that represents a printer on a NetWare network. (8)

printer-recognizable machine code Computer code that runs the printer. Printer drivers are programs that get translated into machine code that the printer can interpret. (8)

print servers Print devices that offer their printing capability to others on a network. (8)

programs Organized sets of computer instructions. (1)

properties Descriptive attributes of an object. (6)

protocol A networking language consisting of a set of rules. Network protocols govern many aspects of network communications. (2)

protocol suite   Groups of protocols working together to accomplish a particular task. (3)

publish   Releasing printer information, such as name, type, and location, through Active Directory to all domain users. (8)

quota   An assigned limit on the amount of network storage space users can use, designed to ensure an equitable distribution of space when such networked resources are limited. (10)

RAID   Acronym for redundant array of independent disks, RAID involves using multiple disk drives, usually to ensure fault tolerance—if one disk drive is damaged, the information is still contained on another disk. (7)

random access memory (RAM)   A series of memory chips linked together inside your computer that act as a "thinking location" for the computer's "thought processes." (2)

Ready Tests   Red Hat's equivalent of Microsoft's extensive component compatibility testing. (4)

relative distinguished names   NDS object names that start with a period and describe the location of an object relative to the user's current context. (6)

replicas   Duplicate pieces of the Directory (in larger networks with multiple file servers) that NDS stores on many of the servers around the network. Replicas provide fault tolerance and backup capability. (10)

report view   The System Monitor view that displays the data for each item being tracked in summary format only. (10)

restore the mirror   On a mirrored volume, the act of replacing the failed hard drive with a new one and copying the information stored on the remaining operational drive. (7)

rheostat   A device used to gradually adjust electrical current instead of using an on/off switch. (3)

rights   An NDS method for granting permission to perform an action on a networked object. (6)

ring topology   A network in which computers are attached to each other in a large circle. The signal flows around the circle to each station in turn, but stops if the circle is broken or a station is not operating properly. (3)

risk   The likelihood that damage or injury may occur. (9)

RJ-45 connectors   Connectors most commonly used to connect the network medium to the networking interface on Ethernet networks. (2)

rootkit   A set of programs that will aid the hacker in returning to the system and hiding his or her presence. (9)

router   The sophisticated network concentrator device that reads specific portions of headers in network packets and directs traffic to destinations beyond the local network. (2)

routing   Selecting a path for sending a message directly to the resource for which it was intended. (3)

schema   Microsoft's term for the whole set of database information (called *properties* and *values* in NDS). (6)

server   In the general sense, an entity that provides customers, or clients, access to resources. More specifically, a computer that plays one or more of several important roles in a network. In all of these roles, it provides services to other computers (which act as clients). (1)

server-based network   A type of network that offers centralized control and is designed for secure operations. (1)

server directory   The index inside the operating system that keeps track of the server objects. (4)

service pack   An update for the operating system, or for another applicable software package. (4)

setup boot disks   A set of floppy disks used to start the Windows XP installation when you are unable to boot from your CD drive. (5)

shared indicator   A small upward-facing hand below a print device's icon indicating that the device is currently being shared. (8)

shares   As a noun, these are the shared resources users control on their computers, such as document folders, printers, and peripherals. As a verb, it means to make a resource, such as a document folder or printer, available on the network. (1)

simple volume   A dynamic storage area that is located on one physical disk and uses all or part of the disk's space for a single volume. (7)

SMTP   Acronym for Simple Mail Transfer Protocol, which defines a set of rules that regulate the sending of e-mail across the Internet, at which point it is stored on a user's mail server. (3)

sneakernet   The process of sharing information by actually walking it to another computer. (1)

sniffing   The process of examining network traffic (possibly obtaining encrypted passwords or other information) as it passes between systems. (9)

SNMP   Acronym for Simple Network Management Protocol, an Internet-standard protocol that facilitates monitoring the network and sending status updates to a central location, called the *network management system* (NMS). (10)

SNMP manager   Another name for the network management system (NMS). (10)

social engineering   A method of gaining unauthorized access to computer systems through non-technical means, such as using lies and deceit to gain passwords or other information about the network. (9)

software   A set of instructions that controls the operation of a computer. *See* programs. (1)

source address   An address where transmitted network information originates. (3)

spanned volume   A system of dynamic storage that provides an efficient way to use numerous disk drives. Combining those multiple spaces—up to 32 individual disks—is done by setting up what are known as *pointers* that give the operating system directions on how to get from one disk to the next. (7)

stand-alone computer   A computer that is operated independently of other computers. (1)

standards   Networking rules. (3)

star topology   The most common type of topology currently used because it is easy to maintain. At the center is the concentrator, typically a hub or switch, and each computer has a direct connection to it. (3)

states   Distinct and discernible conditions, such as on or off. (3)

static address   A system whereby each IP address is individually assigned and manually configured. (3)

straight-through network cable   A commonly used network cable that connects a computer to a concentrator. (2)

striped volume   An efficient way to use storage space in multiple disks by using an equal amount of space (not necessarily the entire drive) from up to 32 disks to create a single storage space. (7)

striped volume with parity   A fault-tolerant arrangement (RAID-5) that produces redundant storage. If one of the volumes fails, the portions of the extra stripe (the parity stripe) that are stored on the remaining disks are used to recreate the failed segment and keep the system in operation while the failed disk is replaced. (7)

switch   A network concentrator device to which media from each computer connects. A switch offers network monitoring and selective configuration, such that it sends a signal only to the destination port. (2)

syntax   A set of formatting rules for correctly entering a command at the command line. The rules include the command name and the parameters that act as instructions to the command. (7)

SYS C: A DOS command line entry that directs the computer to transfer the operating system to the C: drive. (4)

SYS volume   The name of the NetWare operating system drive where the system files are located. (4)

SYS.COM   The full name of the DOS file that transfers the operating system. (4)

System Monitor   The portion of your Performance console utility that allows you to view either current system activities or those recorded using Performance Logs and Alerts. (10)

system partition   The location on a disk drive where the hardware-specific files necessary for starting the operating system are located. (7)

systemroot   The main folder containing the Windows XP operating system files, which is usually C:\Windows (though on Windows 2000 systems, it is C:\WINNT). (5)

system unit   The box-like housing for a computer's essential electronic circuitry, such as the CPU, ROM, and RAM. (2)

Task Manager   A management tool available at the user level through the taskbar that provides a means to not only gather information about a user's computer but also to start or stop most of their own applications. (10)

TCP/IP   Acronym for Transmission Control Protocol/Internet Protocol, which is the name of a suite of network protocols. These two protocols, and the others that make up the suite, allow computers to access the Internet. (3)

terminated Ended with a special attachment that absorbs the signal at the ends of the cable. (3)

terminator A device that absorbs any residual signal at the end of a network and ensures that the signal does not bounce back over the thinnet cabling medium where it could cause signaling errors on the network. (2)

thicknet The first widely used network-cabling medium, consisting of thick coaxial cable. (2)

thinnet The network-cabling medium that generally replaced thicknet coaxial cable. It consists of a thinner coaxial cable. (2)

threat Someone or something that could inflict damage or injury. (9)

topology Physical layout or geometric pattern formed by the arrangement of interconnected computers within a network. (3)

total cost of ownership (TCO) The full amount spent on a particular component over that equipment's usable lifetime, including initial purchase cost and all related costs for maintaining the component and supporting the use of the component. (1)

trap message An SNMP alarm message sent by agents when they are configured to look for specific events (like login failures or other unauthorized access) and report their occurrence. (10)

traverse Navigating through a particular folder on the way to another file or folder that is contained either within or below the original folder. (7)

Trojan horse A program that pretends to be something it is not, usually with malicious intent. (9)

trustees NDS objects with permission to perform specific actions on other objects. (6)

twisted-pair wiring A type of network cabling that is similar to telephone cable. (2)

UDP User Datagram Protocol, a connectionless protocol. (3)

unique address An exact name and storage path that correctly locates the item being sought. (3)

upgradeable system An operating system, such as Windows XP or NetWare 6, that can be upgraded with the current version of the operating system's software. (5)

URL Acronym for Uniform Resource Locator, a convenient method for locating resources—typically on the Internet. (3)

values The specific entries assigned to the descriptive properties of an object. (6)

virtual device driver (VXD) A program for each of the computer's main hardware devices, including the hard disk drive controller, keyboard, and serial and parallel ports. These drivers maintain the status of a hardware device that has changeable settings. Virtual device drivers handle software interrupts from the operating system rather than hardware interrupts. A virtual device driver usually has a filename extension of .vxd. (7)

virus A program, usually of a malicious nature, that piggybacks on another program—viruses are not programs that exist on a system by themselves. (9)

war-dial An attempt to find phone lines that are being answered by computers, accomplished when a malicious act is intended. (9)

wide area network (WAN) A network that spans a larger area than a typical metropolitan city. (1)

Windows NT boot loader The initial segment of the NT operating system that loads into a computer and boots the system in Windows NT, Windows 2000, and Windows XP. (4)

Windows XP Home The version of Windows XP that is recommended for use in typical households and includes only limited networking capability. (5)

Windows XP Professional The version of Windows XP that is recommended for use in company situations and includes extended networking capability. (5)

wireless A networking medium that uses infrared or radio waves between networked components. (2)

workstation A computer used as a location to accomplish work. (1)

workstation administrator account The first account added to an operating system during installation. This is the most powerful account on the workstation. (5)

worms Programs that execute on their own and use their own code to propagate, usually intent on causing malicious damage. (9)

AutoRun feature, Windows XP
  Professional, 139

■ B

back door attacks, 298–301
    See also external threats; security
      overview, 298–299
      physical security, 299, 301
      remote access security, 299–300
      social engineering, 301
      wireless networks, 300–301
backup and restore options,
    NWCONFIG.NLM, 346
Backup tool, 318–319, 320
    See also Windows XP
      Professional workstation tools
backups, 307
    See also network security
      planning
      centralized management, 13–14
      RAID (redundant array of
        independent disks) and, 307
basic Windows file storage, 219–222
    See also Windows file storage;
      Windows file systems
      basic disks, 220
      converting to dynamic storage,
        225–226
      extended partitions, 221
      overview, 219–220
      partitions, 219–222
      primary partitions, 221–222
binary systems, defined, 56
biometrics, 286
    See also authentication; internal
      threats; security
      objections to, 287
bits, digital to analog conversion, 57
BNC T-connectors, coaxial cable, 38, 40
Boot Disk Creation window, Red Hat
    Linux, 127, 159
boot disks
    Windows 2000 Server, 108–110
    Windows XP Professional,
      138, 139
Boot Loader Configuration window,
    Red Hat Linux, 123
Boot Loader Password Configuration
    window, Red Hat Linux, 124
boot loaders, Red Hat Linux, 120

bridges, connection media, 36
broadcasting versus routing,
    communication protocols, 72–73
Broker component, 270–274
    See also iPrint service; NetWare
      network printing
      ENS (Event Notification
        Services), 270
      iManage feature and creation
        exercise, 271–274
      RMS (Resource Management
        Services), 271
      SRS (Service Registry
        Services), 270
brute force attacks, passwords and, 290
bus topology, 80
    See also network design; topology
      daisy chaining, 80
bytes, digital to analog conversion,
    57–58

■ C

cabling, 37–40
    See also installing network
      hardware
      coaxial, 37–38
      communication media, 33–34
      creating, 39, 41–43
      Ethernet signals and, 37
      fiber-optic, 33, 40
      straight-through network, 41–43
      twisted-pair, 39
      wireless as alternative to, 33, 40
cache buffers, MONITOR.NLM
    and, 342
centralized management, 12–14
    See also network benefits
      backups, 13–14
      network maintenance, 13
      software, 13
Change permission, sharing FAT
    partitions, 236
character sets, 58
child objects, NDS container objects
    and, 174–175
chkdsk command, Error-Checking
    tool, 314
client software, 134–165
    See also operating systems;
      workstations

essay quiz, 165
key term quiz, 162–163
key terms, 162
lab projects, 165
multiple-choice quiz, 163–165
Novell Client, 148–154
Red Hat Linux, 154–160
summary, 161–162
Windows XP Professional,
    135–148
client-based networks, 19
    See also network classifications;
      networks
clients
    iPrint service, 276, 277–278
    network components, 32
clusters
    FAT (File Allocation Table), 227
    NTFS, 229–230
coaxial cable, 37–38
    See also cabling; installing
      network hardware
      BNC T-connectors, 38, 40
      daisy chaining, 38
      thinnet and thicknet, 38
common name (CN), NDS object
    naming, 177–178
communication media, 33–34
    See also connection media;
      network components
      fiber-optic cabling, 2.5;, 40
      twisted-pair wiring, 33
      wireless, 33, 40
communication protocols, 69–78
      broadcasting versus routing,
        72–73
      defined, 70
      Internet, 74–77
      intranet/extranet, 77–78
      layered communication, 73–74
      message formatting, 73
      NetBEUI protocol, 70–72
      OSI (Open System
        Interconnection) model,
        73–74
      overview, 69–70
      transmitting messages, 72
communications, 54–91
      addressing, 60–65
      character sets, 58
      digital signals, 55–58

X

INTERNATIONAL CONTACT INFORMATION

AUSTRALIA
McGraw-Hill Book Company Australia Pty. Ltd.
TEL +61-2-9900-1800
FAX +61-2-9878-8881
http://www.mcgraw-hill.com.au
books-it_sydney@mcgraw-hill.com

CANADA
McGraw-Hill Ryerson Ltd.
TEL +905-430-5000
FAX +905-430-5020
http://www.mcgraw-hill.ca

GREECE, MIDDLE EAST, & AFRICA
(Excluding South Africa)
McGraw-Hill Hellas
TEL +30-210-6560-990
TEL +30-210-6560-993
TEL +30-210-6560-994
FAX +30-210-6545-525

MEXICO (Also serving Latin America)
McGraw-Hill Interamericana Editores S.A. de C.V.
TEL +525-117-1583
FAX +525-117-1589
http://www.mcgraw-hill.com.mx
fernando_castellanos@mcgraw-hill.com

SINGAPORE (Serving Asia)
McGraw-Hill Book Company
TEL +65-6863-1580
FAX +65-6862-3354
http://www.mcgraw-hill.com.sg
mghasia@mcgraw-hill.com

SOUTH AFRICA
McGraw-Hill South Africa
TEL +27-11-622-7512
FAX +27-11-622-9045
robyn_swanepoel@mcgraw-hill.com

SPAIN
McGraw-Hill/Interamericana de España, S.A.U.
TEL +34-91-180-3000
FAX +34-91-372-8513
http://www.mcgraw-hill.es
professional@mcgraw-hill.es

UNITED KINGDOM, NORTHERN,
EASTERN, & CENTRAL EUROPE
McGraw-Hill Education Europe
TEL +44-1-628-502500
FAX +44-1-628-770224
http://www.mcgraw-hill.co.uk
computing_europe@mcgraw-hill.com

ALL OTHER INQUIRIES Contact:
McGraw-Hill/Osborne
TEL +1-510-420-7700
FAX +1-510-420-7703
http://www.osborne.com
omg_international@mcgraw-hill.com